THE LARDER CHEF

KU-617-338

THE LARDER CHEF

Food Preparation and Presentation

Fourth edition

M. J. Leto, MHCIMA
W. K. H. Bode, Mphil, MHCIMA DipHot(Göt)

ELSEVIER

AMSTERDAM • BOSTON • HEIDELBERG • LONDON • NEW YORK
OXFORD • PARIS • SAN DIEGO • SAN FRANCISCO
SINGAPORE • SYDNEY • TOKYO
Butterworth-Heinemann is an imprint of Elsevier

BH

Wiltshire College

69512

Butterworth-Heinemann is an imprint of Elsevier
Linacre House, Jordan Hill, Oxford OX2 8DP, UK
30 Corporate Drive, Suite 400, Burlington, MA 01803, USA

First published 1969
Second Edition 1975
Reprinted 1977, 1980, 1981, 1984, 1985, 1986
First published as a paperback edition 1987
Reprinted 1988
Third edition 1989
Reprinted 1990, 1992, 1993, 1995, 1996, 1997, 1998, 2000
Transferred to digital printing 2003
Fourth edition 2006

Copyright © 1969, 1975, 1989, 2006, M. J. Leto and W. K. H. Bode. Published by
Elsevier Ltd. All rights reserved

The right of M. J. Leto and W. K. H. Bode to be identified as the author of this work has been
asserted in accordance with the Copyright, Designs and Patents Act 1988

No part of this publication may be reproduced, stored in a retrieval system or transmitted in any
form or by any means electronic, mechanical, photocopying, recording or otherwise without the prior
written permission of the publisher

Permissions may be sought directly from Elsevier's Science & Technology Rights Department in Oxford,
UK: phone (+44) (0) 1865 843830; fax (+44) (0) 1865 853333; email: permissions@elsevier.com.
Alternatively you can submit your request online by visiting the Elsevier web site at
http://elsevier.com/locate/permissions, and selecting Obtaining permission to use Elsevier material

Notice
No responsibility is assumed by the publisher for any injury and/or damage to persons or property
as a matter of products liability, negligence or otherwise, or from any use or operation of any methods,
products, instructions or ideas contained in the material herein. Because of rapid advances in the medical
sciences, in particular, independent verification of diagnoses and drug dosages should be made

British Library Cataloguing in Publication Data

Leto, M. J. (Mario Jack), 1910–1994
    The larder chef : food preparation and presentation. – 4th ed.
    1. Cookery 2. Quantity cookery
    I. Title II. Bode, W. K. H. (Willi Karl Heinrich), 1931–641.5

ISBN–13: 978-0-75-066899-6
ISBN–10: 0-75-066899-7

Library of Congress Cataloging-in-Publication Data
Library of Congress Control Number: 2006922294

For information on all Butterworth-Heinemann publications
visit our web site at books.elsevier.com

Printed and bound in Great Britain

06 07 08 09 10   10 9 8 7 6 5 4 3 2 1

Working together to grow
libraries in developing countries

www.elsevier.com | www.bookaid.org | www.sabre.org

ELSEVIER   BOOK AID International   Sabre Foundation

Contents

Preface

It is now 35 years since *The Larder Chef* was first published. Since its first edition in 1969 we have had a Second Edition in 1975 with several reprints, then in 1988 the new Paperback Edition was published, and a metric Third Edition followed in 1989, when Jack Leto was still with us for help and guidance.

The Larder Chef has sold worldwide in most English-speaking countries, and some that are not. Personally I have been asked to sign often long-held copies in Boston, Budapest, Hamburg, London, New Orleans, Stockholm, and in the depths of Dorset.

The book was intended as a text for catering students of all types and levels, and we were thus pleasantly surprised when a good percentage of copies were bought by the general public, as well as hotel, restaurant and butchery managers and staff. We have always been grateful for their comments, suggestions for inclusions or changes, and criticisms received over the years. These were always considered when a new edition was prepared.

But for some time now I have felt that *The Larder Chef* needed a more radical update, to reflect the considerable changes that have taken place in our industry. For this purpose I approached 80 chefs and their managers with a questionnaire, asking for answers to 30 questions. I contacted establishments in an area roughly bounded by Exeter and London, Oxford and Bournemouth. I had a remarkable 84% response, with very honest answers and very reflective comments. My grateful thanks to you all.

The results of my survey clearly showed a split in the approach to preparation and service of food in our industry today. Food Service may contrast between the very fast, medium fast and slow, and Food Quality and Presentation may range from the very poor, acceptable to good, and very good and expensive. These different approaches are well expressed in two drawings reproduced here from the observant eye of Swiss artist Paul André Parret.

My survey also showed that today:

- 4% still bought a hindquarter of beef or carcass of lamb on a weekly basis
- 72% bought most of their joints ready for the oven
- 78% bought all of their different types of steak ready cut to required size or weight
- 30% bought their steaks frozen
- 80% bought only frozen fish, a necessity in many places as very little good fresh fish is available.

Given this information, how was I to write or bring up to date a cookery textbook that would be of help to all and meet most needs? Clearly with some difficulties!

Looking at the rest of the answers to my survey, the picture looks much better: 90% of all hors d'oeuvres were prepared fresh, most of the salads, all of the vegetables and most potatoes, and all buffets, if simpler Modern versions, were made fresh in house.

I am well aware that today many of the tasks described in this book have been taken over by manufacturers who, by applying mass production techniques, are able to supply many of the partly prepared needs of the caterer in some form or other. But *The Larder Chef* has been written primarily as a textbook for students, or young chefs who wish to widen their knowledge, or check on facts or approach in respect to a given task in hand. Both should learn to distinguish between a spring chicken or a

The intimidated guest

The intimidated waiter

boiling fowl, a pheasant and a guinea fowl and how to prepare them for the pan or pot. He or she should know the difference between a sardine or a sprat, a lemon sole or a Dover sole, whether fresh or frozen. It will be useful to them to be able to distinguish between a rump and a sirloin, to have a good knowledge of other cuts of meats, their size, weight and cost, the quality, and portions to be had, from said weight. How cuts and joints related to the whole animal and for what method of cookery and dishes they are best suited. *The Larder Chef* aims to help them gain that knowledge.

This Fourth Edition is much enlarged and improved by the addition of nearly 400 coloured illustrations showing various plated presentations of dishes. Many of these came from my work while at Surrey University, others I have prepared and photographed especially for this edition to fill obvious gaps. The slides are of varying standard, new and old, and in making the slides I begged and borrowed plates and dishes to show as many types of presentations in as many ways as space would allow.

I would like to thank all my former colleagues at Bournemouth College of Further Education who, more than thirty years ago, helped and encouraged myself and Jack Leto to get *The Larder Chef* off the ground. Thanks must also go to the many teachers and students, as well as working chefs, who over the years bought the book, and approached us with useful advice and suggestions, and my special thanks to all chefs and managers who answered my survey in such numbers and so promptly.

It is my hope that this new illustrated edition of *The Larder Chef* will be of further benefit and use to young and old for the next 35 years, and that my old colleague, mentor and friend Jack Leto would approve. I think he would.

W. Bode
Christchurch, Dorset 2006

1 The Larder Chef (The Chef Garde-Manger)

THE FUNCTION OF THE LARDER DEPARTMENT

The Cold Larder, or Garde-Manger, is a department set aside for the storage of perishable foods, both raw and cooked, and where foodstuffs such as meat, fish, poultry and game are prepared and made ready for cooking.

In this department too, all 'Cold Elements' found on the menu, such as the hors d'oeuvre, cold fish or meat dishes, all salads, cold sauces and dressings, are prepared and 'dressed'. One particular special duty of this department is the preparation and presentation of all types of cold buffet, which are nowadays a feature of so many functions.

For these departmental functions to be effectively carried out, it is essential that:

(1) The room is separate from the kitchen, and located in a cool place. At the same time, it must be close to the kitchen to avoid undue running about between departments of the kitchen, which are all closely interrelated.

(2) It should be light, airy and well ventilated, and sufficiently spacious to allow the staff to carry out their duties in a clean and efficient manner. It must also be able to store prepared foods and buffets in a cool and hygienic manner.

(3) It must be equipped with the necessary fittings, plant, machinery and tools, in accordance with the volume and/or quality of the trade of the catering establishment in which it is situated.

BREAKDOWN OF WORK

Taking the above into consideration, it naturally follows that the work is broken down into various fields, such as Hors d'oeuvre, Salads, Butchery, Poultry, Cold Buffet etc., and, in effect, in large busy establishments each of these functions or duties is carried out by one or more men or sometimes women, who specialize in the work of that particular sub-department. As an example, the Butcher, Poulterer, or Fishmonger may be an expert in that particular field without being a trained chef or cook, and it sometimes happens that salads or hors d'oeuvres are prepared by (often female) staff trained in those particular duties only.

More frequently, these various duties are allocated by the Chef Garde-Manger, who is in overall charge of the department, to commis or assistant chefs, and they are known as Commis Garde-Manger, whatever duties they are assigned to. Naturally, the busier the establishment, the more Larder-work it entails; therefore more commis are required to staff the department. The smaller the volume of trade the fewer commis required, and so on. In many establishments the Chef Garde-Manger is single-handed and carries out all the various functions personally.

It should be mentioned at this stage that often quality rather than quantity of trade is the determining factor in deciding the number of staff required in the Garde-Manger, or for that matter in the kitchen as a whole.

RESPONSIBILITIES OF THE CHEF GARDE-MANGER

The responsibilities of the Chef Garde-Manger, therefore, are many and varied. This person is responsible to the Chef for the efficient running of the Larder department and for the co-ordination of the work of its staff; for the training and discipline of larder staff; for the foodstuffs in the department, some of which may be stored in refrigerators or even in deep freeze, or preserved by other means. The Chef Garde-Manger is responsible for keeping a record of such foodstuffs and a day-by-day record of issues to kitchen or other departments.

The Chef Garde-Manger must study the menus in advance, so as to be able to order meat, fish, etc., in time for the foodstuff to be prepared and cleaned and made ready for the kitchen in time for it to be cooked; and also to order all necessary stores for the various larder productions such as salads, hors d'oeuvres, sauces, buffets, etc.

The Larder Chef is responsible for the efficient storage of food to avoid deterioration and wastage and for cleanliness and hygiene in the department, to avoid any danger of contamination and possible food poisoning. He should also advise the Head Chef as to what foodstuff items require using to prevent eventual wastage.

LARDER CONTROL

If this department is to be run efficiently and economically, it is essential that the Chef Garde-Manger should exercise the strictest possible control over the foodstuffs received and stored in the department. This involves:

- Checking the quantity and quality of all goods delivered to the larder.
- Ensuring that all foodstuffs are stored at the right temperature and that they can be easily checked.
- Ensuring that the food is protected from contamination by vermin.
- Ensuring that portion control is rigidly carried out, e.g. a given weight of fish, poultry, meat, should always produce the required number of portions.
- Ensuring that food is not overstocked and stocks of food are regularly turned over.
- Making every effort to maintain the highest possible standard of hygiene and to prevent any deterioration in the foodstuffs under his control.
- Taking every precaution to discourage pilfering.
- Ensuring (and this is imperative) that a simple daily stock sheet be kept by each section within the Larder and handed to the Chef Garde-Manger at the end of each day's business to enable him to write out his order for the following day.

STOCK SHEET

The stock and order sheets should be made as simple and easy to keep up to date as possible. A complicated stock sheet, requiring too much writing, will defeat the whole object of the exercise, as it will be neglected during busy rush periods, the very time it is most needed. See the example below.

Department: Larder		Section: Hors d'oeuvre		Day and date: X and Y	
Items	*Unit*	*Stock*	*Unit Price*	*Cost in £*	*Order*
Tomatoes	Kg	3			
Cucumber	No.	4			
Eggs	Doz.	2			
Olive oil	Litre	1½			
Vinegar	Litre	¾			
Sardines	Tins	7			

For some sections, the devising of a simple but effective list is reasonably easy. With others it is not quite as easy. For example, the keeping of the stock of food sent in and returned by the Cold Buffet can be complicated and time-wasting, if one has to measure every gram or millimetre. Therefore, it is necessary to accept some rule of thumb, providing this is well supervised. Note that an experienced Chef du Froid or Chef Garde-Manger should be able to tell at a glance the weight, or number of portions of a given joint or cold dish, within very narrow margins.

The Butchery department also presents some problems and the stock sheet for this department needs careful consideration. Fish, salad vegetables, canned foods and dairy produce, on the other hand, are comparatively easy to control. Naturally, each catering establishment will produce its own system, today in most cases supported by a computer program taking its own problems into account, but the stock/order sheet given here should meet the requirements of most departments, if only to supply the computer with the necessary information.

LIAISON WITH KITCHEN AND PASTRY DEPARTMENT

The Larder is both a storage department for most perishable foods and a preparation department for such foodstuffs. The Larder staff, under the supervision of the Chef Garde-Manger, are responsible for the ordering, storing and preserving of stores, keeping stocks up to date, and accounting for such items as meat, fish, poultry, game etc. which pass through the department on their way from the suppliers to the kitchen and eventually to the restaurant or banqueting rooms. The bulk of such foodstuff needs dissecting or cleaning, dressing, cutting into the required joints or portions, and generally preparing for cooking.

Figure 1.1 shows a typical Larder kitchen layout in a medium to large hotel–restaurant. Figure 1.2 demonstrates a wider layout of a medium to large hotel–restaurant kitchen, showing the relation of the Larder to the rest of the kitchen, as well as the access to all sections of the kitchen by the waiting staff. Section A in Figure 1.2 shows the front view of the kitchen with the three main departments, Larder, Main Kitchen and Pastry, as well as the Wash-up section, as the waiting staff would approach them, having clear access to all service counters and the restaurant. In the back of the kitchen an uninterrupted passage to all sections is clearly visible.

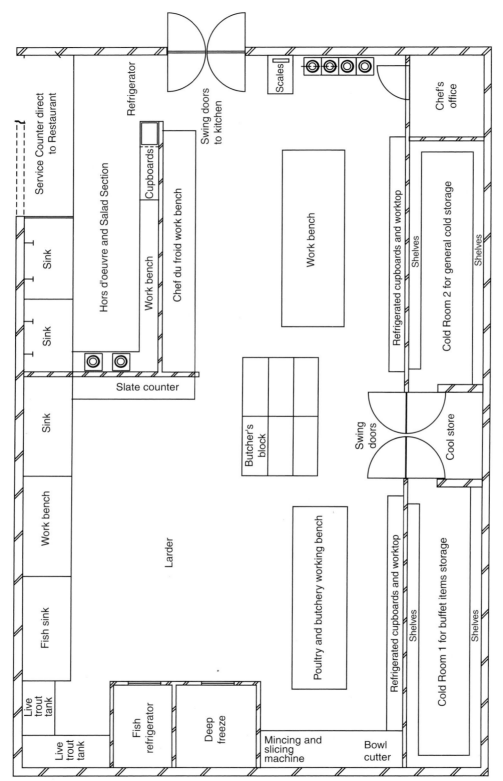

Fig. 1.1 *Larder layout of large hotel–restaurant*

Service Counter direct to Restaurant

Refrigerator

Swing doors to kitchen

Scales

Chef's office

Hors d'oeuvre and Salad Section

Cupboards

Work bench

Chef du froid work bench

Work bench

Refrigerated cupboards and worktop

Shelves

Cold Room 2 for general cold storage

Shelves

Sink

Sink

Sink

Slate counter

Butcher's block

Swing doors

Cool store

Fish sink

Work bench

Larder

Poultry and butchery working bench

Refrigerated cupboards and worktop

Shelves

Cold Room 1 for buffet items storage

Shelves

Live trout tank

Live trout tank

Fish refrigerator

Deep freeze

Mincing and slicing machine

Bowl cutter

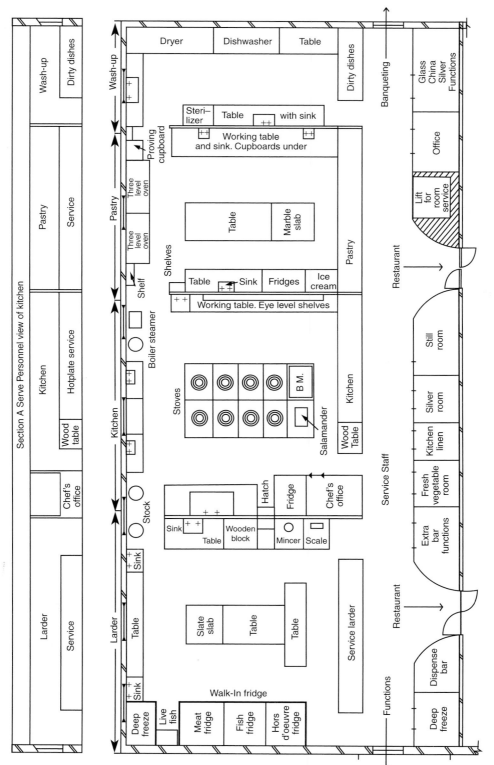

Fig. 1.2 *Wider layout of the kitchen of a large hotel–restaurant*

Section A Serve Personnel view of kitchen

Larder	Chef's office	Kitchen	Pastry	Wash-up
Service		Hotplate service	Service	Dirty dishes
	Wood table			

Larder · Kitchen · Pastry · Wash-up

Deep freeze
Live fish
Sink
Sink
Table
Slate slab
Table
Table
Walk-In fridge
Meat fridge
Fish fridge
Hors d'oeuvre fridge
Service larder

Stock

Sink
Table
Wooden block
Mincer
Scale
Hatch
Fridge
Chef's office

Stoves
B M.
Salamander
Wood Table

Boiler steamer

Shelf
Shelves
Three level oven
Three level oven
Table
Marble slab

Table
Sink
Fridges
Ice cream
Working table. Eye level shelves

Proving cupboard
Sterilizer
Table
with sink
Working table and sink. Cupboards under

Dryer
Dishwasher
Table
Dirty dishes

Pastry · Kitchen

Deep freeze
Dispense bar
Extra bar functions
Fresh vegetable room
Kitchen linen
Silver room
Still room
Lift for room service
Office
Glass China Silver Functions

Functions
Restaurant
Service Staff
Restaurant
Banqueting

To function in an effective manner, the Larder department must operate in harmony with the Kitchen in particular, and in many cases with the Pastry department, too, if confusion and wastage are to be avoided. A good layout of the Larder in relation to the Kitchen will avoid undue running from place to place. Lack of liaison between the departments could result in duplication of work, or sometimes in certain processes not being carried out to the best advantage. For example, certain foods intended for cold service are best cooked in the Kitchen where there are greater facilities for carrying out the operation, as well as being more closely supervised, thus obtaining the best results.

Likewise, pastry for pies or puddings, and various savouries served from the Larder department, are best prepared by the Pastry staff, who will be more skilful in such work, and who are equipped with the necessary apparatus and tools for producing such items. Such tasks as the lining of pudding basins or the covering of meat pies, prior to or after filling by the Larder staff – in readiness for cooking in the Kitchen – are examples of such co-operation between the departments.

On the other hand, such savoury fillings as are required by the Pastry chef for such items as sausage rolls, patties, or pasties, ravioli, etc., will be prepared in the Larder and transferred to the Pastry department as and when required.

Another important function of the Garde-Manger is to process and utilize the 'leftover' element of any meal, and consequently parts of cooked joints, poultry, fish or even eggs, vegetables and potatoes will be transferred from the Kitchen to the Larder at the conclusion of every meal. Naturally, the Head Chef will seek to keep these leftovers to a minimum by careful ordering but, in a busy establishment with a varied menu, a certain amount of leftovers are unavoidable.

It is the task of the Chef Garde-Manger in consultation with the Head Chef to make the best possible use of these. Some will go to the preparation of hors d'oeuvres or salads; others, suitably trimmed and dressed, to the preparation of cold dishes; and some will be used in 'made-up' dishes. All these factors should be, and usually are, taken into account by the Head Chef when planning the menus and the close co-operation of the Chef Garde-Manger can be of the utmost importance.

A number of garnishes or accompaniments to dishes served from kitchen departments are prepared by the Garde-Manger. Such items as stuffings, forcemeats, lardons or bacon rashers, are naturally provided by the Larder, as well as cold sauces for the accompaniment of hot dishes, such as Tartare or Remoulade for fried or grilled fish, mint sauce for roast lamb, Raifort for roast beef, Ravigote or Vinaigrette for calf's head, and many others which are dealt with in Chapter 3. In some instances, the Larder department also prepares savoury butters for use by the kitchen. But such preparations as dumplings and some savoury patties used by the Kitchen for garnishes are prepared by the Pastry department, with the savoury ingredients, chopped suet or fillings, provided by the Larder.

It will be seen from the above that the Chef Garde-Manger must be familiar with the garnishes and accompaniments of all dishes on the menu, in particular the classical fish dishes and entrées and soups. Close liaison, therefore, is essential between these various departments if delays and complications are to be avoided at the time of serving these dishes.

It is advisable, therefore, for students to make themselves familiar with the more commonly used classical garnishes. There are some very good books on this subject, notably Escoffier's *Guide to Modern Cookery*, or *Le Répertoire de la Cuisine*.

USE OF REFRIGERATORS AND FREEZERS

REFRIGERATORS

These play a very important part in the function of the Garde-Manger as they enable perishable foods to be stored at a low temperature and thus prevent deterioration in the food and particularly the growth of harmful bacteria. It should be clearly understood that the refrigerators are not deep freeze compartments and the temperature should be set at a little above freezing point or 0–1 °C (32 °F). A temperature of around 2–3 °C (34–36 °F) is desirable and, as too great a variation in temperature can be harmful to the food in store, an effort must be made to keep the temperature as constant, or as near constant as possible.

The following principles must be observed:

(1) Ensure that the refrigerator is in good working order; check the thermostat to make sure it is functioning; have the refrigerator serviced regularly.

(2) Defrost regularly to enable the evaporator to function efficiently. This is done by switching off the motor and opening the doors to allow the warm air to melt snow, frost and ice, which is clinging to the vanes of the evaporator and the coils. Never in any circumstances should one use an ice pick or a knife to dislodge the ice, as there is a danger of perforating the coils, thus allowing the refrigerant to escape.

(3) Use the door as little as possible and never leave it open longer than is necessary for depositing or withdrawing foodstuffs from the refrigerator. The atmosphere outside the refrigerator will be at a much higher temperature normally and will, therefore, be attracted into the colder temperature causing it to rise rapidly.

(4) Never place hot food into the refrigerator as this will raise the temperature and is harmful to the other foods in cold store.

When the refrigerator is being defrosted, it should be thoroughly cleaned. The racks and bars are removed and scrubbed with hot water containing a grease solvent, rinsed and allowed to dry. The walls, floor and doors should be thoroughly sponged down likewise, with hot water containing grease solvent, then rinsed and dried. During this cleaning and defrosting operation the foodstuffs will naturally have been removed and transferred to alternative storage.

Under-Workbench Fridges

The modern kitchens have today under-workbench fridges to which uncooked foods such as fish and meats portion are transferred in readiness for cooking and service. Positioned in the hot and greasy Kitchen, these fridges are especially in need of frequent and thorough cleaning and service.

USE OF DEEP FREEZERS

With the use of more and more frozen food, in particular fish, in modern catering we have to rely today on freezers. The basic purpose of storing food in deep freeze is to prolong its storage life. Occasionally we wish, or have to, freeze certain food ourselves, for which we have no immediate use for a given time.

Under normal temperatures food will deteriorate rapidly through the action of micro-organisms and also enzymic and chemical reactions. By reducing the temperature it is possible to slow down the growth and multiplication of bacteria, such micro-organisms as moulds, yeasts, etc., and in particular the chemical and enzymic reactions. The lower the temperature, the slower the reactions until, at a temperature of about 20 °C, or lower, all reactions cease. This will ensure that food storage is safe for long periods, that the natural flavours are maintained, and that off-flavours caused by these reactions are prevented.

Quick Freezing

As the term implies, this is a technique whereby the lowering of the temperature in the food to the level mentioned or below is brought about in the shortest period of time possible. The reason for this quick freezing is the existence of a crucial point at which the water content of the food changes to the solid state (ice). At this point, known as the latent heat barrier, the temperature of the food remains static until the latent heat is removed from the food and the water is turned into ice. It is of the greatest importance that this stage be passed through as quickly as possible because, the longer the time taken, the larger will be the ice crystals formed in the intercellular structure of the food and, of course, vice versa.

Large ice crystals cause rupture of the cell structure which causes drip when the food is thawed. Nutrients are drained away by drip that also results in moisture loss and thus poor texture in the food and in turn poor flavour. It will be seen, therefore, that food intended for deep freeze storage should be quick frozen first, then stored at a constant temperature of not more than −20 °C, equal to −4 °F.

The food processing industries have developed many sophisticated and expensive techniques of quick freezing but it is not appropriate to enter into a discussion of the comparative qualities of these, since they are not really relevant to the operation of the Garde-Manger, desirable as they might be. It is sufficient to say that we should be wary of usurping the function of the food industries by attempting to freeze any large pieces or volume of food without the specialized know-how and the capital investment necessary, if we are to retain flavour, texture and nutritional values, all necessary ingredients in good quality food. There is no doubt that in the past ten years or so the deep freeze has become ever-more important in all types of catering establishments as well as in the home.

Whether in a large hotel, or the large refectory with their enormous walk-in deep freezes, or whether in a guest house or small restaurant with only a deep freeze section within a normal refrigerator, all would find it difficult to do their work today without this most excellent long-term storage facility.

The reasons for this increased use of the deep freeze are many and may be placed under the following three headings:

(1) Bulk-buying and subsequent need for storage.
(2) Special offer/seasonal buying and subsequent need for storage.
(3) Irregular supply or delivery and subsequent need for storage.

Let us look at each in turn and assess the respective reasons for use of deep freezing as well as possible advantages and disadvantages.

Bulk Buying

Experience shows that one can usually buy in bulk many foods at a reduction of 10–20% and whenever possible one should take advantage of this. In larger establishments, where usually the correct type of refrigeration and deep freezes are available, these foods should then be stored as and when they are delivered. If brought out of storage according to size and weight two or three days before they are required, they can then slowly defrost and be dissected and prepared for use and cooking over a number of days.

In smaller establishments where limited deep freeze storage is available, it is usually better to buy the foods fresh, and after due dissection and preparation they are placed into storage for use at a later date. These smaller joints and cuts need only be taken out of deep freeze storage the day before use, as required for any particular function or dish. The removal of bones and carcasses from meat, fish and poultry prior to storage will give more space and make the best possible use of the limited storage space available.

Special Offer Purchases

One is advised again and again as to the importance of good purchasing and there is no doubt that both bulk buying, special offer, or seasonal advantage purchasing fall into this category. We find that all suppliers make these offers from time to time for various reasons, and whenever possible one should take advantage of them.

Special or seasonal offers should, however, have a considerable reduction in price and one should make sure that correct and sufficient storage is available before consideration is given to the foods to be purchased and their relative saving. Remember that all foods stored in the deep freeze cost money to keep, both in space and electricity.

In this way the purchase of six hindquarters of beef at 10–15% reduction would be a more advantageous purchase than, say, 24 boxes of frozen vegetables at a reduction of 30% on normal price. Both would take up the same space approximately in the deep freeze, but the very much higher cost of beef and subsequent higher saving in pounds and pence, would make beef the better buy for our purpose.

One of the authors purchased at one time a whole plane-load of 5000 pheasants and 6500 partridges in Stockholm on special offer from Russia at a reduction of 40% of the normal market price at the time. With the existence of a large deep freeze of the walk-in type, there was sufficient space to store this large purchase and the saving was considerable.

The saving was again emphasized when in the following year game prices rose by about 20% which thus paid for the lost interest on capital outlay of the purchase, the running cost of the deep freeze, together with many other items stored for several years. One cannot of course always take inflation into consideration; it may work the other way, but in the last few years these types of purchase have proved to be useful.

Irregular Supply and Deliveries

In all parts of the country, catering establishments, particularly those situated a little remotely or open only for a season, as well as those of small size, have experienced more and more irregular supplies and deliveries in recent years. It may be because of the small amounts required, thus making the cost of deliveries not worthwhile, or for reasons of distance or delivery patterns, but both small and large establishments will find a need for advanced buying under these circumstances.

The storage facilities of a deep freeze, as indeed all other storage space, will be necessary to be able to do normal business in a proper manner and with the necessary supplies available.

TYPES OF DEEP FREEZER

There are three types of deep freezer. Differences between them, however, are only in respect of shape, size and possibly make, for all work by the same principle of compressor, condenser and evaporator.

Built-in Walk-in Type

This type of deep freeze is usually found in larger catering units, such as hospitals, refectories, canteens and large hotels and restaurants. It is also used in the main by hotels and restaurants that do not normally have a large volume of business but do a high-class type of work, with large and varied menus, and need for this reason this type of deep freeze storage.

The average size of deep freezers normally found in catering establishments is 2 × 2 × 2.25 metres, but all sizes are available or can be built, and there are companies that will build purpose-designed deep freezes in many shapes and sizes.

All such freezers will have divisions within them, allowing for separation of meat and fish or vegetables.

Deep Freeze Cabinet

Here we have two types. First, the box or chest type, which is the most popular deep freeze and the cheapest to buy, with some having the advantage of a built-in quick-freeze section, which is separate from the storage section and which allows one to freeze foods quite quickly.

These types of deep freeze have, however, one big disadvantage in that even with some divisions in the form of plastic-coated wire baskets, foods are mixed and often lie on top of one another. Quick access to the food is often difficult, and usually what one is looking for is found on the bottom of the freezer. One has to remove many things before the item one is looking for can be found, even if well marked as to content and amount.

The second type of cabinet is the so-called upright cabinet. It is usually a little more expensive to buy, but by its design and inner shelving it allows easy and quick access to foods required, which is most useful in a busy establishment.

Its disadvantage is in the opening of the upright door, which allows in a lot of warm air, and which warms the inside of the freezer very easily and so it therefore needs more electricity for this reason than the box type freezer.

Manufacturers have of late gone over to fitting two or four doors, which allow for the division of foods from one another and of course only lets warm air into one of several compartments of the freezer, thus reducing the excessive use of electricity for this type. Some of these upright freezers have freeze-cooled shelves which help in

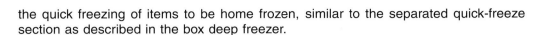
the quick freezing of items to be home frozen, similar to the separated quick-freeze section as described in the box deep freezer.

Fridge–Freezer Cabinet

The last type of deep freeze comprises a combination of normal fridge and freezer in one unit. Originally intended for the larger household, they have been readily bought by small catering units, and have also found good use in back-bar cooking, floor-service cooking and ward-service cooking storage in hospitals. They are available in two types, with two doors one over another, the top usually being the fridge and the lower door being the deep freeze.

They are also available with four doors as a complete unit for the smaller establishment, two fridge doors and two freezer doors where one fridge door is intended to hold any cooked foods and another to hold raw foods. The two freezer doors allow separation of fish from meat or vegetables.

FREEZER MANAGEMENT

Whatever the type of freezer, good organization in use is essential to give the best possible service. This organization must at all times follow a set of basic rules.

Freezer Management Rules
- When buying ready-frozen foods freeze-store only the foods, not the packaging boxes, which take up too much room.
- Foods to be frozen in-house should be sealed in oil-brushed moisture- and vapour-free material, usually plastic bags. For some items oiled greaseproof paper sheets can help to exclude as much air as possible. A near-vacuum is the ideal.
- Only fresh and sound foods should be frozen. Food that smells when you freeze it will smell when you defrost it.
- Mark your package to be frozen with a permanent felt pen as to content, number, weight and date.
- Freeze weights and numbers in accordance with the volume of your business. If on average you serve 20 suprêmes of chicken per meal freeze in 10 or 12 suprêmes per packet; if you serve on average 20 portions of beef stew per meal freeze your diced stewing beef in packs of 2 kg to give you 16–20 portions.
- Frozen food defrosted must never be re-frozen, even after it has been cooked.

Collection

A good reason for the use of a deep freeze in this connection is that of collection. Small amounts of fresh foods not sufficient for a dish or meal can be placed into the deep freeze until there is sufficient for a given meal or dish, e.g. chicken livers may be collected over a period, until there is enough to make a pâté, or skewers of chicken liver and bacon.

Storage and Shelving

Most deep freezes are supplied with a number of shelves according to size, or they are equipped with shelves or baskets, as in the case of box deep freezes. One should if possible reserve one shelf for each item or type of food, e.g. a shelf for beef, one shelf for lamb, one shelf for veal, one shelf for poultry, and so on.

Freezer Stock Control

One should always know what foods and how much of each food is to be found in the deep freeze. This is best done with a stock list on or near the freezer, where staff can easily cross off or add items which are removed from or placed into it.

Thus at a glance one is aware of the stock in hand, and this can be taken into consideration when placing new orders. This stock list should be well laid out and simple to use. If the working of the stock list gets too complicated, any additions or subtraction will not be recorded and in the atmosphere of a busy kitchen, incorrect stock will be shown. This could be disastrous and result in either too much or too little stock.

Once every three or four weeks all the stock should be removed from the deep freeze, excess ice scraped out, and the deep freeze thoroughly cleaned. Every two or three months the deep freeze should be switched off and defrosted, if it is not of the self-defrosting type, and thoroughly cleaned. The guidance given above with regard to defrosting an ordinary refrigerator may be applied equally well to a deep freeze.

WITHDRAWAL

When foods are required from the deep freeze it takes good timing to place them outside the deep freeze for defrosting. The best place for defrosting meats, poultry and fish is of course a normal fridge where the food can defrost slowly and without sudden temperature change. Various weights and sizes need different times, and the amount of bone left in some cuts of meat or fish (as in the case of a rib of beef or halibut steaks) will have some delaying effect on the defrosting.

Foods of any kind should never be defrosted by applying either dry heat or hot water, as they will always lose flavour and appearance. Of late microwave ovens have been used in the defrosting of larger cuts or joints of meat, but not very successfully, as it needs some experience and good timing so that the food is only defrosted and does not actually begin to cook. A guide for defrosting in a normal fridge may be as follows:

Small cuts and portions	overnight
Small joints and poultry	12–24 hours
Small carcasses (lamb)	12–24 hours
Larger carcasses/quarters (beef)	48–72 hours

In the case of small or medium packages, especially those of one's own production and preparation, all wrapping should be removed and food placed on to trays with a wire rack to allow defrosting liquid to seep separately. The slower the defrosting cycle the better the results, especially with red meats like beef and game. These should be defrosted slowly, otherwise they bleed excessively and much of the goodness and blood will be found on the defrosting tray.

Marinating

However carefully we freeze food it will bleed and lose some flavour and sometimes appearance, and we would do well to put some of this back. It is best done in the form of marinades or by some seasonings.

A bag of defrosted prawns is much improved by the following method: when defrosted, wash and drain, then add a little lemon juice, oil, salt and pepper, and let them marinate for 1–2 hours before using. Most flavour and colour will return and make these prawns much more pleasant to use for both hot and cold dishes.

When it is necessary to freeze sirloins for steaks always freeze whole or possibly in two pieces if a large strip-loin, for individual steaks bleed much more excessively in proportion than the whole or piece of sirloin. When the piece for entrecôtes has been defrosted, cut the steaks and place them on a tray for grilling or frying with the addition of a little oil, garlic, salt and pepper marinade. The flavour and appearance will greatly improve and render the entrecôtes ready for grilling or frying at the same time.

The same is the case for fish. If left for an hour or so before cooking in a little seasoning and lemon juice marinade for boiling or poaching fish, or seasoning, lemon juice and oil for all grilling or frying fish, it will improve both in appearance and flavour and much will be added to its final presentation when cooked.

Never force foods when defrosting: give them time. Hanging foods to defrost in a hot kitchen, or leaving them outside in a kitchen overnight will cause deterioration, especially in appearance, and there are also some dangers in respect of contamination.

Many scientists will advise, for various reasons, not to freeze food oneself as normal deep freezes are only intended for storing frozen food, and are not made to freeze fresh foods, which should be done by blast-freezing only. While this advice has a sound scientific basis, there is no law in Great Britain against home freezing in a normal deep freeze, except the rules and regulations applying to ice creams, which are well known.

The practice of doing our own freezing is widespread, both in the home as well as in our industry, and manufacturers of deep freezes have even supplied various types with special quick-freeze sections or coils for quick contact freezing to help us in this, but they are not as effective as the proper blast-freeze units which few can afford to install.

If we only freeze smaller joints and packages, if we only freeze good fresh and sound foods, if we keep our freezers and equipment absolutely clean, and cook our food properly and well, most deep freezes are a most valuable aid in the preparation of food in our industry.

USE AND CARE OF MACHINERY AND UTENSILS

Mincing Machine and Food Processors

These two machines have an important function in the Larder. In the case of the mincer, this includes the mincing of raw meats for sausages, hamburgers, bitoks, meat loafs, mincing of fats prior to rendering for dripping and other minced meat preparation. A food processor (Figure 1.3) is a useful tool in the making of raw and cooked farces, pâtés, mousses and purée mixtures as well as some sauces. It is also handy for

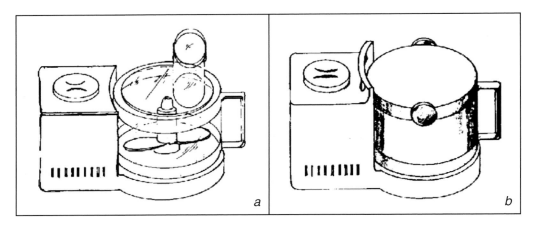

FIG. 1.3 *Food processors: (a) plastic version and (b) metal*

the making of brown breadcrumbs (chapelure) from stale brown bread or fresh white breadcrumbs (mie de pain) from day old crustless white bread. The metal machines are more expensive but usually prove more robust in use.

Both the mincing and processor attachments can be dismantled for cleaning, which should be done with hot water containing grease solvent, then rinsed and dried before re-assembling. Finally, the machine must be lubricated at regular intervals with the lubricating oil provided. The operator should study the instruction chart to become familiar with the oiling points.

The Slicing Machine

This machine is used for cutting slices of cooked meats such as ham or tongue, or any other joint of meat that must, naturally, be boneless. It is also used for cutting bacon or gammon rashers that will, of course, be uncooked. A calibrated scale is fitted to determine the thickness of the slice or rasher and one must ensure that this is returned to zero prior to placing one's hands in the vicinity of the blade to remove or adjust the joint of meat or to clean the machine. The slicer is usually of the gravity feed type but other makes and types are available, e.g. horizontal feed. They may be hand operated, semi-automatic or fully automatic, the latter having both blade and carriage mechanically operated.

For cleaning, the machine should be dismantled in accordance with the instruction chart provided by the manufacturers and all parts washed in hot water containing a grease solvent. They should then be rinsed and dried prior to re-assembly. The parts not removable should be cleaned on the machine and care must be taken to ensure that no foodstuffs are left clinging to any part of it, as this could be the ideal breeding ground for bacteria. Cotton waste and a wooden palette are used for cleaning the edge of the blade.

Remember, the scale must be set at zero before undertaking any of these operations. The blade should be kept sharp by using the grindstone attachment provided, when necessary, but care must be taken not to do this too often or for too long as it will cause wear to the blade.

The machine should be kept lubricated with the oil provided, in accordance with the instruction book.

Scales and Weighing Machines

There are several types, the uses of which are obvious. Large platform scales for weighing large joints of meat or other heavy weights are obtainable. For lesser weights there are smaller scales such as graduated scales fitted with a price chart showing at a glance the prices of the odd grams and/or the price per kilogram. The Inspector of Weights and Measures should inspect and set these periodically.

No maintenance is necessary other than keeping them in a scrupulously clean condition. Sponging them over with a cloth soaked in hot water and then drying thoroughly will do this. The pans of the small scales and the tray of the graduated scales are removable and should be washed in a sink of hot water.

Foodstuff should not be placed directly on to the platform or pans of the scales but should always be on a clean dish or tray or on a sheet of greaseproof paper when being weighed. Naturally, the weight of the container must be taken into account when reckoning the weight of the food.

Electric Grinding Machine

This machine is used for grinding an edge on knives and choppers, or cleavers, as and when required. It should not be abused and should be brought into use only when the steel or the hand carborundum stone fails to set a sufficiently keen edge to the cutting tools. The too frequent use of the grinding machine not only unduly wears the steel of the knives, etc., but has a detrimental effect on the temper of the steel itself.

The following instructions should be carefully observed:

(1) Make sure there is sufficient water in the well and that the water is being pumped on to the grindstone, before using. Never use the stone dry.

(2) Use the guides fitted to the machines for either knives or choppers, as this ensures the correctly set edge.

(3) Hold the handle of the knife, or chopper, in the right hand and draw the edge along the stone from the heel of the knife to the tip, with the stone revolving in the forward position.

(4) Now switch to reverse and reverse your drill; knife handle in the left hand, edge of knife from heel to tip, from right to left. Do not over-grind. Set the edge with steel.

(5) Keep the machine in a clean condition by sponging the stove-enameled parts with a damp cloth, then dry. Change the water frequently to prevent sediment from clogging the pump.

(6) For lubricating, follow the instructions on the chart and learn the lubricating points.

Boiling Plate or Gas Rings

These are used to heat or cook foodstuffs as required, e.g. principally for cooking vegetables for hors d'oeuvres, for rendering fats, and for the making of aspic jelly, sauces, pickles and other Larder preparations. The flame must at all times be controlled to avoid the risk of burning the food and the taps are adjustable to a range of settings to suit all purposes.

Spillings, or boil-overs, should be wiped down immediately to prevent them from baking hard on the hot surfaces. When bars are cooled, remove any crusted matter, and then wash in hot water containing a grease solvent. Periodically, the burners will require the same treatment and must be carefully dried before replacing. The enamel surround should be sponged down with the water. Abrasives should not be used as they damage and scratch the enamel.

Griller/Toaster (Salamander Grill)

As the name implies, this is used for either grilling or toasting foodstuffs. It is used principally for toasting bread for making savouries and canapés, and for grilling sausages, chipolatas or other foodstuffs for savouries.

For cleaning, the burners should be lightly brushed to prevent the holes from clogging up. The metal reflectors should be carefully wiped clean as they are easily damaged. The fat drip tray must be emptied and cleaned daily. A little water in the tray will prevent the grease from baking on. Do not allow crumbs to burn in the tray. The stove enamel parts should be sponged with a damp cloth and wiped dry.

Gas Boiler

The gas boiler is used for cooking large joints such as hams, gammons, tongues, etc., and also for cooking lobsters or crabs. The pan interior must be emptied and cleaned, washed and dried each time it is used.

Butcher's Blocks

These are used for all butchery work: dissecting, jointing and cutting meat, as well as cutting fats, breaking and chopping bones, etc. They are composed of a number of sections of timber in block form, jointed together and framed around with a stout wooden frame. The whole is secured with bolts which pass through the frame and blocks, securing all together.

They have the advantage of being reversible, so that when one surface becomes badly worn, the block can be reversed. They can also be re-surfaced when badly worn by having the surfaces cut by a large saw at a timber yard. The block usually rests on a stout deal frame, into which may be fitted drawers to contain the butcher's tools.

A good general rule is to keep the surface as clean and dry as possible. The top should never be scrubbed. It should be scraped or brushed with the scraper or wire brushes provided and left to dry. Wet meat should not be allowed to lie on the block longer than is necessary, as brine or water can soften the joints or produce wet rot between the blocks. Never wash the tools on the block, as this can add considerably to the moisture content.

Saucepans and Lids

These are mostly aluminium and require the utmost care to keep clean. Certain foods cause bad discoloration of aluminium and the saucepans should be washed in hot soapy water, polished to a bright shine with wire wool and soap, thoroughly rinsed, and dried each time after use. Soda must not be used, as this causes pitting and discolouring. The same treatment is given to aluminium trays and other containers. Enamel trays are washed in hot soapy water, rinsed and dried, as also are china and earthenware bowls and basins and plastic hors d'oeuvres dishes.

Frying Kettles and Frying Pans

The frying kettles are used for deep-frying and for rendering fats into dripping. The frying pans are used for a variety of shallow frying or sauté-ing operations. Both are made of wrought steel and are best cleaned, whilst still hot, with a heavy dry cloth.

Tables, Counters and Floors

Steel tables are used as workbenches but foodstuffs must not be cut on them. Apart from scratching the surface of the table, such malpractice can also blunt the edge of the knife or tool being used. Boards are provided for such a purpose. The tables should be cleaned by sponging with a cloth soaked in hot soapy water, rinsed with clean water and dried. The chopping boards should be well scrubbed and dried after use. In particular, care should be taken not to leave any fish scales clinging to the surfaces. Formica-top tables can be sponged down, as for the steel tables, but the wooden framework must be scrubbed and dried.

At the end of each session, the sinks, counters and floor must be left in a clean condition, together with all the other items mentioned above. Porcelain sinks should be cleansed with scouring powder and rinsed out. Drains should be cleared; cloths washed and hung up to dry. Counters should be scrubbed, windowsills sponged clean and, finally, the floor well swept. If these operations are carried out, the department will always be clean and fresh for the commencement of each session.

Other Larder Tools

The following pieces of small equipment are made of steel or tinned steel and are cleaned by washing in hot water containing grease solvent, then rinsed and dried:

Serving spoons and ladles	For spooning or ladling foods
Sieves	For sieving various foods
Colanders	For draining foodstuffs
Conical strainers	For straining sauces, etc.
Meat presses	For pressing joints etc.
Pie moulds	For pork or veal and ham pies
Whisks	For whisking and stirring food
Egg slicer	For slicing hard-boiled eggs
Steel basins	Containers, etc.
Graters	For grating foods

The following tools are kept clean by washing in hot water, rinsing and drying. Care should be taken to prevent them from rusting or deteriorating:

Cutlet bat	For flattening cuts of meat
Trussing needles	For poultry trussing
Larding needles	For larding cuts of meat, poultry, etc.
Larding pin	For larding joints, etc.

Lemon zesters	For scraping of lemon peel
Lemon decorators	For channeling lemon skin
Vegetable scoops	For shaping vegetables and potatoes
Butcher's hooks	For hanging joints etc.
Skewers	For skewering meat, etc.
Brining syringe	For pumping brine into joints
Brinometer	For measuring density of brine

Polythene Bins – Hygiene

The refuse bins should be emptied daily and washed out with warm water. They must not be exposed to excess heat, otherwise they will lose their shape, or even melt. In particular, no disinfectants must be used in the swill bin, as this could poison the pigs. The bin for brining meat must not be interchanged with either of the other two.

2 Starters (The Hors d'oeuvre)

On any modern menu, the cold hors d'oeuvre will always take first place, except on a cold winter day when a hot soup or hot starter might be preferred.

Hors d'oeuvres as we understand them today were developed by French chefs in Russia, by combining Russian food customs of the day with French know-how and finesse. In Russia as well as in the rest of Europe, in the days of great palaces and mansions or country houses, the aristocratic high society frequently held large receptions, dinners and dances. It must have been a fine sight to see the lords and ladies arrive by carriage. The ladies in high-fashion gowns with wide crinoline skirts, the gentlemen in tight breeches and buckled shoes, both topped with white powdered wigs, and officers in the most colourful uniforms imaginable. Thus, these receptions and dinners were a matter of much pomp and ceremony.

The arrival of so many guests by carriage was a slow business and it often took hours for all guests to arrive and enter, in strict order of importance and standing. During such a lengthy assembly of guests, invariably an orchestra played for the amusement of the visitors or even dancing, and often gaming was provided in the small side room. Great amounts of champagne and other drinks were freely served to the waiting guests, which had the disadvantage that many guests were somewhat unsteady on their feet, if not positively inebriated, before they were asked to sit down for dinner.

During this times French culture, language and *rigueur du table* were very prominent in Russia, as well as Europe, and French cuisine was a must. Every great house in Europe had a French Head Chef, who provided food and dishes of the highest flavour and quality with artistic splendour of presentation and service. But a somewhat drunk, however elegant, assembly was unable, in its shaky state to appreciate the magnificent food presented by the French chefs. Nor were the guests able to offer due appreciation and make the expected compliments to which many French chefs had become accustomed. A method therefore had to be devised to ensure that as sober an assembly as possible sat down to dinner.

To stop the generous service of vodka and champagne would have been considered inhospitable and stingy. The chefs then had the idea of serving the arriving guests something to eat – something, it was hoped, which would give them some base for drinking, some lining for their often empty stomachs. Guests would then arrive at the dinner table somewhat more sober and consequently more appreciative of the delights for the palate the cuisine *à la française* was about to offer.

Thus the modern hors d'oeuvre was born, serving foods represented at first by basic Russian eating habits in the form of the old-established Zakouski, plus such as various breads, with radishes, anchovy, oysters, caviar, smoked fish, sardines, pickled onions, pickled cucumber, pickled eggs, and other titbits, still associated with today's receptions or cocktail parties, including olives, nuts, gherkins etc., and the newly acquired French culinary finesse in the grand houses of Russia.

But these foods were not served in the dining rooms but in the anterooms, from small side-tables placed all around the reception area. From this humble beginning gradually the hors d'oeuvre became established and very fashionable, particularly in the newly emerging hotel and restaurant industry. As it did so, restaurants and their chefs tried to outdo each other in the assortments, combination and presentation of their hors d'oeuvre offering. Through this competition, types of hors d'oeuvre grew substantially in numbers and variety, a trend which has continued to this day. We now see almost daily new hors d'oeuvres proffered on modern restaurant menus; one could list over 10 000 foods and dishes, with their variations of presentation, that could be served as the hors d'oeuvre, or starters, at the beginning of meal.

The translation of the term *hors d'oeuvre* is literally 'outside or before the main work', in our case, before the main meal, which makes good sense in the light of the above explanation of availability before the meal and away from the dining room. This meaning is not always understood. It is therefore not surprising how many and varied translations there are for the French term *hors d'oeuvre* in the different European languages. In England alone this course may be termed 'starters', 'appetizers', 'prelude' or 'overture' and the term 'side dishes' may well relate to the fact, as explained above, that in the old days the 'starters' were offered in small dishes from side-tables of the reception room, or anteroom, while the guests waited to be asked to enter the dining hall for the meal.

Today we do not eat the hors d'oeuvre course as a base for drinking, but to titillate our palate. 'Appetizer' therefore is a very appropriate word for this course, if we then remember that the hors d'oeuvre may only be one course of several to follow. *All hors d'oeuvres should therefore be light and served in modest portions*, to make the mouth water, and not to fill the stomach. The offerings should, at all times, be fresh, colourful, appetizing and piquant, as well as varied and suitable for the time of year and occasion or meal.

There is little doubt that a well-composed and presented hors d'oeuvre will set the tone for any ensuing courses, and nowhere in the region of culinary presentation has the Chef such a unique opportunity to make his or her *first good impression*, which can raise expectations for the rest of the meal to follow.

To help you find your way through this large number of choices when it come to the selection of the right starter for the right occasion, or a given meal, and the right time of the year, we give below a classification of hors d'oeuvres, broken down into types and presented in tables, which should aid readers in a generally better understanding of the subject and hopefully enable the right practical choice in their respective establishments.

CLASSIFICATION OF STARTERS   *Hors d'oeuvres*

We differentiate between three types of starters:

Single starters	or	Hors d'oeuvres singuliers
Mixed starters	or	Hors d'oeuvres variés
Hot starters	or	Hors d'oeuvres chauds

Here we will first consider single starters (hors d'oeuvres singuliers), with the best known and popular examples. These will be followed by examples of some mixed starters (hors d'oeuvres variés), which are less often served today. In both sections some special or foreign examples are included.

Hot starters, according to the modern menu structure, are served after or in place of the soup. These are not produced in the Larder but in the given section of the kitchen according to type, and are therefore not included here.

SINGLE STARTERS *Hors d'oeuvres singuliers*

As the term implies, these appetisers consist of one foodstuff, plus a suitable garnish. This even includes some classic combinations such as Parma Ham with Melon, or Parma Ham with Asparagus. More than two items *plus* a garnish would make it a mixed starter.

Single starters, according to type, may be served on plates, or dishes, in bowls, which can be of glass, crystal, china, earthenware, silver, wood or plastic, and are known as plats russes. Some single side dishes may also be served in crystals or glasses, e.g. Cocktail de crevettes roses, while some lend themselves to be served also in goblets, cocktail cups, or coupes (see Figure 2.2).

For a better understanding of the different types of single starters they have been grouped as follows:

Fruit starters	Hors d'oeuvres singuliers de fruit (for examples see Table 2.1, Plate 2.1)
Egg starters	Hors d'oeuvres singuliers d'oeufs (for examples see Table 2.2, Plate 2.2, Figure 2.1)
Fish starters	Hors d'oeuvres singuliers de poisson (for examples see Table 2.3, Plates 2.3–2.7)
Meat starters	Charcuterie (for examples see Table 2.4, Plates 2.8–2.11)

Under each of the above groups or types of starters are listed those most commonly used today, with a short explanation, a suggested presentation, with some examples with their menu names in both English and French. These lists are intended as guidance only and are by no means comprehensive.

For some selected starters detailed recipes and methods of preparation are given. Books specializing in the preparation and presentation of hors d'oeuvres will add to the knowledge and understanding of the wide scope of modern and classical hors d'oeuvres available to the modern chef.

SOME CLASSICAL SINGLE COLD *Hors d'oeuvres recipes*

Below are given some popular recipes for some of the single starters listed in the tables above. The number of average size portions each recipe will yield has been indicated, but the actual number of portions is very much a matter of the individual establishment as to size of portion to be served and cost.

TABLE 2.1 *FRUIT STARTERS* ✕ *Hors d'oeuvres singuliers de fruit (see Plate 2.1)*

Name	Types	Presentation	Menu examples	French
Artichoke: Globe	Large green Laon Large Camus	Cut off stalks, trim off sharp points with scissors. Tie with string, place in a rondeau. Cover with blanc and cook for 10–15 mins according to size or age. Cool, remove centre and choke, serve hot or cold	Globe Artichokes Vinaigrette Globe Artichokes Mayonnaise Globe Artichokes Herb Sauce Globe Artichokes Cocktail Sauce	Artichauts vinaigrette Artichauts mayonnaise Artichauts fines herbes Artichauts sc. Andalouse
Bottoms		Cook as above, remove leaves and use bottom only	Artichoke Bottoms with Prawns	Fonds d'artichauts aux crevettes
Quarters	Small green Provence	Cut off stalks, trim off sharp points with scissors. If small cook whole or quarter as above	Artichokes Greek Style	Coeur d'artichauts à la Grecque
Avocado	Green Black Crinkly	When ripe, cut in halves, fill with various dressings or fillings, e.g. prawns, or peel and slice in fans	Avocado Vinaigrette Avocado Cocktail Sauce Avocado with Prawns	Avocat vinaigrette Avocat sc. Andalouse Avocat aux crevettes
Grapefruit	Yellow Blood	Serve halves chilled, with segments cut between membrane. Cover halves with brown sugar and grill or serve whole segments served as a cocktail	Chilled Grapefruit Grilled Grapefruit Grapefruit Cocktail	Pamplemousse frappé Pamplemousse grillée Cocktail de pamplemousse

Continued

TABLE 2.1 *FRUIT STARTERS* 🖑 *Hors d'oeuvres singuliers de fruit (see Plate 2.1)—cont'd*

Name	Types	Presentation	Menu examples	French
Fruit juice	Orange Pineapple Grapefruit Tomato	Serve chilled in suitable glass with sugared rim	Chilled Orange Juice Chilled Pineapple Juice	Jus d'orange frappé Jus d'ananas frappé
Melon	Cantaloupe Charentaise Ogen Water	Cut in halves, remove pips, cut large types in portion segment or smaller in halves serve chilled or with various fillings (see below)	Chilled Cantaloupe Melon Ogen Melon with Port Charentaise Melon with Prawns Honeydew Melon with Parma Ham	Cantaloupe frappé Melon au Porto Charentaise aux crevettes Honeydew melon au jambon de Parme
Oranges	Pink Blood	Usually as juice or orange segment salad cocktail	Orange Juice Orange Cocktail Orange Salad	Jus d'orange Cocktail d'orange Salade d'orange
Tomatoes	Medium size and ripe	Cut off tops, halve and core with parisienne cutter. Fill with various fillings, e.g. prawns, fish or meat or vegetable salads	Tomatoes with Crab Meat Tomatoes with Chicken Salad Tomatoes with Ham Salad	Tomates au crabe Salade de tomates au volaille Salade de tomates au jambon
Compound salads	Fruit-, vegetable-, fish- and meat-based	See Salads, Chapter 3	Waldorf Salad Aida Salad Favourite Salad Carmen Salad	Salade Waldorf Salade Aïda Salade Favorite Salade Carmen

Cut lengthwise in half

1 Garnished with asparagus tip

2 Garnished with piped yolk and olive slices

3 Garnished with a cooked turned mushroom head and peas

4 Garnished with piped yolk and stuffed olive slices

5 Garnished with piped yolk and shrimps

6 Garnished with piped yolk and slices of plovers egg

7 Garnished with a large Dublin bay prawn and sliced radish

8 Garnished with trimmed anchovy fillets

9 Garnished with piped yolk and large prawn, parsley

10 Garnished with piped yolk and Bismarck Herring diamond

11 Garnished with piped yolk, cornet of ham or smoked salmon

12 Garnished with piped yolk, blanched tarragon, half a stoned olive

13 Garnished with piped yolk, crossed anchovy fillets and parsley

14 Garnished with piped yolk, gherkin fan and black olive half

15 Garnished with piped yolk and piped circle of pink Danish caviar

16 Garnished with bundle of cooked French beans and strip of paprika

Cut across in half

17 Garnished with piped yolk and prawns

18 Garnished with piped yolk and an anchovy ring and whole olive

19 Crown cut garnished with piped yolk and turned cooked mushroom head

20 Garnished with black caviar

21 Crown cut, garnished with blanched peeled tomato top, cooked peas

22 Crown cut, star cut tomato base including its stalk

Fɪɢ. 2.1 cont'd

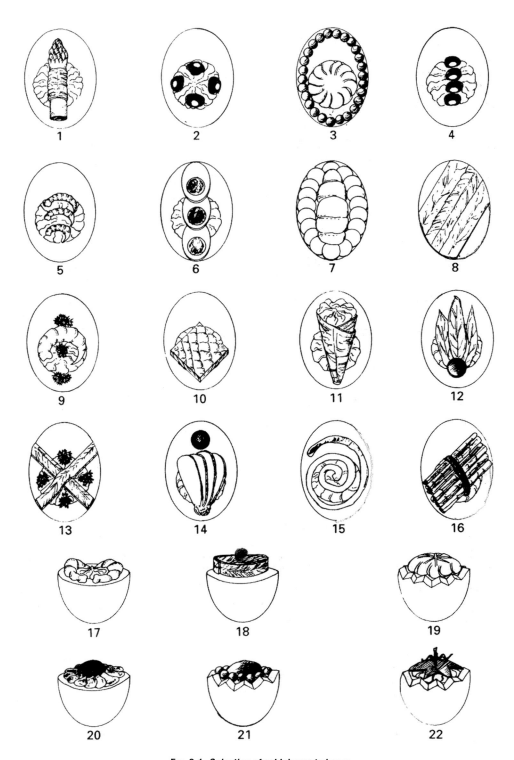

Fɪɢ. 2.1 *Selection of cold decorated eggs*

TABLE 2.2 *EGG STARTERS* ✂ *Hors d'oeuvres singuliers d'oeufs (see Plate 2.2, Fig. 2.1)*

Name	Types	Presentation	Menu examples	French
Stuffed eggs	Usually hen's eggs, others can be used. Hard boiled, shelled, peeled, cut in equal halves, yolk removed and sieved, seasoned and flavoured, mixed with mayonnaise, piped back in empty egg halves	Decorated in various ways, e.g. with prawns, anchovy, smoked salmon, Bismarck herring, asparagus tips, ham, smoked eel, caviar, herbs etc. (see Fig. 2.1)	Stuffed Eggs with Caviar Stuffed Eggs with Smoked Salmon Stuffed Eggs with Anchovy Stuffed Eggs with Prawns	Oeuf farci au caviar Oeuf farci au saumon fumé Oeuf farci au anchois Oeuf farci aux crevettes roses
Egg salad	Usually hen's eggs, others can be used. Hard boiled, shelled, peeled, cut in slices or segments	Placed on shredded lettuce, coated with various vinaigrette, garnished with anchovy capers, tomato, etc.	Egg Salad Plovers Egg Salad	Salade des oeufs Salade des oeufs de pluvier
Egg mayonnaise	Usually hen's eggs, others can be used. Hard boiled, shelled, peeled, cut in slices or segments	Placed on shredded lettuce, coated with vinaigrette, coated with mayonnaise, garnish with anchovy, capers, tomato, etc.	Egg Mayonnaise Plover's Egg Mayonnaise	Mayonnaise des oeufs Mayonnaise des oeufs de pluvier

Continued

TABLE 2.2 EGG STARTERS ⚜ *Hors d'oeuvres singuliers d'oeufs (see Plate 2.2, Fig. 2.1)—cont'd*

Name	Types	Presentation	Menu examples	French
Cold poached eggs	Usually hen's eggs, others can be used. Poached for 4 minutes, cooled, trimmed, dried	Placed on crouton and coated with mayonnaise, or mayonnaise-based sauce, e.g. green (verte), rosée or aspic. Garnish with asparagus, prawns, anchovy etc.	Cold poached Egg with Asparagus Cold Poached Egg Rosé Sauce Cold Poached Egg Green Sauce Cold Poached Egg with Anchovy	Oeuf poché froid d'asperges Oeuf poché froid sc. rosée Oeuf poché froid sc. verte Oeuf poché froid au anchois
Cold eggs in dish	Usually hen's eggs, others can be used. Butter cocotte dish, line with garnish such as asparagus, ham, prawns, peppers, etc. break raw egg on top, cook 2–3 min. in bain marie, cool	Turn out on toast, crouton or brioche base, coat with aspic or serve on mayonnaise base surround.	Cold Cocotte Egg with Ham Cold Cocotte Egg with Prawns Cold Cocotte Egg with Peppers	Oeuf en cocotte froid au jambon Oeuf en cocotte froid aux crevettes Oeuf en cocotte froid Andalouse
Plover's eggs	Quail eggs or others can also be used. Cook for 2–3 min, cool and peel. Easily stored in salted water for 2–3 days	Make a nest of mustard and cress or shredded lettuce, in the indentation place 2–3 eggs, coat with light vinaigrette, serve with mayonnaise based sauces	Plover's Eggs in Nest of Cress Quail Eggs in Nest of Cress	Oeufs de pluvier au nid de cresson Oeufs de caille au nid de cresson

TABLE 2.3 *FISH STARTERS* ✠ *Hors d'oeuvres singuliers de poisson (see Plates 2.3–2.7)*

Name	Types	Presentation	Menu examples	French
Bückling sprats	Warm smoked herring of various types, size and preparation found all over Europe	Loosen skin, remove bones, retaining shape. Place on lettuce base, garnish, serve with creamed horse radish and brown bread and butter (B&B)	Bückling Smoked Herring, Horseradish Smoked Sprats, Horseradish	Hareng fumé sc. raifort
Caviar	Ranges from the best of Russian Black Beluga to lumpfish caviar from Iceland, varying in colour from dark black to bright pink according to type and source	Best served chilled on crushed ice with B&B or possibly toast or blinis (buckwheat pancakes). A squeeze of lemon juice will bring out the flavour. Sieved hard boiled egg yolks and whites and chopped spring onions and Vodka are usual accompaniments	Chilled Beluga Caviar Chilled Osietre/ Ocetra Caviar Chilled Sevruga Caviar Chilled Fresh-water Salmon Caviar (See Plate 2.7)	Caviar de Béluga frappé Caviar de Osietre/ Ocetra frappé Caviar de Sevruga frappé Caviar de saumon frappé
Cured salmon	Gravad Lax, a Scandinavian speciality cured with sea salt, caster sugar, peppercorns and dill for 24–72 hours (see Plate 2.5). See brine recipes (Chapter 7)	Serve in thin slices on a bed of lettuce and dill with its famous mustard sauce served separately, and B&B	Cured Scandinavian Salmon or Gravad Lax with Mustard Sauce	Saumon mariné Suédoise sc. moutarde
Eel	Warm smoked eel or jellied eel. Common in northern Europe	Smoked, serve on lettuce base with creamed horseradish and B&B. Jellied, serve on lettuce base, offer lemon or vinegar, and B&B	Smoked Eel, Creamed Horseradish Jellied Eel	Anguille fumée sc. raifort Anguille à la gelée

Continued

Table 2.3 *FISH STARTERS*   *Hors d'oeuvres singuliers de poisson (see Plates 2.3–2.7)—cont'd*

Name	Types	Presentation	Menu examples	French
Herring	Bismarck, rollmops, soused, are all pickled herrings in various forms and flavours, as commercially prepared or made fresh on the premises	Serve whole or in slices, serve on lettuce base, garnish with onions rings, pickled cucumber and tomato, B&B	Soused Herring Bismarck Herring Swedish Pickled Herrings	Hareng à la Grecque Hareng Bismarck Hareng Suédoise
Mackerel	Warm smoked, found plain or in crushed peppercorns	Trim, cut in sections, place on lettuce base garnish with lemon onion rings and tomato. Serve with creamed horseradish served separately, B&B	Smoked Mackerel Pepper Smoked Mackerel	Maquereau fumé Maquereau fumé au poivre
Smoked salmon	Cold smoked salmon sides, brined and smoked in different woods to gain distinct flavour. Scottish salmon is one of the best in the world	After removing all inner bones it is traditionally cut into paper thin slices tail to head and placed on a lettuce bed and garnished with cress and lemon quarters. Mill pepper should be offered at the table. More modern, thick-cut presentations are shown in Plate 2.6	Smoked Wild Scottish Salmon Smoked Wild Irish Salmon Smoked Canadian Salmon	Saumon fumé Ecossaise Saumon fumé Irlandaise Saumon fumé Canadienne
Smoked trout	Now widely available from local trout farms, or smoked on the premises. A delicate starter	Carefully remove head and skin, remove the fillets from all bones. Serve on a bed of lettuce, garnish with cress, lemon quarters and the trout skin cut in strips and tied into a bow. Serve with B&B and creamed horseradish	Smoked Brown Trout Smoked River Trout Fillets	Truite fumée Filets de truite fumées

TABLE 2.3 *FISH STARTERS* 🔪 *Hors d'oeuvres singuliers de poisson (see Plates 2.3–2.7)—cont'd*

Name	Types	Presentation	Menu examples	French
Shellfish	Crab Lobster Crayfish Crawfish	Cooked in court bouillon, cooled, split and dressed and served on bed of lettuce with mayonnaise, B&B or toast	Dressed Crab Half a Lobster with Mayonnaise Six Crayfish with Mayonnaise Half a Crawfish with Green Sauce	Crabe froid garni Demi-homard sc. mayonnaise Écrevisses froids sc. mayonnaise
Shellfish salad	Crab, lobster, crayfish, crawfish, mussels, cockles and prawns or mixture thereof, e.g. Fruits of the Sea	As above, removed from shells, marinated in light vinaigrette, placed on a lettuce bed and garnished with capers, tomato, hard boiled egg quarters and parsley, B&B. Can be placed in shells or tartlets for neater presentation	Crab Salad Lobster Salad Mussel Salad Fruits of the Sea Salad Fruits of the Sea in Tartlets	Salade de crabe Salade d'homard Salade de moules Salade de fruits de mer Tartelettes de fruits de mer
Shellfish mayonnaise	As above	As above, coat with thinned mayonnaise, then garnish with capers, tomato, hard boiled egg quarters and parsley. Can be placed in shell tartlets for better presentation	Lobster Mayonnaise Crab Mayonnaise Crayfish Mayonnaise	Mayonnaise d'homard Mayonnaise en crabe Mayonnaise écrevisse

Continued

TABLE 2.3 *FISH STARTERS*   *Hors d'oeuvres singuliers de poisson (see Plates 2.3–2.7)—cont'd*

Name	Types	Presentation	Menu examples	French
Fish and shellfish cocktail	As above plus any poached fish pieces	Cut in neat pieces where applicable, marinate in light vinaigrette, place in coupe or suitable wine glasses, coat with cocktail sauce, garnish with a prawn or piece of lobster or crab according to content, lemon and parsley	Prawn Cocktail Mussel Cocktail Lobster Cocktail Fruits of the Sea Cocktail	Cocktail de crevettes Cocktail de moules Cocktail d'homard Cocktail de fruits de mer
Fish mousse	Can be made of most poached soft fish, e.g. salmon, smoked trout, prawns, halibut, lobster etc.	Place cooked fish or shell fish in food processor, add lemon juice and little white wine, cut to fine puree add mayonnaise and galantine dissolved in heated white wine, season, place in bowl, add whipped cream, see recipe below	Salmon Mousse Prawn Mousse Lobster Mousse Salmon and Halibut Mousse	Mousse de saumon Mousse de crevette Mousse d'homard Mousse d'homard et flétan
Oysters	Different types in different parts of Europe, France, British Isles, Belgium	Must be fresh and have closed shell, remove flat shell, remove beard from oyster, place on crushed ice, 6 per portion. Serve with lemon quarters and chopped shallots. Sometimes different vinegars are requested but both are served separately. B&B	½ Dozen Whitstable Oysters ½ Dozen Colchester Oysters ½ Dozen Belon Oysters ½ Dozen Marennes Oysters	6 Huîtres de Whitstable 6 Huîtres de Colchester 6 Huîtres de Belon 6 Huîtres de Marennes

TABLE **2.4** *COLD MEAT STARTERS* 🍴 ***Charcuterie (see Plates 2.8–2.11)***

Name	Type	Presentation	Menu examples	French
Charcuterie	Under this name we have a vast number of cold meat preparations and sausage from all over the world. Europe alone provides more than 3000 specialities ideally suited as a starter to any meal			
Raw smoked or cured meats	Various cured and/or smoked meat specialities from all over Europe, such as hams, turkey, duck, goose, venison, reindeer etc.	Cut into paper thin slices in the case of hams, venison or reindeer and presented on a plate on a lettuce base garnished with gherkins, radish, tomato and parsley. In the case of turkey, goose and duck, cut in neat scallops and garnished on lettuce base with tomatoes, cucumber. In some cases these meats are served in combination with fruits such as melon, kiwi, dates or figs	Parma Ham with Melon Westphalia Ham with Gherkins Smoked Pork Shoulder with Radish Smoked Breast of Goose Smoked Venison with Kiwi Smoked Reindeer with Cranberries Smoked Turkey Breast with Pineapple Bündel-Fleisch with Onions or Asparagus	Jambon de Parme avec melon Jambon Westphalie Poitrine de porc fumé Poitrine d'oie fumée Gigot de chevreuil fumé Épaule de renne fumé Poitrine dindonneau fumé Viande séchée anion ou asperge

Continued

TABLE 2.4 COLD MEAT STARTERS ☆ *Charcuterie (see Plates 2.8–2.11)—cont'd*

Name	Type	Presentation	Menu examples	French
Sausages	These may be smoked or plain, comprising more than 2000 different varieties from all countries in Europe: salamis, garlic sausage, liver sausages, beer sausages and many more, in all shapes, sizes and with many different flavours	Cut into slices in varying thickness according to type, they are usually presented on a bed of lettuce and garnished with gherkins, olives, radishes, pickled cucumber, tomato, onion rings and parley and served with B&B or toast	Italian Salami with Radishes Mortadella with Olives Ham Sausage with Spring Onions Beer Sausage with Onion Rings Smoked Liver Sausage Toast Tongue Sausage with Gherkins Garlic Sausage with White Radish	Salami Italienne Mortadelle avec olives Saucisse de jambon Saucisse de bière Saucisse de foie de porc fumé Saucisse de langue Saucisse de porc d'ail
Liver pâtés	The pâté foie gras is the queen of the pâtés, however very good pâtés are made from most other livers, such as chicken, duck, veal, pork. Bound with eggs and cream and flavoured with herbs and spices as well as fortified wines or brand, they are very tasty and represent a popular starter	Produced either in individual mould portions or loaf moulds, when they have to be cut with a sharp knife dipped in to hot water, they are often covered in aspic, served on a lettuce base and garnished with gherkins, pickled cucumber, tomato, radishes and parsley and always accompanied by hot or possibly Melba toast	Goose Liver Pâté Duck Liver Pâté Turkey Liver Pâté Veal Liver Pâté Pork Liver Pâté Chicken Liver Pâté	Pâté foie gras Pâté de foie de caneton Pâté de foie dindonneau Pâté de foie de veau Pâté de foie de porc Pâte de foie de volaille

Continued

TABLE 2.4 *COLD MEAT STARTERS* 🍴 *Charcuterie (see Plates 2.8–2.11)—cont'd*

Name	Type	Presentation	Menu examples	French
Galantines and terrines	Not dissimilar to pâtés, but made not from livers but from coarsely ground meats, again flavoured with strong herbs and spices fortified with wine or brandy, as well as pistachio nuts or green peppercorns to enhance flavour and appearance. Cooked in skin casings or moulds	They are presented on a base of different dressings, coulis or lettuce and garnished with gherkins, pickle cucumbers, tomato, radish and parsley in case of meats, or with apples, pineapples, kiwi, tomato, radishes and parsley or coriander in the case of the poultry items. Served with B&B or toast they are often presented with cranberries, red currant jelly or mayonnaise-based sauces	Galantine of Chicken Galantine of Turkey Terrine of Veal Terrine of Pork Terrine of Veal and Ham Terrine of Venison	Galantine de volaille Galantine dindonneau Terrine de veau Terrine de porc Terrine de veau et jambon Terrine de gibier
Rillettes, potted meats and brawn	Disappeared almost entirely from the average hors d'oeuvre menu in the last 20 years, but now making a comeback and produced commercially at good quality. Made from diced pork, duck and rabbit, seasoned and fried, after which the fat is separated and the meat torn into shreds with a fork. Placed into small individual stone jars and covered with the fat to set. In the case of brawns the meat is boiled and set again in individual jars in its own jelly	Individual rillettes are placed on a plate and surrounded with radishes or gherkins and served with hot toast. Large rillettes or brawns are cut in slices and placed on a bed of lettuce, served with sauce remoulade or other mayonnaise-based sauce In many mid-European countries the brawn is today often served as a luncheon main course with sauté potatoes and sauce remoulade	Rillette of Pork Rillette of Duck Rillette of Rabbit Pork Brawn Veal Brawn	Rillettes de porc Rillettes de caneton Rillettes de lapin Porc en gelée piquant Veau en gelée piquant

Continued

TABLE 2.4 *COLD MEAT STARTERS* ✝ *Charcuterie (see Plates 2.8–2.11)—cont'd*

Name	Type	Presentation	Menu examples	French
Pies	For cold starters we use the loaf-shaped pies fully surrounded by pastry, and normally made from pork, veal, veal and ham, and game with the fillings not unlike the terrines above	The pies are cut in wedges or slices and placed on a bed of lettuce, and garnished with spring onions, tomato, radish and gherkins. They are often served with strong sharp sauces, such as Cumberland, Ravigote or Niçoise sauce	Veal and Ham Pie Pork Pie Chicken Pie Game Pie	Pâté en croûte de veau et jambon Pâté en croûte de porc Pâté en croûte de volaille Pâté en croûte de gibier
Mayonnaises	Meat mayonnaises are only made from poultry (boiled breast of chicken), cut into neat scallops, marinated with a little vinaigrette and mixed with pineapple pieces or asparagus tips	This mixture is placed on a lettuce base coated with thinned mayonnaise and garnished according to content with either pineapple slices or asparagus tips, tomato, and parsley. Can be placed in small tartlets for better presentation	Chicken Mayonnaise Asparagus Chicken Mayonnaise Pineapple Tartlet of Chicken Mayonnaise	Mayonnaise de volaille d'asperge Mayonnaise de volaille d'ananas Tartelette de mayonnaise de volaille
Meat salads	Many salads can be made from raw or cooked charcuterie sausages and served as starters. The more simple are made by simply cutting cooked meat into julienne and adding strips of onions, pickled cucumber and red peppers, and flavouring this with a vinaigrette. (See Chapter 3 on Compound Salads)	Place the well-marinated salad on a bed of suitable lettuce, garnish with tomato and parsley. Served with B&B or toast	Piquant Beef Salad Garlic Sausage Salad Chicken Salad with Asparagus Salad of Veal with Kiwi Fruit	Salade de bœuf piquant Salade de saucisse d'ail Salade de volaille d'asperge Salade de veau au kiwi

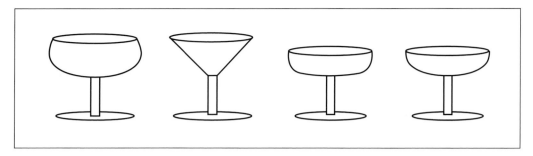

FIG. 2.2 *Various glasses suitable for cocktail presentation*

Potted Shrimps   *Crevettes au beurre*

Ingredients (4–6 portions)
250 g freshly shelled shrimps
  or small prawns
200 g butter
2 tbsp white wine
Salt and freshly milled pepper
Little lemon juice
Pinch of ground mace

Method
1 Heat butter, remove all water, clarify, add
  salt, pepper and mace
2 Add white wine bring to boil
3 Add washed shrimps/prawns, bring to boil,
  correct seasoning
4 With a perforated spoon place shrimps in
  equal amounts into individual moulds,
  evenly divide remaining butter into mould
5 Place into fridge over night to set
6 Carefully remove from mould and present
  on lettuce leaves, garnish with lemon
7 Serve with hot toast or brown bread and
  butter

Prawn Cocktail   *Cocktail de crevettes roses*

Ingredients (4–6 portions)
300 g shelled prawns
500 ml cocktail sauce
  (see p. 94)
3 lettuce finely shredded
4 channelled lemon slices
4–6 unpeeled prawns
1 sprig dill, mint or parsley

Method
1 Select appropriate glasses, coupes, or
  bowls (see Figure 2.2)
2 Equally divide shredded lettuce into
  glasses
3 Divide prawns equally on top of lettuce
4 With a tablespoon, coat the prawns with
  cocktail sauce in each of the glasses
5 Garnish with an unshelled prawn, lemon
  slice and dill, mint or parsley sprig
6 Serve with brown bread and butter or
  toast

Variation on the basic cocktail recipe above can be achieved by replacing the prawns with:

Cooked lobster pieces, making a **Lobster Cocktail/Cocktail d'homard**
Poached flaked fish fillet, making a **Fish Cocktail/Cocktail de poisson**
Cooked mussels, making a **Mussel Cocktail/Cocktail de moules**
A mixture of prawns, scallops, flaked poached fish and mussels etc., making a **Seafood Cocktail/Cocktail de fruits de mer**

Salmon Tartare   *Tartare de saumon* (see Plate 2.3*f*)

Ingredients (4–6 portions)	*Method*
500 g fresh salmon fillet *(must not be frozen)*	1 Coarsely mince fresh salmon flesh *(do not use processor)*
1 tsp sea salt	2 Mix well with salt, pepper and olive oil, leave in fridge for 10 min then shape like a small bitok
1 tbsp olive oil	
Freshly milled white pepper	
½ cucumber	3 Place on plate or platter, garnish on sliced cucumber and grated radish, offer sour cream or crème fraîche separately
150 g white or red radish	

Salmon Cornets   *Cornettes de saumon* (see Plate 2.3*g*)

Ingredients (4–6 portions)	*Method*
12–18 slices smoked salmon according to size	1 Fill the slices of salmon with the salad of your choice
200 g compound salad, e.g. Celery, Waldorf etc.*	2 Trim into even shapes
½ peeled cucumber	3 Dress on sliced cucumber garnish with lemon and dill
Lemon	
Sprigs of dill	

*Salad should be cut in a neat, fine dice; see Chapter 3 on Salads

The Mousses

Salmon Mousse   *Mousse de saumon*

Ingredients (6–8 portions)	*Method*
250 g poached flaked salmon	1 Heat white wine and dissolve gelatine therein, slightly cool
250 ml mayonnaise	

Continued

Salmon Mousse *Mousse de saumon*—cont'd

Ingredients (6–8 portions)
1 cup (300 ml) white wine
250 ml whipped cream or yoghurt
30 g gelatine
500 ml lemon juice
Salt and white pepper to taste

Method
2 Place salmon flakes free of skin and bones in a food processor, cut to fine purée
3 Add mayonnaise, lemon juice, salt and pepper, mix well in processor
4 Add the dissolved gelatine with wine, mix well in
5 Remove mixture from processor into a clean bowl
6 Fold in stiffly whipped cream, correct seasoning
7 While still in pouring consistency, pour into dariol moulds or individual soufflé dishes or loaf-shaped mould, set over night in fridge
8 Carefully remove mousse from moulds by dipping mould in hot water
9 Present individual mousse or slice of large mould on lettuce-base garnish with tomatoes and cucumber and dill, and small diamonds of smoked salmon. Serve with brown bread and butter, toast or Melba toast. Can be dressed with a coulis

Variation on the basic mousse recipes above can be achieved by replacing the salmon with:

Poached flaked halibut fillet, making a **Halibut Mousse/Mousse de flétan**
Poached smoked haddock, making a **Smoked Haddock Mousse/Mousse de aigrefin fumé**
Smoked salmon, making a **Smoked Salmon Mousse/Mousse de saumon fumé**

Carpaccio *Marinated Ox Fillet* (see Plate 2.10*i*)

Ingredients (8–10 portions)
600 g lean trimmed ox/beef fillet
2 tbsp olive oil
1 tbsp sea salt

Method
1 Place beef fillet in a deep china or stainless steel bowl
2 Mix oil with all other ingredients, rub into fillet and place in bowl

Continued

Carpaccio *Marinated Ox Fillet* (see Plate 2.10*i*)—**cont'd**

Ingredients (8–10 portions)
1 tbsp milled black pepper
1 tbsp green peppercorns
2 sprigs fresh thyme

Method
3 Pour over rest of marinade, leave to marinate 24–36 hours in fridge
4 Deep freeze the fillet for easy carving
5 Carve fillet in paper-thin slices on a slicing machine, place on plate in neat pattern, sprinkle with olive oil and crushed green peppercorns. Leave to stand at room temperature for 3–5 min before serving

Vitello Tonnato (see Plate 2.10*k*)

Ingredients (8–10 portions)
600 g lean joint trimmed veal
100 g mirepoix
1 bay leaf
1 clove garlic
250 ml dry white wine
2 litres veal or chicken stock
500 ml mayonnaise
50 g cooked tuna (may be tinned)
12 peppercorns
Salt
1 tbsp capers

Method
1 Place veal in a suitable saucepan, add all other ingredients
2 Bring to the point of boil, skim
3 Simmer gently on side of stove for 1 hour
4 Remove veal into a bowl, strain hot stock over veal, cool
5 Place in fridge for 24–36 hours
6 For service, carve veal in paper-thin slices (best with a machine)
7 Place on a plate in neat pattern, cover with a puree of tuna-flavoured mayonnaise, sprinkle with capers

Ham Mousse *Mousse de jambon*

Ingredients (6–8 portions)
250 g cooked ham cut in even dice
250 ml mayonnaise
1 cup (300 ml) white wine
250 ml whipped cream
30 g gelatine
1 tsp Worcestershire sauce

Method
1 Heat white wine in pan and dissolve gelatine therein, cool
2 Place ham and Worcestershive sauce in a food processor, cut to fine purée
3 Add the dissolved gelatine with wine, mayonnaise and seasoning, mix well in processor

Continued

Ham Mousse  *Mousse de jambon—cont'd*

Ingredients (6–8 portions)
4 tbsp Madeira or port
Salt and milled pepper to
  taste

Method
4 Remove mixture from processor into a
  clean bowl, fold in stiffly whipped
  cream, correct seasoning and add
  port or Madeira
5 While still in pouring consistency, pour
  into dariol moulds, soufflé dishes or
  loaf-shaped mould, set over night in
  fridge
6 Carefully remove mousse from mould
  by dipping mould in hot water
7 Present individual mousse or slice
  from large mould on lettuce base,
  garnish with tomatoes, parsley,
  pickled onions and cucumber slices.
  Serve with brown bread and butter,
  toast or Melba toast. Can be dressed
  with a coulis

Pheasant Mousse *Mousse de faisan*

Ingredients (6–8 portions)
250 g cooked pheasant
  breast, diced
250 ml mayonnaise
1 cup (300 ml) white wine
250 ml whipped cream
30 g gelatine
1 tsp Worcestershire sauce
5 tsp Madeira
50 g white button mushrooms
Salt and milled pepper,
  cayenne to taste

Method
1 Heat white wine in pan and dissolve
  gelatine therein, cool
2 Cut mushrooms in julienne, cook in
  Madeira, cool
3 Place pheasant and Worcestershire
  sauce in food processor, cut to fine
  puree
4 Add the dissolved gelatine with wine,
  mayonnaise and seasoning, mix well
  in processor
5 Remove mixture from processor into a
  clean bowl, fold in stiffly whipped
  cream, mushrooms/Madeira, correct
  seasoning
6 While still in pouring consistency pour
  into dariol moulds or soufflé dishes or
  loaf-shaped mould, set over night in
  fridge
7 Carefully remove mousse from mould
  by dipping mould in hot water

Continued

Pheasant Mousse   *Mousse de faisan*—cont'd

Method

8 Present individual mousse or slice of large mould on lettuce base, garnish with tomatoes and asparagus tips, serve with brown bread and butter or Melba toast. Can be dressed with a coulis

Variation on the basic recipes above can be achieved by replacing pheasant meat with:

Partridge meat, making a **Partridge Mousse/Mousse de perdrix**

Snipe meat, making a **Snipe Mousse/Mousse de bécassine**

Grouse meat, making a **Grouse Mousse/Mousse de grouse**

Venison meat, making a **Venison Mousse/Mousse de chevreuil**

All game mousses are often served with cold sauces and preparations such as Cumberland Sauce, Tomato Coulis and Cranberry Sauce (see sauce recipes in Chapter 3).

Liver Mousse   *Mousse de foie* (see Plate 2.10*e*)

Ingredients (8–16 portions)
500 g liver (veal or chicken), well trimmed, diced
200 g green bacon, cut in neat dice
100 g butter
250 ml whipped cream
1 large clove garlic
100 g diced onions
1 heaped tbsp marjoram
1 tsp ground clove
Salt, milled pepper, cayenne to taste
1 glass Madeira
1 litre Madeira aspic

Method
1 Fry liver of your choice in butter to a good deep brown
2 Do the same with green bacon
3 Place both in a food processor, adding marjoram, garlic, seasoning and Madeira, cutting in to a fine puree
4 Force the purée through a fine sieve in to a bowl (should be very fine) and smooth, mix in a ladle or two of aspic
5 Gently fold in the whipped cream, correct seasoning
6 Pipe into individual dishes or moulds, allow to set well
7 Coat portion with a film of Madeira aspic or melted butter
8 Serve with Melba or warm toast

The Terrines/Potted Meats

Chicken Terrine　　*Terrine de volaille*

Ingredients (12–16 portions)
750 g raw white chicken meat,
　coarsely minced
2 raw chicken breasts cut in
　neat dice
100 g green lean bacon, cut
　in neat dice
100 g chopped shallots,
1–2 glasses white wine
1 generous pinch ground
　thyme
1 tbsp Worcestershire sauce
30 g peeled and blanched
　pistachio nuts
1 litre chicken aspic
Juice of 1 lemon
Salt, cayenne, milled pepper
　to taste
1 large glass brandy

Method
1 Cook shallots in little chicken fat/oil,
　cool
2 Place coarsely minced chicken, bacon
　and chicken dice in a bowl
3 Add onions, wine, thyme and
　Worcestershire sauce and seasoning
4 Mix well, by hand, add pistachio nuts,
　lemon juice, mix
5 Lace mixture into a terrine with
　2–3 bay leaves on top
6 Cook terrine in a tray with water au
　bain marie in a medium–low oven for
　1½–2 hours until all fat has risen to
　the top and is clear. Drain off
　excessive juice and fat
7 Place on a tray, pour brandy over top,
　place in fridge over night to set.
　Flavour will improve by longer storage
　in a cool place
8 Fill the side cavity of terrine with a
　good aspic with a thin layer of aspic
　on top, allow to set in fridge
9 Cut into even portion with a hot knife,
　place on plate with garnish, serve
　with hot toast or Melba toast

Pork Terrine　　*Terrine de porc* (see Plate 2.10*c*)

Ingredients (12–16 portions)
750 g medium lean pork
　coarsely minced
150 g trimmed pork fillet cut in
　neat dice
150 g green bacon, cut in
　neat dice
100 g chopped shallots
1–2 glasses white wine
1 generous pinch ground
　marjoram

Method
1 Cook shallots in little pork fat/oil, cool
2 Place minced pork, bacon and pork
　fillet dice in a bowl
3 Add onions, wine, marjoram,
　Worcestershire sauce, vinegar and
　seasoning
4 Mix well, by hand, add pistachio nuts,
　mix again
5 Place mixture into a terrine with
　2–3 bay leaves on top

Continued

Pork Terrine ⚜ *Terrine de porc* (see Plate 2.10c)—cont'd

Ingredients (12–16 portions)
1 tbsp Worcestershire
  sauce 30 g peeled and
  blanched pistachio nuts
1 litre aspic
Cayenne and milled pepper to
  taste
2 tbsp wine vinegar
1 glass dry sherry

Method
6 Cook terrine in a tray with water au
  bain marie in medium–low hot oven
  for 1½–2 hours until all fat has risen
  to the top and is clear, pour off
  excessive fat, pour sherry over
7 Place on a tray to cool, place in fridge
  over night to set. Flavour will improve
  by longer storage in a cool place
8 Fill the side cavity with a good aspic
  with a thin layer of aspic on top, allow
  to set in fridge
9 Cut into even portion with a hot knife,
  place on plate with garnish, serve
  with hot toast or Melba toast

Game Terrine ⚜ *Terrine de gibier*

Ingredients (12–16 portions)
750 g coarsely minced
  venison shoulder/leg free
  of all skin and sinew
2 trimmed game fillet cut in
  neat dice
150 g green bacon fat, cut in
  neat dice
100 g chopped shallots
200 g very small button
  mushrooms
1 litre aspic
1–2 glasses red wine
1 generous pinch ground
  marjoram
2 tbsp Worcestershire sauce
Cayenne and milled pepper
  to taste
1 tbsp wine vinegar
2 glasses Madeira

Method
1 Cook shallots in little fat/oil, cool
2 Sauté button mushrooms, cool
3 Place minced game, bacon and game
  fillet dice in a bowl
4 Add shallots, wine, marjoram,
  Worcestershire sauce and seasoning
5 Mix well, by hand, add mushrooms,
  lift in carefully
6 Place mixture into a terrine with
  2–3 bay leaves on top
7 Cook terrine in a tray with water au
  bain marie in medium–low oven for
  1½–2 hours until all fat has risen to
  the top and is clear, pour off
  excessive fat pour Madeira over top
8 Place on a tray to cool, place in fridge
  over night to set. Flavour will improve
  by longer storage in a cool place
9 Fill the side cavity with a good aspic
  with a thin layer of aspic on top, allow
  to set in fridge
10 Cut into even portion with a hot knife,
   place on plate with garnish, serve
   with hot toast or Melba toast

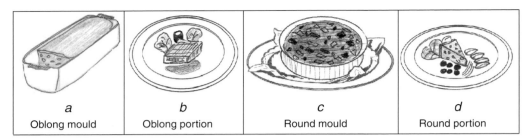

a	b	c	d
Oblong mould	Oblong portion	Round mould	Round portion

Fɪɢ. 2.3 *Terrine shapes and portions. (a,b) Oblong mould and portion; (c,d) round mould and portion*

Savoury Jellies and Brawns

Savoury Meat Jelly   *Aspic de viande*

Ingredients (to produce 2 litres)
150 g lean minced beef
1 litre best quality beef/veal
   stock, cold
2–3 egg whites
   18–20 leaves of gelatine
1 stick celery
1 carrot
1 small onion, not peeled
Some parsley stalks
1 glass red wine
Salt and pepper to taste

Method
1 Soak gelatine in plenty of cold water
2 Place minced meat in saucepan, add egg whites and little cold stock, mix well, add remainder of stock, vegetables, parsley stalks
3 Place on stove and bring to a burst of boil
4 Take aside and very slowly simmer for 30 min, when the solid will rise to top. Add the soft, well squeezed out leaf gelatine, let dissolve, add wine
5 Gently ladle aspic on to sieve with a tummy cloth to drain into a bowl
6 Test setting firmness of aspic by placing a small amount on a saucer and place in fridge to set. If too firm add a little white wine, if too loose add more soaked gelatine, dissolve and re-strain

Note: Ideally suited for the glazing and masking of cold meat and buffet pieces and dishes 'au gelée', see below.
   In hot weather the gelatine might be increased by 2–4 sheets to assure firm setting.
   Can be made with other meats and stock, mostly chicken and game.

Savoury Chicken Jelly   *Aspic de volaille*

Ingredients (to produce 2 litres)
150 g lean minced chicken

Method
1 Soak gelatine in plenty of cold water

Continued

Savoury Chicken Jelly *Aspic de volaille*—cont'd

Ingredients (to produce 2 litres)
1 litre best quality chicken/veal
    stock, cold
2–3 egg whites
    18–20 leaves of gelatine
1 stick celery
1 carrot
1 small onion, not peeled
Some parsley stalks
1 glass red wine
Salt and pepper to taste

Method
2 Place minced chicken in sauce
    pan, add egg whites and little cold
    stock, mix well, add remainder of
    stock, vegetables, parsley stalks
3 Place on stove and bring to a burst of
    boil
4 Take aside and very slowly simmer for
    30 min, when the solid will rise to the
    top. Add the soft, well squeezed out
    leaf gelatine, let dissolve, add wine
5 Gently ladle aspic on to sieve with a
    tummy cloth to drain into a bowl
6 Test setting firmness of aspic by
    placing a small amount on a saucer
    and place in fridge to set. If too firm
    add a little white wine, if too loose add
    more soaked gelatine, dissolve and
    re-strain

Savoury Fish Jelly *Aspic de poisson*

Ingredients (to produce 2 litres)
150 g lean minced white fish,
    e.g. whiting
1 litre best quality fish stock, cold
2–3 egg whites
18–20 leaves of gelatine
1 stick celery
1 carrot
1 small onion, not peeled
1 glass white wine
Salt and pepper to taste
Some parsley stalks and some
    tarragon or dill stalks

Method
1 Soak gelatine in plenty of cold water
2 Place minced fish in saucepan add
    egg whites and a little cold stock, mix
    well, add remainder of stock,
    vegetables, parsley, dill etc. stalks
3 Place on stove and bring to a burst
    of boil
4 Take aside and very slowly simmer for
    30 min, when the solids will rise to the
    top. Add the soft, well squeezed out
    leaf gelatine, let dissolve, add wine
5 Now gently ladle aspic on to sieve
    with a tummy cloth to drain into a
    bowl
6 Test setting firmness of aspic by
    placing a small amount on a saucer
    and place in fridge to set. If too
    firm add a little white wine, if too
    loose add more soaked gelatine,
    dissolve and re-strain

Pork Brawn　*Porc à la gelée*

Ingredients (12–16 portions)
1 kg pork shoulder
2 litres good white stock
1 stick celery
1 carrot
1 small onion not peeled
Some parsley stalks
18–20 leaves of gelatine
2 tbsp malt vinegar
4 sweet and sour pickled
　cucumbers
12 peppercorns
6 allspice corns
Salt and pepper

Method
1 Bring shoulder of pork to boil, strain
　off first water
2 Cover with a good stock, vegetables
　and parsley stalks, bring to boil and
　slowly simmer until tender, about
　1–1½ hours
3 Remove shoulder, set aside and cool
4 Strain stock, which should be clear, if
　not add 2–3 beaten egg whites
5 Bring to boil, add soaked gelatine and
　strain (for method see meat jelly
　above)
6 Cut shoulder and cucumber in neat
　dice, place into clean bowl, add
　strained stock–jelly, correct seasoning
　with salt pepper and vinegar
7 Place into loaf-shaped terrine or
　individual moulds, making sure in the
　latter case to get proportion of meat
　and aspic right
8 Allow to set in fridge over night
9 To serve remove from loaf-shape
　mould and cut into slice with sharp
　knife dipped into hot water, or dip
　individual moulds into hot water for
　1–2 seconds. In both cases place on
　lettuce base garnished with sweet
　and sour cucumber

Veal Brawn　*Veau à la gelée* (see Plate 2.10*h*)

Ingredients (12–16 portions)
As for pork brawn (above),
　replacing shoulder of pork
　with
1 kg shoulder of veal
Omit allspice
Add some chopped tarragon

Method
Follow method above for pork
At stage 6 above add some chopped
　tarragon to jelly for flavour

Prawns in Jelly *Crevettes roses à la gelée* (see Plate 2.3*k*)

Ingredients (15–18 portions)
1 kg freshly peeled prawns
1½ litres savoury fish jelly (see above)
1 bunch dill or tarragon

Method
Best done in individual dariol or similar moulds
1 Place a tablespoon of fish jelly on bottom of mould
2 Place some 2–3 good prawns in pattern in this jelly
3 Place in fridge to set
4 When set, fill moulds in equal amount with remaining prawns
5 Add some chopped dill or tarragon to jelly, and fill moulds to brim, place in fridge to set
6 Serve by dipping moulds in hot water for 2–3 seconds and place on some suitable lettuce leaf base garnish with extra prawns around the base as well as dill or tarragon

Note: Can be prepared with other shellfish, e.g. lobster, crayfish, mussels, scallops etc., as well as flakes of poached fish, e.g. salmon, trout, halibut, tuna.

The Liver Pâtés

All over Europe, the liver pâtés have long been an established starter and remain so to this day. Indeed, today all British supermarkets sell considerable amounts of pâtés, where the Belgian types have made themselves a particularly good name. In many of the modern restaurants they can be and are still easily produced, more often than not from livers that are supplied free with the purchases of chickens or other poultry. The writer's following recipes have proved a favourite in four countries in which they have been produced.

Chicken Liver Pâté *Pâté de foie de volaille* (see Plate 2.10*b*)

Ingredients (10–12 portions)
500 g chicken liver trimmed
125 g lean pork diced
125 g green bacon cut in neat dice
150 g streaky green bacon slices

Method
1 In large frying pan fry liver in butter, add pork dice, fry
2 Add onions, garlic, fry until golden brown, cool slightly
3 Place mixture in food processor, cut to a fine purée

Continued

Chicken Liver Pâté   **Pâté de foie de volaille** (see Plate 2.10*b*)—cont'd

Ingredients (10–12 portions)
100 g butter
250 ml cream
100 g diced onions
Glass of brandy
Heaped tbsp marjoram
Tsp ground cloves
Salt, milled pepper, cayenne
   to taste

Method
4 Add seasoning, marjoram, garlic, half
   the brandy, mix well
5 Fry bacon dice in a little butter until
   golden brown, set aside
6 Pour liver mixture in a large bowl, mix
   in bacon and cream
7 Line a loaf-shaped mould with bacon
   slices, overlapping the edge
8 Pour in liver mixture, lift overlapping
   bacon on top
9 Cook pâté in a water bath tray for
   1½–2 hours until top is clear and
   shows no blood
10 Place on a tray, pour in remainder of
   brandy, cool
11 Place in fridge to set. (Flavour will
   improve with time)

Service:
With hot, small knife cut portion from
   mould (see Figure 2.3) or loosen
   edge with small knife, dip mould into
   hot water for a few seconds then turn
   pâté onto a board and cut in portions
   for faster service. Serve with hot toast
   or Melba toast

This basic recipe used for over 40 years can be applied to other livers, such as:

Pork liver, making a **Pork Liver pâté/Pâté de foie de porc**
Veal liver, making a **Veal Liver Pâté/Pâté de foie de veau**
Turkey liver, making a **Turkey Liver Pâté/Pâté de foie de dindonneau**
Duck liver, making **Duck Liver Pâté/Pâté de foie de canard**
Pheasant liver, making **Pheasant Liver Pâté/Pâté de foie de faisan**

Simple Coarse Cold Liver   *Pâté* (see Plate 2.10*a*)

Ingredients (10–12 portions)
500 g liver (pork, veal,
   poultry) trimmedneat dice

Method
1 In a large frying pan fry the liver in
   pork dripping cut in small dice
   (ensure it is cooked through), lift out
   and set aside

Continued

Simple Coarse Cold Liver   *Pâté* (see Plate 2.10*a*)—**cont'd**

Ingredients (10–12 portions)
200 g green bacon cut in neat
  dice
50 g pork dripping
200 g buttercream
4 large cloves of garlic
100 g diced shallots
3 heaped tbsp marjoram
Salt, milled pepper, cayenne
  to taste
1 glass Madeira

Method
2 Now fry bacon, when brown
  add shallots, garlic and fry until
  golden brown, in the last moments
  add marjoram and cook
  slightly
3 When cool, place in food processor,
  add butter, cream and seasoning,
  cut in processor to an even coarse
  purée, correct seasoning and add
  Madeira
4 Put in an oval or round mould, smooth
  top, cover with little melted butter, set
  in fridge over night
5 With a knife dipped into hot water cut
  into neat portions

Galantines

The stages in the preparation of a galantine are illustrated in Figure 2.4. The boning and preparation of chicken or game for use in galantines is shown in Figure 2.5. Recipes for cold forcemeats (farces) are given in Chapter 7.

Note that nowadays galantines are not always poached in a cloth but are et in loaf-shaped stainless steel tins and poached or steamed therein (see Plate 2.8*a*–*c*).

Raised Pies

For a pie, we first have to make the special pastry, for which the following are two good recipes.

Hot Water Paste

Ingredients (for average-size pie)
1000 g flour
300 g lard
20 g salt
½ litre water

Method
1 Sieve flour and salt in bowl
2 Boil water and lard
3 Pour into flour and mix well with a
  wooden spoon
4 Then knead well, smooth by
  hand
5 Use while still warm

a	Lay a clean kitchen towel across a board, place the chicken skin on to this towel in an oblong shape, overlapping the skin where the removal of breast and leg bones has made a small hole.
b	Carefully spread the first layer of farce (prepared in accordance with the recipe in Chapter 7) on to the skin, being careful not to disturb the latter.
c	Lengthwise lay chicken breast strips on to the farce, alternating with strips of nice pink cooked ox-tongue, ham or strips of bacon in a neat and even pattern. Nowadays we seldom have the luxury of chopped truffles to be added in strips, but a few pistachio nuts will improve the final appearance of the galantine.
d	Now cover these strips carefully with another layer of farce, taking care not to disturb the pattern of strips beneath, pressing a handful of roasted and peeled pistachio nuts into the farce.
e	Normally we add 2–3 layers of farce and garnish; it is a matter of the size of the chicken.
f	Lift the kitchen towel nearest to you and roll the galantine firmly into a neat and even roll, twist and tie first end, twisting again to achieve a neat even shape. Tie the other end in the same way, secure with 3–4 strings around the middle. Place in a suitable pan, cover with a good chicken stock, bring to the boil and simmer very gently for 1–1½ hours. Leave to cool in the stock overnight, remove the string and cloth, trim and place in the fridge to cool and set.
g	The galantine should then be glazed or covered with Chaud Froid sauce, and cut into portion slices and served on a salad base with other suitable garnish and a coulis or cold sauce, such as mild Mustard or Spanish cream sauce or suitable coulis (see Chapter 3). The galantine may be presented whole for a Cold Buffet, as shown in the drawing.

FIG. 2.4 *Stages in the preparation of galantine of chicken*

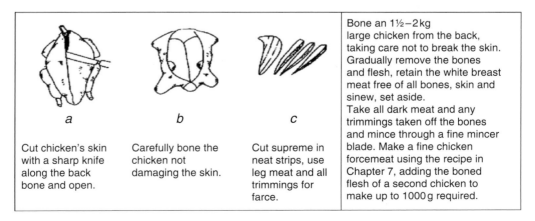

a	*b*	*c*	Bone an 1½–2 kg large chicken from the back, taking care not to break the skin. Gradually remove the bones and flesh, retain the white breast meat free of all bones, skin and sinew, set aside. Take all dark meat and any trimmings taken off the bones and mince through a fine mincer blade. Make a fine chicken forcemeat using the recipe in Chapter 7, adding the boned flesh of a second chicken to make up to 1000 g required.
Cut chicken's skin with a sharp knife along the back bone and open.	Carefully bone the chicken not damaging the skin.	Cut supreme in neat strips, use leg meat and all trimmings for farce.	

FIG. 2.5 *Boning and preparation of chicken and game for galantines and pies*

Pie Pastry ♔ *Pâte à pâté*

Ingredients (for average size pie)
1000 g flour
150 g butter
150 g lard
250 ml water
20 g salt
2 eggs

Method
1 Sieve flour and salt in a bowl
2 Rub in butter and lard to resemble
  fine crumbs
3 Add beaten eggs and as much water
  as is needed to make a smooth
  pastry
4 Rest in cool place before using

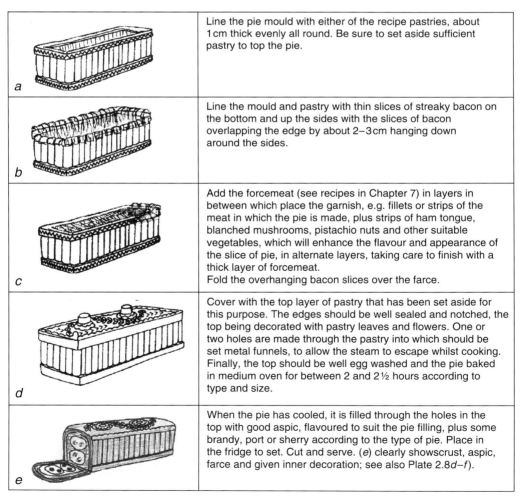

a	Line the pie mould with either of the recipe pastries, about 1 cm thick evenly all round. Be sure to set aside sufficient pastry to top the pie.
b	Line the mould and pastry with thin slices of streaky bacon on the bottom and up the sides with the slices of bacon overlapping the edge by about 2–3 cm hanging down around the sides.
c	Add the forcemeat (see recipes in Chapter 7) in layers in between which place the garnish, e.g. fillets or strips of the meat in which the pie is made, plus strips of ham tongue, blanched mushrooms, pistachio nuts and other suitable vegetables, which will enhance the flavour and appearance of the slice of pie, in alternate layers, taking care to finish with a thick layer of forcemeat. Fold the overhanging bacon slices over the farce.
d	Cover with the top layer of pastry that has been set aside for this purpose. The edges should be well sealed and notched, the top being decorated with pastry leaves and flowers. One or two holes are made through the pastry into which should be set metal funnels, to allow the steam to escape whilst cooking. Finally, the top should be well egg washed and the pie baked in medium oven for between 2 and 2½ hours according to type and size.
e	When the pie has cooled, it is filled through the holes in the top with good aspic, flavoured to suit the pie filling, plus some brandy, port or sherry according to the type of pie. Place in the fridge to set. Cut and serve. (*e*) clearly showscrust, aspic, farce and given inner decoration; see also Plate 2.8*d*–*f*).

Fɪɢ. 2.6 *The stages of making a classic raised pie*

Presentation of terrines, brawns and pâtés

With the advent of the now very common plated service, in most establishments terrines, potted meats, brawns and pâtés are more often than not cooked/set in single portion or in oblong or triangular loaf moulds and cut in portions for better-plated presentation.

In both cases terrines should be assembled in layers in between which are set the marinated fillets of a given meat, plus strips of ham, tongue, bacon etc. plus diced red peppers, button mushrooms, pistachio nuts, olives etc. in a pattern which takes regard of the final appearance.

Not unlike the galantine assembly above, in most cases farce should make up the final layer of the terrine after which it is cooked slowly in a medium oven, cooled and finished with aspic (see individual recipes above).

The preparation and composition of these two preparations is very much the same, the only difference being the receptacle in which they are cooked and the actual cooking. For both, the filling consists of coarsely minced simple forcemeat prepared from the required meat, poultry, or game (see Chapter 7). Between the layers of farces we set marinated fillets of the chosen meats and whatever savoury garnishing, suitable to the particular terrine or pie.

Pickles

Greek Pickle 🔱 *à la Grecque*

Ingredients (sufficient for 1 kg of vegetables, giving 8–12 portions)	*Method*
250 ml olive oil	1 Combine all ingredients
1 litre white wine	2 Bring to the boil, simmer for 10 min
Juice of 1 lemon	3 Correct seasoning
12 peppercorns	4 Cook vegetables in this liquor according to
12 coriander seeds	type between 5 and 10 min. Cool and store in
100 g fennel or celery	fridge for 24–72 hours
1 good sprig thyme	Use as a cold starter or part of a selection of
2 bay leaves	cold starters or as part of a buffet
1 litre water	
Pinch of sugar	The flavour improves with storage in a glass or
Salt to taste	china jar

Menu examples of individual Greek pickles are given in Table 2.5 and Plate 2.12*a–c*.

TABLE 2.5 *Popular Greek Pickles*

Name	Preparation	Menu examples	French
Artichoke quarters	Trim and quarter, wash, cook in pickle (see text), should be firm but cooked. Cool and store in fridge for 24 hours or more	Artichoke Quarters Greek Style	Quartiers d'artichauts à la Grecque
Cauliflower	Trim cauliflowers, cut into neat rosettes, wash, cook in pickle (see text), must be firm. Store in fridge for 24 hours or more	Cauliflower Greek Style	Chou-fleur à la Grecque
Button mushrooms	Trim stalks off mushrooms, wash well, cook in pickle (see text), must be firm. Store as above	Mushrooms Greek Style	Champignons à la Grecque
Celeriac	Peel and wash celeriac, cut into neat dice or strips, cook in pickle (see text), must be firm. Store as above	Celeriac Greek Style	Céleri-rave à la Grecque
Leeks	Trim the leek and cut the lower white part into 3 cm length, wash well, cook in liquor, must be firm, store as above	Leeks Greek Style	Poireau à la Grecque
Button onions	Peel small button onions, wash, cook in pickle (see text), must be firm. Store as above	Onions Greek Style	Oignons à la Grecque

Portuguese Pickle *à la Portugaise*

Ingredients (sufficient for 1 kg of vegetables, giving 8–12 portions)

250 ml olive oil
2 large cloves garlic
200 g finely diced onion
500 g tomato concassé (coarsely chopped)
2 tbsp tomato purée
20 g black milled pepper
2 sprigs fresh thyme
50 g chopped parsley
1 litre white wine
1 litre water
Pinch of sugar
Salt to taste

Method

1 Heat oil in low wide-bottomed pan
2 Add garlic and onion, cook without colour
3 Add tomato purée, cook
4 Add tomato concassé
5 Add white wine and water, bring to the boil
6 Add thyme, sugar, pepper and salt, simmer for 20 min, correct seasoning

Menu examples of individual Portuguese pickles are given in Table 2.6 and Plate 2.12*d–f.*

Scandinavian Herring Pickles (sweet and sour basic recipe)

Ingredients (6–8 portions)
12 freshly filleted salted and soaked herring fillets or ready prepared from commercial jars*
500 ml wine vinegar
500 ml caster sugar
400 g red onion, finely sliced
Coarsely cut allspice corns
Chopped parsley

Method
1 Mix sugar and vinegar and allow to dissolve (best done overnight*)
2 Place sliced red onions in suitable dish for presentation
3 Place herring fillet whole or cut in 3–4 pieces retaining fillets' shape on to onions, or place in suitable dishes
4 Sprinkle crushed allspice corns and parsley on top
5 Cover with sugar and vinegar mixture and leave to stand 4–8 hours

*Note: *This sugar–vinegar mixture is often done in batches and is always ready in the Scandinavian kitchen. It appears to be a curious mixture but combines well with herring fillets and quite a few vegetables (see Salads in Chapter 3). A most popular starter, it has many variations (see examples below).*

Tomato Pickled Herrings

Ingredients (6–8 portions)
As above with the addition of 150 g raw tomato concassé or 6–8 tbsp tomato ketchup

Method
Mix into basic sweet-sour pickle above, pour over fillets

Mustard Pickled Herrings

Ingredients (6–8 portions)
4–6 tbsp Dijon mustard *or*
4–6 tbsp sweet Scandinavian mustard *or*
4–6 tbsp crushed grain mustard
1 tsp caster sugar
A little chopped dill

Method
Mix mustard of your choice, sugar and dill into basic sweet-sour pickle above and pour over fillets

TABLE 2.6 *Portuguese Pickles*

Name	Preparation	Menu examples	French
Vegetables All the vegetables given in Table 2.5 for à la Grecque can also be used for Portuguese Pickle	Follow preparations for à la Grecque	Artichoke Quarters Portuguese Style Cauliflower Portuguese Style Mushrooms Portuguese Style Celeriac Portuguese Style Leeks Portuguese Style Onions Portuguese Style	Quartiers d'artichauts Portugaises Chou-fleur Portugaise Champignons Portugaises Céleri-rave Portugaise Poireaux Portugaises Oignons Portugaises
Mussels	Cook mussels in the normal way, shell and cook in Portuguese pickle. Cool and store	Mussels Portuguese Style	Moules Portugaises
Prawns	Cook frozen or freshly shelled prawns in Portuguese pickle, cool	Prawns Portuguese Style	Crevettes roses Portugaises
Herrings, mackerel, trout	Fillet and skin fish, cut length-wise in half, roll into a paupiettee, secure with toothpick, place in suitable dish, cover with Portuguese pickle and cook gently, to bring to boil. Cool and store	Herrings Portuguese Style Mackerel Portuguese Style Trout Portuguese Style	Hareng Portugaise Maquereau Portugaise Truite Portugaise
Fillet of white fish	Skin and trim fillets of fish, e.g. sole, lemon sole, plaice and cod etc. Cut in 2 cm wide strips, place in a suitable dish, cover with Portuguese pickle and cook, gently, bring to boil. Cool and store	Strips of Sole Portuguese Style Strips of Lemon Sole Portuguese Style Strips of Plaice Portuguese Style Strips of Cod Portuguese Style Strips of Salmon Portuguese Style Trout Steaklet Portuguese Style	Goujon de sole Portugaise Goujon de limande Portugaise Goujon de plie Portugaise Goujon de cabillaud Portugais Goujon de saumon Portugais Petite darne de truite Portugaise

Dressed Crab (see Plate 2.3*d*)

Ingredients (individual portion)

600–750 g portion cooked crab
1 hard boiled egg
20 g fresh white breadcrumbs
4–6 anchovy fillets
A little chopped parsley or dill
A little sweet paprika powder
Salt to taste

Method

1 Boil the egg for 8–10 min, refresh and cool
2 Remove claws from crab, crack and break open, remove all white meat, set aside
3 With a pointed knife open the lower shell along visible line, remove dead man's finger, discard
4 With a spoon now lift out the soft dark flesh (butter), place in a bowl, add breadcrumbs and season with a little salt
5 Break up the white flesh
Assembly:
6 Place the white flesh into the end-corners of the washed and dried shell of the crab
7 Place the dark flesh in the middle of the shell
8 Now garnish the crab with stripes of anchovy and of the chopped-sieved white and yolk of egg and parsley–dill in a neat pattern by placing the same on the edge of a small knife
9 Finally garnish with stripes of sweet paprika powder. Serve chilled, offer mayonnaise

The Presentation of Single Hors d'oeuvres

All cold starters in the past were presented in oblong china dishes called raviers and crystal, china, glass, earthenware, wooden and even plastic dishes, bowls, glasses, or coupes, according to the type of starter to be served. In first-class hotels and restaurants they were then usually served from trolleys or trays at the table, from where guests could make their choice (see Figure 2.13 below).

In recent years, particularly with the advent of the introduction of cuisine nouvelle, cocktails are served as before, but for nearly all other starters plated service, normally on fishplates size, which can be round, square, or oblong, has predominated in the presentation of the first course. Not only does this allow a more focused, attractive and individual presentation by the chef, it gives a much faster service, so important in the modern catering operation.

This plated service in most cases needs a good background before the starter is placed on the plate. Some establishments have gone so far as to use different coloured china plates, but a good and attractive presentation can be achieved in many other ways. In these times of healthy eating, the background is more often than not one of the many leaf-lettuces which are available to us today, details of which can be found in Chapter 3 on Salads, Cold Sauces and Dressings.

It is important to choose a lettuce type best suited for a given hors d'oeuvre when it comes to shape or colour of leaves, to assure compatibility as to taste, and to give contrasting colour when it comes to presentation. For some starters the lettuce chosen should best be shredded, at other times a whole leaf or selection of smaller leaves assures the best presentation, either as background or side garnish (see Figure 2.7).

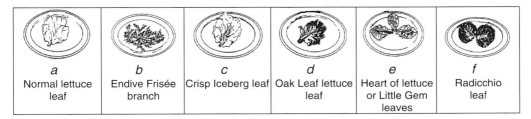

a Normal lettuce leaf	*b* Endive Frisée branch	*c* Crisp Iceberg leaf	*d* Oak Leaf lettuce leaf	*e* Heart of lettuce or Little Gem leaves	*f* Radicchio leaf

FIG. 2.7 *Various lettuce leaf bases for single starters. Shredded lettuce of any of these types can also be used*

On or besides these different lettuce bases we can place the various single hors d'oeuvres, completing the presentation with suitable other garnishes, such as lemon and tomato quarters or slices, cucumber or kiwi slices, sprigs of parsley, dill, tarragon etc. Finally we may add a little of the right dressing, or a coulis or cold sauce suitable to the starter being prepared to enhance presentation, and to make that important first impression at the start of a given meal.

Various presentations of other cold single starters are illustrated in Figures 2.8–2.12.

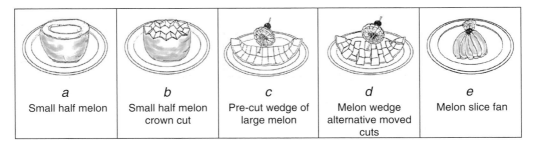

a Small half melon	*b* Small half melon crown cut	*c* Pre-cut wedge of large melon	*d* Melon wedge alternative moved cuts	*e* Melon slice fan

FIG. 2.8 *Presentation of chilled melon*

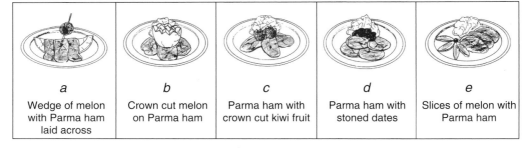

a Wedge of melon with Parma ham laid across	*b* Crown cut melon on Parma ham	*c* Parma ham with crown cut kiwi fruit	*d* Parma ham with stoned dates	*e* Slices of melon with Parma ham

FIG. 2.9 *Various presentations of Parma ham or other charcuterie with fruits*

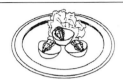

a	*b*	*c*
Stuffed eggs	Egg mayonnaise	Plover's eggs
Here the three halves of stuffed eggs have been placed on a bed of sardine oil flavoured mayonnaise garnished with small sardines and presented for contrast with radicchio lettuce leaves and lemon slices	An egg mayonnaise where three egg halves have been placed on a tartlet, coated with mayonnaise, garnished with a cross of anchovy fillets and some capers against a background of lettuce leaf and segment of blanched, peeled and pipped tomato quarter	The presentation of two whole plover's eggs on a nest of mustard and cress, with the four half-shells of the eggs used as decoration, and covered with a little French dressing. A mayonnaise-based sauce can be offered separately

Fig. 2.10 *Presentation of cold egg starters*

a	*b*	*c*
A ham mousse garnished with lettuce, cress, quarters of peeled and pipped tomatoes and an orange quarter	A two-layered white fish and salmon mousse, garnished with lettuce cress, slices of cucumber and lemon quarter	A three-layered fish mousse, white, salmon pink and spinach flavoured green, garnished with lettuce, lemon, and pickled mushroom slices

Fig. 2.11 *Individual meat and fish mousse presentations*

a	*b*
Two-layered loaf-set chicken and ham mousse, garnished with lettuce, cress, slices of kiwi and lemon quarter	Three-layered loaf-set chicken, ham and venison mousse, garnished with lettuce, cress, slices of tomatoes and/or orange wedges

Fig. 2.12 *Presentation of meat or fish mousses set in a loaf mould and cut into portion slices*

MIXED STARTERS   ***Hors d'oeuvres varié s***

As the term implies, we speak here of a selection or mixture of different cold starters offered to the guest as a portion. How many items are included in a selection of starters is very much determined by the cost of the items and the price charged on the menu.

A selection of starters can be combined from a thousand and one things: for example, a half portion of any of the single starters listed above, plus two or three of the many salads, simple or compound, listed in Chapter 3, plus condiments such as pickled onions, gherkins, pickled cucumber and different types of olives etc.

In days of old a selection of hors d'oeuvres would never be less than four and up to forty items. Single as well as mixed starters were served from trolleys or from trays (Figure 2.13). These were taken to the table and the guests could make their choice from among the proffered delicacies. Some modern restaurants today offer both single and mixed hors d'oeuvres from specially constructed starter buffet tables.

Plated Service for a Mixed Starters   *Hors d'oeuvres variés*

Most selection of hors d'oeuvres, like the single starters, are nowadays served plated. A better portion control can be assured, reducing costs, and service is that much faster for guests.

If we add to this the most attractive plate presentation possible, which came into being with the introduction of cuisine nouvelle, the plated presentation and service of the first course can be most attractive. Some examples of assembly are shown in Figure 2.14 and Plate 2.13. Some mixed salad starters are shown in Plate 2.11.

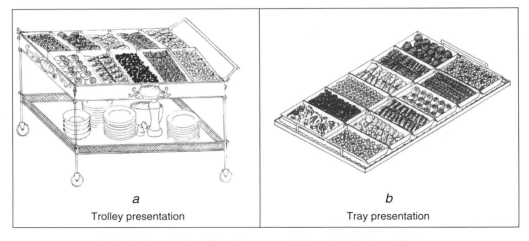

a	b
Trolley presentation	Tray presentation

Fɪɢ. 2.13 *Presentation of hors d'oeuvres variés from (a) a trolley or (b) a tray*

Cocktail hors d'oeuvres

These consist usually of canapés, petites bouches, sausage rolls, bridge rolls, tartlets, Duchesse Carolines, dartois, quiches, sandwiches etc.

Salted nuts, crisps, pretzels, gherkins, olives, pearl onions, plus any other items given under Finger Buffets in Chapter 8 may be offered, the consideration being very much a matter of price paid.

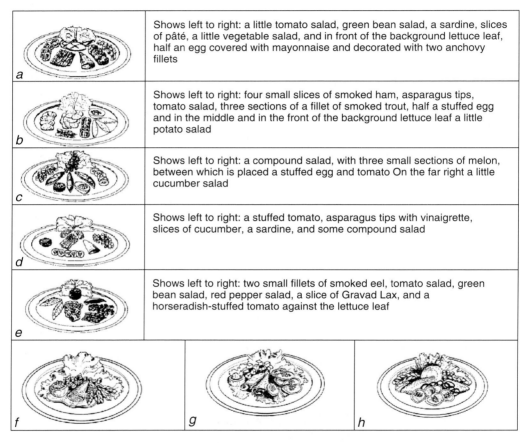

a	Shows left to right: a little tomato salad, green bean salad, a sardine, slices of pâté, a little vegetable salad, and in front of the background lettuce leaf, half an egg covered with mayonnaise and decorated with two anchovy fillets
b	Shows left to right: four small slices of smoked ham, asparagus tips, tomato salad, three sections of a fillet of smoked trout, half a stuffed egg and in the middle and in the front of the background lettuce leaf a little potato salad
c	Shows left to right: a compound salad, with three small sections of melon, between which is placed a stuffed egg and tomato On the far right a little cucumber salad
d	Shows left to right: a stuffed tomato, asparagus tips with vinaigrette, slices of cucumber, a sardine, and some compound salad
e	Shows left to right: two small fillets of smoked eel, tomato salad, green bean salad, red pepper salad, a slice of Gravad Lax, and a horseradish-stuffed tomato against the lettuce leaf

FIG. 2.14 *Examples of assembly of plated mixed starters. The drawings are of course unrealistic as a presentation in that there is too much space between each item making up the selection of hors d'oeuvres. This is simply to show how the whole may be assembled. Normally the food items are much closer, if not overlapping. The example drawings in (f), (g) and (h) give a much more realistic plated presentation of a mixed starter, as do the three examples shown in Plate 2.13*

Salads, Salad Dressings and Cold Sauces

3 (Les Salades, Assaisonnements et Sauces Froids)

There is no doubt that in the past ten years or so the availability and service of all kinds of salads in every type of catering establishment has gained a now long overdue importance. Modern catering, with an emphasis on healthier eating and the desire for lighter, more balanced meals, has made the service of salads at all meal times very popular.

Particularly in the early part of the year, when most fresh vegetables are not yet available or very expensive, many types of salads could and should take the place of vegetables as an accompaniment to all types of hot and cold dish. It would be ridiculous to serve frozen vegetables at that time of the year when fresh salads could take their place, often at a fraction of the cost. The variety of salads available almost all the year round is considerable. If we then vary their dressings and presentations we can satisfy the taste of most of our guests without much repetition.

SALAD DRESSINGS *Assaisonnements pour les salades*

A good salad needs a good dressing to bring out the best flavour, and in the list below we find one or more suitable to any salad we care to produce. To help with this, we differentiate between four basic dressings types, with many variations on the basic theme.

These four are:

> Vinaigrette and its variation
> Mayonnaise-based dressing and its variations
> Acidulated cream and its variations
> Scandinavian sweet and sour dressing

Most, but not all of the variations of dressing are based on the vinaigrette, others on mayonnaise. Some are based on cream, sour cream, or latterly crème fraîche and yoghurt. Even the sweet and sour Scandinavian dressing is getting very popular, as it adds a distinctive new taste to salads.

The list of 25 dressings below should help you to find the right dressing for any given salad. The Vinaigrette is presented first, as Dressing No. 1, as befits the most commonly used dressing. Variations on a vinaigrette are then listed in Table 3.1. Other types of dressing are detailed in Table 3.2. Any establishment will also be able to add their own specialities to our list.

No. 1　Vinaigrette

Ingredients (for an average of 24–30 portions)
750 ml olive oil or other vegetable oil*
250 ml vinegar of your choice*
1 tsp sugar
1 tsp salt 1 tsp white ground pepper

Method

Place vinegar into a china bowl
Add salt and pepper and dissolve
Beat in the oil gradually until it
　　forms an emulsion
Place into bottle with perforated top
　　for sprinkling on salad
Always shake bottle well before use

Vinegars
White wine vinegar
Red wine vinegar
Strawberry vinegar
Raspberry vinegar
Cider vinegar
Malt vinegar
Rice wine vinegar
Distilled vinegar
Light and dark balsamic vinegars of
　　various age
Spiced vinegars

Many of above vinegars are available
　　flavoured with herbs and spices, e.g.
　　chilli, thyme, tarragon, mixed herbs

Oils
Extra Virgin olive oil
Fine Virgin olive oil
Virgin olive oil
Sunflower oil
Groundnut oil
Walnut oil
Hazelnut oil
and others

Variations are very much a matter of choice and according to with what salad the dressing may be used. The basic vinaigrette is usually made with olive oil and wine vinegar, but quite a number of guests find some olive oils too strong. Here sunflower oil is a good bet. Some nut oils should be avoided for reasons of possible allergies.

SALAD PRESENTATIONS

For ease of description and understanding, we have grouped the salads as follows:

　　　Leaf salads:
　　　　　Green leaf salads　　Salades vertes
　　　　　Mixed green leaf salads　　Salades vertes panaches
　　　　　Mixed green and coloured leaf salad　　Feuilles de laitue panaches
　　　Vegetable salads:
　　　　　Simple or single vegetable salads　　Salades de légumes simples
　　　　　Mixed vegetable salads　　Salades de légumes panaches
　　　Compound salads　　Salades composées
　　　Special salads　　Salades spéciales

TABLE 3.1 *Dressings Based on Vinaigrette*

No.	Name	Method (additions to basic recipe of 1 litre of vinaigrette dressing as in text)
2	**Lemon Dressing**	As above, using half the amount of lemon juice, in place of vinegar
3	**English (Mustard) Dressing**	As for vinaigrette, with the addition of 2–3 tsp of English mustard
4	**French (Mustard) Dressing**	As for vinaigrette, with the addition of 3–4 tsp of French mustard
5	**Herb Dressing**	As for vinaigrette, with the addition of 3–4 tsp freshly chopped herbs (one of a type or a mixture of several according to season)
6	**Marseillaise Dressing**	As for vinaigrette, with the addition of 3–4 tsp of garlic paste
7	**Swiss Dressing**	Cut 150 g of green bacon cut into small dice, fry until golden brown, add vinegar to hot pan than mix with oil and other ingredients of basic vinaigrette
8	**Tomato Dressing**	Add 150 g of raw tomato concassé to basic vinaigrette recipe
9	**Paprika Dressing**	Gently heat/cook 50 g of sweet paprika powder in little of the oil, cool, then mix with the rest of the oil and other ingredients of basic vinaigrette
10	**Gasconne Dressing**	As for Marseillaise with the additions of garlic fried bread croutons
11	**Anchovy Dressing**	Paste 4–6 fillets of anchovy and add to basic vinaigrette recipe
12	**Plaça Dressing**	English Mustard Dressing with the addition of little Tabasco sauce and chutney
13	**Chiffonnade Dressing**	Vinaigrette with the addition of chopped, hard-boiled egg, and chopped parsley and fine brunoise of beetroot
14	**Roquefort Dressing**	Add 100 g of Roquefort cheese, pressed through a sieve, to the basic vinaigrette
15	**St Regis Dressing**	English Mustard Dressing with the addition of little Worcestershire sauce and a tsp of paprika

TABLE 3.2 *Other Types of Dressing*

No.	Name	Method
16	American Dressing	Place 2 yolks of egg in a bowl, add the following tsps to bowl: 3 of salt, 1 of ground white pepper, 1 of sugar, 2 of English mustard, 4 of sweet paprika powder, 1 of Worcestershire sauce. Mix well, add 250 ml of the vinegar and 750 ml of the oil of your choice, mix well
17	Cream Dressing	Mix four parts of fresh double cream with one part of wine vinegar, salt and pepper, and a little sugar to taste
18	Cream Mustard Dressing	Mix four parts of fresh cream with one part of wine vinegar, and 3 tsp of French mustard plus salt and pepper
19	Escoffier Dressing	To one litre of mayonnaise add the juice of half a lemon, a dash of Worcestershire sauce and Tabasco and sweet paprika powder
20	Thousand Island Dressing	To one litre of mayonnaise add a 150 g mixture of small 0.5 cm dice of red and green peppers, 250 ml single cream, flavour with Tabasco sauce
21	Chatelaine Dressing	Mix equal amounts of fresh cream and mayonnaise, flavour with lemon juice and salt and pepper
22	Russian Dressing	To one litre of mayonnaise add the following: 2 tsp finely chopped beetroot, 2 tsp diced red and 2 tsp diced green peppers, plus a tsp each of finely chopped parsley and chives, plus 2 tbsp of caviar
23	Dill Dressing	To a litre of mayonnaise add 150 g freshly chopped dill, 250 ml single cream and some lemon juice, salt and pepper
24	Italian Dressing	To one litre of mayonnaise add 250 ml single cream, 100 g of ketchup and 150 g of tomato concassé and freshly chopped herbs
25	Scandinavian Dressing	Dissolve 1 litre of wine vinegar with 1 litre of caster sugar overnight or bring mixture to boil and cool. When cold add 125 ml oil of your choice, pour over salads with chopped dill, parsley or chives

SUITABLE DRESSINGS

Table 3.3 suggests suitable dressings (by number from the 25 dressings detailed above) for green or leaf salads.

TABLE 3.3 *GREEN SALADS* **Les salades vertes (see Plate 3.1)**

Salad example	Suggested dressings	French
Batavian	1, 2, 3, 4, 5, 10, 20, 23, 24	Salade d'escarole
Chicory	1, 2, 3, 4, 5 , 6, 7, 10, 14, 15, 23, 24	Endive Belge
Crest	1, 2, 3, 4, 5, 6, 7, 9, 16, 18, 21, 24	
Cos	1, 2, 3, 4, 5, 6, 7, 10, 14, 15, 23, 24	Salade Romain
Dandelion	1, 2, 3, 4, 5, 6, 7, 9, 16, 18, 21, 24	Salade Pissenlit
Endive	1, 2, 3, 4, 5, 6, 7, 10, 14, 15, 23, 24	Salade Chicorée, Frisés
Iceberg	1, 2, 3, 4, 5, 6, 7, 20	
Lambs Lettuce	1, 2, 3, 4, 5, 6, 7, 10, 11, 23, 24	Salade Mâche
Lettuce	1, 2, 3, 4, 5, 10, 23, 24	Salade Laitue
Lolla Rosso	1, 2, 3, 4, 5, 10, 23, 24, 25	Lolla Rosso
Mustard and Cress	1, 2, 3, 4, 5, 10, 20	Cressonnette
Oak Leaf	3, 4, 5, 7, 10, 23, 24, 25	Salade de feuille de chêne
Red Lettuce	1, 2, 3, 4, 5, 7, 10, 23, 24, 25	Radicchio
Rocket	1, 2, 3, 4, 5, 7	Roquet
Sorrel	1, 2, 3, 4, 5, 7, 202	Salade d'oseille
Spinach	2, 3, 4, 5, 7, 20	Épinard
Spring Onions	1, 2, 3, 4, 816	Oignons printemps
TatsoiLeaves	1, 2, 3, 4, 5, 7	Feuille de Tatsoi
Watercress	1, 2, 3, 4, 5, 7, 20	Crès de fontaine

Table 3.4 suggests suitable dressings (by number from the 25 dressings detailed above) for single ingredient (simple) salads.

LEAF SALADS

Preparation of Most Leaf Salads

(1) Always wash lettuce in cold water. Hold by roots, plunging into water to force water to centre, thus removing dirt and grit. Repeat process several times, each time in clean water.

(2) Remove bad or discoloured outer leaves.

(3) Trim roots and carefully inspect inside for slugs and insects.

(4) Remove coarse ribs, from outer leaves with fingers, remove excess stalks.

(5) Place into iced water to crisp if necessary.

TABLE 3.4 *SINGLE SALADS*   *Salades simples*

Salad example	Suggested dressings	French
To be prepared and served raw		
Cabbage Salad	1, 3, 4, 7, 9, 20	Salade de choux
Cucumber Salad	1, 3, 4, 7, 9, 16, 17, 25	Salade de concombre
Coleslaw Salad	4, 7, 16 and/or mayonnaise	
Radish Red Salad	1, 2, 3, 5	Salade de radis rouge
Radish White Salad	1, 2, 3, 5	Salade de radis blanc
Tomato Salad	1, 4, 5, 6, 11	Salade de tomate
Sweet Peppers Salad	1, 4, 5, 7, 25	Salade de piment
To be prepared and served cooked		
Artichoke Salad	1, 4, 11, 24	Salade d'artichauts
Asparagus Salad	1, 4, 11	Salade d'asperge
Beetroot Salad	1, 4, 11	Salade de betterave
Celeriac Salad	1, 4, 11, 20	Salade de céleri-rave
Celery Salad	1, 4, 11, 20	Salade de céleri anglais
French Bean Salad	1, 4, 6	Salade de haricots verts
Haricot Bean Salad*	1, 4, 5, 6, 20	Salade de haricot blanc*
Potato Salad	1, 4, 7, or mayonnaise	Salade de pommes

*Today many other pulses are used for salads, for example butter beans, haricot beans, chickpeas, flageolets, green and brown lentils etc

(6) Drain thoroughly. Shake well in a salad basket or colander.

(7) Avoid bruising leaves. Place on clean cloth cover with cloth.

(8) Keep in a cool place until required.

(9) Serve neatly in china, glass or wooden bowls or plate add dressing in last moment.

(10) Whole washes and prepared salad heads keep better than loose leaves
Plate 3.2 shows the preparation of whole salad heads.

SINGLE GREEN SALAD   *Salade verte*

When serving salad most think of a mixture of various different salad types on a plate or in a bowl. Few consider serving just one type of leaf. Yet, a bowl of just green leaves with a suitable dressing is ideal for say a grilled steak or fillet of fish, or indeed roast poultry of all types.

MIXED GREEN SALAD   *Salade verte panache*

If we think a single green salad is too simple, we may go up one step and serve a mixed green salad, that is to say a mixture of any green leaves available such as Batavian, Lambs Lettuce, Rocket, Endive Frisés or whatever is available in the range of green.

MIXED LEAF SALAD *Feuilles de laitue panaches (see Plate 3.3)*

With the availability of Oak Leaf, Lolla Rossa, Radicchio and Endives, all of various colours, plus any of the green salad listed above, we can now really go to town and make a mixed salad of all types of leaves, green or coloured.

Free Combination Green Leaf Salads

See Plate 3.4 for some examples of free additions to green leaf salads.

Named Leaf-Based Salads

The next group of salads is the named salads, that is to say, their name implies that we should follow a given recipe with *always the same ingredients* of different leaves and other additions, as well as dressing.

Tarragon Salad ﾏ Salade d'estragon (Plate 3.5*a*)

Any green leaves with the addition of freshly chopped tarragon leaves sprinkled on the top plus vinaigrette. Served as a side salad with roast and grilled meats, poultry and fish.

Mimosa Salad ﾏ Salade de Mimosa (Plate 3.5*b*)

Green leaves with the sieved hard-boiled egg yolk sprinkled on top to give the appearance of the Mimosa blossom.
Served as a side salad with roast and grilled meats, poultry and fish.

Orange Salad ﾏ Salade d'orange (Plate 3.5*c*)

Green lettuce leaves with the addition of orange segments and blanched orange peel cut julienne sprinkled on the top. Served as a side salad with roast meats, poultry and game, particularly roast duck and saddle of venison.

New Orleans Salad ﾏ Salade New Orléans (Plate 3.5*d*)

Sliced raw button mushrooms on young spinach leaves, dressed with strong garlic dressing. Served as a side salad with roast meats, poultry and grilled steaks and fish of all types.

SINGLE VEGETABLE SALADS 🕴   **Salades de légumes simples**

The single salads, sometimes also called in French the simple salads, are produced from vegetables or fruits rather than from leaves, although some of the latter are often used as a base decoration. Single salads may have small additions/garnish, such as lettuce leaves, onion rings, chopped or sprigs of herbs, to give flavour and help presentation. Vegetables and garnishes for single salads are shown in Plate 3.6.

They fall into two groups:

Single **raw** salads:	Such as cucumber, radish, tomato etc. (Table 3.5, Plate 3.7).
Single **cooked** salads:	Which are cooked or blanched before dressing, such as asparagus, beetroot, celeriac, French beans, potato and pulses, pasta salads etc. (Table 3.6, Plate 3.8).

Preparation of Single Salads

No general rule can be given for the preparation of single (simple) salads except to use only the freshest of vegetables, which if of the cooked type, should be cooked al dente and be of good natural colour. To achieve the best flavour, they should be marinated in a vinaigrette dressing while still warm and allowed to cool therein.

Simple salads can be dressed on their own or on a bed of shredded or whole lettuce leaves of various types and colours to add contrast. Onion rings, chopped blanched shallots, sprigs of parsley, dill, mint, tarragon or sage will all help to give our simple salads a most appetizing look. Figures 3.1 and 3.2 illustrate the preparation of onion dice and fruit segments for garnish.

MIXED VEGETABLE SALADS 🕴   **Salades de légumes panaches**

Named Mixed Salads

Certain named mixed salads should always have the same ingredient content. For example:

Bagatelle Salad/Salade bagatelle (see Plate 3.9*a*): julienne of mushrooms, carrots, asparagus tips with French dressing.

Cress Salad/Salade cressonnière (see Plate 3.9*b*): sliced cooked potatoes, watercress leaves, chopped parsley and chervil with French dressing.

French Salad/Salade à la Française (Plate 3.9*c*): selection of salad consisting of green leaves, cucumber slices, tomato quarters, spring onions and quarters of hard-boiled eggs with French dressing.

Other mixed salads which can be found in good cookery books are: Niçoise, Hungarian, Italian, Lords, Marie Stuart, Mercédès, Palois, Provençale etc.

TABLE 3.5 *Single Simple Raw Salads (See Plate 3.7)*

Menu example	Preparation and recommended dressing	French
Cabbage Salad	Shred cabbage very fine, sprinkle with salt, add caraway seeds, knead in well. Leave to stand for 30 min. Squeeze off excess liquid and salt, add one of the following dressings: 1, 2, 3, 4, 7, 12, 18, 25. Leave to stand for 1 hour. Dress in a suitable dish or on a plate	Salade choux blanc
Red Cabbage Salad	Shred cabbage very fine, sprinkle with salt and little wine vinegar, knead in well. Leave to stand for 30 min. Squeeze off excess liquid. Add a little ground clove and one of the following dressings: 1, 2, 3, 4, 7. Leave to stand for 1 hour. Dress in a suitable dish or on a plate	Salade de choux rouges
Cucumber salad	Peel cucumber, slice fine on mandolin, sprinkle with salt, knead in well. Leave to stand for 30 min. Squeeze off excess liquid. Add one of the following dressings: 1, 2, 3, 5, 25. Leave to stand for 1 hour. Dress in a suitable dish or on a plate	Salade de concombre
Russian Cucumber Salad	Peel cucumber, slice fine on mandolin, sprinkle with salt, knead in. Leave to stand for 30 min. Squeeze off excess liquid. Mix 2 sliced cucumbers with 250 ml sour cream or crème fraîche, correct seasoning and leave to stand for 1 hour. Sprinkle with chopped chives. Dress in a suitable dish or on a plate	Salade de concombre Russe
Coleslaw	Shred cabbage very fine, sprinkle with salt, knead in well. Leave to stand for 1 hour. Squeeze off excess liquid. To 1 kg of cabbage add 150 g of julienne of carrots and 100 g finely chopped shallot, a tsp of English mustard and mix with 125 ml vinaigrette. The addition of 125 ml mayonnaise is optional. Correct seasoning and leave to stand for 1 hour. Dress in a suitable dish or on a plate	
Radish Salad	Tail radish. Holding on green top cut into fine slices on mandolin, sprinkle with salt, mix in well. Leave to stand for 1 hour. Squeeze off excess liquid. Add dressing of your choice, e.g. 1, 2, 3, 4, 5. Leave to stand for 1 hour. Serve sprinkled with chopped chives or parsley. Dress in a suitable dish or on a plate	Salade de radis
Tomato Salad	Cut a small cross into top and bottom of tomato, place in bowl, cover with boiling water for 6–8 seconds, drain, cover with cold water to refresh, peel off skin. Cut tomato in neat slices, lifting each tomato into a neat pattern on a tray. Sprinkle with chopped shallots and/or chives and the dressing of your choice (suggest 1, 3, 4, 5). Dress in a suitable dish or on a plate as a base of leaves	Salade de tomate

Table 3.6 *Single Simple Cooked Salads (see Plate 3.8)*

Menu example	Preparation and recommended dressings	French
Artichoke Bottom Salad	Cook the artichoke bottoms in normal way (available cooked from tins), cut in strips or quarters, add dressing of your choice (suggest 1, 3, 4, 5, 6, 8, 12, 16). Leave to stand for 1 hour. Dress in a suitable dish or on a plate	Salade de fonds d'artichauts
Asparagus Salad	Cook asparagus in the normal way, drain, pour over dressing of your choice while still warm (suggest 1, 2, 3, 4, 6 and 20, 23 only after asparagus is cold). Leave to stand for 1 hour. Dress in a suitable dish or on a plate	Salade d'asperges
Beetroot Salad	Wash beetroot well without damaging skin, cook until tender, cool, peel and cut into slices, dice or julienne. Add dressing of your choice while still warm (suggest 1, 2, 3, 4, 5, 6, 12, 13, 21). Leave to stand for 1 hour. Much suited for Scandinavian sweet and sour dressing. Dress in a suitable dish or on a plate	Salade de betterave
Celeriac Salad	Peel celeriac, cut into slices, dice, or julienne, cook for 5 min. Drain and add dressing of your choice while still warm (suggest 1, 2, 3, 4, 5). Leave to stand for 1 hour. Dress in a suitable dish or on a plate	Salade de celerie-rave
French Bean Salad	Cook beans in the normal way. Drain and add dressing of your choice while still warm (suggest 1, 2, 3, 4, 5). Leave to stand for 1 hour. Dress in a suitable dish or on a plate	Salade d'haricots verts
Haricot Bean Salad	Cook haricot beans until tender. Drain and add dressing of your choice and 200 g of tomato concassé while still warm suggest 1-2-3-4-5. Leave to stand for 1 hour. Add some chopped herbs. Dress in a suitable dish or on a plate	Salade d'haricots blancs
Red Bean Salad	Cook haricot beans until tender. Drain, add dressing of your choice while still warm (suggest 1, 2, 3, 4, 5). Leave to stand for 1 hour. Dress in a suitable dish or on a plate	Salade d'haricots rouge
German Potato Salad	Cook small to medium potatoes in their jacket, peel while still warm. Place vinaigrette into a bowl, slice warn potatoes into dressing, add chopped chives and shallots, toss, taking care not to break potato slices. The warm potatoes	Salade Allemande

Continued

Table 3.6 *Single Simple Cooked Salads (see Plate 3.8)*—cont'd

	and vinaigrette should make an emulsion. Dress in with suitable garnish in dish or on plate	
Swiss Potato Salad	As for German Potato Salad above using Swiss dressing (with bacon)	Salade de pommes Suisse
Hot Potato Salad	As either German or Swiss Potato Salad above but served warm by heating and keep warm over a bain marie	Salade de pommes de terre chaud
Potato Salad	Cook small to medium potatoes in their jacket, partly cool, peel, cool, mix with a splain vinaigrette. To 1 kg of potatoes add 250 ml mayonnaise. Mix in carefully not to break the slices of potato. Dress in a suitable dish or on a plate garnished with chopped chives or parsley	Salade de pomme de terre
Sweet Corn Salad	Mix cooked fresh sweetcorn grains (or from tins) with the dressing of your choice (suggest 1, 3, 4, 5, 9, 16, 22, 23). Dress in a suitable dish or on a plate	Salade de mais
Sweet Pepper Salad	Choose red, green or yellow peppers or a mixture thereof. Cut in even halves, wash away all pips/seeds, cut into neat dice, strips, squares or diamond shapes, place in a bowl, cover with boiling water for 3 min. Drain, while still hot cover with dressing of your choice (suggest 1, 3, 4, 5, 6, 7). Cool. Sometimes also dressed with sour cream. Dress in a suitable dish or on a plate	Salade de piment
Lentil Salad	Soak lentils overnight. Bring to boil, drain off water, cover with stock and gently simmer for 30–40 min. When cooked drain, cover with the dressing of your choice while still warm (suggest 1, 3, 6, 7, 8, 10, 12). Leave to stand	Salade de lentilles
Flageolets Salad	Cook flageolet in the normal way (available cooked in tins). Drain, cover with the dressing of your choice while still warm (suggest 1, 3, 6, 7, 8, 10). Leave to stand for 1 hour. Finally add some freshly chopped herbs	Salade flageolets
Chickpeas Salad	Soak chickpeas overnight. Bring to boil, drain off water, cover with stock and gently simmer for 30–40 min. When cooked, drain and cover with the dressing of your choice while still warm (suggest 1, 3, 6, 7, 8, 10, 12). Leave to stand for 1 hour. Add 200 g of tomato concassé and some freshly chopped herbs	Salade de pois de chiche

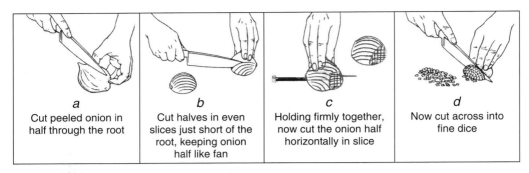

a	b	c	d
Cut peeled onion in half through the root	Cut halves in even slices just short of the root, keeping onion half like fan	Holding firmly together, now cut the onion half horizontally in slice	Now cut across into fine dice

FIG. 3.1 *Cutting of shallots/onions for salad garnish*

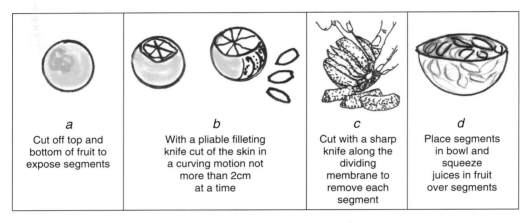

a	b	c	d
Cut off top and bottom of fruit to expose segments	With a pliable filleting knife cut of the skin in a curving motion not more than 2cm at a time	Cut with a sharp knife along the dividing membrane to remove each segment	Place segments in bowl and squeeze juices in fruit over segments

FIG. 3.2 *Cutting segments of citrus fruits for cocktail salads and garnish*

Free Combination Mixed Salads

Any two or three of the leaf salads, according to season, may be combined with some two or three single salad ingredients raw or cooked, whatever is in season. Of late, many of the raw grated fruit or/and vegetables salads have become very popular. Here the choice of dressing is requested when ordering or at the table. Plate 3.10 illustrates a range of free combination salads.

COMPOUND SALADS   *Salades composées*

Our third basic group of salads are the compound salads made from a combination of foods such as fruit, vegetables, fish, shellfish, poultry and meats, of which one ingredient should dominate, sometimes giving the salad its name. Plate 3.11 illustrates some examples.

For a better understanding when best to serve a given compound salad, they are grouped in the recipes below according to the main base ingredient of their preparation, i.e.:

Fruit-based
Vegetable-based
Fish-based
Poultry-based
Meat-based.

All are marinated in light vinaigrette and thereafter bound with acidulated cream, sour cream, mayonnaise or one of its variations, or, of late, crème fraîche.

In Britain these types of salads were until quite recently much underused, only a few such as Waldorf Salad being really well known. On the Continent of Europe and in America they are very popular and found in daily use in all types of catering establishments, served as:

A single hors d'oeuvre
Part of a mixed hors d'oeuvre
A side salad in place of vegetables (vegetable- and fruit-based only)
Part of a mixed salad
Part of a cold buffet.

The preparation of compound salads, as well as the ingredients used, varies considerably from one compound salad to another. Again, only the best materials should be used, well washed, clean and dry. Their preparation, particularly the cutting of the various food items that make up the salads, is the most important. Care should be taken in the cutting of very neat and even dice, strips or batons (see Plate 3.12).

First, we feature the detailed preparation of eight classical compound salads, including two of the best-known and popular – the Waldorf Salad and Dutch Herring Salad. Many of the points made here can be applied to other salads listed. Other examples of each of the base types are then given below.

Preparation of Some Classical Compound Salads

Waldorf Salad (fruit-based) (see Plate 3.11*b*)

Ingredients (10–12 portions)
500 g celeriac
6 large Russet apples
500 ml mayonnaise
24 walnut halves
Juice of half a lemon
Green leaves
Salt and pepper to taste

Method
1 Peel and cut the celeriac in neat ½ cm dice, blanch drain and cool
2 Peel the apples, place in lemon water, dice again into neat ½ cm dice. Immediately place in to a bowl and mix with mayonnaise
3 Add the now cooled and drained celeriac, salt and ground white pepper, mix
4 Leave to stand for 1–2 hours, loosen with a little water if necessary

Continued

Waldorf Salad (fruit-based) (see Plate 3.11*b*)—cont'd

Ingredients (10–12 portions)

Method

5 Dress in portions by pressing salad in ring on suitable plate, decorate with walnut halves and a little rocket, parsley or watercress. For a buffet place in a large bowl (see Plate 3.11*k*)

Note: In the past some walnuts were chopped and incorporated in the salad and some used as decoration. Today, when guests often wish to avoid nuts, garnish on top for easy removal.

Aida Salad (vegetable-based) (see Plate 3.11*g*)

Ingredients (8–10 portions)
4 chicory yellow or red
4 tomatoes
4 artichokes bottoms
1 green pepper
250 ml mustard dressing
2 hard-boiled eggs

Method
1 Trim chicory cut across in slices, for salad, save chicory tips for garnish
2 Cut green peppers in julienne, blanch, drain and cool
3 Blanch and peel tomatoes, cut in slices or quarters
4 Cook fresh artichokes bottoms or use from tin, cut into eighths
5 Mix all ingredients, marinate in mustard dressing, leave to stand for 30 min
6 Dress individually on plate or in bowl, garnish with quarters of hard-boiled eggs

Serve as a starter or on a buffet

Dutch Herring Salad (fish-based) (see Plate 3.11*d*)

Ingredients (8 portions)
6 large Russet apples
200 g cooked beetroot
200 g cooked potatoes
4–6 salted herring fillets or rollmops
250 ml mayonnaise
Some green leaves
Salt and pepper to taste

Method
1 Cut all ingredients in neat ½ cm dice
2 Mix with mayonnaise, leave to stand overnight for best red colour
3 Season with salt and pepper
4 Dress as individual portion in ring (see Waldorf Salad above) or on a plate or platter on a bed of green leaves. Can be decorated with quarters of hard-boiled eggs or sieved egg whites or/and yolks

Serve as a starter or on a buffet

Avocado and Prawn Salad (shellfish-based) (see Plate 3.11*a*)

Ingredients (8 portions)
4 ripe avocados
600 g peeled prawns
100 g red onions, diced and
  blanched
Juice of half a lemon
250 ml American dressing
Some green leaves

Method
1 Blanch onions, drain and cool, place in
  a bowl
2 Peel avocado, cut away the two even
  outer slices to make a semi or full
  circle, cover with lemon juice
3 Cut rest of avocado in dice or strips, place
  in bowl with onions
4 Add most prawns to bowl, mix with
  American dressing
5 Dress prawn–avocado–red onion mixture
  in avocado circle, garnish with
  a few prawns

Serve as a starter or on a buffet

Carmen Salad (poultry-based) (see Plate 3.11*j*)

Ingredients (8–10 portions)
2 red peppers
2 cooked chicken breasts
200 g cooked rice
50 g cooked peas
250 ml American dressing
Chopped tarragon to garnish
Green leaves

Method
1 Cut peppers in halves, wash away all pips,
  cut into ½ cm dice, blanch, cool
2 Cut chicken breasts into small scallops
3 Place rice into a bowl, add peas, pepper
  and chicken dice, tarragon and dressing
4 Mix well, leave to stand for 30 min
5 Dress on leaves of your choice, garnish
  with tarragon leaves and pepper
  diamonds

Serve as a starter or on a buffet

Hungarian Salad (meat-based) (see Plate 3.11*e*)

Ingredients (8–10 portions)
400 g lean bacon or ham
3 kg cooked potatoes
300 g white cabbage
125 ml mayonnaise
125 ml paprika dressing
2 tbsp horseradish
Chopped parsley
Green leaves

Method
1 Shred cabbage very fine, sprinkle with
  salt, mix in, leave to stand
2 Grill bacon crisp, cool and set aside
3 Cut potatoes into julienne, place into
  a bowl
4 Squeeze out water from cabbage add to
  potatoes
5 Add paprika dressing and mayonnaise,
  horseradish, half of bacon cut in julienne
  and chopped parsley. Mix all well and
  leave to stand

Continued

Hungarian Salad (meat-based) (see Plate 3.11*e*)—cont'd

Ingredients (8–10 portions)

Method

6 Dress on green leaves sprinkling rest of bacon julienne on top

Serve as a starter or on a buffet or as a side salad to steaks

Mascot Salad (meat-based) (see Plate 3.11*h*)

Ingredients (8–10 portions)
250 g cooked ham
150 g chicken liver
100 g diced shallots
16 asparagus tips
8 crayfish tails
250 ml cream mustard
   dressing
Green leaves

Method
1 Trim and cut liver in neat pieces, sauté in little butter, set aside to cool
2 Blanche shallots, drain and cool
3 Cut ham into neat dice, cut crayfish tails into halves, place in bowl
4 Add shallots, chicken livers and dressing, mix, leave to stand
5 Dress individually or in larger bowl on bed of leaves or cress. Garnish with asparagus tips

Serve as a starter or on a buffet

Genoa Salad (poultry-based) (see Plate 3.11*c*)

Ingredients (8–10 portions)
400 g poached chicken
100 g small pasta, cooked
1 tin Cannelleni beans
100 g shallots, diced, cooked
250 ml mayonnaise
150 g tomato concassé
I tsp tomato ketchup
Salt and pepper to taste
Green leaves, extra tomato

Method
1 Cut chicken into scallops or strips, place in bowl
2 Add pasta, concassé, shallots, beans, ketchup and mayonnaise. Mix well, leave to stand
3 Dress on green leaves or in half tomatoes, or on slices of tomato

Serve as a starter or on a buffet

Preparation of Various Fruit-Based Compound Salads

Alice Salad   Salade Alice

Ingredients (8 portions)
8 medium Russet apples
100 g redcurrants off
   branches

Method
1 Peel and core apples, place in lemon water
2 Cut one-third off the top of each apple, return the two-thirds part to lemon water

Continued

Alice Salad Salade Alice—cont'd

Ingredients (8 portions)
8 redcurrant branches
50 g split almonds
250 ml sour cream
Juice of 1 lemon
Leaves for decoration
Salt and pepper

Method
3 Cut the tops of the 8 apples into ½ cm dice
4 Mix with loose redcurrants, cream, lemon juice, salt and white pepper
5 Drain and dry the 8 apple bases, place on some green leaves
6 Divide apple/currant mixture equally and heap onto each apple base
7 Garnish with redcurrant branch sprinkled with roasted split almonds

Serve as a starter or side salad with roast or grilled fish, meats and game

Apple Salad  Salade de pommes

Ingredients (8 portions)
8 medium Russet apples
150 g finely sliced shallots
500 ml mayonnaise
Juice of 1 lemon
Leaves for decoration
Some tarragon leaves
Salt and pepper

Method
1 Blanch sliced shallots, cool
2 Peel and core apples, place in lemon water
3 Place mayonnaise, half the lemon juice, salt and pepper into a bowl
4 Add shallots, then slice apples into thin slices into the bowl
5 Gently mix, add a little water if necessary, leave to stand for 30–60 min
6 Dress on leaves and garnish with tarragon leaves

Serve as a starter or side salad with roast or grilled fish, meats and game

Creole Salad Salade Créole

Ingredients
1 large melon
150 g cooked cold rice
250 ml sour cream
50 g fresh ginger
Juice of 1 lemon
Leaves for decoration
Salt and pepper

Method
1 Cut melon in quarters, remove all flesh, cut into neat segments into bowl
2 Add cooked rice, part grated ginger, cream, lemon juice, salt and pepper
3 Gently mix, leave to stand for 30–60 min
4 Dress on leaves and garnish with grated ginger. (Can be made with small scooped melons and mixture filled in cavity.)

Serve as a starter or side salad with roast poultry, meats and game, or include on a buffet

Eve Salad   Salade Eve

Ingredients (8 portions)
1 small pineapple
4 apples
2 bananas
250 ml fresh cream
Leaves for decoration
Salt and pepper

Method
1 Peel and cut pineapples in segments, peel and cut apples in segments
2 Place in bowl, add sliced bananas, cream, salt and pepper
3 Gently mix, leave to stand for 30 min
4 Dress on leaves and garnish with water-cress or rocket

Serve as a starter, or with roast poultry, meats and game, or on any buffet

Columbia Salad   Salade Columbie

Ingredients (8 portions)
1 Russet apple
2 medium bananas
200 g seedless grapes
250 ml mayonnaise
Juice of 1 lemon
50 g pistachio nuts
Leaves for decoration
Salt and pepper

Method
1 Peel, core and slice apples, sprinkle with some lemon juice
2 Place mayonnaise in to a bowl, mix in apples
3 Slice in bananas and grapes cut in halves, add salt and pepper
4 Gently mix, leave to stand for 30 min
5 Dress on individual cups of lettuce leaves or in a bowl, sprinkle with roasted pistachio nuts

Serve as a starter or side salad with roast poultry, meats and game, or include on a buffet

Japanese Salad   Salade Japonaise

Ingredients (8 portions)
500 g tomatoes
1 small pineapple
250 ml sour cream or crème fraîche
Juice of one orange
Leaves for decoration
Salt and pepper

Method
1 Peel and cut tomatoes in quarters, remove pips, cut into large dice
2 Peel and cut pineapple in largish dice
3 Make julienne of skin of orange
4 Place in bowl, add little salt and pepper, juice of orange, cream
5 Gently mix, leave to stand for 30 min
6 Dress on individual cups of lettuce leaves or in a bowl, sprinkle with julienne

Serve as a starter or side salad with roast poultry, meats and game, or include on a buffet

Windsor Salad Salade Windsor

Ingredients (8 portions)
8 apples
1 small pineapple
500 ml mayonnaise
4 tomatoes
Juice of half a lemon
Leaves for decoration
Salt and pepper

Method
1 Peel and core apples, place in lemon water, cut one-third off the top of each apple
2 Cut the tops of the 8 apples into neat 1 cm dice, mix into mayonnaise
3 Peel and cut pineapple into 1 cm dice, add to apple and mayonnaise, season with lemon juice and salt and pepper
4 Place salad mixture into bottom two-thirds of apple.
5 Dress on individual cups of lettuce leaves surrounded by tomato slices

Serve as a starter or side salad with roast poultry meats and game, or include on a buffet

Preparation of Various Vegetable-Based Compound Salads

American Salad Salade Américaine

Ingredients (8 portions)
6 tomatoes
500 g cooked potatoes
250 g small onions
½ stick of celery
250 ml vinaigrette/cream
Leaves for decoration
2 hard-boiled eggs

Method
1 Blanch and peel tomatoes, slice, add sliced potatoes and sliced celery
2 Finely slice onions, blanch, drain and cool, add to above
3 Mix all ingredients, marinate with vinaigrette, leave to stand for 30 min
4 Dress individually or in a bowl on shredded lettuce, sprinkle top with julienne of egg whites and yolk

Serve as a starter or side salad with roast and grilled meats and fish, or include on a buffet

Andalusia Salad Salade Andalouse

Ingredients (8 portions)
6 tomatoes
2 red peppers
200 g boiled rice

Method
1 Blanch and peel tomatoes, cut in quarters
2 Cut peppers in halves, wash away all pips, cut into neat strips, blanch

Continued

Andalusia Salad Salade Andalouse—cont'd

Ingredients (8 portions)
4 medium onions
250 ml garlic dressing
1 bunch watercress

Method
3 Place cooked rice in a bowl, add tomatoes and pepper strips
4 Marinate with garlic dressing, leave to stand for 30 min
5 Dress individually or in bowl on watercress leaves

Serve as a starter or side salad with roast and grilled fish and meats or include on a buffet

Bagatelle Salad Salade Bagatelle

Ingredients (8 portions)
200 g young carrots
200 g button mushrooms
24–32 asparagus tips
250 ml vinaigrette
Juice of half a lemon
50 g mixed chopped herbs
2 boxes of mustard and cress

Method
1 Peel and coarsely shred young carrots, slice mushrooms very fine
2 Place in bowl, mix well with lemon juice to retain colour, add vinaigrette
3 Mix well again, leave to stand for 30 min
4 Dress on bed of cress individually or in bowl
5 Garnish with 3–4 asparagus tips per portion, sprinkle with chopped herbs

Serve as a starter or a side salad with roast and grilled fish and meats, or include on a buffet

Russian Salad Salade Russe

Ingredients (8 portions)
150 g diced carrots, cooked
150 g diced turnips, cooked
150 g green peas, cooked
100 g cooked French beans cut into diamonds
500 ml mayonnaise
Seasoning

Method
1 Drain all cooked vegetables well, place in bowl
2 Add mayonnaise and seasoning, including a little sugar
3 Mix well, leave to stand for 1 hour
4 Dress in a suitable dish for a cold buffet, use as part of a mixed salad or base in tartlets

Can be used as a salad in its own right dressed with hard-boiled eggs, smoked salmon, caviar etc.

Preparation of Various Fish-Based Compound Salads

Salad Beauty of the Night   Salade Belle de Nuit

Ingredients (8 portions)
32 crayfish tails
50 g truffles
250 ml lemon dressing
2 medium lettuce
2 hard-boiled whites of
  egg

Method
1 Cut crayfish tails in halves, place in bowl
2 Slice truffles in very thin slices, add to
  crayfish tails, marinate with lemon dressing,
  leave to stand for 30 min
3 Trim outer leaves of lettuce, wash whole, drain,
  cut into 16 sections, held together by stalk
4 Dress by placing two lettuce sections on a plate
  or around a large bowl, place crayfish truffle
  mixture on top or in middle of bowl, sprinkle with
  chopped or julienne of egg whites

Serve as a starter or ideal to include on a buffet

Francillon Salad   Salade Francillon

Ingredients (8 portions)
1 kg mussels
500 g potatoes
150 g shallots
50 g chopped parsley
250 ml vinaigrette/cream
Green leaves

Method
1 Cook mussels in the normal way, cool, open
2 Cut potatoes in neat 1 cm dice, cook in mussel
  stock, drain and cool
3 Cut shallots very fine, blanch, cool
4 Mix mussels, potatoes, shallots and parsley with
  dressing, leave to stand for at least 1 hour
5 Dress on leaves in individual portions or in a
  larger bowl

Serve as a starter or ideal to include on a buffet

Prawn Salad   Salade de crevettes

Ingredients (8 portions)
1 kg shelled prawns
750 g tomatoes
⅓ litre cocktail sauce
Juice of 1 lemon
Green leaves

Method
1 Wash prawns, drain, marinate in half the lemon
  juice and a little salt
2 Blanch and peel tomatoes, cut in halves, wash
  off pips, cut into neat dice
3 Mix prawns and tomato flesh with cocktail sauce,
  leave to stand for at least 1 hour
4 Dress in individual portions or in a large bowl on
  green leaves of your choice

Serve as a starter or ideal to include on a buffet

Salmon Cucumber Salad　　Salade de saumon et concombre

Ingredients (8 portions)
600 g fillet of salmon
1 large cucumber
Sprigs of dill
8 large tomatoes
125 ml vinaigrette
250 ml mayonnaise
Salt and pepper
Green leaves

Method
1 Poach salmon fillet in the normal way, cool
2 Peal cucumber, cut in half, remove pips with a
  teaspoon
3 Cut in slices, place in bowl, sprinkle with salt,
  add 1 tsp chopped dill and vinaigrette, mix
4 Flake cooked salmon onto cucumbers, add
  mayonnaise, mix, leave to stand for
  at least 1 hour
5 Cut tops off tomatoes, scoop out flesh with
  parisienne cutter, salt and pepper
6 Fill tomatoes with salmon–cucumber mixture
7 Place on leaves, garnish with sprigs of dill
  on top

Serve as a starter or ideal to include on a buffet

Preparation of Various Meat-Based Compound Salads

Beatrice Salad　　Salade Beatrice

Ingredients (8 portions)
cooked chicken
  breasts
16 cooked asparagus
  tips
500 g peeled potatoes
⅓ litre mayonnaise
1 tsp English mustard
Green leaves
8 slices of truffles

Method
1 Cut potatoes into julienne, cook, strain and,
  cool place in bowl
2 Cut chicken breasts into julienne, add to
  potatoes
3 Mix mustard into mayonnaise, add to chicken
  and potatoes, mix well
4 Dress on leaves of your choice in individual
  portions or large bowl
5 Garnish with asparagus tips and slice of truffle

Serve as a starter or include on a buffet

Egyptian Salad　　Salade Égyptienne

Ingredients (8 portions)
150 g chicken livers
150 g cooked ham
100 g button
  mushrooms, sliced

Method
1 Trim and cut liver in neat pieces, sauté in little
  butter, add mushrooms, cook, cool
2 Cut ham in neat dice, cut artichoke bottoms
  each in 8 pieces, place in a bowl

Continued

Egyptian Salad   Salade Égyptienne—cont'd

Ingredients (8 portions)
4 artichokes bottoms
100 g cooked rice
250 ml vinaigrette
Green leaves

Method
3 Add cooked rice, cooked liver and mushrooms
  and dressing, mix well, leave to stand for
  at least 1 hour
4 Dress in a pyramid on leaves

Serve as a starter or include on a buffet

Fauchette Salad   Salade Fauchette

Ingredients (8 portions)
4 cooked chicken
  breasts
250 g button
  mushrooms
4 endives
25 g truffles
250 ml vinaigrette
Juice of half a lemon
25 g chopped chives

Method
1 Cut mushrooms in very thin slices, place in bowl,
  add lemon juice and vinaigrette
2 Cut endives across in slices, add to mushrooms,
  add chives
3 Cut chicken into neat small scallops, add to bowl,
  mix well, leave to stand for at least 1 hour. Dress
  on leaves of your choice, garnish with julienne
  of truffles on top

Serve as a starter or include on a buffet

Florida Salad   Salade Florida

Ingredients (8 portions)
1 medium pineapple
4 cooked chicken
  breasts
2 grapefruit
330 ml American
  dressing
Red lettuce leaves

Method
1 Peel, core and slice pineapple, cut in neat 2 cm
  dice, place in bowl
2 Cut chicken into neat scallops, add to bowl, add
  dressing, leave to stand for at least 1 hour
3 Peel grapefruit, cut out neat segments, set aside
4 Dress individually or in a bowl on red lettuce
  leaves, surrounded by segments of grapefruit

Serve as a starter or include on a buffet

Presentation, Garnishes and Borders for Compound Salads

Some presentations have been suggested with each of the compound salads above, but the final appearance is often a very personal thing or restricted by the equipment available in any given establishment. The following items, where and when suitable, may be used to enhance the appearance of the salad:

> Dice, julienne, diamonds, triangles, etc. – of the main ingredient of the salad
> Neat, blanched or raw rings of onion – not suited everywhere
> Hard-boiled eggs sliced, quartered, as well as coarsely chopped or sieved
> Beetroot cut into diamonds, triangles or half-moon shapes – only with beetroot dishes
> Julienne of whites of eggs, pimentos, mushrooms, ham, tongue – suitable for most salads
> Bouquets of fresh watercress, mustard and cress or rocket – suitable for many salads
> Quartered hearts of lettuce, whole sliced radishes, cucumber, tomatoes and spring onions

On occasion tartlets, banquettes, puff-pastry bases as well as croutons or fleurons are very helpful as a base in the presentation of compound salads, particularly when these are served as a starter in individual portions.

SERVICE OF SALADS

In the olden days all salads, simple or compound, were served in individual or larger crystal glass, china or wooden bowls, earthenware saladiers etc. Whereas the green and simple salads should be served on the flatter type of saladier, this will allow more room for border and garnishes, which often surround this type of salad. Some of the more expensive types of compound salads can be served on crushed ice. Surrounding the salads with folded or artistically shaped serviettes completes the picture, especially when served on a buffet.

Nowadays, the large majority of salads are served plated and most, whether green, mixed green, single or mixed and compound, are served on side or fish plates.

Final Note

Remember: fruit- and vegetable-based compound salads can be served as side salads with a main course in place of vegetables. Fish- and meat-based compound salads are usually served as an hors d'oeuvre or on buffets of all types.

HOT SALADS

Hot salads have been found on menus for more than a hundred years, but in the past few years they have gained new popularity, especially at lunchtime and with women, by whom they are considered a less filling meals. Some examples of modern hot salads are given in Plate 3.13. The question may perhaps be posed as to whether they are really a salad or more of a hot entrée?

Basically, the hot salad consists of a largish plate with mixed leaves plus some, cucumbers, shredded carrots, tomatoes, slices of red or spring onion etc.

The fish, poultry and meats to be used should be of very good quality, cut into neat strips and are best marinated before cooking (see marinades below). The foods are then sautéed in butter, drained and placed on the salad at the very last moment before serving.

COLD SAUCES **Les sauces froides**

This section concerns itself with the various types of cold sauces as well as coulis which have become so much a part of modern food presentation, and the cold savoury butters served with grilled fish, poultry and meats.

We shall start with the most famous of the cold sauces, the mayonnaise. If the Hollandaise is called the Queen of all sauces, the mayonnaise is most certainly the Princess of the cold sauces. As we have seen, it is used as a base for some of the dressings above and as base for many other sauces.

MAYONNAISE

Basic Mayonnaise (see Plate 3.14)

Ingredients (12–16 portions)
8 yolks of eggs
2 tbsp vinegar
2 tsp English Mustard
1 litre oil (olive or other)
1 tsp caster sugar
500 ml lemon juice
2 tbsp hot water
Salt and ground white
  pepper

Method
1 Place eggs yolks into a bowl or food processor, add vinegar, mustard, sugar, salt and pepper, mix well
2 Gradually add in the oil, first a drop at a time, stirring all the time. If using a processor use the pulse button. When half the oil has been added, add the rest of the oil more boldly
3 Finally add the lemon juice and hot water mix and correct the seasoning
4 The sauce should be thick and like butter of piping consistency for piping through a piping bag for decoration of cold foods. For other purposes the mayonnaise can be thinned down with water

Variations on mayonnaise (see Plate 3.15*b,c,d*)

Sauce
Tartare Sauce

Rémoulade Sauce

Method
Add 150 g of sweet and sour cucumber/ gherkins, 50 g of capers and 50 g of parsley all finely chopped to mayonnaise above, mix well, leave to stand

Add 150 g of sweet and sour cucumber/ gherkins, 50 g of capers and 50 g of parsley, anchovy fillet and 3 hard-boiled egg, all finely chopped, to mayonnaise above, mix well, leave to stand*

Continued

Variations on mayonnaise (see Plate 3.15*b,c,d*)—cont'd

Sauce	Method
Andalouse Sauce	To 750 ml of mayonnaise plus 250 ml of tomato ketchup add 200 g of finely diced and blanched red peppers, mix well, leave to stand
Green Sauce/ Sauce verte	Add 150 g of mixed herbs, parsley, dill, chives, chervil, tarragon, all finely chopped, to mayonnaise above; 100 g of freshly cooked and cooled finely sieved spinach can much improve the colour, especially at a time when dried herbs have to be used
Gribiche Sauce	To 1 litre of Tartare sauce above add 3 finely chopped hard-boiled eggs*
Mayonnaise Colée	Strain 6 leaves of gelatine dissolved in a little hot water to the above basic recipe, allow to cool and set. Use for covering cold fish and egg portions

For the Rémoulade and Gribiche sauces, in the old days sieved cooked egg yolks were used in place of raw egg yolks, following the method for mayonnaise above. This practice is seldom followed today.

COCKTAIL SAUCE (see plate 3.15a)

There are three methods of preparing cocktail sauces, all equally good and popular.

Sauce	Method
Cocktail Sauce (mayonnaise-based)	To 1 litre of mayonnaise add 250 ml of tomato ketchup, a little cayenne and Worcestershire sauce and a little water, combine well and use as required. Must be running but covering at a same time
Cocktail Sauce (cream-based)	Whip 1 litre of cream,* add 250 ml of tomato ketchup, a little cayenne, Worcestershire sauce, and salt and pepper, combine well and use as required
Cocktail Sauce (cream/ mayonnaise)	To 750 ml mayonnaise add 250 ml cream,* 250 ml ketchup, a little cayenne and Worcestershire sauce and a little grated horseradish, salt and pepper, combine well and use as required

Of late crème fraîche is often used in place of normal cream.

THE COULIS

Coulis are Small Sauces made from fruits and vegetables. They have a long history but were almost forgotten or underused until they came into renewed use with the advent of the plated service associated with cuisine nouvelle.

Sweet or sharp, or often a combination of the two (think of the famous Cumberland Sauce), they should always be of a succulent flavour. They are served as a sauce–dressing with all manner of food, such as hot or cold savoury fish and meat dishes, mousses and salads.

Others are sweeter made with the addition of extra sugar, and piped or ladled around sweets such as cakes, pancakes, gateaux, cheese cakes, stewed fruit etc.

In both cases they can give extra flavour and useful contrast for our modern plated presentation.

Asparagus Coulis

Ingredients (10–12 portions)
12 asparagus spears
    cooked
100 g shallots
2 tbsp olive oil
250 ml white wine
4 tbsp double cream
1 clove garlic
A little lemon juice
Salt and pepper

Method
1 Cook shallots in oil, cool, add asparagus cut in small pieces, garlic, lemon juice, white wine and salt and pepper
2 Cut to a fine puree in a processor, or force through a sieve
3 When cold, add cream and correct seasoning

Suitable to be served with cold salmon and other cold fish portions, fish mousses, smoked trout, eel, cold ham, tongue etc. and salads

Apricot Coulis

Ingredients (10–12 portions)
500 g dried apricots
100 g shallots
2 tbsp olive oil
500 ml white wine
4 tbsp double cream
1 clove of garlic
A little lemon juice
Salt, pepper, cayenne

Method
1 Place apricots in pan with garlic, lemon juice and white wine, cayenne and salt and pepper, cook until tender, cool
2 Cook shallots in oil, cool
3 Cut shallots with apricot mixture to a fine puree in a food processor, or force through a sieve
4 When cold add cream and correct seasoning

Suitable to be served with cold meats, game and poultry of all types, roast hot meats, and entrées, e.g. fillet, medallion etc. and salads

Cucumber Coulis

Ingredients (10–12 portions)
2 cucumbers
150 g shallots
2 tbsp olive oil
500 ml white wine
4 tbsp double cream
1 clove of garlic
A little lemon juice
Salt, pepper, cayenne

Method
1 Cook shallots in oil, cool
2 Peel and cut cucumbers in half, lengthwise, remove pips, cut in small chunks
3 Add to shallots with garlic, lemon juice and white wine, cayenne and salt and pepper, and cut to a fine puree in a food processor or force through a sieve, add cream and correct seasoning

Suitable to be served with poached salmon, smoked trout, eel, mackerel etc. and salads

Plum Coulis

Ingredients (10–12 portions)
750 g stoned plums
100 g shallots
2 tbsp olive oil
250 ml white wine
4 tbsp double cream
1 clove garlic
1 tsp English mustard
A little lemon juice
Salt and pepper
A little lemon juice
Salt and pepper

Method
1 Place plums in pan with garlic, lemon juice and white wine, cayenne and salt and pepper, cook until tender, drain most cooking liquor, cool
2 Cook shallots in oil, cool
3 Cut shallots with plums to puree in a food processor, when cold add cream, mustard and plum liquor to get a covering consistency, correct seasoning

Suitable to be served with cold meats, game and poultry of all types, roast hot meats and entrées, e.g. fillet, medallions etc.

Tomato Coulis

Ingredients (10–12 portions)
1 kg tomatoes for concassé
150 g shallots
2 tbsp olive oil
250 ml white wine
1 clove garlic
50 g tomato puree
A little sugar
Salt and pepper, cayenne
A little Worcestershire sauce

Method
1 Cook shallots in oil, add tomato puree, sweat, cool
2 Blanch, cool and peel tomatoes, cut in quarters, wash away pips, cut into dice, add to shallots, wine, garlic, sugar, salt and pepper in pan, bring to the boil for a few minutes
3 Place all in a food processor and cut to a fine puree or force through a sieve, cool, correct seasoning and add Worcestershire sauce

Suitable to be served with cold meats, game and poultry of all types and salads

DIVERS COLD SAUCES

We have a number of different cold sauces, sometimes called the English Sauces, although they are not all of English origin. The list below gives a number of the best known.

Cumberland Sauce

Ingredients (12–16 portions)
2 jars redcurrant jelly
250 ml port
4 tsp English mustard
100 g shallots
3 oranges
1 lemon
Zest of 1 orange
Salt and milled pepper

Method
1 With a peeler, peel oranges, cut peel into fine julienne, blanch
2 Squeeze juice from oranges
3 Warm and melt jelly with orange juice, reduce somewhat
4 Add shallots, bring to point of boil, cool slightly
5 In a bowl mix English mustard with lemon juice, add the still warm jelly mixture, salt and pepper, and finally the julienne
6 Correct seasoning, should be sharp and sweet

Serve with cold meats, e.g. ham, tongue, roast game, beef and lamb

Horseradish Sauce

Ingredients (12–16 portions)
500 g freshly grated horseradish
250 g fresh white breadcrumbs
500 ml milk
500 ml cream
A little cayenne
Salt and white pepper

Method
1 Soak breadcrumbs in milk
2 Grate horseradish, place in bowl with cream, add breadcrumbs
3 Mix well, season with cayenne, salt and pepper

Serve with warm smoked fish, e.g. trout, eel, mackerel, and roast beef

Horseradish Sauce 2

Ingredients (12–16 portions)
2 jars ready horseradish
500 ml whipping cream
A little cayenne
Salt and white pepper

Method
1 Whip cream medium firm, add ready horseradish, fold in well
2 Correct seasoning with cayenne, salt and pepper

Serve with warm smoked fish, e.g. trout, eel, mackerel, and roast beef

Mint Sauce

Ingredients (12–16 portions)
3 bunches of fresh mint
250 g caster sugar
250 ml vinegar
250 ml water
Pinch of salt

Method
1 Place water and ⅔ sugar in a pan, bring to boil and dissolve, set aside and cool
2 Pick leaves off stalks, chop very fine on board with ⅓ of sugar, or in a processor
3 Mix mint with sugar syrup, add vinegar to required sweetness, and correct salt to taste

Serve with roast lamb

Oxford Sauce

Ingredients (12–16 portions)
As for Cumberland Sauce but replacing oranges with lemon, and using only 2 lemons for both juice and julienne

Method
Proceed as for Cumberland Sauce

Mustard (Scandinavian) Sauce

Ingredients (12–16 portions)
1 bunch fresh dill
500 ml vegetable oil
125 ml wine vinegar
1 small jar Dijon mustard
1 tbsp sugar
Salt and milled pepper

Method
1 Place mustard, salt, pepper, sugar and vinegar into a bowl and mix well
2 Gradually work in the oil, should be slightly thickening
3 Remove stalks from dill, chop dill leaves very fine
4 Add chopped dill to sauce, stand for 1 hour, may need seasoning correction. Sauce can separate, give an occasional stir before serving

Serve with Gravad Lax and other cold fish

Niçoise Sauce

Ingredients (12–16 portions)
1 litre French dressing
50 g capers
100 g stoned olives
150 g tomato concassée
50 g parsley
2 cloves garlic

Method
1 Chop capers, parsley, olives, garlic reasonably fine, place in a bowl
2 Add French dressing and tomato concassée, mix well and correct seasoning

Serve with cold meats, fish and eggs, use as a dressing for meats or poultry salads

Ravigote

Ingredients (12–16 portions)
1 basic vinaigrette
150 g finely diced shallots
100 g mixed chopped herbs,
    parsley, chervil, tarragon
2 hard-boiled eggs
8 anchovy fillets
2 tbsp anchovy essence
Pinch of sugar

Method
1 Blanch copped shallots, drain and cool
2 Chop anchovy and capers, sieve eggs
    through coarse sieve
3 Mix all ingredients in a bowl, add sugar
    and correct seasoning

Serve with cold meats and fish, calfs head
    or use as a dressing for beef salad

Persillade Sauce

Ingredients (12–16 portions)
As for Ravigotte with the
    addition of garlic

Method
Proceed as for Ravigotte

Serve with cold meats, fish and eggs or use
    as a dressing for meats or poultry salads

Swedish Sauce

Ingredients (12–16 portions)
1 kg apples, not too sweet
500 ml white wine
150 g grated horseradish
1 lemon juice
100 g sugar
250 ml mayonnaise

Method
1 Peel, core and quarter apples, place in
    pan with lemon juice, wine and sugar
2 Bring to the boil, cook until tender, set
    aside and cool
3 Grate horseradish or use equivalent
    from ready jar
4 Place with apples in a food processor, or
    pass through a sieve to a fine puree, cool
5 When cold add mayonnaise, correct
    seasoning

Serve with warm smoked fish, e.g. trout,
    eel, mackerel, and cold meats

Aioli (see Plate 3.16)

Ingredients (12–16 portions)
6 egg yolks
3 large cloves of garlic
500 ml olive oil

Method
1 Crush garlic to a fine puree with the salt
2 Add egg yolks and pepper

Continued

Aioli (see Plate 3.16)—cont'd

Ingredients (12–16 portions)
Salt and ground white
   pepper to taste

Method
3 Mix in well
4 Gradually whisk in the olive oil
Larger amounts can be made in a food
   processor

Use as a dip or like mayonnaise for dishes
   such as grilled fish

COMPOUND BUTTERS   *Beurres composés*

Compound butters are a very useful addition to the flavouring and presentation of our dishes, particularly in the case of grilled fish and meats, where they take the place of sauces.

Parsley Butter or Beurre Maître d'hôtel is the best known. However, they come in two types, mainly those with a savoury flavour and a few with the addition of sugar for sweet dishes such as pancakes. The preparation of the most popular types is given below.

Parsley Butter   Beurre Maître d'hôtel (see Plate 3.17)

Ingredients (for 1 kg butter,
gives 24–36 portions)
1 kg soft butter
Juice of 1 lemon
4 tbsp Worcestershire sauce
A little salt and milled pepper
150 g finely chopped parsley

Method
1 Combine all ingredients in a bowl or food
   processor, mix well and correct seasoning
2 Divide into 3–4 batches, place on wet
   greaseproof paper, wrap and roll into a
   neat roll about 5 cm in diameter, twist
   ends to create sausage shape. Place in
   fridge to harden
3 Cut into 1–2 slices per portion

Serve with grilled fish and steaks of all types

Butter
Dill Butter/Beurre l'aneth

Method
As above, replacing parsley with equal
   amount of chopped dill

Serve with grilled fish and veal

Tarragon Butter/Beurre
  estragon

As above, replacing parsley with equal
   amount of chopped tarragon

Serve with grilled fish, veal, lamb

Continued

Butter	Method
Mixed Herb Butter/Beurre fines herbes	As above, replacing parsley with equal amount of chopped freshly chopped mixed herbs, e.g. parsley, chives, tarragon, basil, chervil
	Serve with grilled fish, veal, lamb and all steaks
Anchovy Butter/Beurre anchois	As above, replacing parsley with 15–20 anchovy fillets finely chopped or forced through a sieve, mix well, proceed as above
	Serve with all grilled fish and some meats
Lemon Butter/Beurre au citron	As above, replacing parsley with 2 further lemons (3 in all). Wash, dry and grate zest of all lemons, place with butter and all other ingredients in bowl then add the juice of all lemons and mix well. Proceed as for first recipe
	Serve with grilled fish
English Mustard Butter/ Beurre moutard Anglaise	Add 2–3 tbsp English mustard to recipe ingredients
	Add 4–5 tbsp French mustard to recipe ingredients
French Mustard Butter/ Beurre moutard Française	Omit parsley in both cases
	Serve with grilled herring and other grilled fish
Horseradish Butter/Beurre Raifort	As basic recipe but replacing parsley with 150 g freshly grated horseradish or 250 g ready horseradish. Mix well and proceed as above
	Serve with grilled fish and steaks of all types
Red Wine Butter/Beurre vin rouge	Cook 500 g of chopped shallots in 750 ml red wine until almost dry and cool. Add these now dark red shallots to butter with all other ingredients but omitting the parsley. Proceed as above
	Serve with grilled or fried fish, steaks, cutlets, medallions, escalopes etc.

MARINADES

Marinades are intended to flavour all manner of fish and meats before cooking. In the olden days they were mostly applied to fish and meat portions to be grilled, especially if a little bland, such as poultry. As today we have increasingly to use more chilled and frozen fish and meats, marinating helps to give back flavour and even colour that has been lost in the defrosting process.

Marinade for fish and shellfish

Ingredients
500 ml white wine
250 ml oil
Juice of 2 lemons
Salt and milled pepper
Parsley stalks

Method
Mix all ingredients well, brush on fish portions
    and prawns etc. an hour or so before cooking

Ideal whether fish is to be grilled, fried or deep
    fried. Prawns will much improve even for
    cocktails

Marinade for poultry (especially chicken and veal)

Ingredients
500 ml white wine
250 ml oil
Juice of 1 lemon
2–3 tbsp honey
Salt, milled pepper,
    cayenne, paprika
    powder

Method
Mix all ingredients well, brush on fish portions
    and prawns etc. an hour or so before cooking

Marinade for red meats and game

Ingredients
500 ml oil
1 glass of port
2–3 crushed cloves garlic
Salt, milled pepper and
    cayenne

Method
Mix all ingredients well, brush on fish portions
    and prawns etc. an hour or so before cooking

Brine for pickled/brined salmon (Gravad Lax) (see Plate 2.5)

*Ingredients (for both sides
of a 3 kg salmon)*
200 g sea salt
150 g caster sugar
30 g black peppercorns,
    coarsely crushed
2–3 bunches of dill stalks
    only (keep most dill
    itself for sauce)

Method
1 Pick best dill off stalks and set aside
2 Crush dill stalks with bat (most flavour inside)
3 Mix salt, pepper and sugar well, rub into
    the flesh sides of the salmon, place on top
    of one another into a stainless steel tray
    with the crushed dill stalks in between,
    store in fridge
4 Marinate for 48–72 hours, turning the
    sides several times

Serve cut in thin slices garnished with sprigs
    of dill and with mustard sauce

4 Fish, Shellfish and Crustaceans (Poissions, Fruits de Mer and Crustacé)

FISH 🍴 *Les poissons*

Most fishes are edible and the world of fish represents an enormous source of good food. Of the most nourishing types of fish, many come from the rivers, such as the eels and the lamprey family, salmon, salmon trout, trout and char, and from the sea we have mackerel, fresh herrings, turbot and the conger-eel family. Among the less nourishing are such as sole, lemon sole and bream, etc., but they are nevertheless well liked for their good taste and easy adaptation to the many different methods of preparation and cooking.

This chapter is concerned with the preparation, for cooking, and presentation of fish and fish dishes in particular and the importance of the fish course on our menu in general. In most parts of the world, and in particular in Europe, fish and shellfish have always been a valuable source of protein, whether they came from the sea or the lakes and rivers of Europe. The reasons for this are the increased popularity of fish dishes, both in the home and in restaurants, in a more prosperous and health conscious Europe, which has led to a trebling of fish consumption in less than twenty years. This need for more and more fish for the table has subsequently led to over-fishing of all types of popular fish, which in the British Isles are cod, haddock, herring, turbot, halibut, plaice and sole as well as salmon, trout and shellfish, such as crab, lobster, oysters, mussels, etc.

All these very popular fish types have trebled in price and in many cases the cost of fish can now be double or more that of meat, if we equate it to equal food value. Even quality and size of all types of fish is not as good as it was in the past, and we now have to accept smaller fishes, with a subsequent higher preparation loss and further increase in price.

To be able to bring a reasonable supply of fish to these shores, very much larger fishing boats have to go further and further on to the high seas, with long voyages for the ships. To compensate for the cost of these long and expensive trips, and to keep the crew occupied, many fishing boats have been turned into factory-ships, filleting, portioning and generally preparing and chilling or freezing the fish on board on the way back to ports. In this process, the fish bones are often thrown overboard, and it is getting increasingly difficult to get fresh fish bones to make the fish stocks which are such a very important part in the majority of classical poached fish dishes with their famous sauces and presentations.

Recent trends such as the pollution of rivers and the sea, coupled with concern for over-fishing, followed by the imposition of European fishing quotas and limits, have made many popular fish types now a rarity and very expensive. For this reason we have had to adopt new fish types, or accept more frozen fish from all parts of the world, which only a few years ago would not have been acceptable in most British or European restaurants.

Nearly all good cookery books give almost as much space and consideration to the preparation and presentation of fish dishes as they do to meat. Although these recipes are numerous and varied, and it is true to say that most of them are limited to the most popular types of fish, they are nowadays often applied to those new types of fish which of late we have had to accept and use in our kitchens.

NUTRITIONAL VALUE

All fish consist of nearly 75% water and also the albuminoids content varies little from fish to fish, at about 18%. In fat the variation is much wider: about 26% for the conger-eel family, 12% for salmon and salmon trout, 9% for trout, 8.2% for shad and 6% for herring.

From this it can clearly be seen that fish flesh does not vary much from that of land animals. Proportions of fat, minerals and albuminoids are very much the same. Where the fish has the advantage is in the contents of phosphorylated compounds and in the fact that fish, especially the leaner fishes, are much more easily digestible and so represent an excellent food for the sedentary worker and the sick.

From the practical point of view it is interesting to note that the quantity of waste in preparing fish is very high, about 35–50%, according to the kind and size of fish and the methods employed in preparation and cooking.

TYPES OF FISH

In general terms, for recognition purposes, fish can be divided into two groups or types; the flat fishes, which are to be found near the bottom of the sea, and the round fishes which are commonly found swimming near the surface. There are also, of course, shellfish (crustaceans and molluscs). All of these are further sub-divided, first into sea or freshwater fish, white fish, oily fish, etc.; and then into distinct families or groups.

TABLE 4.1 *Classification of Fish*

White fish, round	Cod, hake, haddock, whiting etc.
White fish, flat	Sole, halibut, lemon sole, plaice, turbot, brill
Oily fish, round	Eel, herring, mackerel, salmon, trout
Oily fish, flat	None
Shellfish/crustaceans	Crab, crawfish, crayfish, lobster, prawns, shrimps
Molluscs	Cockles, mussels, oysters and scallops

With the exception of shellfish, all fishes have a number of fins. In some cases these can be used as a means of distinguishing one fish from another. The fins are to be found either in pairs or singly. The paired fins are the pectoral, found on the sides of the fish just behind the gills, and the pelvic, which are found on the underside or belly of the fish. The single or unpaired fins are the dorsal, which runs along the back, the caudal or tail, and the anal, which is found on the underside of the fish near the tail.

QUALITY AND STORAGE OF FISH

Fresh Fish

Good fresh fish is recognized by the following points:

- Good clear smell of fish and sea
- Wet and slimy to the touch
- Clear, bright eyes
- Flesh firm and resilient to the touch
- Good, bright bloody gills
- Scales, if any, firm and plentiful

Frozen Fish

Available types of frozen fish can be classified as follows:

- Individually frozen small fishes, e.g. trout, herring, mackerel, or individually frozen portions of larger fish, such as fillets, steaks, or suprêmes of cod, halibut, brill, etc.
- Block frozen fish, usually fillets of small and large fish, often with skin still attached (at times with skin removed), available in 2 kg, 3 kg, 5 kg and 10 kg blocks. These are only really suitable for larger catering operations. The block amount purchased should be in keeping with daily business of a given establishment. Once the block of fish is defrosted; this fish must be used within 24 hours.
- Whole large fish, mostly salmon, halibut, pike, tuna, etc.

Individually frozen fish is usually of better quality, with even portion size, for use in the kitchen of a good standard of restaurant. Block frozen fish can be of lesser quality when it comes to cuts and preparation, and of uneven portion size. It is best used in fish and chip shops, fish restaurants or possibly banqueting operations when large amounts are required.

All frozen fish will lose some flavour during the process of defrosting. Defrosting should be carried out slowly. Fish should never be left to defrost in a warm kitchen or forced in warm water or a microwave oven as this will spoil the flavour and appearance even more, and it could be particularly dangerous in regard to food poisoning for fish incorrectly defrosted. It is best done slowly overnight in a normal fridge.

After defrosting, most frozen fish can be improved in flavour and appearance by marinating in a marinade of a little lemon juice, salt and oil for an hour or two before cooking, particularly so if the fish is intended for shallow or deep frying. Frozen fish intended to be poached or boiled will benefit by a marinade of lemon juice and a little salt for an hour or so before cooking. (For marinades see Chapter 3.)

Farmed Fish

To compensate for the reduction of the general fish harvest, all over Europe and in particular the British Isles, many fish farms have come into operation, both in rivers and lakes in the case of trout, carp, grey and red bass, and in the sea around the Scottish Isles, mostly for salmon.

These farms have secured a steady supply of fish of these types. Experts however consider these fish not as good in texture and flavour as the wild versions. The comments in this chapter about the quality and storage of fish, and the methods of preparation and cooking to follow, apply equally to farmed fish.

Storage of Fish

All fresh fish is best stored in a separate fish-fridge on crushed ice, with a kitchen cloth to separate the fish and the ice, with a perforated tray base for drainage.

Frozen fish is best stored in its closed packaging, although not necessarily in their cartons as these can take up too much room in freezers.

CLASSIFICATION OF FISH

In Tables 4.2, 4.3 and 4.4 descriptions and approximate sizes are given for the most popular types of European fish and shellfish.

PREPARATION OF FISH FOR COOKING

(1) Remove scales (most, but not all, fishes have scales) with a knife, scraping from tail towards head on a slant, on both sides.

(2) With a pair of scissors cut away all dorsal and steering fins as close to the body as possible.

(3) Remove the eyes by inserting the point of a small knife, and twist these out of the socket.

(4) In the case of some fish, remove the white inner skin and congealed blood by rubbing with salt.

(5) Wash well under running cold water, drain well, store for further preparation or use in fish-fridge on crushed ice.

More detailed fish preparations and cuts are given below.

Preparation of Whole Fishes

Some of the smaller round or flat fishes of portion size are prepared to be eaten whole, such as herring, sprats, trout, mackerel, small plaice, sole, lemon sole etc. Some large fishes, such as cod, haddock, turbot, halibut or salmon, can be cooked and presented whole on buffets or may be cut into steaks for poaching or grilling.

After they have been scaled and cleaned, the fish should be prepared according to type or the cooking method (see Figures 4.1–4.5). Some individual and more elaborate fish preparations are described in Figures 4.6 and 4.7 and illustrated in Plate 4.1.

TABLE 4.2 *Classification of Fish: Group A – Flat Fish*

White saltwater fish	English	French	Weight range	Description
	Plaice	La plie	2–12 kg	Dark grey–brown with orange spots, lateral line almost straight
	Dab-Flounder	Le carrelet	2–12 kg	Resembles plaice, rougher to the touch, bright white underside not orange spots, lateral line curves
	Sole Slip Sole	La sole Petit sole	500–1000 g 200–300 g	Both eyes on right side, brownish with dark markings, bright white underside
	Lemon Sole	La limande	500–1000 g	Blue–grey colour, almost oval in shape, small head and mouth, bright firm flesh

Continued

TABLE 4.2 *Classification of Fish: Group A – Flat Fish—cont'd*

White saltwater fish	English	French	Weight range	Description
	Halibut	Le flétan	3–20 kg	Can be quite a large fish, dusky brown/olive colour, white and smooth on opposite, both eyes on right/dark side
	Turbot	Le turbot	3–8 kg	No scales, but wart-like tubercles/stones in black skin, yellowish-white on underside, almost round
	Brill	Le barbue	2–5 kg	Smooth skin darker in colour than turbot, more elongated shape

TABLE 4.3 *Classification of Fish: Group B – Round Fish*

Round saltwater fish	English	French	Weight range	Description
	Cod	Le cabillaud	2–6 kg	Brownish-olive colour with yellowish-brown spots, white lateral line, near human expression
	Haddock	L'aigrefin	2–6 kg	Large black patch either side of body just behind the gill, black lateral line, available smoked
	Hake	La merluche	1–3 kg	Eel-like appearance, dark-grey to silver colour, two rows of sharp teeth, inside of mouth dark
	Whiting	Le merlan	2–12 kg	Greenish-grey with white underside, black spots at pectoral fins, indistinct lateral line, loose flesh

Continued

TABLE 4.3 *Classification of Fish: Group B – Round Fish—cont'd*

Round saltwater fish	English	French	Weight range	Description
	Pike*	Le brochet	1–4 kg	Silver–grey freshwater fish with straight lateral line, found in rivers and lakes bony, but firm white flesh, ideally suited for fish-farce, quenelles
	Sea Bream	Brème de la mer	500 g–3 kg	Red to pink in colour on back with silver belly, large scales, white firm flesh
	Salmon**	Le saumon	3–12 kg	Plump and clear-looking with bright silvery scales, steel blue at back and head, pink to red flesh, now often from farms
	Salmon Trout	La truite saumonée	1–12 kg	Trout which lived in the sea; lighter, pink in colour, softer sweet flesh
	River Trout*	Truite de rivière	1–2 kg	Brown or grey–green on back, silver belly of sweet flesh, full of scales, freshwater fish from rivers and lakes and now fish farms

*Freshwater fish.
**Oily fish.

TABLE 4.4 *Classification of Fish: Group B cont. – Small Round Fish*

Small round fish (all are oily fish)	English	French	Weight range	Description
	Mackerel	Le maquereau	300–1000 g	Silvery back with blue stripes, white silvery belly, dark oily flesh
	Herring	Le hareng	250–400 g	Silvery blue back, silvery white belly, pronounced dorsal fin
	Sprat	Le sprat	100–200 g	Small herring-type fish, bright silvery in colour, seldom larger then 15 cm (6 in.)
	Pilchard	Le pilchard Le pélamide	100–200 g	Small herring-type fish with a more rounded body, large scales, deep grey-green in colour
	Anchovy	L'anchois	150–200 g	Small herring-type fish with green silver skin, broad silver band on side, projecting snout
	Whitebait	Les blanchailles	15–25 g	Very small baby fish of herring or sprat type, bright silvery colour about the size of a little finger, a small handful as a portion

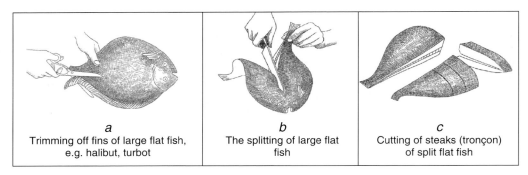

a	*b*	*c*
Trimming off fins of large flat fish, e.g. halibut, turbot	The splitting of large flat fish	Cutting of steaks (tronçon) of split flat fish

Fɪɢ. **4.1** *Preparation of large flat fish for cooking*

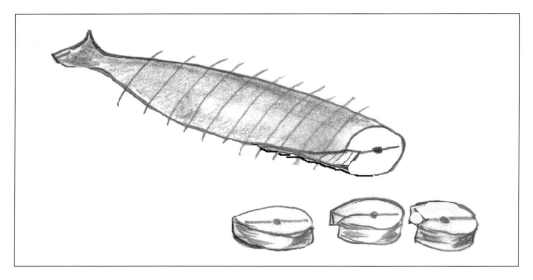

Fɪɢ. **4.2** *Cutting steaks (darnes) of whole large round fish, e.g. cod, whiting, salmon*

Cuts and Preparations from Small and Large Fillets of Fish

When the various fillets of small and large fishes have been completed, we can make further portion-size preparations, many of which have their own description or name, of which those in Figure 4.8 are the best known. (See Figures 4.8–4.12.)

SHELLFISH AND CRUSTACEANS   *Les fruits de mer et les crustacés*

We now look at the best-known and liked shellfish available in the British Isles. Being surrounded by the sea, we are lucky that most fresh shellfish is still available in good quantities, particularly crab, lobster, mussels, scallops, scampi, shrimps and cockles,

Round Fish

The filleting of round fish will yield *two* fillets whether the fish is a small fish such as herring or mackerel, or a large fish such as a salmon or cod.

In the case of a round fish it is best to first remove the head, and fillet with a large filleting knife from the back of the head towards the tail, along the back bone, which acts as a guide. When one fillet has been removed turn the fish over to the other side and repeat the procedure.

Flat Fish

The filleting of a flat fish will always yield *four* fillets whether this is a small fish such a sole, plaice, or lemon sole, or whether it is a larger flat fish such as a halibut, turbot or brill.

In the case of a flat fish the head can first be removed but it is not necessary. Make an incision along the middle of the fish from head to tail, filleting one fillet to the right and one fillet to the left. Turn the fish over and repeat the procedure, giving four fillets.

It will be noted that the two fillets from the back of the fish will be larger than those from the belly.

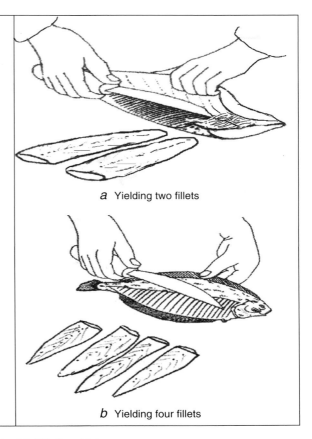

a Yielding two fillets

b Yielding four fillets

FIG. 4.3 *Filleting of fish*

The skinning of large or small fillets of fish is much the same. Loosen the skin 1–2 cm at the tail end with a small knife. Firmly hold by the loosened skin in one hand, place the knife between skin and flesh and with a wriggling motion against the knife remove skin gradually from the flesh/fillet. Draw the skin towards you and push the filet away from you.

Notes: The larger the fillet the bigger the filleting knife you should use. Some small whole fish are skinned differently, see Figure 4.5.

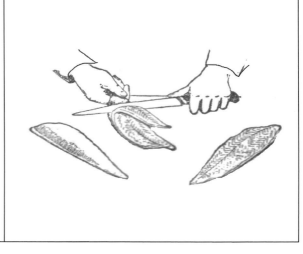

FIG. 4.4 *The skinning of fillets, large or small*

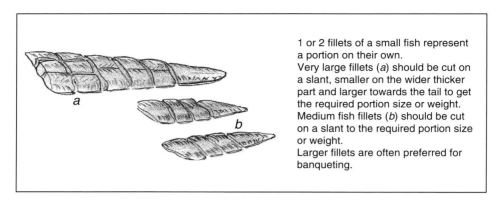

1 or 2 fillets of a small fish represent a portion on their own.
Very large fillets (*a*) should be cut on a slant, smaller on the wider thicker part and larger towards the tail to get the required portion size or weight.
Medium fish fillets (*b*) should be cut on a slant to the required portion size or weight.
Larger fillets are often preferred for banqueting.

FIG. 4.5 *The cutting and portioning of medium and large flat fish fillets (see also Figure 4.8 d,e)*

either alive or cooked. In the case of prawns, most of these come from further away and they are always cooked. More often than not they are frozen either in their shell, or already shelled. For the catering industry we should look at available sizes, quality and flavour of prawns, and choose the best quality at the best price for our operation. Tables 4.5 and 4.6 give a classification of the most used shellfish.

DIFFERENT PREPARATIONS FOR CULINARY USE

The Larder department prepares fish for many uses in the kitchen. In a smaller establishment the task may be shared between Larder and Kitchen; in larger establishments the Larder may be asked to carry out varied and complex tasks. This is particularly so when large banquets are part of the operation.

BOILED/POACHED FISH

Table 4.7 explains some of the uses on the menu of boiled or poached fish. Figure 4.13 shows three buffet preparations which are cooked in a court bouillon or stock.

For smaller fishes and fish portions, such as fillets, suprêmes, délices or paupiettes, we use buttered trays of various sizes according to numbers (Figure 4.14)

Type of fish	Use	Method	Appearance
Trout/Truite poché bleu	Poaching blue trout	Clean and prepare trout as above. With a string and trussing needle, bring head and tail together and bind, gently poach in court bouillon, remove string before serving. Serve with melted butter or Hollandaise.	a 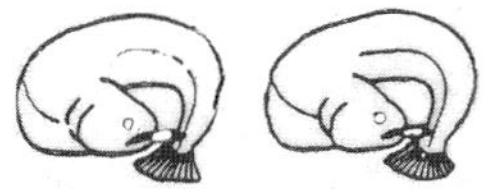
Trout/Truite grillée Truite meunière	For grilling or shallow frying	Clean and prepare trout as above, make 2–3 shallow incisions in the skin, season, roll in flour, brush with oil, and grill on both sides; for meunière, roll in seasoned flour and shallow fry in oil and butter.	b 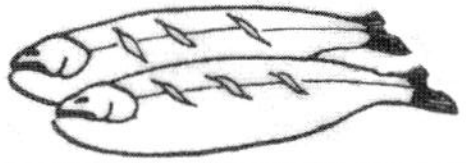
Trout/Truite St Germain	For split grilling	Make a mixture of soft butter, chopped herbs, breadcrumbs and seasoning, mix well, now split the trout along the backbone removing the bone, and spread the mixture all over the inside of the trout. Place in fridge to set, grill to order, garnish with parsley and lemon wedge.	c 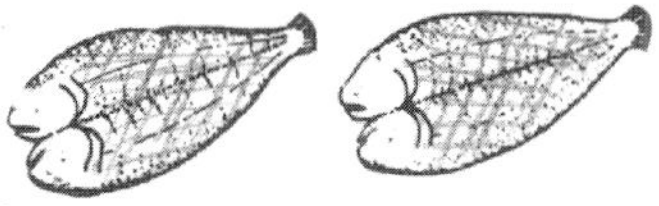
Herring, sprat, anchovy/ Hareng grillée	For grilling	Clean and prepare herring etc. as for trout above, make 2–3 incisions in the skin, season, roll in flour, brush with oil and grill on both sides. Serve 2 per portion with mustard sauce. Treat sprats and anchovy the same way, see drawing for trout above.	d 
Whole poached salmon/ Saumon pochée	Poaching for cold buffet presentation	Place salmon on a perforated base, tie with string, place in saumonière, cover with court bouillon, bring to boil, simmer for 15 min per kg, cool in bouillon over night; or place a turbot in turbotière, cover with fish stock, poach and continue for salmon as above.	e 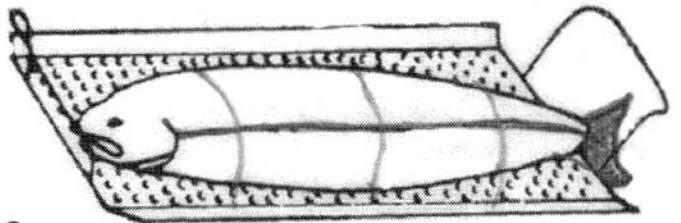
Escalope of fish	Shallow fried. Occasionally poached	With more and more à la minute cooking and plated service the old escalope cut usually associated with meats has been applied to large fillets of fish, particularly salmon, cut from the fillet almost horizontally. In large thin slices it can easily be shallow fried in 2 minutes, if poached it needs careful handling as it can easily break.	f 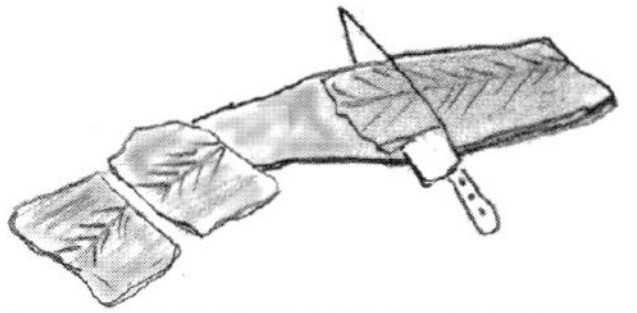

Fig. 4.6 *Individual fish preparations*

Type of fish	Use	Method	Appearance
Curled Whiting	For deep frying	This preparation is used for small portion whiting, 350–450g. First the whiting is carefully skinned, and a point of knife pushed through both eye sockets for a passage. Now the whole whiting is rolled in seasoned flour, egg wash and breadcrumbs and the tail is pushed through the eye socket and secured with a cocktail stick. It is deep fried and served with any of the mayonnaise-based sauces, e.g. Tartare, Rémoulade, Verte.	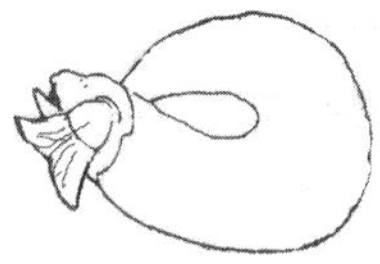 a
Mad Whiting/Merlan colère	For deep frying	Much the same as above, but the tail is put into the mouth like a mad dog biting its tail. Experience has shown that the tail should be secured to the mouth with a cocktail stick, as it otherwise can come easily apart during cooking process. It is deep fried and served as above.	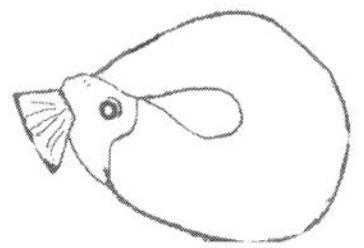 b
Goujons of fish	For shallow frying or deep frying	Cut fillets of fish on the slant into small strips, the size of a little finger, pass through seasoned flour, shallow fry in oil and butter, or pass through seasoned flour, egg wash and breadcrumbs and roll each goujon to firmly attach breadcrumbs, allow to rest. Deep fried and served as above (see Plate 4.1j).	 c
Plaited fish fillet/Filet en tresse	For deep frying	Take one or two small fillets of fish according to size (150g in all), cut into three strips, keeping it together on the top end. Pass through seasoned flour, egg wash and breadcrumbs (press on firmly to the fillet strips), now plait the strips into a neat plait, place in fridge to set for one hour, then deep fry to order. Serve as above. Best suited for smaller fillets of fish, such as sole, plaice, lemon sole etc.	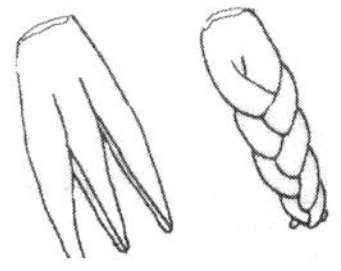 d

Fig. 4.7 *More elaborate fish preparations*

Preparation	Appearance
Fillet/Filet: This is the normal fillet from a small fish about 100–150 g in weight, trimmed and ready for cooking. If the fish is very small it well might be two smaller fillets. For the menu we would of course add the name of the fish, e.g. Fillet of Plaice or Filet de brème (see Plate 4.1*l*).	*a* 
Délice: This is one fillet or two fillets per portion, neatly folded in half, sometimes with a filling, or shaped, or the tail end put through an incision, see drawings. In French *délice* means 'delight'; on the menu we would of course add the name of the fish, e.g. Délice of Sole or Délice de sole.	*b* 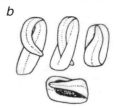
Paupiette: This is a fillet which is stuffed with fish farce (white), salmon farce (pink), chopped creamed spinach, duxelles and other stuffings, rolled and stood up. It is invariably poached in a good fish stock and served in a rich fish sauce. It should appear on the menu as Paupiette of Lemon Sole or Paupiette de limande (see Plate 4.1*c*).	*c* 
Suprême: This is a portion of fish cut on a slant from a large fillet of fish; without bones and skin it represents the supreme piece of fish, usually poached, it can also be shallow fried meunière or occasionally deep fried. On the menu it would appear as Supreme of Cod or Suprême de cabillaud (see Plate 4.1*k*).	*d* 
Pavé: This is a portion of fish similar to the suprême above, but not cut on the slant, thicker and more square (flagstone), often grilled or shallow fried. On the menu it would appear as Pavé of Salmon or Pavé de saumon.	*e* 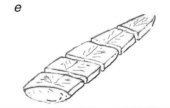

FIG. 4.8 *Individual fish cuts and preparations*

a	*b*
Skin portion-size whiting by cutting along the edge of the fish on both sides and draw skin off towards the tail. Split whiting from tail to head, leave fillets attached to head, remove bone and skin.	Pass whiting through flour, egg wash and breadcrumbs. Press on firmly. Roll crumbed filets towards the head. Secure with a skewer or cocktail sticks. Ready to deep fry.

FIG. 4.9 *Preparation of a small-portion fish – a whiting en lorgnette*

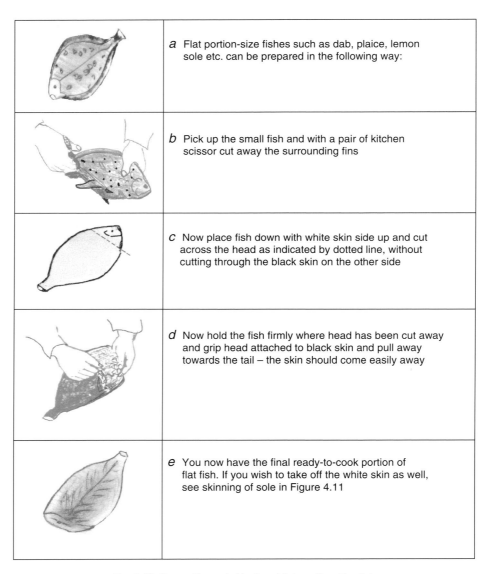

	a Flat portion-size fishes such as dab, plaice, lemon sole etc. can be prepared in the following way:
	b Pick up the small fish and with a pair of kitchen scissor cut away the surrounding fins
	c Now place fish down with white skin side up and cut across the head as indicated by dotted line, without cutting through the black skin on the other side
	d Now hold the fish firmly where head has been cut away and grip head attached to black skin and pull away towards the tail – the skin should come easily away
	e You now have the final ready-to-cook portion of flat fish. If you wish to take off the white skin as well, see skinning of sole in Figure 4.11

FIG. 4.10 *Preparation and skinning of flat small-portion fish*

	*a* Cut half-way through the sole's tail and with a small knife loosen the tail skin on both sides about 2 cm up towards the flesh
	*b* Grip the loosened skin firmly in one hand and the tail of the sole in the other. With a sharp pull draw off the skin in one motion. Repeat with the skin on the opposite side
	*c* With a sharp knife cut away the head on a slant and trim the fins on the sides of the sole with a pair of scissors
	*d* The sole is now ready for poaching, shallow frying, deep frying and other preparations, e.g. Sole Colbert (see Figure 4.12)

FIG. **4.11** *Preparation and skinning of slip and Dover sole*

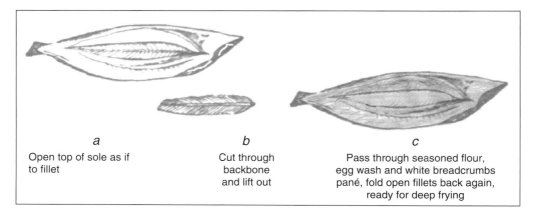

a	*b*	*c*
Open top of sole as if to fillet	Cut through backbone and lift out	Pass through seasoned flour, egg wash and white breadcrumbs pané, fold open fillets back again, ready for deep frying

FIG. **4.12** *Preparation of Sole Colbert*

TABLE 4.5 *Classification of Shellfish Types: Crustaceans*

Appearance	English	French	Weight/size range	Description
	Shrimps	Les crevettes	2.5–3 cm	Found in shallow waters around British coast. Greyish-green with brown spots. Cook 3–5 min, now pink–brown in colour
	Prawns	Les crevettes roses	5–8 cm long. long-toothed snout projecting over body	Found around northern coasts mostly imported from Scandinavia. If fresh, cook for 8–10 min, turn pink or red after cooking, hence French name 'rose'
	Dublin Bay Prawns (Scampi)	Les langoustines	8–15 cm long	Like small lobster, also found in the Mediterranean, here known as scampi. Claws are empty only tail is used, widely available, fresh cooked or cooked and frozen
	Crayfish	Les écrevisses	12–15 cm long	Black–green, long-tailed, smaller freshwater cousin of the lobster available from Scottish and Scandinavian rivers or lakes. Best cooked in a court bouillon (see below), bright red when cooked, mostly eaten as a starter

Continued

TABLE 4.5 *Classification of Shellfish Types: Crustaceans—cont'd*

Appearance	English	French	Weight/size range	Description
	Lobster	L'homard	Best at 500–750 g	Black with grey–green spots, 10 legs, claws of different size. Best cooked in court bouillon, then bright red. Best eaten cold in cocktail, salad Mayonnaise or as several hot dishes
	Crawfish	La langouste	Best at 1–2 kg	Black–greenish brown in colour, a lobster-like shellfish with no claws and a spiny body. Best cooked in a court bouillon 15 min per kg, will appear brown–pink after cooking. Nearly all recipes applied to lobster are suitable
	Crab	Le crabe	Best at 750–1000 g	Light brown in colour, 10 legs, of which the first is an uneven pair of claws. Full of white tasty meat in claws and legs, creamy dark meat in body. Mostly used as starters, e.g. Dressed Crab, Crab Salad and Mayonnaise, but also used in some hot dishes

Table 4.6 *Classification of Shellfish Types: Molluscs*

Appearance	English	French	Description
	Oysters	Les huîtres	Best eaten raw fresh from the sea, can be poached in a little fish stock and lemon juice, treated like poached fish served with white sauces or fried. Many types, basic difference wild or cultivated. In England best known are Whitstable, Colchester and Helford
	Mussels	Les moules	Both salt and some freshwater types, of bluish-black colour, an oblong shape about 3–5 cm. Must be well cleaned with a hard brush, and beard removed. Cooked in their own juice with some shallots and white wine, Moules marinière (see Plate 4.1*e*) is a dish in its own right or is used as a starter, salad, soup or as part of several fish-garnishes
	Scallops	Les Coquilles St Jacques	A hard shell, beige-brown in colour, nearly twice as large as an average oyster. To open place on a hot stove which will relax the muscle for easy opening, exposing white and orange meats. Cook in a little fish stock with lemon juice. Serve poached or fried, often in its own shell, or as part of several fish-garnishes
	Clams	Les palourdes	Name applies to several edible bivalve molluscs found under this name. In the raw state eaten like oysters. Very popular in North America, where it is mostly eaten fried. It is used as part of several fish-garnishes or fruits de mer mixture

Continued

TABLE 4.6 *Classification of Shellfish Types: Molluscs—cont'd*

Appearance	English	French	Description
	Cockles Winkles	Les clovisses Les bigorneaux	Small molluscs, eaten as starters, or a seaside treat. Used as part of several fish-garnishes or fruits de mer mixture
	Snails*	Les escargots	The only terrestrial mollusc of the gastropod family, cultivated on farms in France. When of the right size, they are starved and then fed with flour to clear the intestines, cooked in a court bouillon, cooled and removed from the shell. Eaten as a starter with rich garlic butter returned to shell. In England usually bought in cans of a dozen
	Frogs Legs**	Les pieds de grenouilles	Green or common frog cultivated in France as a delicacy. Only the legs are used, with skin and feet removed. Soaked in cold running water, when white, drained and dried, cooked deep fried à l'Anglaise or shallow fried meunière. In England only available frozen

*Although terrestrial, the snail is a mollusc and for this reason has been included here for completeness.
**The frog is, of course, not a mollusc but because it lives partly in water and has a fishy taste it has been included here.

TABLE 4.7 *Uses for Boiled/Poached Fish*

Explanation	Menu example	French

Applies mostly to whole fishes, such as carp, salmon and occasionally turbot, halibut or salmon–trout, when these are to be eaten cold, or to be served decorated on a cold buffet presentation
 	
All shellfish, e.g. lobster; crab, scallops cockles etc., can also be boiled. Boiling methods are:
 	
In a good fish stock: for the white fishes, e.g. turbot, halibut, cod etc.
 	
In a court bouillon: for the oily fishes, e.g. salmon and shellfish (see recipe for court bouillon below)
 	
Marinière: a mixture of fish stock, white wine and shallots, mostly used for poached/boiled molluscs such as mussels, scallops, oysters, etc.
	Cooked Salmon
	  Sandwiches
	Fish Canapés
	Cold Starters
	  Fish Mayonnaise
	  Fish Salad
	  Lobster Salad
	  Seafood Salad
	Buffet Presentation
	  Cold Decorated
	  Salmon
	  Cold Decorated
	  Crawfish
	  Cold Decorated Turbot
	  Cold Trout in Fish Jelly
	Cold Lobster
	Dressed Crab
	Cold Salmon Steaks
	Boiled Scallops
	Boiled Mussels
	Boiled Crayfish
		Sandwich de saumon
		
		Canapés de poisson
		
		Mayonnaise de saumon
		Salade de poisson
		Salade d'homard
		Salade fruits de mer
		
		Saumon chaud froid
		
		Turbot froid belle vie
		Truite froide en gelée
		Homard froid
		Crabe belle vie
		Darne de saumon froid
		Coquilles St Jacques
		Moules marinière
		Écrevisses en marinade

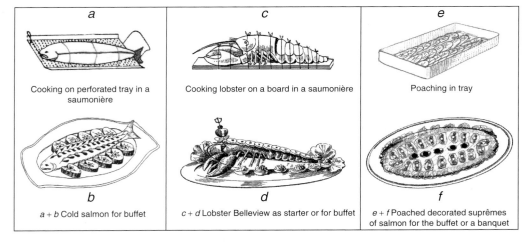

FIG. 4.13 *Typical items to be cooked in court bouillon (a–d) or stock (e,f)*

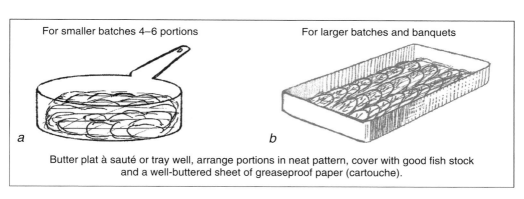

For smaller batches 4–6 portions

For larger batches and banquets

a

b

Butter plat à sauté or tray well, arrange portions in neat pattern, cover with good fish stock and a well-buttered sheet of greaseproof paper (cartouche).

FIG. 4.14 *Poaching trays for fish*

Fish Stock and Court Bouillon

Fish stock   Fond de poisson

Ingredients (for 5–6 litres)
3 kg fish bones free of fish roes and well washed; best to use white fish bones of sole, plaice, turbot, halibut
1 kg onions cut in fine slices
1 bottle (750 ml) white wine
200 g butter or margarine
1 bouquet garni of parsley stalks, bay leaves, white peppercorns and thyme
Juice of 2–3 lemons
7 litres of fresh cold water

Method
1 Melt butter in a rondeau – flat low round pan
2 Add the onions and sweat, cooking without colour
3 Add well-washed small cut fish bones, sweat
4 Add white wine, cover with lid, continue sweating, add water, bring to the boil, skim of froth
5 Gently simmer for 20–25 min
6 When ready, strain through a fine sieve, cool and store in fridge until required

Note: *In the case of fish stock we only make white stocks*

Court bouillon

Ingredients
3 litres water
50 g sea salt
1 large carrot sliced
2 large onions sliced

Method
1 Combine all ingredients, bring to the point of boil, simmer for 10–15 min
2 Strain onto the fish or shellfish to be cooked therein

Continued

Court bouillon—cont'd

Ingredients	*Method*
3 sticks of celery 3 bay leaves 24 peppercorns Generous bunch of parsley stalks 3–4 sprigs of thyme 1 tbsp sugar 250 ml wine vinegar	3 Can be cooled and stored in the fridge until required

GRILLED AND FRIED FISH

The Larder prepares many types of fish for grilling. Table 4.8 gives a good selection with various accompaniments. Grilled fish should always be marinated (see Chapter 3).

TABLE 4.8 *Grilled Fish and Fish Cuts with Accompaniments*

Menu example	French
Best suited to grill-bar grilling (heat from below)	
Grilled Cod Steak with Choron Sauce	Darne de cabillaud sauce Choron
Grilled Dover Sole with Red Wine Butter	Sole grillée beurre vin rouge
Grilled Halibut Steak with Béarnaise Sauce	Tronçon de flétan sauce Béarnaise
Grilled Herrings with Mustard Sauce	Hareng grillé sauce moutard
Grilled Lemon Sole with Herb Butter	Limande grillée beurre fines herbes
Grilled Mackerel Fillets with Anchovy Sauce	Filet de maquereau sauce anchois
Grilled Plaice with Lemon Butter	Plie grillé beurre de citron
Grilled Salmon Steak with Hollandaise Sauce	Darne de saumon sauce Hollandaise
Grilled Sardines with Lemon	Sardine grillée aux citrons
Grilled Sprats with Lemon	Sprats grillés aux citrons
Grilled Trout with Parsley Butter	Truite grillée beurre Maître d'hôtel
Grilled Turbot Steak with Mousseline Sauce	Tronçon de turbot sauce mousseline
Best suited for salamander grilling (heat from above)	
Grilled Fillet of Cod with Tarragon Butter	Filet de cabillaud grillé beurre estragon
Grilled Step of Haddock with Thyme Butter	Pave l'aigrefin grillé beurre de thym
Grilled Fillet of Salmon with Cucumber Sauce	Filet de saumon grillé sauce concombre
Grilled Fillets of Sole Dill Butter	Filets de sole grillés beurre l'aneth
Grilled Fillets of Trout with Caviar Butter	Filets de truite grillés beurre caviar
Grilled Cod Fillet Saint Germain	Filet de cabillaud Saint Germain

Deep-fried fish should again be marinated and is thereafter coated in either:

Pané = passed through flour–egg wash and fresh breadcrumbs
Orly = passed through flour and dipped in one or other of the batters below

Beer batter

Ingredients (10–15 portions)
300 g plain flour
1 litre Lager beer
1 egg
1 tbsp oil
Pinch of salt and pepper

Method
1 Combine all ingredients to a smooth paste, pass through a sieve if not smooth, cover with a cloth, place in a warm place until it begins to rise (about 1 to 1½ hours)
2 Pass marinated portions of fish through seasoned flour, dip into batter, fry until golden brown

Egg batter

Ingredients (10–12 portions)
250 g strong flour
1 litre milk
1 egg yolk
2 egg whites
Pinch of salt and sugar

Method
1 Combine all ingredients except white of egg into a smooth paste, store in cold place for 1–2 hours
2 When ready to cook fish, beat whites of egg until very stiff, fold into batter
3 Pass marinated portions of fish through seasoned flour, dip into batter, fry until golden brown

Yeast batter

Ingredients (10–12 portions)
300 g plain flour
1 litre milk or half water
30 g yeast
Pinch of salt and sugar

Method
1 Heat milk to hand warm, dissolve yeast therein
2 Sieve flour, salt and sugar into a bowl, gradually add yeast–milk, mix to a smooth paste, keep in a warm place covered with a cloth for 30 min until it begins to rise
3 Pass marinated portions of fish through seasoned flour, dip into batter, fry until golden brown

OTHER PREPARATIONS

En Papillote

The term en papillotte describes a means to cook small portions of fish, or occasionally whole small fishes, free of skin and bones enveloped in a sheet of greaseproof paper. For method, see Figures 4.15 and 4.16.

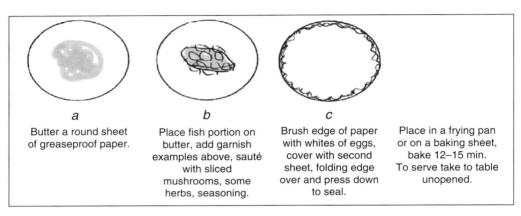

a	*b*	*c*	
Butter a round sheet of greaseproof paper.	Place fish portion on butter, add garnish examples above, sauté with sliced mushrooms, some herbs, seasoning.	Brush edge of paper with whites of eggs, cover with second sheet, folding edge over and press down to seal.	Place in a frying pan or on a baking sheet, bake 12–15 min. To serve take to table unopened.

FIG. **4.15** *Preparation for en papillote: Version 1*

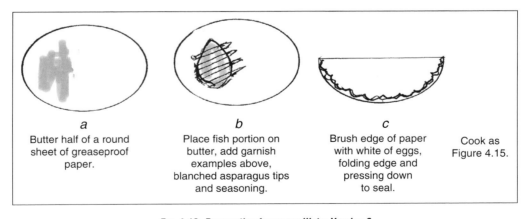

a	*b*	*c*	
Butter half of a round sheet of greaseproof paper.	Place fish portion on butter, add garnish examples above, blanched asparagus tips and seasoning.	Brush edge of paper with white of eggs, folding edge and pressing down to seal.	Cook as Figure 4.15.

FIG. **4.16** *Preparation for en papillote: Version 2*

Skewers

Figures 4.17 and 4.18 illustrate two presentations utilizing skewers.

Lobster Presentation

Figure 4.19 illustrates the stages in cutting a lobster.

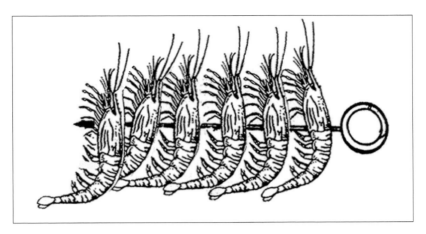

Fig. 4.17 *Large prawn or scampi skewer*

Fig. 4.18 *Mixed fish skewer*

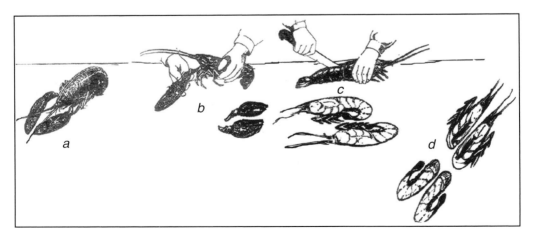

Fig. 4.19 *The cutting/quartering of raw or cooked lobster: a, whole lobster; b, removing claws; c, splitting body; d, quartering body*

5 Poultry and Game (La Volaille et Le Gibier)

POULTRY 🐓 *La volaille*

Present breeds of fowl originate from wild or jungle birds and there is evidence that the prevalence of cock fighting in the past contributed to the various breeds and their general distribution. Breeders invariably take into account the qualities best suited to their requirements or market. Although there are many dual-purpose breeds, in the main they seek either egg production or meat-bearing types. Modern methods of poultry-rearing have revolutionized the market and, all too often, weight and tender flesh are sought at the expense of flavour.

Some of the better-known breeds of table birds are:

Chicken:	Sussex, Old English Game, Indian Game, Dorking, Bresse, Courtes Pattes, Crève Coeur, La Flèche, etc.
Turkeys:	different types originate from Norfolk, Cambridgeshire, Devon, Scotland, Ireland and America
Ducks:	Aylesbury, Peking, White Campbell, Stanbridge White, Rouen, Nantes, Huttegem, Blue Swedish
Geese:	Emden, Toulouse, Roman, Chinese-White, Strasbourg

QUALITY

A pliable breast-bone is probably the best indication when choosing young birds. Other indications are: pliable beak, smooth feet with slender claws, light comb and undeveloped flight muscles. Old birds will have a hard, brittle breast-bone and beak, scaly feet and legs with strong claws and long spurs and well-developed flight muscles. The flesh too will be much darker and the legs hairy.

The following points are the best indication of quality:

- Flesh firm but pliable, with a fine texture.
- Not too much fat, especially in abdominal cavity.
- White or yellow skin, according to breed.
- No cuts, scores, rubbed portions on skin or blood patches.
- The breast should be straight, broad and well fleshed.
- Wings compact, small head, with neat comb and wattles.
- The bones fine, legs short and well fleshed.

MARKET TYPES

The term 'poultry' (volaille) applies in general to all domesticated birds, whether bred for table purposes or for their eggs. Table 5.1 gives a useful list of details.

TABLE 5.1 *Market Types of Poultry*

English	French	Average weight*	Average age*	Approx. portions
Poussin	Le poussin	250–300 g	4–6 weeks	1
Double poussin	Le poussin double	400–600 g	4–8 weeks	2
Cockerel	Le jeune coq	350–600 g	6–8 weeks	2
Chicken	Le poulet reine	1–2 kg	4–6 months	4–6
Boiling fowl	La poule	2–3 kg	12 months	6–8
Young fat chicken	La poulardin	1–1.5 kg	4–6 months	3–4
Capon**	Le chapon	2–4 kg	5–8 months	4
Fat chicken**	La poularde	2–4 kg	5–6 months	4–6
Turkey cock	Le dindon	6–12 kg	6–10 months	18–24
Turkey hen	La dinde	4–7 kg	6–10 months	12–16
Young turkey	Le dindonneau	3–4 kg	5–6 months	8–10
Guinea fowl	La pintade	750 g–1.5 kg	4–6 months	2–4
Duck	Le canard	2–3 kg	3–4 months	4–6
Duckling	Le caneton	1.5–2 kg	2–3 months	4
Goose	L'oie	4–7 kg	6–9 months	10–12
Gosling	L'oison	2–3 kg	4–6 months	6–8
Pigeon	Le pigeon	300–500 g	6–10 weeks	1

*It will be appreciated that the weights and ages given above are the optimum for fresh, farm-bred and reared poultry and are not necessarily related to the broiler or frozen poultry which is becoming increasingly popular on the market.
**The capon and the fat chicken are de-sexed birds (castrated cocks and ovariotomized hens).

PREPARATION OF CHICKEN

Killing

Killing is usually carried out by dislocation of the neck. In some cases the jugular vein can be severed from inside the mouth; this method is known as 'sticking', special pliers being used for the purpose. Kosher killing is carried out by cutting the throat from the outside. With the exception of Kosher, the birds are commonly stunned electrically prior to killing.

Plucking

Plucking is normally done immediately after killing. The legs are held firmly and the wings are spread back between the knees. A firm motion, in the direction opposite to which the feathers grow, is used and the breast of the bird plucked first, followed by the back, wings and legs. Care must be taken not to damage the skin. Stub feathers must be removed, using the tip of a small knife for the purpose.

Scald or semi-scald methods can be employed, plunging the bird for periods into water varying in temperature between 60 and 100 °C for up to 18–20 seconds or 5–6 seconds, according to the water temperature. Nowadays plucking is usually done by machine, either wet or dry, and is very seldom carried out in catering establishments, with the exception perhaps of the occasional pheasant or grouse sent in by one of the guests.

Hanging

The muscles or flesh of poultry will stiffen and toughen as soon as rigor mortis sets in, usually 3–4 hours after killing. Following this, tenderizing takes place rather quickly up to 24 hours and this should be the maximum time required to hang any poultry for the purpose of tenderizing.

If the bird is cooked during the onset of the process of stiffening, it results in tough and rubbery flesh. It is important that fresh killed poultry be cooled as quickly as possible if the birds are to be stored. If left at normal atmospheric temperature for 2 days or more, 'off' flavours will develop very quickly and greening will appear at the vent and in the region of the kidneys. Seepage from the gall bladder will likewise spoil the liver. Stored at between 3 and 5 °C, poultry should keep in good condition if un-drawn. At 0–1 °C it will keep for a week or so.

Singeing

Hold the bird by the head and feet, stretch it well and pass it over a gas jet quickly. Turn it around, so that every part is properly singed, including the underparts of the wings. Take care not to scorch the skin. Scorch the feet over the flame to enable the scales to be wiped off with a cloth. Shorten the toes and cut off any spurs.

Cleaning

Follow the instruction in Figure 5.1. In the process of preparing your poultry or game the entrails (offal) shown in Figure 5.2 will be available. These are most useful in the making of stocks, liver and heart for pâté, sauté, farce and stuffing. Winglets may not be available according to the preparation of the bird.

Cuts

Figures 5.3–5.8 illustrates some of the cuts most commonly used in poultry preparation.

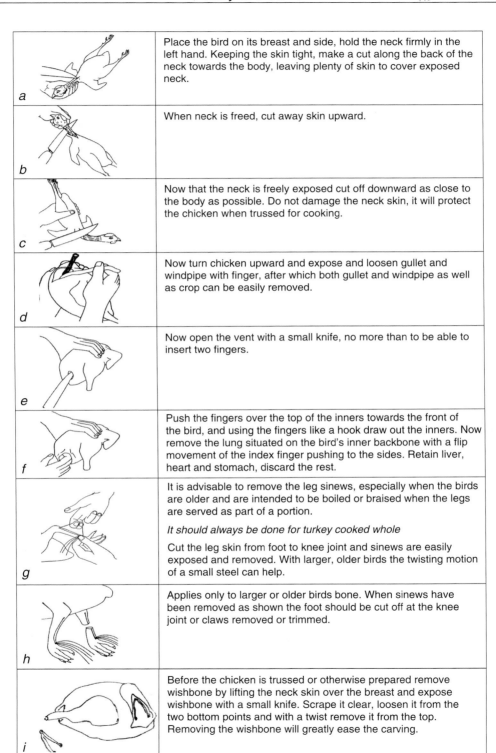

a	Place the bird on its breast and side, hold the neck firmly in the left hand. Keeping the skin tight, make a cut along the back of the neck towards the body, leaving plenty of skin to cover exposed neck.
b	When neck is freed, cut away skin upward.
c	Now that the neck is freely exposed cut off downward as close to the body as possible. Do not damage the neck skin, it will protect the chicken when trussed for cooking.
d	Now turn chicken upward and expose and loosen gullet and windpipe with finger, after which both gullet and windpipe as well as crop can be easily removed.
e	Now open the vent with a small knife, no more than to be able to insert two fingers.
f	Push the fingers over the top of the inners towards the front of the bird, and using the fingers like a hook draw out the inners. Now remove the lung situated on the bird's inner backbone with a flip movement of the index finger pushing to the sides. Retain liver, heart and stomach, discard the rest.
g	It is advisable to remove the leg sinews, especially when the birds are older and are intended to be boiled or braised when the legs are served as part of a portion. *It should always be done for turkey cooked whole* Cut the leg skin from foot to knee joint and sinews are easily exposed and removed. With larger, older birds the twisting motion of a small steel can help.
h	Applies only to larger or older birds bone. When sinews have been removed as shown the foot should be cut off at the knee joint or claws removed or trimmed.
i	Before the chicken is trussed or otherwise prepared remove wishbone by lifting the neck skin over the breast and expose wishbone with a small knife. Scrape it clear, loosen it from the two bottom points and with a twist remove it from the top. Removing the wishbone will greatly ease the carving.

Fɪɢ. 5.1 *Basic poultry and game bird preparation: cleaning*

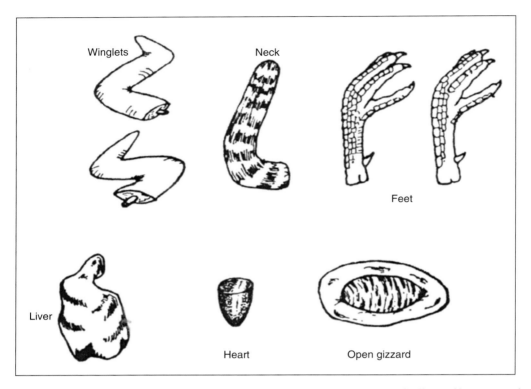

Winglets

Neck

Feet

Liver

Heart   Open gizzard

Fig. 5.2 *Poultry and game offal (abats de volailles). Most are usable for the making of stocks; liver and heart are used for pâté, sauté, farce and stuffing. The winglet may not be available according to preparation of the bird*

The Sauté Cut

One of the most popular chicken preparation is that of cutting the chicken for sauté (Figure 5.10). In this way it can be used for the following much liked dishes:

Blanquette of Chicken	Banquette de volaille
Fricassee of Chicken	Fricassée de volaille
Chicken in Red Wine	Coq au vin
Deep Fried Chicken Pieces	Volaille aux frites or Frites de volaille

Trussing

If poultry or game birds are not to be cut-prepared as above but rather cooked whole, all birds benefit by trussing or binding to retain their shape during cooking, which in turn allows better, neater carving and portion control. Trussing is illustrated in Figures 5.3 and 5.4.

Larding and Barding

Many birds, particularly game birds as well as other cuts and joints of meat, are often barded or larded. See section on Game for this procedure.

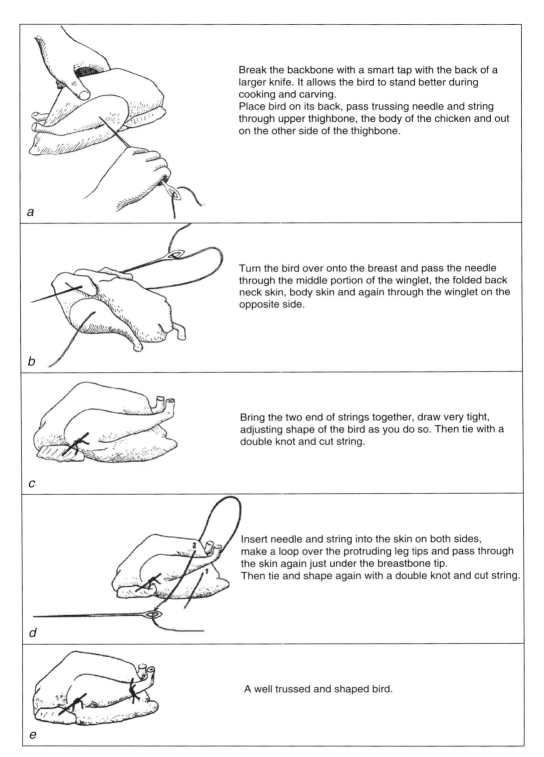

Break the backbone with a smart tap with the back of a larger knife. It allows the bird to stand better during cooking and carving.
Place bird on its back, pass trussing needle and string through upper thighbone, the body of the chicken and out on the other side of the thighbone.

a

Turn the bird over onto the breast and pass the needle through the middle portion of the winglet, the folded back neck skin, body skin and again through the winglet on the opposite side.

b

Bring the two end of strings together, draw very tight, adjusting shape of the bird as you do so. Then tie with a double knot and cut string.

c

Insert needle and string into the skin on both sides, make a loop over the protruding leg tips and pass through the skin again just under the breastbone tip.
Then tie and shape again with a double knot and cut string.

d

A well trussed and shaped bird.

e

Fɪɢ. 5.3 *The standard method of trussing of poultry and game birds*

a b	**For braising or boiling** Cut off all claws and spurs, remove wishbone as shown in Figure 5.1*i*. (*a*) Truss with needle and string through winglets and thigh, shape and tie securely. Make a small band incision through the skin about half way at the side of the leg; push drumstick through skin, repeat on other side. (*b*) Or push leg all the way through skin band to secure shape.
 c	**For roasting, table d'hôte and banqueting** Prepare poultry/game as shown in Figure 5.1, including removing wishbone. Break the backbone in the region of the wing with a tap with the back of the knife so that the bird will lie flat on the board or dish for carving. See trussing above.
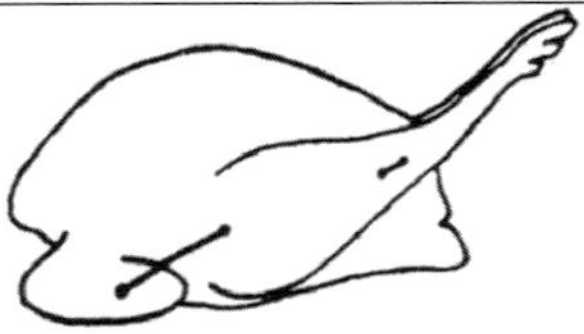 d	**For roasting for guéridon or buffet** Prepare as for (*c*) above but leave legs attached, which is helpful when carving on guéridon or buffet presentation.

Fig. 5.4 *Variations on trussing or binding of poultry and game birds*

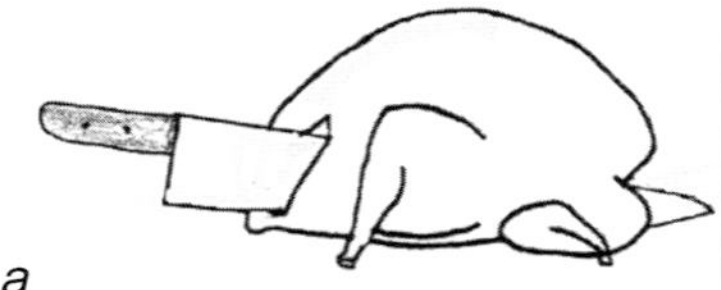 a	Open the chicken along the backbone with a large narrow knife, passing the knife through the body with the chicken on its back from parson's nose to the neck. Give this motion a strong clean cut along the back bone.
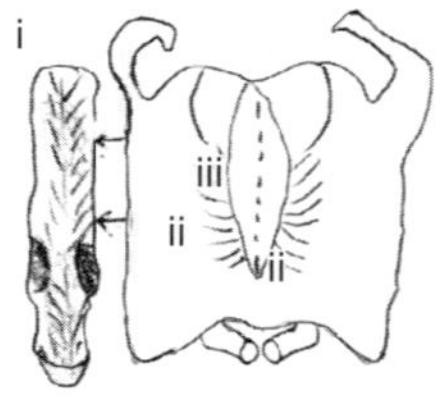 b	Open the chicken and again with a clean cut remove the backbone (i). Lift out the breastbone (iii). Place the chicken on a very hot grill for 1–2 min, this will tighten the small rib bones (ii) and help to remove these bones more easily. Season chicken, brush with oil and mustard or use any other suitable house marinade.
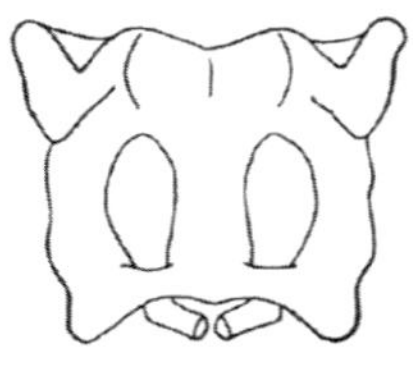 c	When chicken is ready turn it over on the skin side and tuck legs in an incision in the skin as shown and place winglets under body again as shown. Grill first from the inside and then from the outside with a good brown colour, to make sure that especially the legs are well cooked. Rest in the oven for a few minutes. The spatchcock chicken can be grilled, on grill bars, salamander or barbeque.

Fig. 5.5 *Preparation of grilled spatchcock chicken*

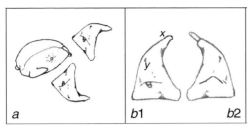

		Cut the skin between breast and leg with a sharp knife assuring that both breast and leg have an equal covering of skin. Trim the leg with small sharp knife by cutting first around the bone *b1x* and scraping away the skin, resulting in *b2*. For some preparations the upper thigh bone *b1y* may also be removed giving a cavity for stuffing with forcemeat.
a	*b1*　　　　*b2*	

Fig. 5.6 *Removing, dissecting and preparing legs. Chicken legs may be grilled, fried, braised or often stuffed (see ballotin)*

a	The prepared cut off chicken leg with exposed thigh bone.
b	Take leg into your hand and with a small knife scrape the bone clear to the knee joint. Give the bone a twist and it should easily come away from the knee joint.
c	Push back the thigh flesh to expose the knee joint knuckle. Cut close to the drumstick bone cartilage, now push the flesh back and the bone can be easily drawn out of its cavity. Remove any remaining gristle or cartilage.
d	The hollow drumstick cavity and the thigh flesh can be filled with the farce or stuffing of your choice after which bring the two sides of thigh skins together enclosing the filling.
e　　　*f*	Fix a cocktail stick in crisscross pattern through the skin (*e*) or shape and hold together with a needle and string (*f*).

Fig. 5.7 *Preparation of stuffed chicken legs (ballottin de volaille). Other poultry and game birds may be prepared in much the same way*

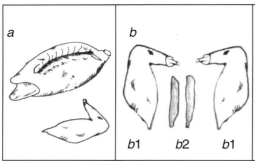

| | | With a sharp knife make an incision on either side of the breast bone, holding knife toward the breast to cut away all flesh. Glide the point of the knife toward the wing bone joint and draw suprême off carcass, assuring good skin cover.
Attached to the suprêmes (*b*1) are little fillets (*b*2), which can come off. Remove small sinew, make a small incision in suprême and tuck fillet in this incision.
Occasionally, fillets are removed to use for farce or sauté. |

FIG. 5.8 *Preparation of poultry breasts (suprêmes de volaille). Suprêmes can be poached, shallow fried or deep fried, the latter usually in a batter or breadcrumbs*

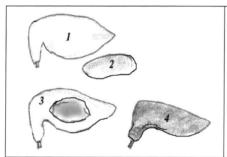

| | Bat out the suprême and fillet (**1** and **2**).
Place the farce/stuffing of your choice onto middle of suprême, cover with batted fillet to surround farce (**3**).
Roll suprême slightly to encircle stuffing-farce (**4**)
Sometimes tied with a string or secured with cocktail stick.
Stuffed suprêmes can be poached, shallow fried or deep fried, in this case they are surrounded by seasoned flour, egg wash and fresh breadcrumbs (pané). |

FIG. 5.9 *Preparation of stuffed poultry suprême (suprême de volaille farcie). For different forcemeats see Chapter 7. The most famous of the stuffed suprêmes is the Suprême de volaille Kiev (Chicken Kiev) with garlic butter*

PREPARATION OF TURKEY

Turkeys are usually delivered with some feathers on the neck and wings. Pluck carefully and remove fine feathers as for chicken. Singe and draw the sinews from the legs. This operation is essential as the sinews will spoil the flesh of the legs and make it impossible to carve them. Cut the skin all round, just above the feet, break the bone, twist the foot, place it in a sinew hook (which used to be found in every Larder) and pull steadily on the leg, pulling all the sinews out attached to the foot or insert a steel and twist (see Plate 5.1*a* and Figure 5.1*g,h*).

The rest of turkey preparation and trussing is much the same as that given for chickens above (see also Plate 5.2). The turkey may also be stuffed.

Turkeys, like most poultry and game, have the tender white breast meat and the tougher dark meat on the legs, taking longer to cook/roast. With the small birds this is more easily overcome, by placing the legs uppermost in the roasting tray to expose them to more intense heat. An alternative is to remove them and use a different cooking method, such a stewing or braising.

Modern Turkey Preparation for Roasting

In this modern method we separate the legs from the turkey, bone out the legs and stuff them with a farce of choice, usually a combination of pork and turkey trimmings

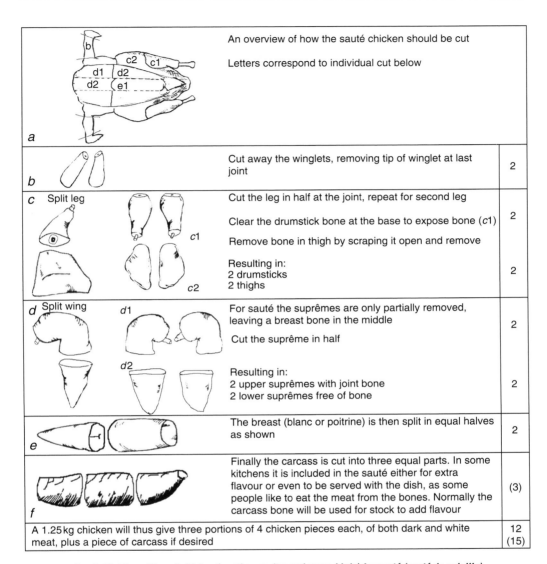

a	An overview of how the sauté chicken should be cut Letters correspond to individual cut below	
b	Cut away the winglets, removing tip of winglet at last joint	2
c Split leg	Cut the leg in half at the joint, repeat for second leg Clear the drumstick bone at the base to expose bone (*c1*) Remove bone in thigh by scraping it open and remove	2
c1 *c2*	Resulting in: 2 drumsticks 2 thighs	2
d Split wing *d1*	For sauté the suprêmes are only partially removed, leaving a breast bone in the middle Cut the suprême in half	2
d2	Resulting in: 2 upper suprêmes with joint bone 2 lower suprêmes free of bone	2
e	The breast (blanc or poitrine) is then split in equal halves as shown	2
f	Finally the carcass is cut into three equal parts. In some kitchens it is included in the sauté either for extra flavour or even to be served with the dish, as some people like to eat the meat from the bones. Normally the carcass bone will be used for stock to add flavour	(3)
A 1.25 kg chicken will thus give three portions of 4 chicken pieces each, of both dark and white meat, plus a piece of carcass if desired		12 (15)

Fɪɢ. 5.10 *The cutting of chicken (or other poultry and game birds) for sauté (sauté de volaille)*

and chestnuts (although if left whole the latter can make carving of the leg difficult; they must be added to the farce coarsely chopped or served as garnish separately). For detailed modern preparation see Plate 5.2.

The roasting of separated turkeys is illustrated in Figure 5.11.

DUCKS AND DUCKLINGS

Ducklings should reach the market at between 8 and 9 weeks old and before developing any adult feathers. Fatness can be tested by pinching the flesh along the side of the breast, just behind the legs. In young birds the breast will be pliable, the feet soft and small and the underside of the wings downy. Soft flexible quills with a decided point

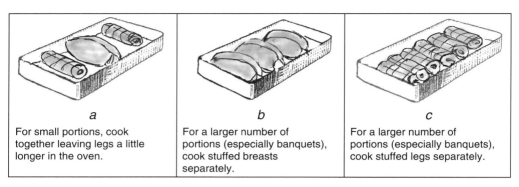

a	*b*	*c*
For small portions, cook together leaving legs a little longer in the oven.	For a larger number of portions (especially banquets), cook stuffed breasts separately.	For a larger number of portions (especially banquets), cook stuffed legs separately.

FIG. 5.11 *The roasting of turkey breast and legs separately*

are also a good indicator. The older the bird, the more rounded the tips. Cleaning and dressing etc. is carried out as for chicken above.

GEESE

To test the age of geese, press the windpipe where it enters the body. In young birds it should be yielding and pliable. In older birds, well-developed wing muscles and a strong beak are evident. Cleaning and dressing is carried out as for chicken above.

GUINEA FOWL AND PIGEON

Quality is judged and preparation is much the same as all other poultry. Note that guinea fowl originally was a wild bird and it is nowadays bred on special farms and is thus classified under the poultry rather than game.

Plate 5.3*a–e* shows various attractive presentations of cooked poultry dishes.

GAME ♟ **Le gibie**

The French word *gibier* applies to all animals being hunted and eaten. It is derived from the verb *gibercer*, which means 'to hunt'.

In the old days on the great estates a day of hunting was a day of joy and feasting. As the evening drew to a close the beaters and hunters carried the game home on their backs – the small-feathered game strung around their necks, the heavier furred game over their shoulders with the two fore and hind legs firmly held in each hand. This made the hunters appear like hunchbacks, relating to the Latin word *gibbosus* ('hunchback'), from which the French perhaps derived their word for hunting.

The gourmet considers game an excellent food – warming and healthy and fit for the most delicate palates. In the hands of an experienced chef, game properly hung and prepared will give dishes of the highest quality and allows variations in one's daily menus.

We differentiate between two types of game – **feathered** and **furred.**

TABLE 5.2 *Feathered Game in Season*

English	French	Season
Pheasant	Le faisan	Oct – 1 Feb
Partridge	La perdrix	Sept – 1 Feb
Young Partridge	Le perdreau	Sept – Dec
Rock Partridge	La bartavelle	September
Woodcock	La bécasse	Oct – 31 Jan
Snipe	La bécassine	12 Aug – 31 Jan
Hazel Hen	La gelinotte	Sept – Dec
Mountain Cock	Le coq de bruyère	Sept – Dec
Grouse	La grouse	12 Aug – 10 Dec
Wild duck	Le canard sauvage	Sept – 31 Jan
Teal	La sarcelle	Dec – Jan
Plover	Le pluvier	Sept – 31 Jan
Lapwing	Le vanneau	Sept – Dec
Goose	L'oie	Sept – 31 Jan
Quail	La caille	July – Sept
Corncrake	Le râle	July – Sept
Fieldfare	La grive	Sept – Dec
Ortolan	L'ortolan	Sept – Dec
Lark	L'alouette	Sept – Dec

Note: In some countries and regions some of the above wild birds are now protected.
Guinea fowl and pigeon, which may strictly be considered as game, are widely available and in some cases farmed and so are included under poultry.

FEATHERED GAME   *Le gibier à plumage*

Table 5.2 lists the seasons when game birds are at their best or allowed to be shot. Game of all types was formerly only offered in British restaurants during the shooting season or shortly thereafter. With modern deep freezing they are often available all the year round, but never of the best quality or flavour. Duck and geese are now considered domesticated birds. Very few wild birds are used in the catering industry.

With all feathered game the flavour will improve by hanging for a few days in a cool, well-ventilated place. Care should be taken with water birds not to get them too 'high' (a certain smell from hanging).

Preparation of Feathered Game

After plucking, game birds are prepared very much like poultry (see Figure 5.1). Some of the preparations and cuts given for poultry in Figures 5.2 to 5.6 can be applied to game birds, especially when older and only really suitable for pot-roasting or braising.

Most game, whether feathered or furred, has very little fat and needs protection under any method of cooking so as not to get too dry. This protection is afforded by covering with or inserting fat (speck) or green bacon fat (smoked bacon fat would impair the flavour of the game). This operation is called barding (see Figures 5.12–5.14).

Other cuts for the preparation of feathered game are shown in Figure 5.15.

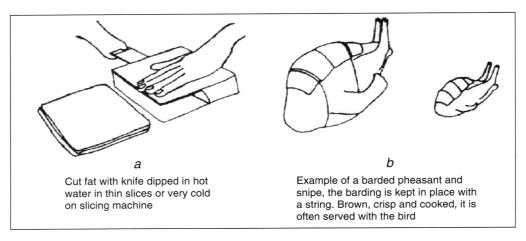

a

Cut fat with knife dipped in hot water in thin slices or very cold on slicing machine

b

Example of a barded pheasant and snipe, the barding is kept in place with a string. Brown, crisp and cooked, it is often served with the bird

Fɪɢ. 5.12 *Barding of poultry and feathered game*

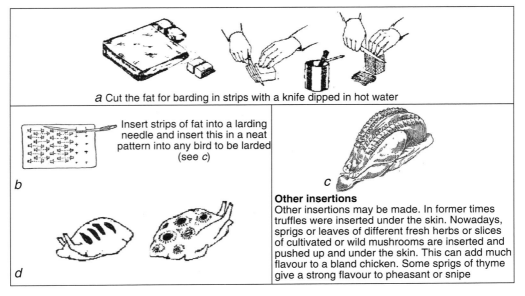

a Cut the fat for barding in strips with a knife dipped in hot water

b Insert strips of fat into a larding needle and insert this in a neat pattern into any bird to be larded (see *c*)

c

Other insertions
Other insertions may be made. In former times truffles were inserted under the skin. Nowadays, sprigs or leaves of different fresh herbs or slices of cultivated or wild mushrooms are inserted and pushed up and under the skin. This can add much flavour to a bland chicken. Some sprigs of thyme give a strong flavour to pheasant or snipe

d

Fɪɢ. 5.13 *Larding of poultry and feathered game*

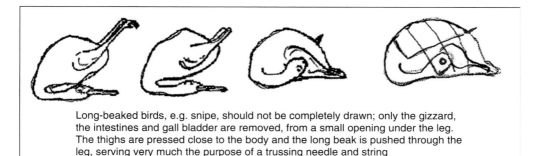

Long-beaked birds, e.g. snipe, should not be completely drawn; only the gizzard, the intestines and gall bladder are removed, from a small opening under the leg. The thighs are pressed close to the body and the long beak is pushed through the leg, serving very much the purpose of a trussing needle and string

FIG. 5.14 *Example of beak-trussed and barded small game bird – the snipe*

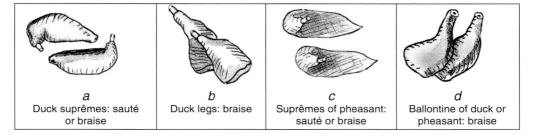

a	*b*	*c*	*d*
Duck suprêmes: sauté or braise	Duck legs: braise	Suprêmes of pheasant: sauté or braise	Ballontine of duck or pheasant: braise

FIG. 5.15 *Cuts and preparation of other poultry or game*

FURRED GAME 🍗 *Le gibier à poil*

Furred game animals are varied in kind and large in number. Table 5.3 shows the most common furred game of Central Europe, the majority of which are now found or are available in the British Isles.

Preparation of Furred Game

Hoofed game such as **venison** is at its best at the age of 4–5 years. The fat should be bright and clear and the cleft of the hoof smooth and closed.

The larger furred game, like stag and roebuck, are usually supplied skinned but, for those who receive their game directly from the hunter, Figure 5.16a shows how to remove the skin reasonably easily.

Once the skin is removed, the venison should be rubbed with a mixture of salt, flour and crushed black pepper and hung up to dry in a cool, well-ventilated room, where it should be allowed to tenderize and to develop a good gamey flavour, for up to 3 weeks. As game is mostly in season in the cold winter months, this should present no great difficulties.

The carcass of venison should be dissected like a carcass of lamb (see Figure 5.16b and Chapter 6 on butchery). Table 5.4 gives the basic cuts, of which the most important are illustrated in Figure 5.17.

TABLE 5.3 *Furred Game*

English	French
Deer or doe	La chevrette
Young deer or stag	Le cerf
Roebuck	Le chevreuil
Hind	La biche
Chamois or mountain goat	Le chamois
Reindeer	Le renne
Wild boar	Le sanglier
Young wild boar	Le marcassin
Young hare	Le levraut
Hare	Le lièvre
Rabbit	Le lapin
Wild rabbit	Le lapin de garenne

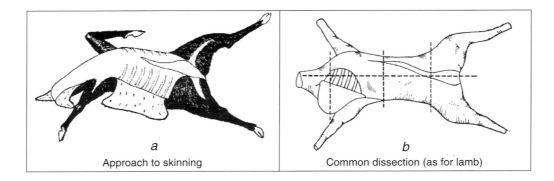

a	*b*
Approach to skinning	Common dissection (as for lamb)

FIG. 5.16 *Approch to skinning and dissecting larger furred game*

Venison and also hare or rabbit saddle has a very fine silvery tough skin which must be removed before cooking. This it best done with a sharp, small filleting knife (see Figure 5.18).

All furred game should, after hanging, be marinated, usually from between 12 and 24 hours according to the type of game and size of joint. Marinating will much improve and bring out the characteristic flavour of the game. (See marinades in Chapter 3.)

Because there is very little fat on venison, the larding of venison cuts comes into its own for flavour and moisture (see Figure 5.19).

Wild boar should be dissected very much like a carcass of pork (see Chapter 6 on butchery). Boar is both roasted and braised; some joints would benefit by larding and marinating.

Hares (August to March) have very tender ears which tear easily, they have short, easily broken claws; the harelip is only faintly defined. They are best at the age of

TABLE 5.4 *Cuts of Venison*

Cut	French	Approx. weight	Best uses
Scrag end	Le cou de chevreuil	1 kg	Boned used for ragouts, farces, pâtés and terrines
Middle neck	Les basses côtes de chevreuil	2.5 kg	Boned used for ragouts, farces, pâtés and terrines
Best end	Le carré de chevreuil	3 kg	Roasting, grilling and frying, or as part of saddle
Long saddle	La selle de chevreuil	2–3 kg	Roasting, braising
Legs (2)	Le gigot de chevreuil	3 kg	Roasting, braising
Shoulder (2)	L'épaule de chevreuil	2.5 kg	Braising, roasting
Breast (2)	La poitrine de chevreuil	1–2 kg	Stew-ragout, minced for farces
Any trimmings			Boned used for ragouts, farces, pâtés and terrines
Bones	Les os		Stocks and sauces

7–8 months, weighing then about 2.5–3 kg. Hang the hare by its forelegs for about a week to collect the blood, which is used in the making of sauces and, of course, jugged hare.

Young hares are best used for roasting, frying, sauté and poêlé, as well as for the making of pies and casseroles. Older hares are best used for jugged hare, pies, terrines and soups.

Rabbits (August to March) are best at 3–4 months old. They are smaller than hare and tamed rabbit. The under-jaw is tender and very easily broken; there is a very short neck and large joints; the paws are well developed in proportion to size. Hang by its forelegs for 1 week. Rabbit flesh is often flavoured by wild thyme, on which it feeds.

To skin, hang hare or rabbit from two hooks, one through each leg sinew, and spreading legs apart. Make an incision upwards on the inside of one of the legs, cut around the paws and draw each leg out of the skin. Cut through the tail and draw the skin downwards, towards the head, using the tip of the knife to cut the tissue between skin and flesh. At the forelegs, loosen skin around the shoulder blades, cut around the front paws and continue to draw the skin over the head. Cut through the ears and take care to trim the skin off the head, making use of the tip of the knife.

Make an incision from vent to ribs, along the middle of the belly, inserting middle and index finger into the cut and cutting between them, so as not to perforate the intestines. Split the pelvic bone and remove intestines, which are disposed of. Next, break through the skin of the diaphragm, separating the belly from the organs, and lift out the lungs, liver and heart and place in a bowl together with the blood that will run from the cavity. A few drops of vinegar will keep the blood fluid till required.

Hare and rabbits are jointed as in Table 5.5. Figure 5.20 shows the cuts for braising or stewing.

Plate 5.3*f–k* show various attractive presentations of cooked game dishes.

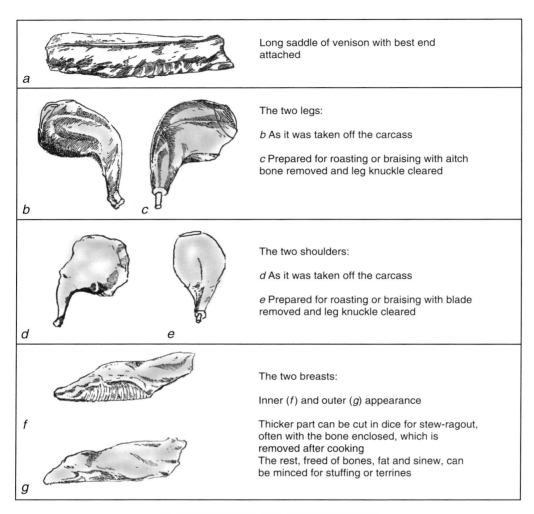

a	Long saddle of venison with best end attached
b c	The two legs: b As it was taken off the carcass c Prepared for roasting or braising with aitch bone removed and leg knuckle cleared
d e	The two shoulders: d As it was taken off the carcass e Prepared for roasting or braising with blade removed and leg knuckle cleared
f g	The two breasts: Inner (f) and outer (g) appearance Thicker part can be cut in dice for stew-ragout, often with the bone enclosed, which is removed after cooking The rest, freed of bones, fat and sinew, can be minced for stuffing or terrines

FIG. 5.17 *Important venison cuts and preparations*

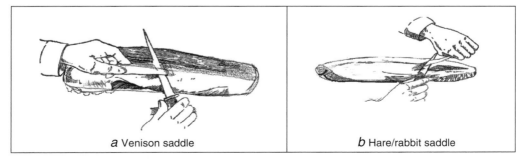

a Venison saddle	*b* Hare/rabbit saddle

FIG. 5.18 *Skinning saddles of venison and rabbit/hare. Taking about a centimetre at a time, draw the knife upward to either side so as not to damage the tender flesh below*

a Larded saddle of venison		*b* Larded shoulder/leg	*c* Larded joint

FIG. 5.19 *The larding of various venison cuts*

TABLE 5.5 *Hare and Rabbits Joints*

Cuts	Rabbit	Hare	Uses
Legs	Les cuisses de lapin	Les cuisses de lièvre	Roast and braise, ragout
Saddle with best end, excluding scrag	La râble de lapin	La râble de lièvre	Roast and braise, ragout
Shoulders	La poitrine de lapin	La poitrine de lièvre	Roast and braise, ragout
Middle neck	Basses côtes de lapin	Basses côtes de lièvre	Bone for stew, stock
Neck	Le cou de lapin	Le cou de lièvre	Bone for stew and stock
Head, breast bones and trimmings	For stocks and sauces		

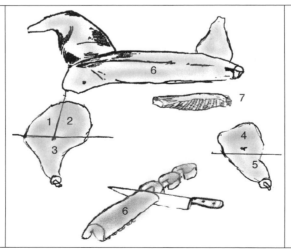

Cut off the two hind legs. Cut in half between the thigh and leg bone and cut the wider upper part in half and trim, resulting in three reasonably even pieces (**1**, **2**, **3** in figure).

Cut off the two front legs and again cut in half at the joint and trim, resulting in two reasonably even pieces (**4,5**).

Now remove the breast on either side of the remaining saddle and set aside. Skin the saddle (**6**) (see Figure 5.18a) and thereafter cut into eight even slices. This preparation results in six hind leg pieces, plus four front leg pieces, plus eight saddle pieces, making 18 pieces in all or three portions.

FIG. 5.20 *Cutting hare or rabbit for jugged hare, braising or stewing, pies and fricassee*

6 Butchery (Le Boucherie)

The function of the Butchery department (Le Boucherie) in the Larder of a catering establishment is the preparation of all raw meat for the kitchens. This involves the breaking down of wholesale cuts of meat, or carcasses, into joints and small cuts for entrées, such as stews, pies, minces, steaks, escalopes, cutlets, fillets, medallions etc., as required for the menus of the day or for banquets.

All preparations requiring raw meat, such as sausages, hamburger steaks, minced shin of beef for clarification etc., are naturally the province of the Butcher. Offal likewise comes into this class. Unlike the shop butcher, who is concerned with selling his meat to his best advantage and, therefore, cannot trim his prime cuts too closely, the Butcher in the catering trade has to prepare and trim each cut carefully so that it should be ready for the different methods of cooking without further trimming of any kind. This involves removing all excess fat, all gristle and sinew, and any bones, which might interfere with easy carving and correct portion control of the meat when cooked.

These by-products should, of course, be carefully sorted and made use of to their best advantage for stocks, dripping etc., and wastage must be kept to its lowest possible level. Careful storage, and the maintenance of all tools in an efficient condition will contribute to the elimination of waste in this very expensive product.

It follows from the above that the Butcher should be familiar with the various meats, should be able to distinguish quality, should have some knowledge of the bone formation of the carcasses to enable him to dissect efficiently, should know the various cuts of meat or joints and their best utilization, the number of portions obtainable from each and the cost per portion. He must also be familiar with the French names of each cut of meat, joint, entrée or grill.

'Fresh meat' includes all meat not salted or cooked. It may be fresh, killed, chilled or frozen. Only chilled meat is imported. It is produced chiefly in Argentina and Uruguay and EU countries. After slaughter beef is cooled, graded, quartered and sheeted and it is hung during transit in a non-freezing temperature in a sterile refrigeration chamber. It must be sold and used quickly after arrival in port. Storage temperature is approx. -1 to $-2\,°C$ (28–30 °F).

Frozen beef is imported from New Zealand, Australia, Argentina, Uruguay and Brazil. Lamb and mutton come mainly from New Zealand and Australia. After slaughter the carcasses are inspected, graded, stamped and sheeted, frozen solid, packed in layers in store refrigerators and in refrigerated ships at $-29\,°C$ ($-20\,°F$). This enables all the space to be filled and therefore makes for cheaper rates of transport than chilled beef. On arrival at British ports it is kept frozen in cold stores and distributed by insulated rail or road containers to various parts of the country.

BEEF   *Le boeuf*

Best home-killed beef comes from Scotland, Norfolk and Devon. Beef is classified as below and the classification can easily be distinguished by reference to the
hindquarters of the carcass.

Male	Female
Entire = Bull calf up to 1 year	**Heifer calf**
Castrate = Castrated bull	**Heifer** = Not calved
Yearling = Bull in first year	**Cow-heifer** = Young female after calving
Steer calf = Castrated yearling	**Cow** = After calving
Bull = Adult bull	
Steer ox = Castrated adult	

Identification:
Steer: Steer will have a curved pubic bone and a relatively narrow pelvic
cavity; the cod fat will be heavy.
Heifer: Heifer will have a flat pubic bone and a relatively wider pelvic cavity;
the udder fat will be firm.
Cow: Cow pubic bone is flat and light with a wide pelvic cavity.
Bull: The bull pubic bone will be large, the pelvic cavity narrow and cod fat
almost non-existent.

Carcass quality is judged under three main headings: conformation, finish and quality. **Conformation** relates to the proportion of good joints in relation to bone and is
rather more important in beef than other animals. **Finish** refers to an outer covering of
fat, which should be smooth, evenly distributed over the carcass and creamy white in
colour.

Quality of beef can be judged by these points:

- The meat should be firm and bright red.
- It should have a good showing of dots or flecks of white fat, what we call marbled.
- The fat should be firm and brittle in texture, and creamy white in colour.
- Yellowish fat is always a sign that the animal is older or of a dairy breed.

Beef should be fresh, or only chilled: frozen beef is never quite as good.

Steer beef is considered best but in some districts heifers are preferred as these
are smaller and the bones are lighter. The texture, too, is finer. Cow or bull beef is
usually sold to the manufacturing industry.

SKELETAL FORMATION

Cattle, sheep and pigs are similar in structure. The body consists of head, neck,
trunk and tail, and is divided into the front part, 'forequarters', and the rear part,
'hindquarters'. The diaphragm forms a division between the chest or thorax and the
abdomen or belly. Figure 6.1 shows the bones to be found in a side of beef.

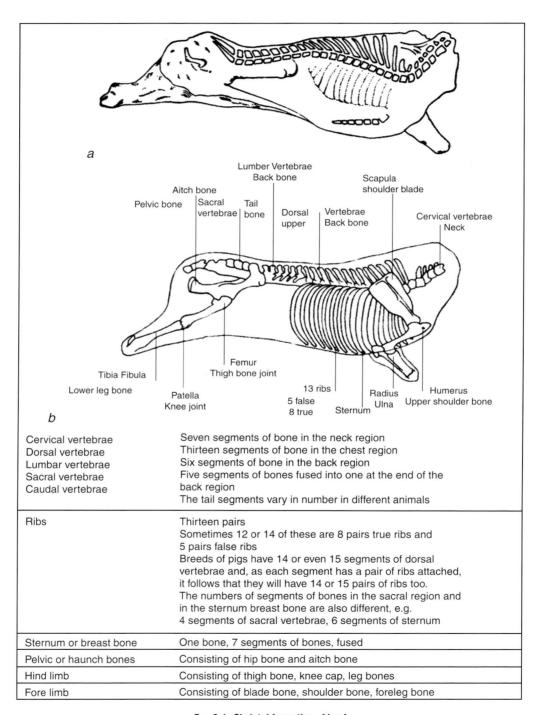

Cervical vertebrae	Seven segments of bone in the neck region
Dorsal vertebrae	Thirteen segments of bone in the chest region
Lumbar vertebrae	Six segments of bone in the back region
Sacral vertebrae	Five segments of bones fused into one at the end of the
Caudal vertebrae	back region
	The tail segments vary in number in different animals
Ribs	Thirteen pairs
	Sometimes 12 or 14 of these are 8 pairs true ribs and
	5 pairs false ribs
	Breeds of pigs have 14 or even 15 segments of dorsal
	vertebrae and, as each segment has a pair of ribs attached,
	it follows that they will have 14 or 15 pairs of ribs too.
	The numbers of segments of bones in the sacral region and
	in the sternum breast bone are also different, e.g.
	4 segments of sacral vertebrae, 6 segments of sternum
Sternum or breast bone	One bone, 7 segments of bones, fused
Pelvic or haunch bones	Consisting of hip bone and aitch bone
Hind limb	Consisting of thigh bone, knee cap, leg bones
Fore limb	Consisting of blade bone, shoulder bone, foreleg bone

Fig. 6.1 *Skeletal formation of beef*

JOINTING OR DISSECTION

The method of jointing described here is based on the skeleton of the animal. No one would take the trouble to chop through a bone if a joint could be found which, with very little effort, one could cut through. Even in these days of mechanical saws, use is still made of the skeletal structure to facilitate jointing.

For convenience a side of beef quartered between the tenth and eleventh ribs and cut straight across is described. This provides a 10 rib forequarter and a 3 rib hindquarter. All imported chilled beef is quartered in this manner, and so is all-local beef.

A whole side of beef (as shown in Figure 6.1) is very seldom supplied to hotels and restaurants. Figure 6.2 shows the cuts available from a side when divided into forequarter and hindquarter. The average weight of a side of beef is about 175–180 kg (350–380 lb) but it could, in certain cases, be heavier or lighter. For this reason, the weights given below for the different cuts are only approximately correct. The methods of cutting vary considerably in certain parts of the world, even in Great Britain. There is, however, a broad correlation between the various systems based on the skeleton of the animal. The method given here is known as the 'London and Home Counties'.

Dissection of a Hindquarter of Beef

(1) Place the quarter on the block with the inside uppermost and remove the kidney knob and rump suet carefully, taking care not to cut into the fillet that lies under the kidney suet.

(2) Remove the cod or udder fat and the goose skirt that is part of the inner muscle of the belly wall and is situated below the cod fat. Make a light incision where it joins the rump, and then make a clean cut, removing the cod fat at its natural seam with the rump and flank.

(3) Remove the thin flank, estimating a point twice the length of the eye muscle from the chine at the wing end to just below the small external muscle, found below the cod fat. Use the knife as far as the ribs and complete the division by sawing through the three rib bones.

(4) The hindquarter is now divided into rump and loin and top piece, taking a line three fingers' width below the round part of the aitch bone (approx. 5 cm and the same height above the end of the rump bone). Cut through the fillet, if not previously removed, saw across the bone and complete the division by making a clean straight cut with the steak knife. This cut must be absolutely square, as sloping towards the top piece will mean cutting into a bone, whilst sloping towards the loin will result in a loss of rump steak.

(5) Remove the fillet, or undercut, carefully, if it is intended for steaks. Use a boning knife and commencing at the chine follow the bones of the lumbar vertebrae closely, avoiding any cuts into the fillet muscle.

(6) Separate the rump from the loin at the cartilage between the sacral and lumbar vertebrae. Using this as a guide, locate the cartilage on the end of the rump bone (ilium) with the point of a knife. Make a cut just through the cartilage and sloping the knife towards the rump, to the point between the vertebrae, complete the separation by sawing through the bone. If not previously removed, remove the fillet head carefully from the rump with the skirt attached.

Wholesale ordering cuts

Hindquarter

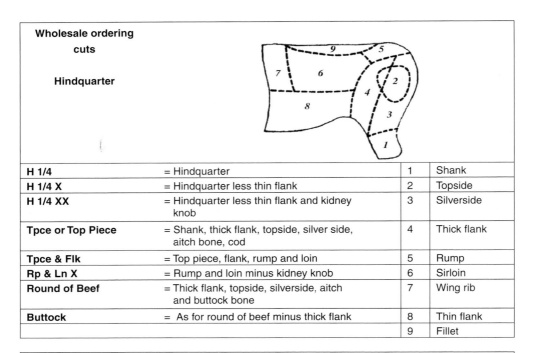

H 1/4	= Hindquarter	1	Shank
H 1/4 X	= Hindquarter less thin flank	2	Topside
H 1/4 XX	= Hindquarter less thin flank and kidney knob	3	Silverside
Tpce or Top Piece	= Shank, thick flank, topside, silver side, aitch bone, cod	4	Thick flank
Tpce & Flk	= Top piece, flank, rump and loin	5	Rump
Rp & Ln X	= Rump and loin minus kidney knob	6	Sirloin
Round of Beef	= Thick flank, topside, silverside, aitch and buttock bone	7	Wing rib
Buttock	= As for round of beef minus thick flank	8	Thin flank
		9	Fillet

Wholesale ordering cuts

Forequarter

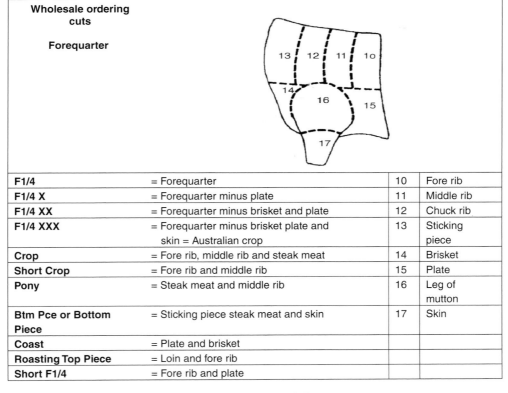

F1/4	= Forequarter	10	Fore rib
F1/4 X	= Forequarter minus plate	11	Middle rib
F1/4 XX	= Forequarter minus brisket and plate	12	Chuck rib
F1/4 XXX	= Forequarter minus brisket plate and skin = Australian crop	13	Sticking piece
Crop	= Fore rib, middle rib and steak meat	14	Brisket
Short Crop	= Fore rib and middle rib	15	Plate
Pony	= Steak meat and middle rib	16	Leg of mutton
Btm Pce or Bottom Piece	= Sticking piece steak meat and skin	17	Skin
Coast	= Plate and brisket		
Roasting Top Piece	= Loin and fore rib		
Short F1/4	= Fore rib and plate		

FIG. 6.2 *Beef wholesale ordering cuts*

(7) Remove the wing end from the loin by cutting between the dorsal and lumbar vertebrae and in a straight line across the loin keeping the loin square. This will necessitate sawing through the tops of two of the ribs and the chine, to complete the division. Use the saw on the bones only and cut through the muscle with a clean stroke of a sharp steak knife.

(8) Remove the aitch bone from the top piece. Starting from the outside, lay back the thin layer of muscle and fat from the surface, baring the bone completely. Pass the point of the knife along the underside of the bone to loosen the muscle, follow the line of the hole with the tip of the knife and cut down the back of the surface, cutting the tendon in the ball to socket joint and remove the bone cleanly.

(9) To remove the thick flank, find the leg end of the patella with the point of the knife and make a straight cut down on to the thigh bone (femur). Insert the point of the knife under the skin covering the bone and draw back the thick flank from the bone. Here will be found the seam of the silverside. Cut open the seam till the silverside muscle is reached, then cut through the skin with a clean cut to remove the thick flank.

(10) Remove the shank–hind shin by cutting through the cartilage and tendon at the joint, between the tibia–fibula and femur.

(11) The topside is now separated from the silverside at the seam. Start from the bone side of the buttock by cutting round the bone until the seam is located, following it until the external fat is reached, then cutting through the fat to remove the topside, leaving the bone clean and attached to the silverside.

Note: Several of these joints (as well as from the forequarter) can be bought vacuum-packed. They are fine for pot roasting, braising and stewing, but they make very poor roast as they are too wet when unpacked.

Dissection of Forequarter of Beef

(1) Remove the shin at the elbow joint with a boning knife. Push the shin forward and downwards whilst loosening the joint with the knife. With frozen beef it is advisable to saw through the tip of the elbow to facilitate 'breaking' the joint.

(2) Remove the plate and brisket taking a line some 5 cm (2 in.) from the end of the skirt to the first bone of the sternum. Saw through the rib bone, followed by cutting, taking care, when removing the brisket end, to find the seam between it and the leg of mutton cut. The plate and brisket are divided by cutting between the 6th and 7th rib bones.

(3) Remove the sticking piece by finding the joint of the clod (humerus) and the blade bone (scapula). To find the cup bone of the blade, cut between the cervical and dorsal vertebrae. Saw across and remove the clod and sticking, in one piece. The clod is separated from the sticking at the natural seam between the muscles, leaving the fat on the clod.

(4) Remove the forerib by cutting between the 6th and 7th ribs with a steak knife drawn between the ribs towards the chine. Finish by sawing through the chine. Keep the joint absolutely rectangular.

(5) The remaining portion is known as the 'pony' and from this remove the middle rib. Cutting between the 3rd and 4th ribs, drawing the knife towards the chine till the blade bone is reached, cutting the muscle over the bone, and then sawing through the blade bone does this. The cut between the ribs is then completed and the chine bone is sawn through.

(6) The remaining portion consists of chuck, blade bone and leg of mutton cut. With the joint on its back, saw through the 3 ribs and follow with a knife cut, just missing the blade bone to separate the leg of mutton cut from the chuck and blade bone. Divide these at the seam, leaving the fat on the chuck.

Note: In most catering establishments the top part of the foreribs and middle ribs are cut off to give a strip of rib tops, known as the flat-ribs. For this a line is drawn from the base of the 1st rib close to the cervical vertebrae to the end of the forerib, keeping the rib joints absolutely rectangular. Saw across the rib bones and finish with a clean stroke of a sharp knife. Naturally, this has the effect of giving a short cut forerib, which is not always convenient, particularly if it is put on display in a restaurant.

Modern Meat Purchases

Since *The Larder Chef* was last published, in its third edition in 1989, much has changed in the purchasing of meats of all types. Very few and only the larger establishment will today purchase quarters of beef, or indeed other whole carcasses. The tendency is to buy smaller sections of the animal (see the different wholesale cuts in Figure 6.2), or indeed particular joints required for a given dish or operation. Furthermore, these required joints or cuts are often oven-ready and need very little butchery preparation. However, on advice from teachers and practising chefs, the section on dissection has been retained for this new edition. First because there are hardly any books which give the dissection in such detail, and secondly, as this is mainly a textbook for colleges and schools, it will be a useful help for teachers and students.

PREPARATION AND USE OF JOINTS AND CUTS

The following pages will give the various joints and cuts, approximate weight and best uses of beef, concentrating more on individual preparations for oven pan or grill (see summary Figure 6.3). Plate 6.1 illustrates some prepared beef dishes.

Individual Preparations and Uses for Joints of the Hindquarter

SHANK   *La jambe/le jarret*

On the inner side of the shank the leg bone is clearly visible; if one follows this clearly visible seam around the bone with a sharp boning knife, the shank is easily boned out. Thereafter, one has only to remove the very tough sinews and some excessive fat, and the meat of the shank is ready for use. Cut into large cubes; it can be coarsely minced for clarification or beef tea. The upper, tender part, of the shank can also be used for stews, especially goulash. This meat can be cooked for a very long time to get it nice and tender, but it will never fall apart, as some of the other stewing meats do.

TOPSIDE   *La tranche tendre*

The topside represents one of the leanest pieces of meat of the whole beef. Reasonably tender, the topside has many excellent uses. Cut into dice, it will make a fine stew; cut into steaks, it gives some of the finest braising steaks. If the meat is of a very

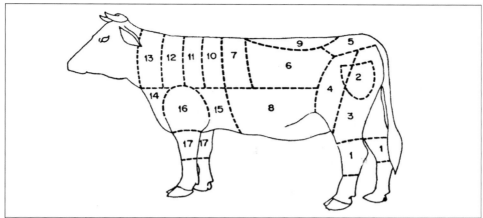

Cuts/Joints	French	Best uses	Approximate weight
Hindquarter			
1 Shank	La jambe Le jarret	Clarification, beef tea, stews and mince	7–8 kg
2 Topside	La tranche tendre	Braising, stewing, second-class roast	9–10 kg
3 Silverside	La plate de cuisse	Boiling, brined and boiled, stewing, mince	12–13 kg
4 Thick flank	Le gîte à la noix	Braising, stewing	11–12 kg
5 Rump	La culotte	Grilling, shallow frying (rump steak)	9–10 kg
6 Sirloin	L'aloyau	First-class roast, grilling, frying (entrecôtes)	10–12 kg
7 Wing rib	Les côtes d'aloyau	Good roast, grilling, frying (côtes de boeuf)	4–5 kg
8 Thin flank	La bavette d'aloyau	Boiling, stewing, mince, sausages	9–10 kg
9 Fillet	Le filet	Roasting, (Wellington), grilling, frying	3–4 kg
Forequarter			
10 Forerib	Les côtes premières	Good roast, grilling, frying (côtes de boeuf)	7–8 kg
11 Middle rib	Les côtes découvertes	Second-class roast and braising	9–10 kg
12 Chunk rib	Les côtes du collier	Braising, stewing, mince	13–15 kg
13 Sticking piece	Le collier coud	Stewing, mince, sausages	8–9 kg
14 Brisket	La poitrine	Boiling, brined and boiled (pressed beef)	17–19 kg
15 Plate	Le plate de côtes	Braising, stewing, mince, sausages	9–10 kg
16 Leg of mutton	L'épaule macreuse	Braising whole and as steaks, stewing, mince	10–11 kg
17 Skin	Le jarret devant	Clarification, beef tea, second-class stews and mince	6–7 kg
Kidney	Le rognon de boeuf	Stews, puddings and pies	700 g
Fat	La graisse	First-class dripping	2.5–3 kg
Marrow	La moelle	Sauce, soups and garnish	400–500 g
Bones	Les os	White and brown stocks	10–12 kg

FIG. 6.3 *Joints, cuts and best uses of beef from a side weighing approx. 180 kg*

good quality, the topside will make a reasonable roast (especially when surrounded by a layer of beef-fat suet). One of the best uses for the topside is for the making of roulades or beef olives. (See Figures 6.10, 6.11 below.)

SILVERSIDE   *Le plat de cuisse*

This piece of meat is very coarse and needs a long cooking time; it is often brined and boiled (e.g. Boiled Beef and Carrots) but it can also be cut into slice for very good braising steaks, or dice and used for a good stew, or minced to give a very good mince. The silverside consists really of two pieces of meat, which are separated by a seam; one is of a wide oblong shape, the other long and round, very much like a large sausage. This latter piece is often brined and boiled, and then served cold for cold meats, salads, sandwiches, etc. (see Figure 6.9 below).

THICK FLANK   *Le gîte à la noix*

Again, a nice lean and tender piece of meat, which, because of its tenderness, is not very good for braised steaks and stews, as it will easily disintegrate if cooked in this way. It is very suitable for pot roasting or braising in a large piece and could, for this method of cooking, even be larded with fat bacon and even marinated in a red wine marinade. Example dishes are Boeuf polé sauce vin rouge or Boeuf braisé aux champignons.

THIN FLANK   *La bavette d'aloyau*

This joint consists of about equal quantities of coarse meat and fat and is not a good cut; at best, it is used for boiling (remove excess fat, bat out, trim and roll neatly, tie with a string); stewing (remove excess fat, cut into neat dice); or mincing (remove most fat and put through the mincing machine) for bitok, sausages, hamburgers etc.

KIDNEY   *Le rognon de boeuf*

For sauté, steak and kidney pies or puddings, stews and soup.

MARROW   *La moelle*

For garnish in soups and sauces.

FAT/SUET   *La graisse*

Used for coverings, dumplings, first-class dripping.

BONES   *Les os*

White and brown stocks and subsequent soups and sauces.

RUMP, SIRLOIN, WING RIB, FILLET   *La culotte, l'aloyau, les côtes d'aloyau, le filet*

For more detailed preparation and use of these first-class joints, see Figures 6.4–6.8.

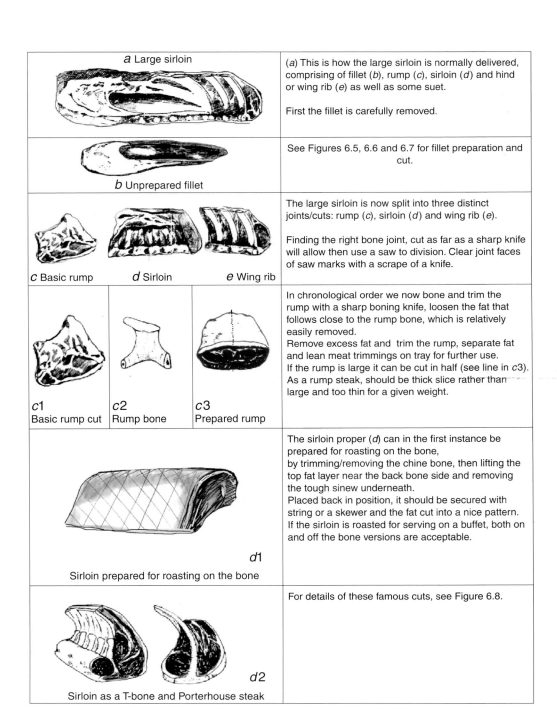

a Large sirloin	(*a*) This is how the large sirloin is normally delivered, comprising of fillet (*b*), rump (*c*), sirloin (*d*) and hind or wing rib (*e*) as well as some suet. First the fillet is carefully removed.
b Unprepared fillet	See Figures 6.5, 6.6 and 6.7 for fillet preparation and cut.
c Basic rump *d* Sirloin *e* Wing rib	The large sirloin is now split into three distinct joints/cuts: rump (*c*), sirloin (*d*) and wing rib (*e*). Finding the right bone joint, cut as far as a sharp knife will allow then use a saw to division. Clear joint faces of saw marks with a scrape of a knife.
*c*1 Basic rump cut *c*2 Rump bone *c*3 Prepared rump	In chronological order we now bone and trim the rump with a sharp boning knife, loosen the fat that follows close to the rump bone, which is relatively easily removed. Remove excess fat and trim the rump, separate fat and lean meat trimmings on tray for further use. If the rump is large it can be cut in half (see line in *c*3). As a rump steak, should be thick slice rather than large and too thin for a given weight.
*d*1 Sirloin prepared for roasting on the bone	The sirloin proper (*d*) can in the first instance be prepared for roasting on the bone, by trimming/removing the chine bone, then lifting the top fat layer near the back bone side and removing the tough sinew underneath. Placed back in position, it should be secured with string or a skewer and the fat cut into a nice pattern. If the sirloin is roasted for serving on a buffet, both on and off the bone versions are acceptable.
*d*2 Sirloin as a T-bone and Porterhouse steak	For details of these famous cuts, see Figure 6.8.

FIG. **6.4** *Preparation of cuts from the large sirloin of beef*

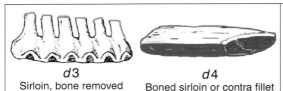	With the bones facing you, carefully remove the flat part of the bones first, gradually working down the back bone, loosening the contra fillet completely.
*d*3 Sirloin, bone removed *d*4 Boned sirloin or contra fillet	Remove part of the top fat with the sinew underneath and the boned sirloin is ready for roasting or cutting for sirloin steaks or entrecôtes (see Figure 6.8).
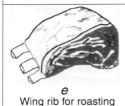 *e* Wing rib for roasting	The wing rib can in the first instance, like the sirloin, be prepared for roasting on the bone, by trimming/removing the chine bone then lifting the top fat layer near the back bone and removing the tough sinew underneath. Placed back in position, it should be secured with string or a skewer and the fat cut into a nice pattern. If the wing rib is roasted for serving on a buffet, the meat between the long bones should be trimmed for better appearance.

FIG. 6.4—*cont'd*

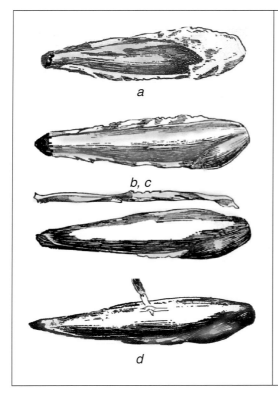

a Carefully remove the suet lump at the head of the fillet

b, c This leaves the fillet and its string, which runs parallel to the fillet. Remove the string carefully, not damaging the fillet. A sharp knife is needed to cut some sinews

d Now with a sharp fillet knife remove the tough silver skin, taking a centimetre or so a time, drawing the knife upward so as not to cut into the fillet

FIG. 6.5 *Preparation of fillet of beef. The average fillet falls into three parts, each in turn ideal for the cuts/steaks shown*

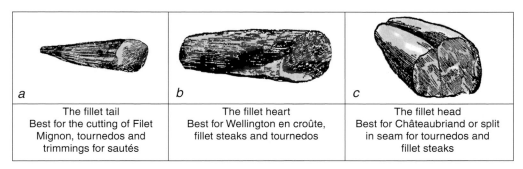

a	b	c
The fillet tail Best for the cutting of Filet Mignon, tournedos and trimmings for sautés	The fillet heart Best for Wellington en croûte, fillet steaks and tournedos	The fillet head Best for Châteaubriand or split in seam for tournedos and fillet steaks

FIG. 6.6 *The fillet parts (see also Figure 6.7). Note that fillets come in all sizes. From very small fillets we could cut all tournedos, whereas a very large fillet could be cut into two Wellington joints or six Chateaubriands*

Fillet Mignon/Filet Mignon de boeuf a	Cut from the fillet tail or the heart of a smaller fillet, usually 2 per portion, about 75 g each.
Tournedos b	Cut from the fillet tail or narrow fillet heart, about 125 g and 5–6 cm high, usually bound with string to retain shape during cooking. In the olden days 2 were served, now only one.
Fillet of beef/ Filet de boeuf c	Cut from the heart of the fillet, about 125 g, 3–4 cm high and 8–10 cm in diameter. Like the tournedos it can be bound with string to retain shape, but not always necessary.
Chateaubriand d	Cut from the wide head or heart of fillet, as a little joint slightly oval in shape, about 400–500 g in weight. Always intended for two person and usually carved at the table.

FIG. 6.7 *Cuts from the fillet of beef*

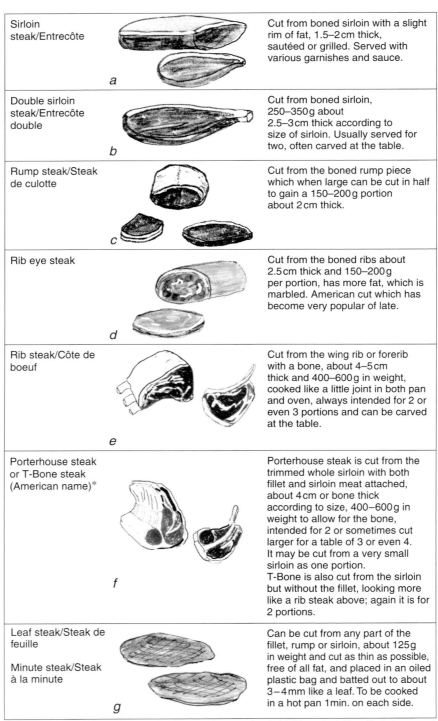

Sirloin steak/Entrecôte		Cut from boned sirloin with a slight rim of fat, 1.5–2 cm thick, sautéed or grilled. Served with various garnishes and sauce.
	a	
Double sirloin steak/Entrecôte double		Cut from boned sirloin, 250–350 g about 2.5–3 cm thick according to size of sirloin. Usually served for two, often carved at the table.
	b	
Rump steak/Steak de culotte		Cut from the boned rump piece which when large can be cut in half to gain a 150–200 g portion about 2 cm thick.
	c	
Rib eye steak		Cut from the boned ribs about 2.5 cm thick and 150–200 g per portion, has more fat, which is marbled. American cut which has become very popular of late.
	d	
Rib steak/Côte de boeuf		Cut from the wing rib or forerib with a bone, about 4–5 cm thick and 400–600 g in weight, cooked like a little joint in both pan and oven, always intended for 2 or even 3 portions and can be carved at the table.
	e	
Porterhouse steak or T-Bone steak (American name)*		Porterhouse steak is cut from the trimmed whole sirloin with both fillet and sirloin meat attached, about 4 cm or bone thick according to size, 400–600 g in weight to allow for the bone, intended for 2 or sometimes cut larger for a table of 3 or even 4. It may be cut from a very small sirloin as one portion. T-Bone is also cut from the sirloin but without the fillet, looking more like a rib steak above; again it is for 2 portions.
	f	
Leaf steak/Steak de feuille Minute steak/Steak à la minute		Can be cut from any part of the fillet, rump or sirloin, about 125 g in weight and cut as thin as possible, free of all fat, and placed in an oiled plastic bag and batted out to about 3–4 mm like a leaf. To be cooked in a hot pan 1 min. on each side.
	g	

Note: *The Americans confuse these English terms by preparing their T-Bone steak like a Porterhouse and calling it a T-Bone, which, with their large portion sizes, is always served as one portion.

Fig. 6.8 *Other butcher's cuts for entrées from beef*

Other Beef Cuts and Preparations

Some other cuts from the hindquarter are shown in Figures 6.9–6.12.

Individual Preparations and Uses for Joints of the Forequarter

FORERIB *Les côtes premières*

This is perhaps the only first-class cut for roasting from the forequarter, consisting of usually four ribs. Again the chine bone is cut in two or four places and excess fat and sinews removed. Before roasting, the back flat chine bone should be broken with the back of a chopper. This will make it easier when the joint is cooked to take the bones away and allow for easier carving. The cut can also be boned, similar to the sirloin, and can be roasted without the bone, or cut into steaks for Kosher forequarter cooking.

Braising steaks may be cut from the silverside (*a*). If the silverside is large, it can be split. The topside (*b*) is usually split in half. In both cases the steak is slightly butted out.	
	a When large can be split *b* Usually split in half

FIG. 6.9 *Braising steaks*

Cut from topside or silverside (*a*), thinly butted out (*b*) and filled with various forcemeats, plus other aromates such as peppers, mushrooms, gherkins. Rolled and secured with string or cocktail sticks (*c*), sealed and braised.	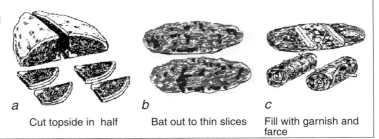
	a Cut topside in half *b* Bat out to thin slices *c* Fill with garnish and farce

FIG. 6.10 *Preparation of beef olives*

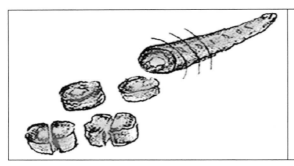	Cut the oxtail between the joint cartilages; the wider ones may be split in half to give even-size pieces. Braised as a stew, flavoured with Madeira or used for clear and thick oxtail soup.

FIG. 6.11 *Cutting of oxtail*

This lesser cut, after boning and trimming off sinew and excessive fat, is ideally suited rolled and tied for **French-Style Boiled Beef**.
If the animal is small it is not split into brisket and plate and is rolled for boiling in one piece.

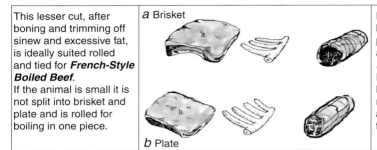

a Brisket

b Plate

Brisket and plate are often brined and made into pressed brisket, or rolled and brined and served as **Boiled Beef and Carrots**. It may be diced and minced. Brisket and plate make a reasonable minced beef but a poor diced stew as it often falls apart.

FIG. 6.12 *Preparation of brisket and plate*

MIDDLE RIB ⚚ *Les côtes découvertes*

Bone out, remove heavy sinews, cut into joints about 2.5 kg and tie firmly with string. Use for second-class roast or for pot roast or braising or stew.

CHUCK RIB ⚚ *Les côtes du collier*

The chuck rib is usually boned out and its meat used for braising en pièce or braising steaks; cut into dice, it makes an excellent stew.

STICKING PIECE ⚚ *Le collier cou*

This is a mass of good lean beef around the neck bone. It is difficult to bone out; one should keep as close to the bone as possible. Diced, the meat makes a good stew; minced it is very good for any dishes where minced beef is used.

Bones are excellent for a good stock.

BRISKET ⚚ *La poitrine*

A popular cut from the forequarter, which is usually brined and boiled and served as Pressed Beef. Boned in both cases, it can also be rolled and boiled fresh as Boiled Beef French Style.

PLATE ⚚ *Le plate de côtes*

Boned and cut into dice, it is quite useful for stews and good minced beef, but only in rare cases can it be used for boiled beef, when it should be of exceptionally good quality.

LEG OF MUTTON CUT ⚚ *L'epaule macreuse*

A good lean piece of meat which is very useful for braising cut in braising steaks. It may also be diced for stews or minced.

SHIN ⚚ *Le jarret de devant*

Like the shank, the shin is carefully boned around the leg bone. Excess fat and all sinews must be removed and it will find a good use for clarification, beef tea and second-class mince.

Fat and Bones

Used as for hindquarter above.

VEAL 🐃 *Le veau*

Veal is the flesh of the calf. Its meat is at its best when the calf is about 2–3 months old. The calf is solely fed on milk, and its meat should be white with a slight tinge to green. If there is any sign of red coloration, it usually indicates the calf has been fed with solids, or has been grazing. Veal can be sold in a full carcass, like lamb, but more often it is split into two halves, like beef. Hotels and restaurants usually purchase the hindquarter or fillet only.

Classification of veal is as follows:

Slink veal: Unborn or stillborn carcass
Calf: Young cattle from birth to six months
Stirk: Weaned calf of both sexes
Baby beef: Beef between 12 and 18 months

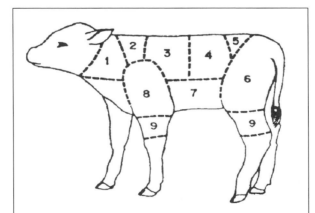

Cuts and joints	French terms	Best uses	Approx. weight
1 Scrag	Le cou	Stock, stewing	2–3 kg
2 Neck end	Les basses côtes	Braising, stewing, stock	3 kg
3 Best end	Le carré	Frying, roasting, pot roasting, braising	3–4 kg
4 Loin (Saddle)	La longe ou la selle	Frying, roasting, pot roasting, braising	3–4 kg
5 Chump or rump	Le quasi	Roasting, braising, grilling	2.5 kg
6 Leg	Le cuissot	Frying, roasting pot roasting, braising*	15–20 kg
7 Breast	La poitrine	Stewing, roasting when stuffed	3 kg
8 Shoulder	L'épaule	Roasting, braising, stewing	5–7 kg
9 Knuckle	Le jarret	Minced, stewing, braising (Osso Bucco)	3–4 kg

*According to dissection, see below

FIG. 6.13 *Joints, cuts and best uses of a side of veal, giving approximately 42–50 kg*

Conformation: The carcass is compact, plump and well fleshed; the loins are well fleshed, legs rounded and well developed; knuckles are short; neck, short and thick; shoulders, deeply fleshed.

Finish: There should be signs of white fat around the kidneys. The inside of the ribs should show indications of fat, which should be white in colour, the flesh should be firm with distinctive pale pinkish colour, described as white. In older animals the flesh can extend to a thin layer over the rump and back.

Quality: The meat is very lean, with a pleasant smell of milk. If the calf is killed too young, its meat is very loose and gelatinous and, as such, is very low in nutritional value.

The usual wholesale cuts of veal are as follows:

Side	Seldom supplied to hotels and restaurants
Forequarter	Seldom supplied to hotels and restaurants
Hindquarter	Common purchase of hotels and restaurants
Leg	Leg less chump, a very commonly purchased cut by hotels and restaurants
Fillet	Leg less chump and knuckle, the most commonly purchased cut by hotels and restaurants
Baby calf	Whole small calf; if purchased dissect as carcass of lamb below

Figure 6.13 shows the basic cuts or joints with their approximate average weight and summarizes the best uses of veal.

DISSECTION

(1) Remove the leg, by cutting straight across, just above the aitch bone.

(2) Separate the knuckle from the fillet by jointing just above the patella.

(3) Bone out the fillet in the same way as the round of beef. This will produce three distinctive cuts: the cushion (topside), the under cushion (silverside) and the thick flank.

(4) Separate the loin from the chump between the lumbar and sacral vertebrae.

(5) Remove the shoulder in the same way as mutton shoulder and joint the fore knuckle from the oyster.

(6) Remove the breast in the same manner. The portion of the breast corresponding to the beef 'plate' is known as the tendons.

(7) Separate the best end from the middle neck between the 6th and 7th ribs.

(8) Divide the neck end from scrag, leaving about five to six bones on the neck end.

PREPARATION AND USE OF JOINTS AND CUTS

The main joints, cuts and their uses are discussed below and illustrated in Figures 6.14–6.18. Plate 6.2 shows various prepared veal dishes.

THE SCRAG ⚶ *Le cou de veau* (Figure 6.14a)

The neck of veal is not a very exciting cut. It is usually cut and chopped, with the bones, into 2–4 cm (1–2 in.) pieces and used for Veal Blanquettes. It can also be boned and

The scrag/Le cou de veau		Usually cut and chopped into pieces or boned and diced
Neck end/Les basses côtes de veau		Usually split and cut into secondary cutlets
Saddle of veal/La selle de veau		This can only be cut from a whole carcass of veal. It is boned, rolled and usually roasted
Loin of veal/Longe de veau		A prime cut with many excellent uses
		The loin can also be cut into veal chops (*i*) for frying or braising Boned and trimmed, noisettes of veal (*j*) are cut from the loin, which are usually shallow fried

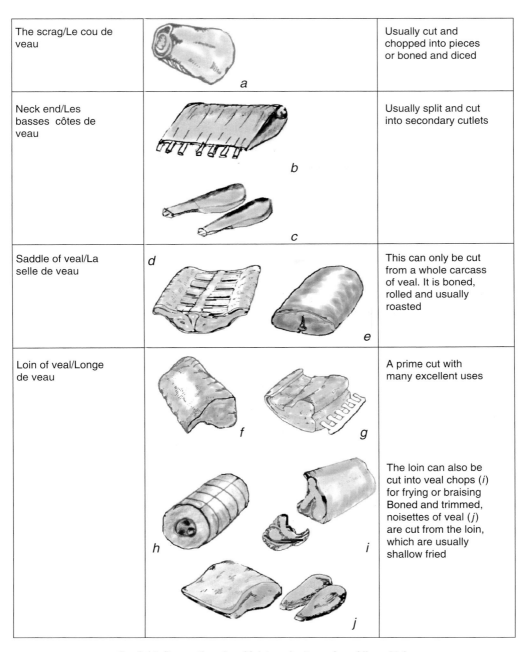

FIG. 6.14 *Preparation of veal joints and cuts: neck, saddle and loin*

then cut into dice of about 2 cm (1 in.) for other white and brown veal stews, or minced. Quite often scrag can be put to very good use in the preparation of first-class white or brown veal stocks.

NECK END *Les basses côtes de veau* (Figure 6.14b,c)

This is a slightly better cut than the scrag but still quite bony. Usually split and cut into secondary cutlets for braising, or cut with the bones into 2–4 cm (1–2 in.) pieces and used for Blanquette. Boned it can be used for other white and brown veal stews, or minced and used in the preparation of pojarskis.

SADDLE *La selle de veau* (Figure 6.14d,e)

This can of course only be cut from a whole carcass of veal and not a side as described here (see notes on Lamb). Once the saddle is jointed, excess kidney fat and the kidneys are removed and, in certain cases, the tenderloin. Now the saddle flaps are cut short, according to their length, by 2–4 cm (1–2 in.), and folded under the saddle, which is tied with string in three or four places to keep the shape. It is used for roast, pot roast, sometimes braised, often larded, and served hot or cold on a buffet.

LOIN *La longe de veau* (Figure 6.14f–j)

One of the prime cuts and with many excellent uses. Usually roasted or pot-roasted whole, it can also be cut into chops. These are not much suited for grilling or frying because of the leanness of the meat; they are therefore braised. For roasting or pot roasting, neatly loosen the bones from the loin; do not actually remove, leave in place as a trivet; remove back sinew, trim and roll to a neat roll, tie with a string in two or three places and it is ready for use.

BEST END *Le carré de veau* (Figure 6.15a,b)

The second prime cut, it too can be roasted or pot-roasted whole. For this purpose, one removes the chine bone and back sinew, cutting approximately 4 cm of meat away from the narrower part of the best end, cleaning meat and sinews between the bones and scraping the bone absolutely clean. After the above procedure, the veal best end can be cut into cutlets between the bones. In turn each of the rib bones is cut to a point on a slight angle, to allow cutlet frills to be fitted.

CHUMP OR RUMP *Le quasi de veau*

This is not really a joint in its own right. According to requirements, it is often left on the loin to gain a larger loin, or on the leg to use when cutting escalopes or grenadines. When jointed, however, the rump of veal cuts into excellent steaks or chops for braising or, when boned, its tender lean meat is most useful for sauté de veau, with its many recipes.

SHOULDER *L'epaule de veau* (Figure 6.15c–f)

Most suitable for pot roast and for this the shoulder must of course be boned. The shoulder is now batted slightly and filled, usually with a lemon and thyme stuffing. Stuffings based on forcemeats, duxelles, rice or a combination of these, will give the chef scope for variation in preparing this dish. The shoulder, boned entirely, may also

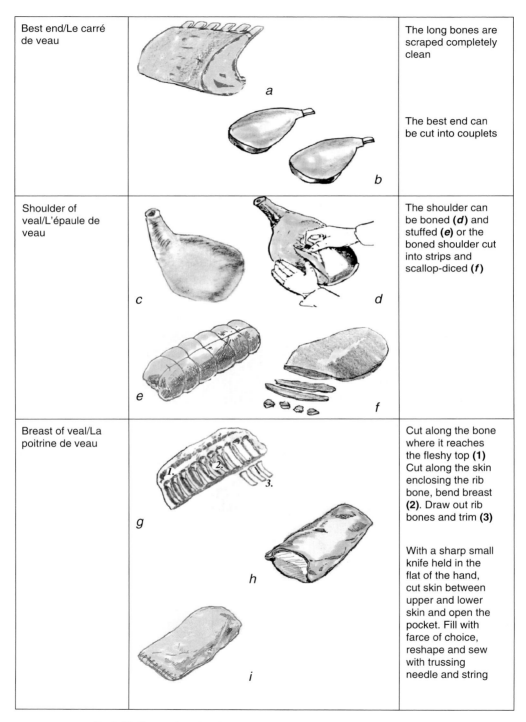

Best end/Le carré de veau		The long bones are scraped completely clean
		The best end can be cut into couplets
Shoulder of veal/L'épaule de veau		The shoulder can be boned (*d*) and stuffed (*e*) or the boned shoulder cut into strips and scallop-diced (*f*)
Breast of veal/La poitrine de veau		Cut along the bone where it reaches the fleshy top (**1**) Cut along the skin enclosing the rib bone, bend breast (**2**). Draw out rib bones and trim (**3**)
		With a sharp small knife held in the flat of the hand, cut skin between upper and lower skin and open the pocket. Fill with farce of choice, reshape and sew with trussing needle and string

FIG. 6.15 *Preparation of veal joints and cuts: the best end, shoulder and breast*

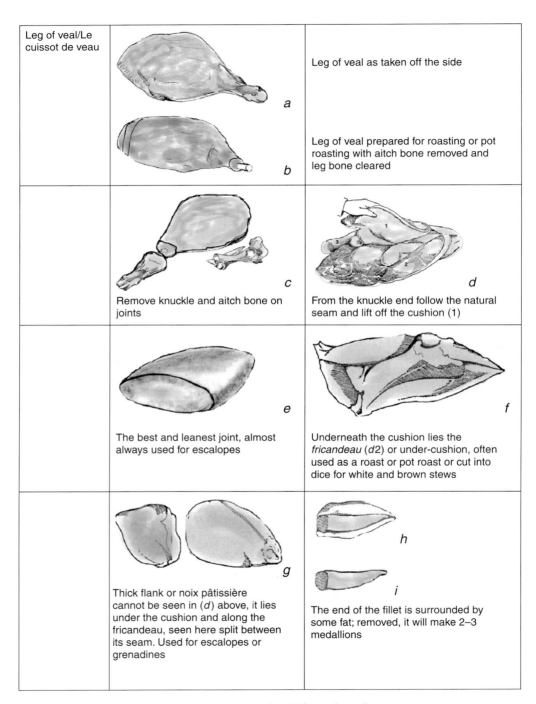

Leg of veal/Le cuissot de veau		
	a	Leg of veal as taken off the side
	b	Leg of veal prepared for roasting or pot roasting with aitch bone removed and leg bone cleared
	c Remove knuckle and aitch bone on joints	*d* From the knuckle end follow the natural seam and lift off the cushion (1)
	e The best and leanest joint, almost always used for escalopes	*f* Underneath the cushion lies the *fricandeau* (*d*2) or under-cushion, often used as a roast or pot roast or cut into dice for white and brown stews
	g Thick flank or noix pâtissière cannot be seen in (*d*) above, it lies under the cushion and along the fricandeau, seen here split between its seam. Used for escalopes or grenadines	*h* *i* The end of the fillet is surrounded by some fat; removed, it will make 2–3 medallions

Fig. 6.16 *Preparation of veal joints and cuts: leg*

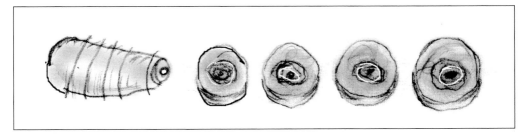

FIG. 6.17 *Preparation of veal knuckles*

Grenadines/ Noisettes de veau	a	Cut from thick flank or cushion, often larded. Shallow fried or braised
Veal escalopes/ E scalopes de veau	b	Cut from the cushion, sometimes need batting out. Cooked shallow fried nature or floured, egg washed and breadcrumbs pané for the famous Wiener Schnitzel
Medallions/ Médaillions	c	Cut from the trimmed fillet of veal, usually 2 per portion, shallow fried
Veal Olives/ Paup iettes de veau	d	Cut slice from the fricandeau or thick flank, bat out, fill with farce of your choice, secure with string or cocktails stick, then braised
Veal Cordon bleu (sometimes called Swiss Schnitzel or Schweizer Schnitzel)	e *Note: originally always made for two persons and carved at the table. Of late, for plated service, prepared for one portion by cutting an escalope in half*	1 Cut two thin escalopes, bat out if need be 2 Cover with thin slice of cooked ham 3 Place slice of Gruyères cheese on top 4 Cover again with thin slice of cooked ham 5 Carefully pass through seasoned flour, egg wash and fresh white breadcrumbs 6 Slowly shallow fried

FIG. 6.18 *Other well-known veal cuts and preparations*

be used for such dishes as fricassee, goulash, Hongroise and sautéd veal when cut in strips across and scallop-diced.

BREAST   *La poitrine de veau* (Figure 6.15g–i)

The breast of the medium to larger calf is ideal for stuffed breast of veal (see below). For this purpose, the breast should be carefully denuded of all bones and gristle, without cutting through the thin skin or flesh. The breast thus prepared can be opened like a pocket; this must be done very carefully in order to avoid tearing the skin. The pocket is filled with a forcemeat, made mainly of minced veal but with the addition of some pork, or pork fat. Fillings of a duxelles, rice or bread base are also often used for this excellent dish. The stuffed veal breast should, whenever possible, be pot roasted and barded to avoid drying out while roasting.

LEG   *Le cuissot de veau* (Figure 6.16a–j)

Representing the best and leanest cut of the whole veal, the leg has many uses and some of the most famous veal dishes come from this joint. If not too big, the leg of veal may be roasted or pot roasted whole. For this purpose the aitch bone is carefully removed and the lower knuckle cleared, tied two or three times with string, where the aitch bone was removed. The leg is then ready for use. As veal is very lean and tends to get dry in roasting or pot-roasting, it is advisable to lard or bard the leg for better results (for technique see Chapter 5 on game). More commonly the leg is boned and the cuts used as shown in Figure 6.16e–i.

KNUCKLES   *Les jarrets de veau* (Figure 6.17)

The most common use for the knuckles of veal of both fore and hind legs is for a dish called Osso Bucco. For this preparation, the knuckles are sawn into slices of 2–4 cm, with the bone in the middle. Freed of sinews and excess bones in relation to meat, this is a famous Italian dish that is liked all over the world.

On the Continent, especially in Germany, Switzerland and Sweden, the hind knuckle of veal is featured often on the menus of hotels and restaurants as a roasted joint/portion for one, usually served with salads, known as Veal Haxe.

Other Well-known Veal Preparations

Cuts for grenadines (noisettes), the famous escalopes de veau and Wiener Schnitzel, medallions and veal olives (paupiettes) are illustrated in Figure 6.18.

LAMB AND MUTTON   *L'agneau et le mouton*

A **lamb** is a young animal before it is one year old. After one year incisor teeth have appeared and it is called a yearling. In the catering sense we differentiate between milk-fed lambs or baby-lambs, sometimes also called Easter lamb, all young animals that have not been weaned and put out to graze. The so-called Easter lamb was eaten during the Easter Festivities, often the first fresh meat after a long winter passed living on salted or smoked meat, if any.

Good quality lamb shows broad, well-shaped loins well covered with flesh and neat whiteness of fat, especially around the kidneys. Various regions in Europe pride themselves on so-called Field, Heather or Marsh lambs, especially when they have had rich feeding on pastures full of wild aromatic herbs, which some say they can taste in the flesh. The French Pauillac and British Welsh and Devon and others in different regions are especially highly regarded.

Mutton is considerably larger and darker and fatter than lamb, almost like beef meat in colour. Several breeds are used, of which the Dishley, Dorset and Southdown mutton or crossbreeds have a very good name for flavour. Many prefer mutton to lamb because of its characteristic stronger flavour, particularly in Irish Stew, blanquette, fricassee and the many lamb or mutton ragoûts. Others consider it to have too much of a wool-grease taste.

Mutton is sold in both carcass or side and the cuts are much the same as for lamb, although somewhat larger and in need of more fat trimming for comparable use to lamb. Leg and shoulder can be roasted, but are often pot-roasted or braised or even boiled, having given us the famous British dish, Boiled Mutton and Caper Sauce. Much chilled and frozen lamb is imported from Australia and New Zealand whole or in joints and of late various cuts such as legs, shoulders

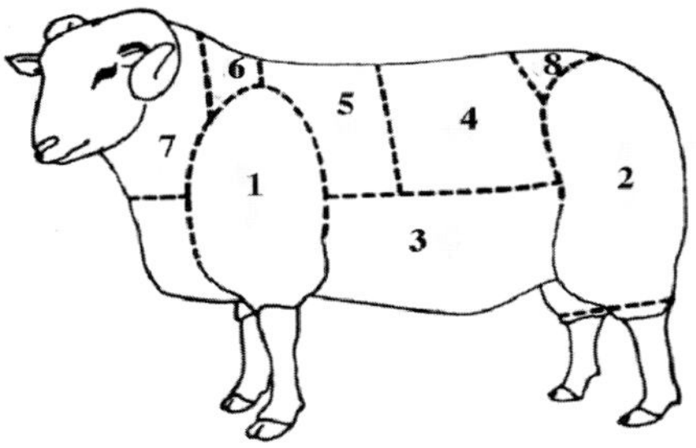

Cuts and joints	French term	Best use	Approx. weight lamb	Approx. weight mutton
1 Shoulder (2)	L'épaule	Roasting, stewing	3 kg	4 kg
2 Legs (2)	Le gigot	Roasting, braising	3.5 kg	5 kg
3 Breast (2)	La poitrine	Roasting, stewing	1.5 kg	2.5 kg
4 Saddle	La selle	Roasting, grilling, frying	3.5 kg	5 kg
5 Best end	Le carré	Roasting, grilling, frying	2 kg	3 kg
6 Middle neck	Les basses côtes	Stewing	2 kg	3 kg
7 Scrag end	Le cou	Stewing, broth	½ kg	1 kg
8 Chump chops*			1 kg	2 kg

Note: *Available only when dissected with short saddle, a long saddle incorporates the chump.
Bones should be chopped down and use for stocks and sauce. Fat rendered down can be used as second-class dripping

FIG. 6.19 *Joints, cuts and best uses of lamb, giving approximately 16 kg of lamb or 20–24 kg of mutton*

and loins have appeared on the market in vacuum packs, often ready prepared for the oven.

Quality of lamb can be judged by the following points:

- Compact and evenly fleshed
- Firm lean meat
- A pleasing dull red colour, fine texture and grain
- Even distribution of white fat
- Bones in a young animal should be pink and porous
- Bones in older animals become hard, white and splinter.

The usual wholesale cuts of lamb are as follows:

Haunches	Pair of legs with chumps attached
Saddle or chine	Pair of loins
Chines and ends	Chines with pair of best ends
Hinds and ends	Pair of legs, loins and best ends
Hinds	Pair of legs and loins
Fores	Pair of forequarters and best ends
Short fores	Forequarters
Jacket	Carcass legs and shoulders
Trunk	Carcass, legs

DISSECTION

(1) (a) Remove the shoulder by incising at a point where the shoulder bulges at the neck and along the back to a point between the 6th and 7th ribs, where the cartilage of the top of the blade bone can be easily cut through.
  (b) The shape of the shoulder can vary from round to almost square.
  (c) Continue the incision along the line of the rib bone to a point parallel with the elbow.
  (d) Then curve the incision some 4–6 cm (2–3 in.) below the elbow and join it to the starting point.
  (e) Now, starting at the neck, find the natural seam between the shoulder and neck muscle with the point of the boning knife and strip off the shoulder without damaging the underlying neck muscle.
(2) (a) Remove the legs, by first dividing the aitch bone, then by cutting through the cartilage in the case of lamb or chopping or sawing in the case of mutton.
  (b) Now cut a small portion of the flap or flank on to the leg and saw through the bone at a slight angle towards the legs.
  (c) The actual point will depend on the amount of chump one requires to leave on the saddle but a point varying from the base of the tail to some 5 cm above the base of the tail should be a fair guide.
(3) Remove the breasts, taking a line from 2 cm below the neck bone on the 1st rib to a point taking equal parts of fat and lean at the chump end (a fold in the flank will act as a good guide); join the two points in a straight line, saw across the ribs and finish by cutting along the line with a clean stroke of a sharp knife.

(4) Remove the saddle at the cartilage pad between the 12th and 13th vertebrae, cut through the cartilage and saw through the bone, keeping both joints rectangular.

(5) Remove the pair of best ends by cutting between the 6th and 7th dorsal vertebrae, cut through the cartilage and saw through the bone.

(6) The middle neck and scrag or neck are now separated, cutting between the cervical vertebrae and the 1st dorsal vertebrae. Keep the middle neck joint rectangular.

PREPARATION AND USE OF JOINTS AND CUTS

The main joints, cuts and their uses are discussed below and illustrated in Figures 6.20–6.25. Plate 6.3 shows various prepared lamb dishes.

SCRAG END　*Le cou* (see Figure 6.20*a*)

This cut is usually only used for stocks and stewing. Sometimes it is boned out for stew or mince.

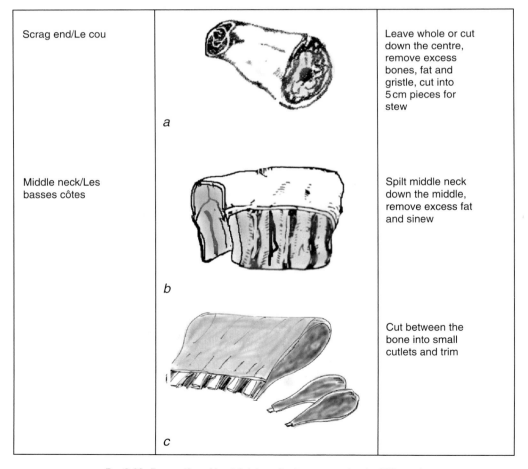

Scrag end/Le cou		Leave whole or cut down the centre, remove excess bones, fat and gristle, cut into 5 cm pieces for stew
Middle neck/Les basses côtes		Spilt middle neck down the middle, remove excess fat and sinew
		Cut between the bone into small cutlets and trim

Fig. **6.20** *Preparation of lamb joints and cuts: scrag end and middle neck*

MIDDLE NECK   **Les basses côtes** (see Figure 6.20*b,c*)

Ideally suited for stews, particularly the famous Navarin. If correctly butchered, this joint can give good uncovered second-class cutlets, called in French côte seconde or côte découverte, usually for braising.

BEST END   **Le carré** (see Figure 6.21*a–e*)

Best end can serve as a roast, cooked whole and served half per person. It also gives us two very attractive presentations, Guard of Honour and Crown of Lamb, which are useful for parties or buffets.

SADDLE   **La selle d'agneau** (Figure 6.21*f–j*)

Occasionally we cut a long saddle for small dinner parties and buffets. In most cases, however, the saddle is split into short saddle and best end.

LOIN   **La longe d'agneau** (see Figure 6.22*a–d*)

The loin is the split short saddle. It is used for roasting, can be cut into chops, boned for noisettes, or may be boned, rolled and stuffed.

LEG   **Le gigot d'agneau** (see Figure 6.22*e,f*)

A very popular roasting joint, the leg can also be boned and stuffed and of late it is boned and cut into slices or steaks and cooked à la minute.

BREAST   **Le poitrine d'agneau** (see Figure 6.23*a–c*)

May be used as a roast, boned, stuffed and rolled. Remove skin, excess fat and hard edge, bone and stuff. Roll and tie with string or sew (as for veal breast above). After removal of excess fat and hard edge it may be cut into pieces for stewing. It is ideal for dishes such as blanquette or Navarin. The bones are easily removed after cooking.

SHOULDER   **L'epaule d'agneau** (Figure 6.24)

The joint may be used for roasting on the bone or it may be boned, rolled and stuffed. Boned shoulder sliced and scallop-diced finds use in blanquette, fricassee, ragoût and curry. It is also ideal for mincing and farces.

Other Cuts and Presentations of Lamb

Figure 6.25 shows three other cuts of lamb that may be used: rosettes, which are a popular grill cut, haunch and baron of lamb, both of which are often cooked on a spit or nowadays in a baker's oven.

Best end/Le carré	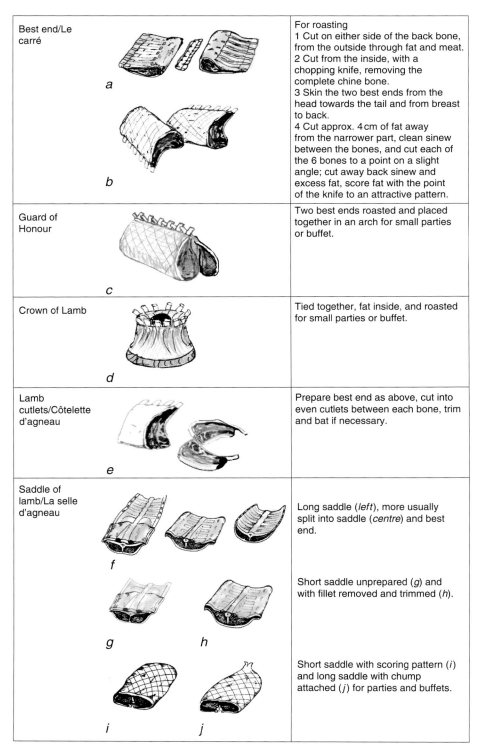	For roasting 1 Cut on either side of the back bone, from the outside through fat and meat. 2 Cut from the inside, with a chopping knife, removing the complete chine bone. 3 Skin the two best ends from the head towards the tail and from breast to back. 4 Cut approx. 4 cm of fat away from the narrower part, clean sinew between the bones, and cut each of the 6 bones to a point on a slight angle; cut away back sinew and excess fat, score fat with the point of the knife to an attractive pattern.
Guard of Honour		Two best ends roasted and placed together in an arch for small parties or buffet.
Crown of Lamb		Tied together, fat inside, and roasted for small parties or buffet.
Lamb cutlets/Côtelette d'agneau		Prepare best end as above, cut into even cutlets between each bone, trim and bat if necessary.
Saddle of lamb/La selle d'agneau		Long saddle (*left*), more usually split into saddle (*centre*) and best end. Short saddle unprepared (*g*) and with fillet removed and trimmed (*h*). Short saddle with scoring pattern (*i*) and long saddle with chump attached (*j*) for parties and buffets.

FIG. 6.21 *Preparation of lamb joints and cuts: the best end and saddle*

The loin/La longe d'agneau	To prepare for roasting, chop saddle neatly down the centre of the back bone, inserting a skewer in the marrow cavity helps. Shorten the flap by 2–4 cm, skin from flap to back and tail. Loosen back bone, but leave in place as a trivet, score the fat

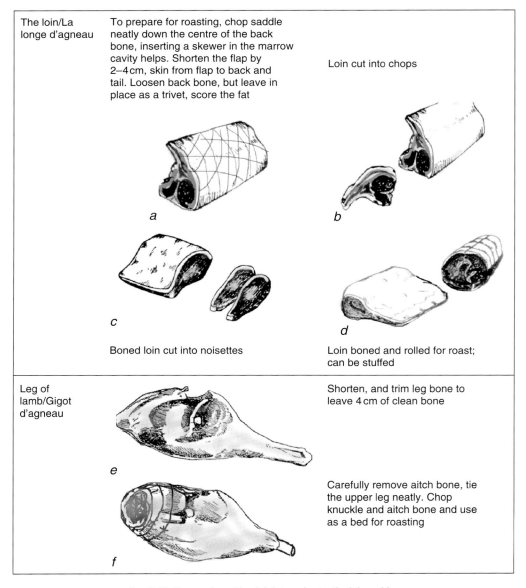

Loin cut into chops

a   b

c

Boned loin cut into noisettes

d

Loin boned and rolled for roast; can be stuffed

Leg of lamb/Gigot d'agneau

Shorten, and trim leg bone to leave 4 cm of clean bone

e

Carefully remove aitch bone, tie the upper leg neatly. Chop knuckle and aitch bone and use as a bed for roasting

f

FIG. 6.22 *Preparation of lamb joints and cuts: the loin and leg*

Breast of lamb/La poitrine d'agneau		Lamb breast, inner and outer view
	a	
	b	Stuffed lamb breast
	c	For stews, cut across into strips, 2 bones at a time, cut across strip to give a piece $4 \times 4\,$cm

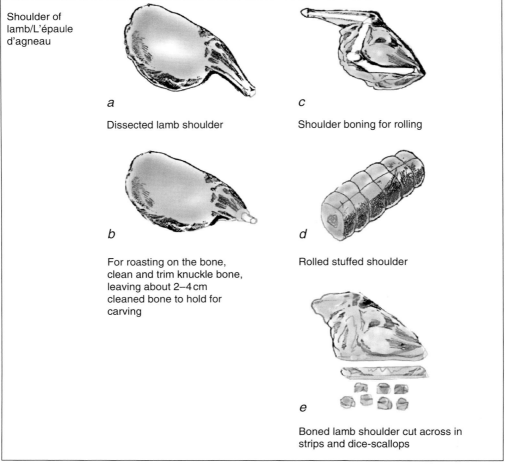

FIG. 6.23 *Preparation of lamb joints and cuts: the breast*

Shoulder of lamb/L'épaule d'agneau

a

Dissected lamb shoulder

c

Shoulder boning for rolling

b

For roasting on the bone, clean and trim knuckle bone, leaving about 2–4 cm cleaned bone to hold for carving

d

Rolled stuffed shoulder

e

Boned lamb shoulder cut across in strips and dice-scallops

FIG. 6.24 *Preparation of lamb joints and cuts: the shoulder*

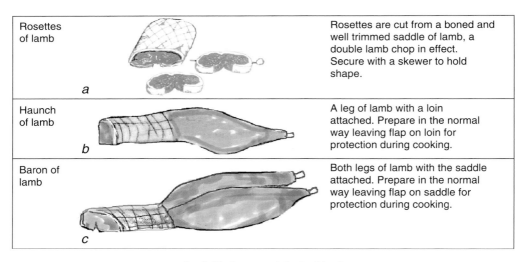

Rosettes of lamb		Rosettes are cut from a boned and well trimmed saddle of lamb, a double lamb chop in effect. Secure with a skewer to hold shape.
a		
Haunch of lamb		A leg of lamb with a loin attached. Prepare in the normal way leaving flap on loin for protection during cooking.
b		
Baron of lamb		Both legs of lamb with the saddle attached. Prepare in the normal way leaving flap on saddle for protection during cooking.
c		

Fɪɢ. 6.25 *Some special cuts of lamb*

PORK *Le porc*

The rearing of pigs has changed more than any other domestic animal. The big pig of 200–250 kg has gone and the average weight today is about 55–60 kg per side. The change to a very much smaller, narrower and leaner animal reflects the modern healthy attitude.

Many, however, consider this a retrograde step, saying that the pork has much less flavour, and gets much drier in the cooking process, especially so for the pan-fried cuts of cutlets, chops and escalopes. The term 'pork' is only used after slaughter. Most pork sides come from castrated animals called figs or stags according to sex.

Younger animals are sold as porker, piglet or suckling pig; the latter should be called so only if fed on milk alone. Pork is either eaten fresh or in cured form, as it lends itself very well to curing, brining and smoking.

Many breeds are available, such as Yorkshire (giving us the famous Yorkshire Ham), Ulster, Tamworth, Wessex, Berkshire, Cumberland etc.

The basic cuts and joints from a side of pork, with their approximate average weights and a summary of their best uses is given in Figure 6.26.

The common ordering wholesale cuts of pork are:

Loin, long loin	Loin including neck end
Short loin	Loin
Hog meat	Loin, rind, some back fat
Hand and belly	Hand-spring, belly
Fore-end	Neck and hand-spring
Hand	Hand-spring
Jacket	Side and leg (part of belly with leg)
Pig X	Whole carcass with head
Neck end	Spare rib and blade bone
Middles	Short loin and belly
Side	Side without head

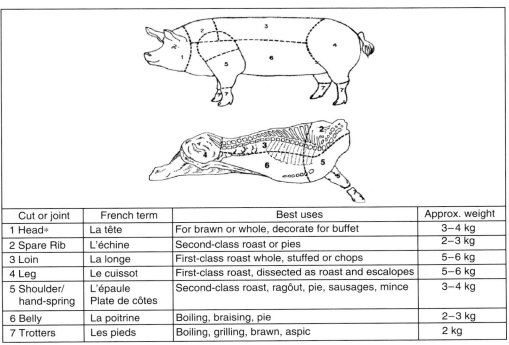

Cut or joint	French term	Best uses	Approx. weight
1 Head*	La tête	For brawn or whole, decorate for buffet	3–4 kg
2 Spare Rib	L'échine	Second-class roast or pies	2–3 kg
3 Loin	La longe	First-class roast whole, stuffed or chops	5–6 kg
4 Leg	Le cuissot	First-class roast, dissected as roast and escalopes	5–6 kg
5 Shoulder/ hand-spring	L'épaule Plate de côtes	Second-class roast, ragôut, pie, sausages, mince	3–4 kg
6 Belly	La poitrine	Boiling, braising, pie	2–3 kg
7 Trotters	Les pieds	Boiling, grilling, brawn, aspic	2 kg

Note: *From whole carcass only

FIG. **6.26** *Joints, cuts and best uses of a side of pork, weighing approximately 50–60 kg*

DISSECTION

(1) Lay the side on the cutting block and break the trotter by cutting across the back and pressing the trotter forward sharply.

(2) Cut away the head as close to the ears as possible.

(3) Remove the leg by marking across the joint 1 cm below the round part of the aitch bone, to a point slightly diagonally some 4 cm above the base of the tail. Saw through the bone and follow with a clean cut with the knife. This gives a square cut leg that could leave the tail on the leg.

(4) Separate the hand-spring and belly from the long loin by finding the joint between the blade bone and humerus and, from this point, mark down over the ribs and cut through the belly wall down to the chump end. Saw through the ribs and finish with a sharp knife. Avoid sawing through the meat. The line can be varied according to the amount of chump end required on the loin.

(5) Only the belly and long loin remain now from the carcass. The two are split in a straight line proportion of about ⅓ to ⅔.

PREPARATION AND USE OF JOINTS AND CUTS

The main joints, cuts and their uses are discussed below and illustrated in Figures 6.27–6.31. Plate 6.4*a–e* shows various prepared pork dishes.

Note: All lean trimmings are ideal for pies or mincing, pork fat rendered down makes good dripping, all bones are ideal for brown stocks.

TROTTERS   *Les pieds* (see Figure 6.27)

After thorough cleaning, the pig trotters are boiled, usually in a seasoned blanc to gain a good white colour. Cooled in the stock in which they were boiled, pig trotters can be used for several tasty dishes. For grilling, the trotters are boiled as above and cooled, the gelatinous meat of the trotters is removed from the bones in one piece. Seasoned, brushed with mustard and oil, they are then grilled to a golden brown. For pig's trotters salad, cook in a blanc and cool, remove the meat from the trotters, cut into fine julienne, mix with onions and herbs and flavour with a vinaigrette.

Because of their gelatinous texture and binding, pig trotters can be put to various uses in the making of brawns. For this purpose the trotters should be boiled, not in a blanc but in clear salted water with some seasoning and mirepoix to get a clear stock (see Chapter 8).

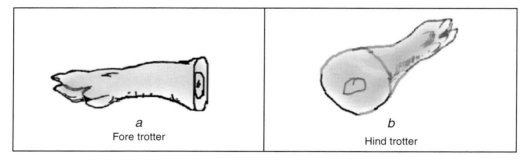

a
Fore trotter

b
Hind trotter

FIG. 6.27 *The trotters*

PIG'S HEAD   *La tête*

From a side, bone out the head for the making of brawn or second-class mince. For the preparation of a whole boar's head for the buffet, see later in the chapter.

LEG   *Le cuissot* (see Figure 6.28a,b)

To prepare for roasting, remove aitch bone and tail if any, clear the knuckle bone and give a good scoring pattern through the crackling. It can also be boned (see below).

SHOULDER/HAND-SPRING   *L'epaule/plate de côtes* (see Figure 6.28c,d)

After boning, the shoulder can be trimmed and rolled to make a second-class roast. With the crackling removed it makes good meat for stews, e.g. Hungarian goulash, pies, brawns or minced for sausages. (For more detail of preparation see boning of veal and lamb shoulder above.)

BELLY AND LONG LOIN   *La poitrine et la longe* (see Figure 6.29)

The belly (Figure 6.29a–c) is usually split and the best and most popular use for belly of pork is in the making of pork sausages, as well as other German or French

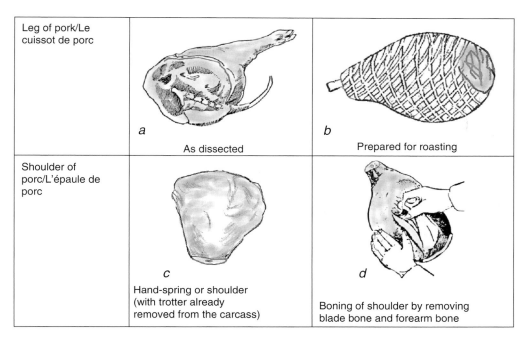

Leg of pork/Le cuissot de porc	a — As dissected	b — Prepared for roasting
Shoulder of porc/L'épaule de porc	c — Hand-spring or shoulder (with trotter already removed from the carcass)	d — Boning of shoulder by removing blade bone and forearm bone

FIG. 6.28 *Preparation of pork joints and cuts: the leg and shoulder*

sausages. Boned and freed of its rind, it is also useful for the making of forcemeats, not necessarily of pork only, but of other meats where some fat pork is required. As a joint, it really has only one use, i.e. to be brined and boiled and served with various vegetables, or pease puddings, and even Sauerkraut, which should always be cooked with a piece of fat, brined pork or bacon.

The long loin is split as shown in Figure 6.29*d*. The long loin gives the loin, cutlet piece and spare ribs. The actual loin is an excellent piece for roasting. It should be carefully boned but the bones are left in place. After removing the back sinew and scoring the rind, the loin has only to be tied in two or three places to be ready for roasting.

Cuts from a Boned Leg of Pork

A leg of pork is boned in very much the same way as a leg of veal, the cuts being similar. Because of being fatter, the dividing seams on the leg of pork are not so easily found and the boning should be carried out with care. The instructions given for boning a leg of veal (see Figure 6.16) can otherwise be followed for pork. The joints can, as for veal, be roasted whole or cut into pork escalopes or steaks (see Figure 6.30). The three best cuts from the dissected leg of pork are the cushion, giving escalopes, the thick flank, giving escalopes and steaks, and the under-cushion, which can be used for roasting, braising and paupiettes.

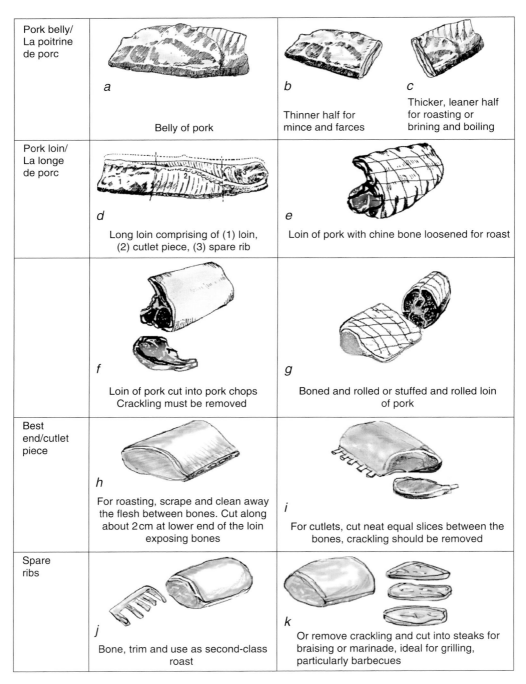

Pork belly/ La poitrine de porc	*a* Belly of pork	*b* Thinner half for mince and farces	*c* Thicker, leaner half for roasting or brining and boiling
Pork loin/ La longe de porc	*d* Long loin comprising of (1) loin, (2) cutlet piece, (3) spare rib	*e* Loin of pork with chine bone loosened for roast	
	f Loin of pork cut into pork chops Crackling must be removed	*g* Boned and rolled or stuffed and rolled loin of pork	
Best end/cutlet piece	*h* For roasting, scrape and clean away the flesh between bones. Cut along about 2cm at lower end of the loin exposing bones	*i* For cutlets, cut neat equal slices between the bones, crackling should be removed	
Spare ribs	*j* Bone, trim and use as second-class roast	*k* Or remove crackling and cut into steaks for braising or marinade, ideal for grilling, particularly barbecues	

FIG. 6.29 *Preparation of pork joints and cuts: belly and long loin*

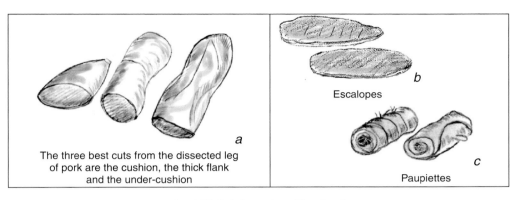

The three best cuts from the dissected leg of pork are the cushion, the thick flank and the under-cushion

a

Escalopes

b

Paupiettes

c

FIG. 6.30 *Cuts from a boned leg of pork*

If the leg of pork is required for ham, it must of course be brined. For this purpose one usually removes the aitch bone and trotter and immerses the leg in brine (see section on 'Brines' or purchase ready brine).

THE PORK FILLET — *Le filet de porc* (see Figure 6.31)

The pork fillet (with kidney) runs along the long loin. Carefully loosen from the loin, clear fillet of string, fat and silver skin (see beef fillet preparation, Figure 6.5). The lean and tender pork fillet can be roasted whole for two persons or more likely cut into medallions to be shallow fried, two per portion.

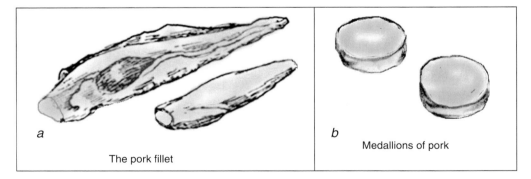

a

The pork fillet

b

Medallions of pork

FIG. 6.31 *Preparation of pork fillet*

PREPARATION OF A BOAR'S HEAD FOR BUFFET DISPLAY

The stages in preparation are described in Figure 6.32. Allow three days. For the preparation and decoration, see Chapter 8 on Buffets.

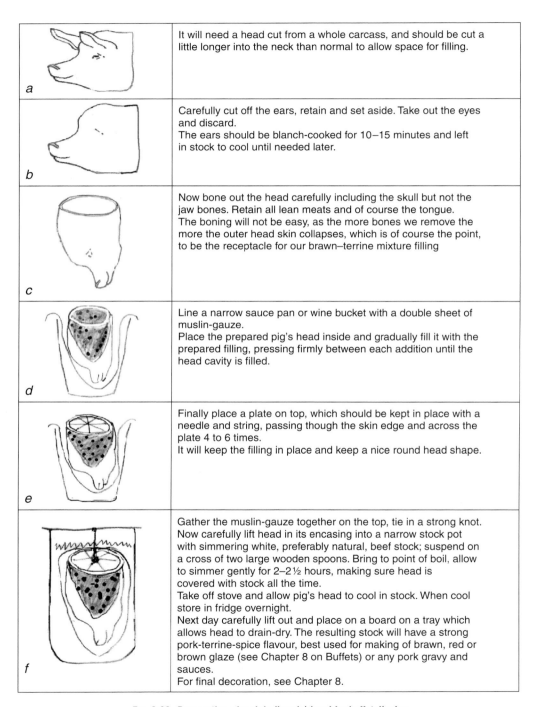

a	It will need a head cut from a whole carcass, and should be cut a little longer into the neck than normal to allow space for filling.
b	Carefully cut off the ears, retain and set aside. Take out the eyes and discard. The ears should be blanch-cooked for 10–15 minutes and left in stock to cool until needed later.
c	Now bone out the head carefully including the skull but not the jaw bones. Retain all lean meats and of course the tongue. The boning will not be easy, as the more bones we remove the more the outer head skin collapses, which is of course the point, to be the receptacle for our brawn–terrine mixture filling
d	Line a narrow sauce pan or wine bucket with a double sheet of muslin-gauze. Place the prepared pig's head inside and gradually fill it with the prepared filling, pressing firmly between each addition until the head cavity is filled.
e	Finally place a plate on top, which should be kept in place with a needle and string, passing though the skin edge and across the plate 4 to 6 times. It will keep the filling in place and keep a nice round head shape.
f	Gather the muslin-gauze together on the top, tie in a strong knot. Now carefully lift head in its encasing into a narrow stock pot with simmering white, preferably natural, beef stock; suspend on a cross of two large wooden spoons. Bring to point of boil, allow to simmer gently for 2–2½ hours, making sure head is covered with stock all the time. Take off stove and allow pig's head to cool in stock. When cool store in fridge overnight. Next day carefully lift out and place on a board on a tray which allows head to drain-dry. The resulting stock will have a strong pork-terrine-spice flavour, best used for making of brawn, red or brown glaze (see Chapter 8 on Buffets) or any pork gravy and sauces. For final decoration, see Chapter 8.

FIG. 6.32 *Preparation of a pig's (boar's) head for buffet display*

BACON, GAMMON AND HAMS

The old French word bacon has passed into the English language like so many others. It meant pork generally and was used especially when talking about the pig's salted back-fat, which was used extensively for all sorts of larding and barding as well as for the making and flavorings of soups and certain sauces.

In Britain, bacon means a side of pork partly boned, salted and cured or cured and smoked. If only salted or cured it is called 'green bacon', which is used in much the same way as the smoked type. Bacon has a very high protein value, and one can make many tasty dishes from it by frying, grilling or boiling. The main cuts of bacon are illustrated in Figure 6.33.

Side		Named cut	Approximate weight	Use
	1	Hock of gammon	2 kg	Boiling
	2	Middle of gammon	3 kg	Grilling and frying
	3	Corner of gammon	2 kg	Grilling and frying
	4	Back gammon	4 kg	Grilling and frying
	5	Thick end of back	3 kg	Grilling and boiling
	6	Collar	4 kg	Boiling
	7	Fore hock	4 kg	Boiling shoulder ham
	8	Best streaky	4 kg	Grilling and frying
	9	Thin streaky	2 kg	Grilling and frying
	10	Flank	1 kg	Boiling and frying
	A side of bacon from modern pigs will weigh approximately 30 kg. A gammon cut from the side will weigh between 5 and 7 kg.			

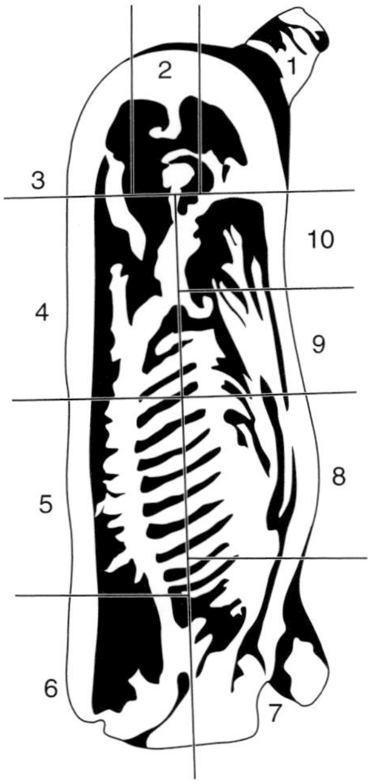

Fig. 6.33 *Joints and cuts of a side of bacon*

PREPARATION OF JOINTS AND CUTS FROM A SIDE OF BACON

After removing the gammon from the side of bacon, the whole side is split lengthwise in half. This is usually done by marking a line of the long cut to be made, with the point of a sharp knife. Follow this line with the knife to cut a straight line right through the side as far as the rib bones will allow. A flat saw is now used to saw through the bones, continuing with a clean cut by a knife. At all times, one should avoid sawing through the actual meat. Once the side of bacon is split lengthwise, the two narrow parts, 'back' and 'streaky', are jointed as indicated in Figure 6.33.

The best uses for the cuts and joints are as follows:

Hock of gammon: Really the knuckle of bacon, good use can be made of it in the making of sauces, soups, stews etc.

Middle of gammon: Ideal joint for gammon steaks. For this purpose, the thigh bone should be carefully removed, before cutting into slices.

Corner gammon: Slightly trimmed of excess fat, the corner cut is most suitable for the cutting of gammon steaks.

Back bacon: The joint with the leanest back bacon: after removing the part of the small chine bone and slicing it is ideal for grilling (breakfast).

Thick end of bacon: This joint is still good back bacon although slightly more fatty and broad. When sliced, it can also be used for braising in one piece.

Collar: Boned and rolled, it is usually boiled or braised. Boiled, it is (as ham) often used for the making of sandwiches (shoulder ham).

Fore hock: Boned and rolled, it can be used for boiling or braising. The fore knuckle is removed for this purpose and used as for collar above.

Best streaky: After boning this joint with a piece of string, or wire, and removing the bacon rind, it is cut into thin slices for grilling, or used as a supplement to back bacon. Many people prefer streaky bacon to the leaner back because of its good flavour. Best streaky can also be used for lardons, cromesquis, pâtés and potted preparations.

Thin streaky: Although much narrower than the best streaky, its use is much the same.

Flank: Flabby and quite fat, the flank of bacon finds its best use in pies, pâtés and other potted preparations where fat pork or bacon is required.

Gammon: A gammon is always the hind leg of a side of bacon, whether it is green or smoked. Gammons are suitable for boiling, braising and baking and may be served hot or cold (see Plate 6.4*f*–*l*). The best-known gammon types are Danish (green and smoked), Wiltshire (green and smoked) as well as many other local gammons.

GAMMON

Boiling

Soak the gammon in cold water for at least 24 hours, and then scrub with a hard brush, especially around the aitch bone and knuckle. For boiling, place the gammon into a jambonnière or similar type of pan. Cover with fresh cold water and bring to the boil. Skim and draw to the side of the stove. Allow the gammon to gently simmer for 40–50 minutes per kilogram. Leave it to cool in its own cooking liquor.

Cold Gammon Service

Prepare and cook the gammon as above. When cooked, remove all rind and excess fat and clean knuckle bone to a handle for carving. Brush the gammon with made-up English mustard and sprinkle with freshly fried breadcrumbs. Surround with a ham-frill and the gammon is ready for carving.

A second method may be employed, which is more commonly used on the Continent: brush the prepared gammon, as above, with English or French mustard, then sprinkle with caster or brown sugar and place in a hot oven to achieve a good even brown glaze. Allow the gammon to cool, surround with ham-frill and the gammon is ready for carving.

Gammon Chaud Froid

See Chapter 8 on Buffets and Figure 8.17.

Braising

For braising, the gammon is prepared as for boiling. The cooking time should be cut down to only about 30 minutes per kilogram of gammon. Slightly cool, then remove rind and excess fat. Place the gammon whole, or boned and cut into neat joints, on a bed of root vegetables in a jambonnière and neatly stud with a pattern of cloves. Now cover the gammon with demi-glace, or espagnole, plus some of its cooking liquor (about half way) and place in the oven to braise until cooked.

Baking

Prepare and boil the gammon, as above, for 15–30 minutes per kilogram of gammon. Remove rind and excess fat and leave gammon to cool on the outside. Now fold gammon into a large sheet of short, puff or bread paste-dough (the crust must meet underneath the gammon). Garnish with a design, using the pastry trimmings. Egg wash well, bake in a medium to hot oven to set the pastry for about 20 to 30 minutes, then turn the oven low and continue to bake for another 40–60 minutes. This type of gammon is invariably served on cold buffets but it can also be served hot with section of pastry-crust on the plate.

HAMS

Ham is always the hind leg of a side of pork and, as such, removed beforehand. The ham is in most cases cut rather long into the loin to give a banjo shape. Dry cured by the rubbing in of salt, or wet cured in brine, most hams are smoked and hung to dry. There are three basic types:

- Those which are usually cured in a brine, slightly smoked or dried and invariably cooked and served hot or cold, e.g. Jambon Glacé, Hamburger Schinken, Danish Hams
- Those dry or wet cured hams, always smoked (often very deep), hung to dry over a period of months or years, always served raw or slightly sauté, e.g. Jambon de Bayonne, Jambon Toulouse, Black Forest Ham
- Dry or wet cured hams but not smoked, hung to dry and to mature for a month and then cooked and served hot or cold, e.g. York Ham, Gothaer Schinken OR cured and dried and hung to mature for a long time, always served raw, e.g. Westphalia Ham, Parma Ham

There are also many other hams from many countries or regions in the world, with their own often unique brines.

AMERICAN HAMS *Jambon d'amérique*

American hams are invariably of the green type and cured in a brine (wet cure) with the addition of molasses that makes them rather sweet. Often very large, they are suitable for boiling, braising and baking and can be served hot or cold.

BRITISH HAMS *Jambon d'angleterre*

This type of ham is wet cured, with the addition of black treacle; this, together with smoking, gives the ham its very dark colour. British ham is slightly sweet in flavour, suitable to be served hot or cold.

The best known of the British hams is York Ham. It is of long cut and distinct banjo shape. Cured, it is hung up to dry in cool cellars for up to 3–4 months. During this period a green mould grows on the ham, especially around the aitch bone and knuckle. This mould growth adds to the flavour and is easily washed off before cooking. York ham is considered to be one of the finest hams and is well known and appreciated as a delicacy on the Continent and elsewhere.

CZECHOSLOVAKIAN HAMS *Jambon de bohème*

Of the Czechoslovakian hams, the Jambon de Prague is the most famous. Cured, smoked and dried, it is usually eaten raw but can be sautéd and served with egg dishes. Its appearance and flavour are similar to the raw German hams.

DANISH HAMS *Jambon danois*

With the Danish hams, the curing starts while the pigs are still alive. That is to say, they are fed on a special diet. Wet cured in a special brine, the Danish hams are hung to dry and are available smoked or green. Danish ham has a very fine meat grain and is most suitable for boiling, braising and baking. It can be served hot or cold.

FRENCH HAMS *Jambon français*

Jambon de Campagne is slightly sweeter in cure than most French hams, it is well smoked and invariably served raw. It can be sautéd and served with egg dishes and forms part of garnishes for several sauces and stews. It should not be boiled.

Jambon de Bayonne is a dry cured ham, smoked and hung to dry and mature. Usually served raw in very thin slices, it is not suitable for boiling but it may be used as garnishes with certain sauces and stews, or slightly sauté with egg dishes.

Jambon de Toulouse is cured and dried, at times even smoked; it is usually eaten raw. It can be used in cooking but, again, must not be boiled. Jambon Blanc, Jambon Demi-sel and Jambon de Paris are of the same type and usually green, but in certain cases they can be found slightly smoked, sweet in flavour. They are suitable for boiling and to be served cold but, more often than not, they are braised or baked and served hot. It is for this reason that these three hams are known as jambon glacé.

GERMAN HAMS *Jambon d'allemagne*

Six famous German hams are Gothaer Schinken, Hamburger Schinken, Stuttgarter Schinken, Mainzer Schinken, Westphalian Schinken and Schwarzwälder Schinken. All can be eaten raw but the first three are often boiled, braised or baked and served hot

a Crown of small melon	*b* Artichoke Vinaigrette	*c* Melon fan with fruit
d Asparagus salad with anchovy dressing	*e* Artichoke hearts with herb dressing	*f* Simple orange cocktail

PLATE 2.1 *Examples of fruit and vegetable starters*

a Simple egg salad	*b* Simple egg mayonnaise
c Stuffed eggs with anchovies	*d* Poached plovers eggs with cherry tomatoes

PLATE 2.2 *Examples of presentation of egg starters*

a Simple rollmops	**b** Oysters on ice	**c** Warm smoked trout
d Dressed crab	**e** Pyramid of crayfish	**f** Salmon Tartare
g Cornets of smoked salmon	**h** Salmon terrine-jelly	**i** Seafood salad (fruits de mer)
j Gravad Lax	**k** Prawns in jelly	**l** Prawn and asparagus mayonnaise

PLATE 2.3 *Examples of various fish starters*

a	b	c	d
Matches herrings on ice	Sweet and sour pickled herring	Tomato pickled herring	Mustard pickled herring

PLATE 2.4 *Examples of pickled herrings*

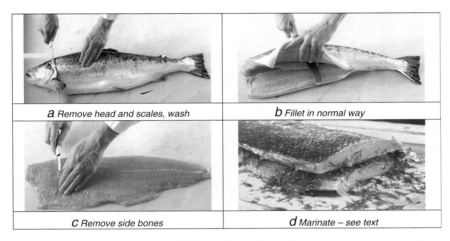

a Remove head and scales, wash	*b* Fillet in normal way
c Remove side bones	*d* Marinate – see text

PLATE 2.5 *Preparation of Gravad Lax*

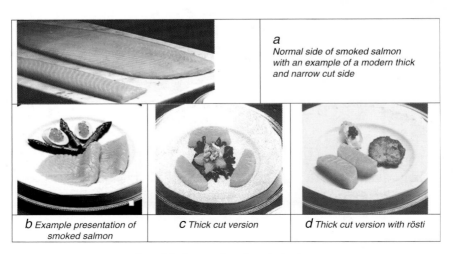

a
Normal side of smoked salmon with an example of a modern thick and narrow cut side

b Example presentation of smoked salmon	*c* Thick cut version	*d* Thick cut version with rösti

PLATE 2.6 *Presentation of smoked salmon*

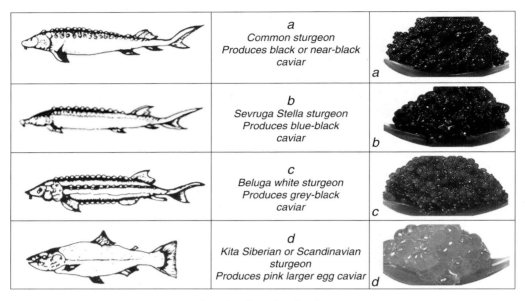

	a Common sturgeon Produces black or near-black caviar	
	b Sevruga Stella sturgeon Produces blue-black caviar	
	c Beluga white sturgeon Produces grey-black caviar	
	d Kita Siberian or Scandinavian sturgeon Produces pink larger egg caviar	

PLATE 2.7 *Examples of caviar*

a Modern mould galantines	b Chicken and vegetable galantine	c Veal and herb galantine
d Modern form pies	e Veal and ham pie	f Game pie

PLATE 2.8 *Pies and galantines*

(i) Smoked or dried sausage

a. Coarse salami
b. Cervelat
c. Italian salami
d. Danish salami
e. German salami

(ii) Scalded sausages

a. Garlic sausage
b. Beer sausage
c. Hunters sausage
d. Lyon sausage
e. Ham sausage

(iii) Boiled sausage

a. Coarse liver sausage
b. Calfs liver sausage
c. Fine liver sausages
d. Slices of coarse liver paté

(iv) Dried or smoked ham

a. Shoulder ham
b. Westphalian ham
c. Bayonne ham
d. Black Forest ham
e. Pork loin ham

PLATE 2.9 *Charcuterie*

a Coarse liver paté	**b** Fine liver paté	**c** Terrine of pork
d Italian salami	**e** Veal liver mousse	**f** Tomato with ham and sweet corn salad
g Parma ham with persimmon	**h** Veal brawn terrine	**i** Carpaccio
j Cornets of ham with Waldorf salad	**k** Vitello Tonnato	**l** Parma ham with asparagus
m Parma ham with avocado fan	**n** Ham tartlet with grain mustard dressing	**o** Viande sechée: dried beef presented as raw ham

PLATE 2.10 *Examples of meat-based hors d'oeuvres*

a Ham and gherkin
salad on tomatoes

b Chicken Mayonnaise with
endive and rocket

c Pepper and ham salad

d Sauté beef salad

e Ham and egg salad

f Mushroom and ham salad

PLATE 2.11 *Examples of meat starter salads*

a Onions	*b* Mushrooms	*c* Celery
d Onions	*e* Herring fillets	*f* Mushrooms

PLATE 2.12 *Examples of à la Grecque pickles (a–c) and Portugaise pickles (d–f)*

a Ham salad (rocket and endive), artichoke heart, potato and tomato salad	*b* Large prawns, stuffed tomato, tartlet of piped paté, salami, Parma ham roll, salad garnish	*c* Tartlet with caviar, stuffed egg, Parma ham roll, triangular paté, tomato salad

PLATE 2.13 *Examples of plated mixed hors d'oeuvres*

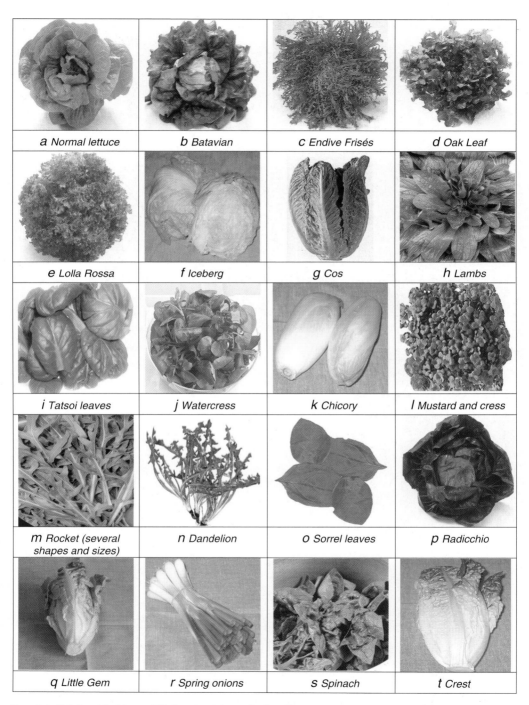

a Normal lettuce	*b* Batavian	*c* Endive Frisés	*d* Oak Leaf
e Lolla Rossa	*f* Iceberg	*g* Cos	*h* Lambs
i Tatsoi leaves	*j* Watercress	*k* Chicory	*l* Mustard and cress
m Rocket (several shapes and sizes)	*n* Dandelion	*o* Sorrel leaves	*p* Radicchio
q Little Gem	*r* Spring onions	*s* Spinach	*t* Crest

PLATE 3.1 *Salad and leaf types. This is only a token selection. There are many more and new types appearing on the market yearly*

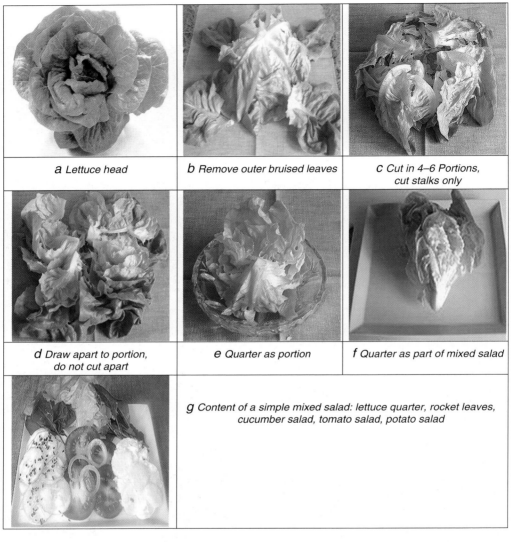

a Lettuce head	*b* Remove outer bruised leaves	*c* Cut in 4–6 Portions, cut stalks only
d Draw apart to portion, do not cut apart	*e* Quarter as portion	*f* Quarter as part of mixed salad

g Content of a simple mixed salad: lettuce quarter, rocket leaves, cucumber salad, tomato salad, potato salad

PLATE 3.2 *Preparation of salad heads*

a Single green salad	*b* Mixed green salad	*c* Mixed coloured leaf salad

PLATE 3.3 *Examples of different leaf salads with variations*

a Green leaf, walnuts and yoghurt dressing

b Lambs lettuce, egg quarters and mustard dressing

c Mixed leaves, croutons and Swiss dressing

d Mixed leaves with polenta

PLATE 3.4 *Examples of free additions to a green leaf salad*

a Tarragon Salad

b Mimosa Salad (French Dressing)

c Orange Salad (Vinaigrette)

d New Orleans Salad (strong garlic dressing)

PLATE 3.5 *Named green leaf salads: these must always have the same content but presentation is up to the individual*

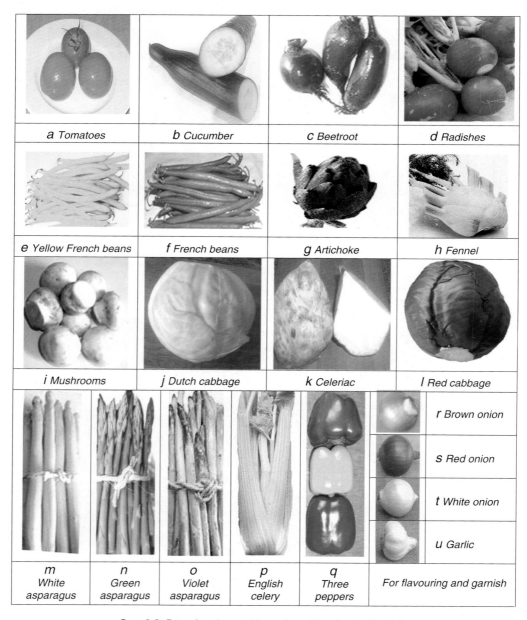

a Tomatoes	*b* Cucumber	*c* Beetroot	*d* Radishes
e Yellow French beans	*f* French beans	*g* Artichoke	*h* Fennel
i Mushrooms	*j* Dutch cabbage	*k* Celeriac	*l* Red cabbage

					r Brown onion
					s Red onion
					t White onion
					u Garlic
m White asparagus	*n* Green asparagus	*o* Violet asparagus	*p* English celery	*q* Three peppers	For flavouring and garnish

PLATE 3.6 *Examples of vegetables and garnishes for single salads*

a Tomato salad with basil	*b* Cucumber salad (Vinaigrette)	*c* White cabbage salad
d Russian cucumber salad with sour cream	*e* Sweet and sour cucumber salad (Scandinavian dressing)	*f* Cucumber salad (mint and yoghurt dressing)
g Radish salad (Vinaigrette)	*h* Sauerkraut with blue grapes	*i* Pomodorina tomato salad (French dressing)
j Coleslaw	*k* Yellow pepper salad (red onion Plaza dressing)	*l* Chicory salad (cream dressing with chives)

PLATE 3.7 *Examples of raw single salads*

a Diamond-cut celeriac salad (Vinaigrette)	b Sweet corn salad (cream and mustard dressing)	c Farfalle with cream and lime dressing
d Beetroot sweet and sour (Scandinavian dressing)	e French bean salad (Vinaigrette)	f Beetroot salad
g Plain potato salad	h Potato salad with Swiss dressing	i Potato salad with mayonnaise
j Haricot bean salad (Swiss dressing)	k Green lentil salad (mustard dressing)	l Red pepper salad (sour cream dressing)

PLATE 3.8 *Examples of cooked single salads*

| a Bagatelle Salad (French dressing) | b Cress Salad (French dressing) | c French Salad (French dressing) |

PLATE 3.9 *Examples of named mixed salads*

a Chicory, rocket, tomato, cucumber	b Lambs lettuce, rocket, haricot beans, tomato, asparagus tips	c Haricot beans, Oak Leaf lettuce, rocket, celeriac, tomato
d Several leaves, peppers, asparagus, cucumbers, radish, tomato, two dressings at front	e Bean sprouts, carrots, peaches, white radish, celery (all raw), dressing of guest's choice	f Lambs lettuce and julienne of beetroot, white radish and apple, herb dressing on side
g Mixed leaves, cucumber, mushrooms tomatoes, two mini rösti	h Lambs lettuce, tomato, mixed vegetable celery, beetroot	i Marinated batons of carrots, celeriac, mushrooms, broad bean, tomato and bouchée with dressing

PLATE 3.10 *Free combination mixed salads using best items in season*

a Avocado and prawns

b Waldorf Salad

c Genoa Salad

d Dutch Herring Salad

e Hungarian Salad

f Creole Salad

g Aida Salad

h Mascot Salad

i Beatrice Salad

j Carmen Salad

k Buffet bowl Waldorf Salad

l Prawn salad

PLATE 3.11 *Examples of compound salads. For recipes, see text. Presentation is always a matter of personal or establishment choice*

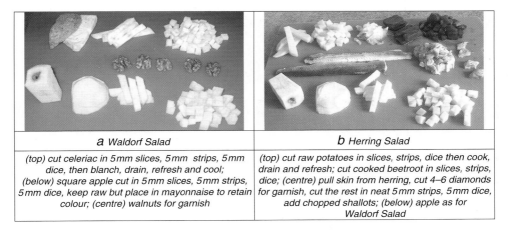

a Waldorf Salad	b Herring Salad
(top) cut celeriac in 5mm slices, 5mm strips, 5mm dice, then blanch, drain, refresh and cool; (below) square apple cut in 5mm slices, 5mm strips, 5mm dice, keep raw but place in mayonnaise to retain colour; (centre) walnuts for garnish	(top) cut raw potatoes in slices, strips, dice then cook, drain and refresh; cut cooked beetroot in slices, strips, dice; (centre) pull skin from herring, cut 4–6 diamonds for garnish, cut the rest in neat 5mm strips, 5mm dice, add chopped shallots; (below) apple as for Waldorf Salad

PLATE 3.12 *Neat cutting of compound salads: Waldorf Salad and Herring Salad (for recipes see text and for presentation see Plate 3.11)*

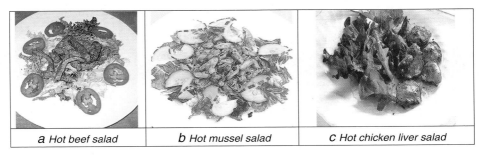

a Hot beef salad	b Hot mussel salad	c Hot chicken liver salad

PLATE 3.13 *Examples of modern hot salads*

a Seasoning: salt, pepper, mustard, vinegar	b Add egg yolks	c Mix well
d Gradually add oil a drop at a time first	e Emulsion achieved	f Final mayonnaise: correct seasoning, store

PLATE 3.14 *Stages of making mayonnaise*

| a Cocktail Sauce | b Sauce Rémoulade | c Sauce Tartare | d Sauce Verte |

PLATE 3.15 *Derivative sauces of mayonnaise*

| a Crush salt and garlic cloves | b Add egg yolks and pepper | c Mix in well | d With whisk gradually add olive oil |

PLATE 3.16 *Stages of making aioli (larger amounts may be made in a foodprocessor)*

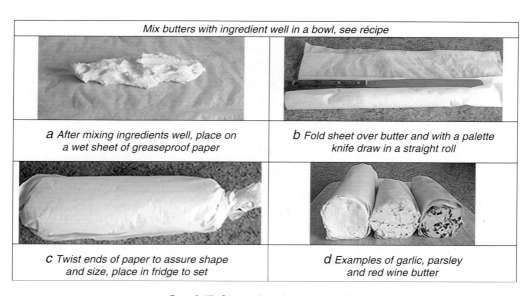

Mix butters with ingredient well in a bowl, see récipe

a After mixing ingredients well, place on a wet sheet of greaseproof paper

b Fold sheet over butter and with a palette knife draw in a straight roll

c Twist ends of paper to assure shape and size, place in fridge to set

d Examples of garlic, parsley and red wine butter

PLATE 3.17 *Stages of making savoury butter*

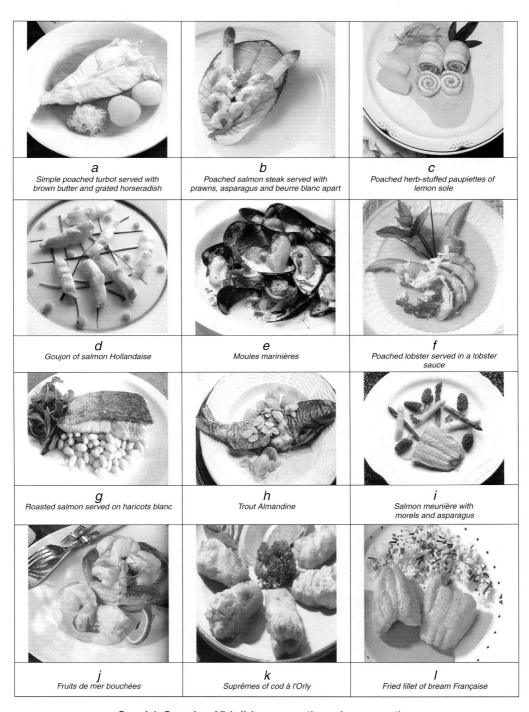

a *Simple poached turbot served with brown butter and grated horseradish*	**b** *Poached salmon steak served with prawns, asparagus and beurre blanc apart*	**c** *Poached herb-stuffed paupiettes of lemon sole*
d *Goujon of salmon Hollandaise*	**e** *Moules marinières*	**f** *Poached lobster served in a lobster sauce*
g *Roasted salmon served on haricots blanc*	**h** *Trout Almandine*	**i** *Salmon meunière with morels and asparagus*
j *Fruits de mer bouchées*	**k** *Suprêmes of cod à l'Orly*	**l** *Fried fillet of bream Française*

PLATE 4.1 *Examples of fish dishes representing various preparations*

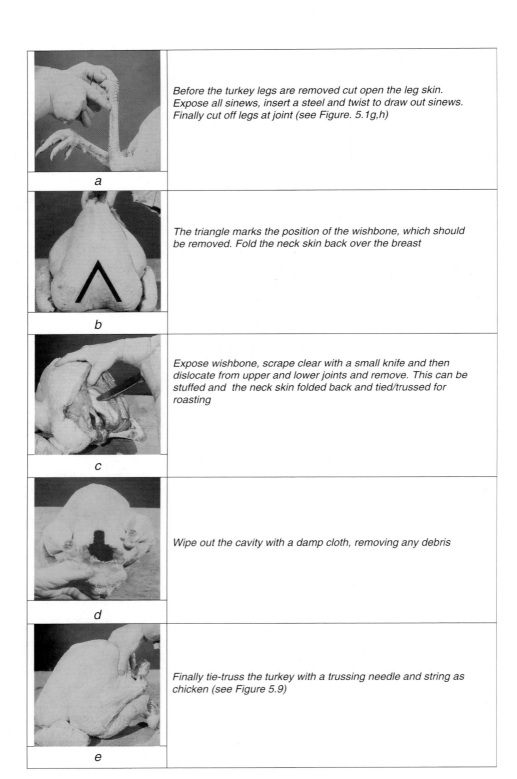

a

Before the turkey legs are removed cut open the leg skin.
Expose all sinews, insert a steel and twist to draw out sinews.
Finally cut off legs at joint (see Figure. 5.1g,h)

b

The triangle marks the position of the wishbone, which should
be removed. Fold the neck skin back over the breast

c

Expose wishbone, scrape clear with a small knife and then
dislocate from upper and lower joints and remove. This can be
stuffed and the neck skin folded back and tied/trussed for
roasting

d

Wipe out the cavity with a damp cloth, removing any debris

e

Finally tie-truss the turkey with a trussing needle and string as
chicken (see Figure 5.9)

PLATE 5.1 *Preparation of turkey for roasting whole*

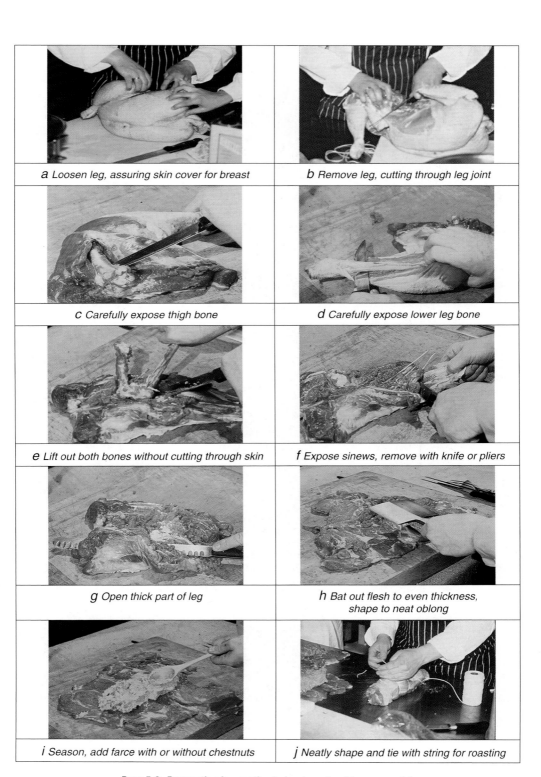

a Loosen leg, assuring skin cover for breast

b Remove leg, cutting through leg joint

c Carefully expose thigh bone

d Carefully expose lower leg bone

e Lift out both bones without cutting through skin

f Expose sinews, remove with knife or pliers

g Open thick part of leg

h Bat out flesh to even thickness, shape to neat oblong

i Season, add farce with or without chestnuts

j Neatly shape and tie with string for roasting

PLATE 5.2 *Preparation for roasting turkey breast and legs separately*

a Roast poussin with oyster mushrooms	*b* Poached poussin on Supreme parsley sauce	*c* Roast duck with braised red cabbage and chestnuts
d Roast breast of goose with baked apples and red currant	*e* Roast pigeon on purée of wild mushrooms	*f* Roast snipe on saffron rice
g Roast quail on green leaf and orange salad	*h* Roast stuffed saddle of venison with chanterelles and stewed plums	*i* Venison cutlet with red wine sauce
j Paupiettes of venison celeriac	*k* Braised leg of venison with Madeira sauce and dumpling	*l* Sauté venison leg steaks with apple quarters and cranberries

PLATE 5.3 *Example of poultry and game dishes*

a Beef olives	*b* Boeuf Bourguignonne	*c* Braised beef steak
d Beef goulash	*e* Grille côte de boeuf	*f* Filet Mignon
g Sauté of beef	*h* Filet Wellington	*i* Boiled beef French style
j Roast sirloin of beef	*k* Fillet steak with roasted vegetables	*l* Entrecôte Lyonnaise

PLATE 6.1 *Examples of beef butchery dishes*

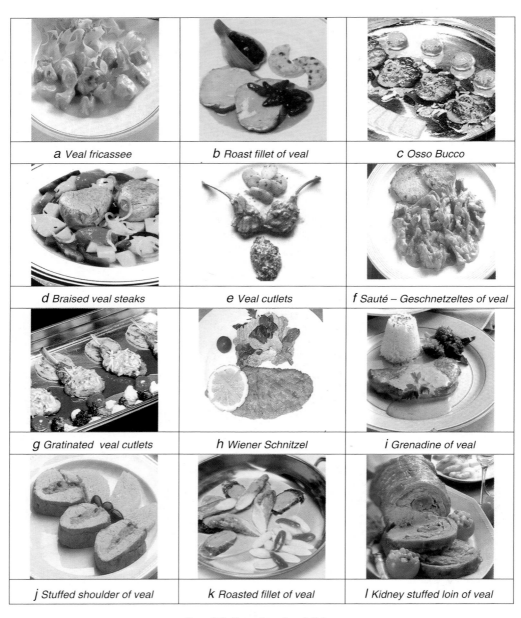

a Veal fricassee	*b* Roast fillet of veal	*c* Osso Bucco
d Braised veal steaks	*e* Veal cutlets	*f* Sauté – Geschnetzeltes of veal
g Gratinated veal cutlets	*h* Wiener Schnitzel	*i* Grenadine of veal
j Stuffed shoulder of veal	*k* Roasted fillet of veal	*l* Kidney stuffed loin of veal

PLATE 6.2 *Examples of veal dishes*

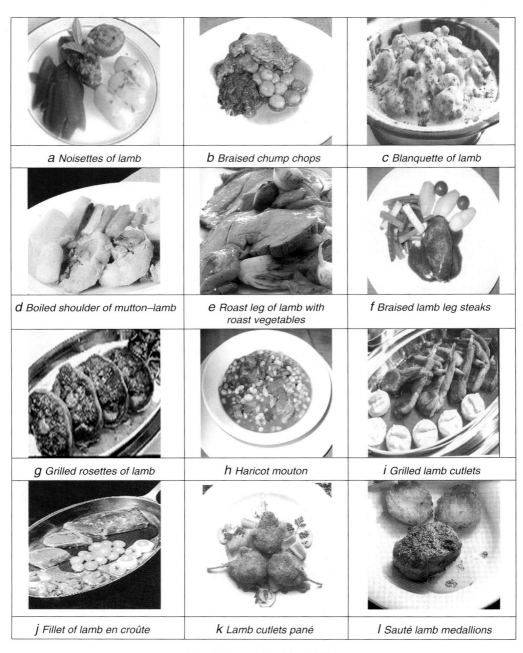

a Noisettes of lamb	*b* Braised chump chops	*c* Blanquette of lamb
d Boiled shoulder of mutton–lamb	*e* Roast leg of lamb with roast vegetables	*f* Braised lamb leg steaks
g Grilled rosettes of lamb	*h* Haricot mouton	*i* Grilled lamb cutlets
j Fillet of lamb en croûte	*k* Lamb cutlets pané	*l* Sauté lamb medallions

PLATE 6.3 *Examples of lamb dishes*

a Pork goulash	*b* Braised pork chops with mushrooms	*c* Roasted ribs of pork
d Boned loin of pork en croûte	*e* Escalope de porc nature	*f* Boiled Kassler cutlets
g Boiled ham with sauerkraut	*h* Braised shoulder of ham	*i* Boiled ham with parsley sauce
j Braised ham in Madeira sauce	*k* Closed ham quiche	*l* Boiled ham with mustard sauce

PLATE 6.4 *Examples of pork and gammon dishes*

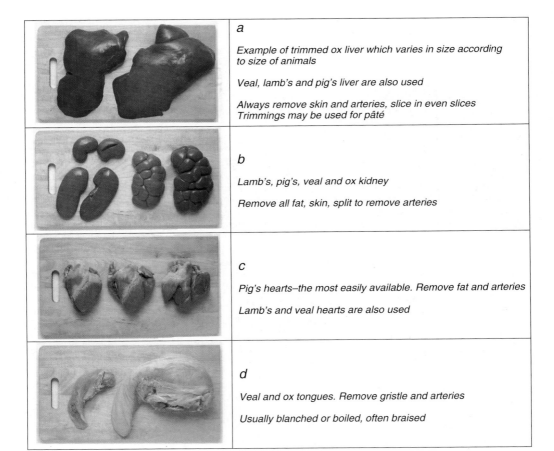

	a Example of trimmed ox liver which varies in size according to size of animals Veal, lamb's and pig's liver are also used Always remove skin and arteries, slice in even slices Trimmings may be used for pâté
	b Lamb's, pig's, veal and ox kidney Remove all fat, skin, split to remove arteries
	c Pig's hearts–the most easily available. Remove fat and arteries Lamb's and veal hearts are also used
	d Veal and ox tongues. Remove gristle and arteries Usually blanched or boiled, often braised

PLATE 6.5 *Examples of Offal*

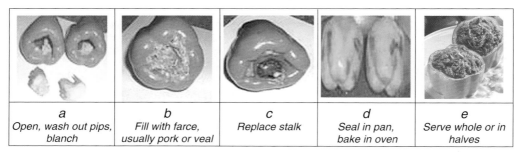

a	b	c	d	e
Open, wash out pips, blanch	Fill with farce, usually pork or veal	Replace stalk	Seal in pan, bake in oven	Serve whole or in halves

PLATE 7.1 *Preparation of stuffed peppers*

a Hamburger Maryland	*b* Lamb meatballs with caper sauce	*c* Bitoks Provençale
d Veal cutlets tomato sauce	*e* Game medallions in red wine sauce	*f* Lamb medallions on creamed mushrooms
g Fish quenelles in white wine sauce	*h* Quenelles of pike in lobster sauce	*i* Quenelles of veal in Supreme sauce served on glass plate

PLATE 7.2 *Examples of modern simple and finer forcemeat-based dishes*

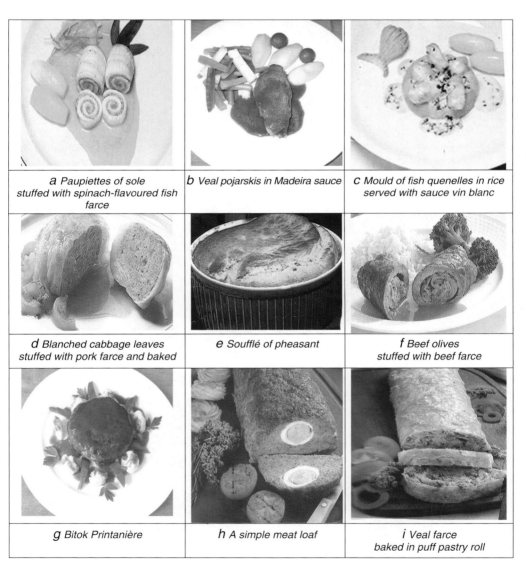

a Paupiettes of sole stuffed with spinach-flavoured fish farce	*b* Veal pojarskis in Madeira sauce	*c* Mould of fish quenelles in rice served with sauce vin blanc
d Blanched cabbage leaves stuffed with pork farce and baked	*e* Soufflé of pheasant	*f* Beef olives stuffed with beef farce
g Bitok Printanière	*h* A simple meat loaf	*i* Veal farce baked in puff pastry roll

PLATE 7.3 *Examples of farce dishes or use of farce as a stuffing*

a
Carved rib of beef with glazed vegetables

b
Fillet Wellington

c
Parma ham to be carved at buffet table

d
Poached slices of salmon

e
Ham quiche

f
Rib of beef to be carved at table

PLATE **8.1** *Some examples of Modern Buffet pieces*

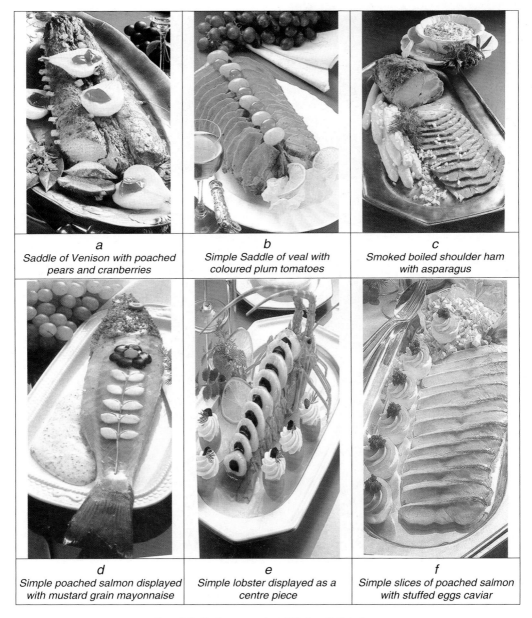

a *Saddle of Venison with poached pears and cranberries*	*b* *Simple Saddle of veal with coloured plum tomatoes*	*c* *Smoked boiled shoulder ham with asparagus*
d *Simple poached salmon displayed with mustard grain mayonnaise*	*e* *Simple lobster displayed as a centre piece*	*f* *Simple slices of poached salmon with stuffed eggs caviar*

PLATE 8.2 *Further examples of Modern Buffet pieces*

a *Decorated fish mousse garnished with asparagus bundles and crayfish*	*b* *Poached farce stuffed with salmon steaks; mayonnaise-filled bouchées, cups of prawns*

c *Poached farce-stuffed salmon steaks set around head and tail bouchées filled with artichoke salad barquettes with green asparagus tips*	*d* *Boned stuffed salmon cooked en croute (cooled overnight cut with very sharp knife), set on aspic garnished with cucumber puree, set in cucumber-shell, heart-shaped croutons*
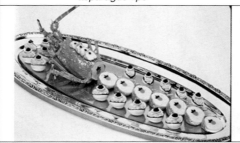	
e *Lobster Belleview: lobster body sliced, chaud froid glazed and placed on body surrounded by stuffed eggs*	*d* *Boned saddle of veal stuffed with veal farce and spinach leaves, roasted, cooled carved and glazed, garnished with fritters and mange tout salad*

PLATE 8.3 *Examples of Classical Buffet pieces*

PLATE 8.4 *The Scandinavian Smörgåsbord: a very commercial example from a large Stockholm hotel serving 100–150 luncheons per day. The barrel in the middle contains two to four schnapps of different regional flavours, one or two of which are included in the price. The other barrel shape is a pile of crisp bread*

PLATE 9.1 *Examples of white cheeses*

a Cottage cheese

b Quark plain and herbs

c Philadelphia block or tub

d Fresh Mozzarella

e Feta

f Fresh Ricotta

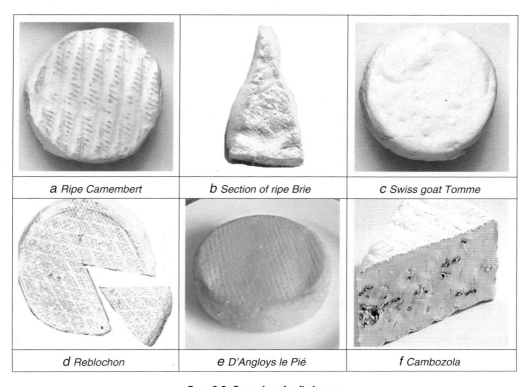

PLATE 9.2 *Examples of soft cheeses*

a Ripe Camembert

b Section of ripe Brie

c Swiss goat Tomme

d Reblochon

e D'Angloys le Pié

f Cambozola

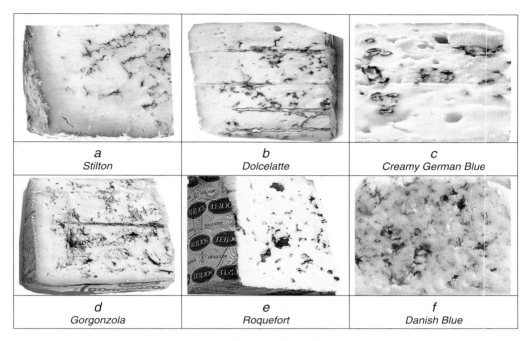

| a
Stilton | b
Dolcelatte | c
Creamy German Blue |
| d
Gorgonzola | e
Roquefort | f
Danish Blue |

PLATE 9.3 *Examples of blue cheeses*

| a
Bel Paese | b
Red rind Fondue | c
Tallegio |
| d
Smoked herb cheese | e
White veined Brie | f
Tilsiter |

PLATE 9.4 *Examples of fondue cheeses*

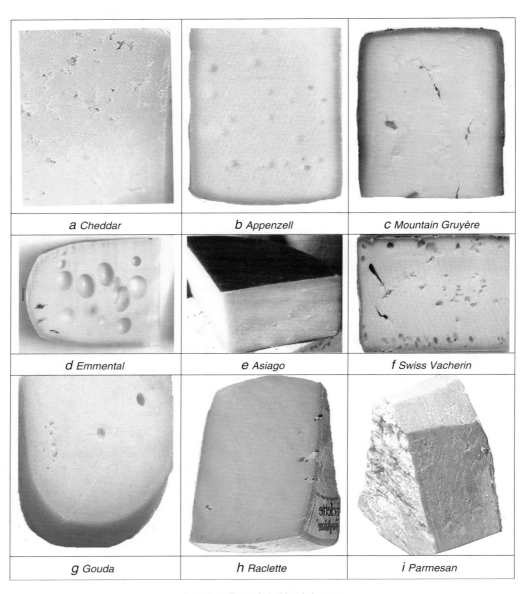

a Cheddar	*b* Appenzell	*c* Mountain Gruyère
d Emmental	*e* Asiago	*f* Swiss Vacherin
g Gouda	*h* Raclette	*i* Parmesan

PLATE 9.5 *Examples of hard cheeses*

or cold. The last three are always eaten raw. Of delicate sweet cure and deep smoked, with selected woods, they are cut into paper-thin slices and eaten as an hors d'oeuvre. The Germans will eat these hams at any time of day together with rye bread and a glass of lager. Lightly fried, they are delicious with all kinds of egg dishes.

HUNGARIAN HAMS *Jambon de hongrie*

Hungarian hams, like the German, are also served raw and are also similar in appearance and flavour. Some Hungarian hams are red or pink in colour; this is because they are rubbed with paprika before and after smoking, then hung to dry for several months. Here the hams from Gynlai and Esterhazy are the best known.

ITALIAN HAMS *Jambon d'italie*

There are a great number of Italian hams, of which Parma Ham (Jambon de Parme) is the most famous of all. The Parma ham is cured and hung to dry for several months and served, invariably, raw. Lightly fried in butter, it is also served with a number of egg and pasta dishes. In Britain it can be bought in round flat tins, ready sliced, with a sheet of greaseproof paper between each slice to allow an easy service. Other Italian hams are suited for boiling, braising and baking and can be served hot or cold.

SPANISH HAMS *Jambon d'espagne*

The Spanish hams are usually mild in cure, with a delicate flavour and invariably smoked and dried. All Spanish hams are suitable for boiling, braising and baking and may be served hot or cold. The best known is the Jambon de Asturies.

Note: The description of curing and smoking of these different hams is necessarily very vague, since the methods used, employing selected woods and special

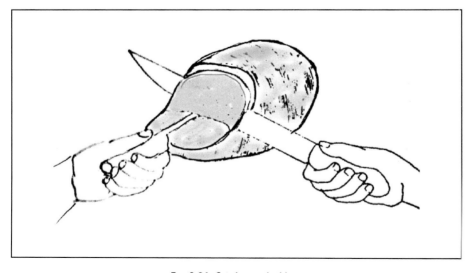

Fɪɢ. **6.34** *Carving cooked ham*

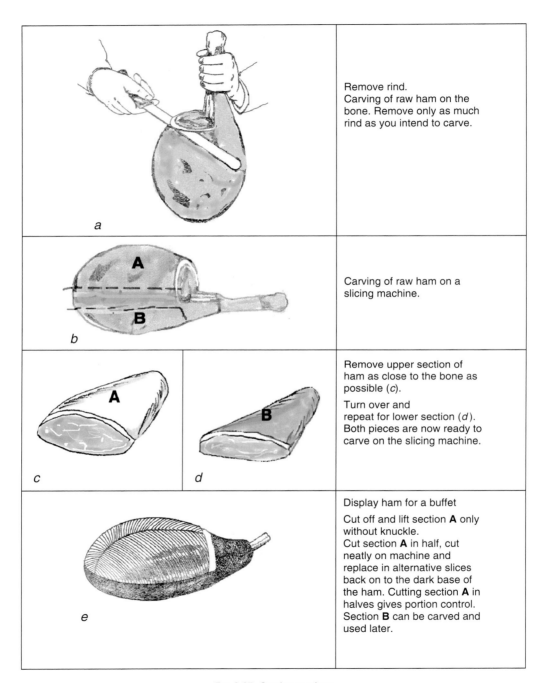

a	Remove rind. Carving of raw ham on the bone. Remove only as much rind as you intend to carve.
b	Carving of raw ham on a slicing machine.
c *d*	Remove upper section of ham as close to the bone as possible (*c*). Turn over and repeat for lower section (*d*). Both pieces are now ready to carve on the slicing machine.
e	Display ham for a buffet Cut off and lift section **A** only without knuckle. Cut section **A** in half, cut neatly on machine and replace in alternative slices back on to the dark base of the ham. Cutting section **A** in halves gives portion control. Section **B** can be carved and used later.

Fig. 6.35 *Carving raw ham*

drying techniques, are closely guarded secrets of the respective countries and manufacturers; quite often these recipes are known only to a handful of people.

Carving

After placing a cooked gammon or ham on a ham holder, it is best carved by clearing the knuckle and thereafter carving upwards with a sharp long knife, making neat cuts with a sawing motion (see Figure 6.34). Alternatively, the upper and lower section may be cut off the bone and sliced on a machine. When the aitch bone part is reached, the ham is turned around and cut in the same way. Many bone the ham or gammon in advance to allow for easier cutting without a bone, but there is no doubt that a ham cooked and carved on the bone has a much better flavour.

A raw ham is always surrounded by a rind. For carving (see Figure 6.35), the rind should be carefully removed. For smaller establishments it is advisable only to remove as much rind of the ham as is required for a particular order, after which the ham is hung again in a cool place. For larger establishments, where large quantities of raw hams are served each day, the whole ham may be freed of its rind and cut. With modern slicing machines, the raw ham may be boned and the rind removed beforehand, then sliced on the machine. The trimmings are then used for garnishes in sauces and stews.

THE OFFALS 　*Les abats*

The offals find many good culinary uses, as described in Tables 6.1–6.5. These include the grills (see Figure 6.37*b,c*), which are mixed meat and offal preparations, and contain elements from every section of this chapter.

TABLE 6.1 *BEEF OFFAL* 　*Les abats de boeuf*

English	French	Preparation and use
Brain	Cervelle de boeuf	Soak well in cold water, clean and remove membranes that cover brain, re-soak to whiten. Place in boiling strained court bouillon. Poach for 15–20 min, cool in liquor. Use as ravioli filling, hot and cold brain sauces, in slices fried as entrée
Heart	Coeur de boeuf	Open the heart without separating halves, trim off excess fat and tubes, remove clots of blood, sprinkle with olive oil and lemon juice, marinate for 30 min, season with salt and pepper, stuff, if required, with pork forcemeat or savoury stuffing. Wrap in bacon cut paper-thin, or pigs cauls, tie with string, always braised
Kidney	Rognon de boeuf	Trim off all fat and tubes. Remove membranes and skin. Cut into slices or dice, as required. Used in pies and soup

Continued

TABLE 6.1 *BEEF OFFAL*   ***Les abats de boeuf—cont'd***

English	French	Preparation and use
Liver	Foie-de-boeuf	Skin, trim off tubes and sinew, cut into thin slices. Usually braised, very young ox liver can be pan-fried
Muzzle	Museau de boeuf	Soak in salt water for 6–8 hours, boil, cool, and cut into thin slices/dice, season with vinaigrette, chopped fine herbs, and chopped onion. Used in hors d'oeuvres and salad, but seldom today
Palate	Palais de boeuf	Soak in cold water for 6–8 hours, blanch, refresh, drain, remove skin and cook in a blanc. Used in hors d'oeuvres or salad, but seldom used today
Oxtail	Queue de boeuf	Trim skinned tail of excess fat, cut into chunks through cartilage between segments of bone, split the wider part to even sizes. Used for soup or stew (see Figure 6.12)
Tongue	Langue-de-boeuf	Can be used fresh or pickled Fresh: soak in salt water for 24 hours, trim Pickled: trim, soak in cold water for a few hours, prick all over, rub with salt and saltpeter. Steep in brine for 6–8 days. Soak in cold water, to remove excess salt In both cases boil for 2–3 hours. Can be served hot, usually braised in Madeira Sauce, or cold for salads and sandwiches
Tripe	Grass-double Tripe de boeuf	Usually bought ready clean and blanched, if not, wash and blanch. In both cases cook in a salt court bouillon and cut into neat pieces or strips. Used for Tripe and Onions, sometimes made into a salad as a starter

TABLE 6.2 *VEAL OFFAL*   ***Les abats de veau***

English	French	Preparation and use
Spinal marrow	Amourette	Prepare as for beef brain
Brain	Cervelle de veau	Prepare as for beef brain
Calf's head	Tête de veau	Bone out, see Fig. 6.36 Soak in acidulated water overnight, blanch, refresh, cool. Rub all over with a cut lemon, particularly inside the mouth, nostril and neck. Cut into 2 × 2 cm squares, cook in a white court bouillon/blanc. Serve hot or cold – a speciality
Calf's heart	Coeur de veau	Prepare as lamb's heart in Table 6.3
Calf's kidney	Rognon de veau	Skin, trim off tubes and excess fat, leave whole or in halves to braise. Cut in slices like an escalope, to shallow fry more often than not in breadcrumbs, or cut in neat dice for the popular kidney sauté

Continued

TABLE **6.2** *VEAL OFFAL* 🍴 *Les abats de veau—cont'd*

English	French	Preparation and use
Calf's liver	Foie de veau	Considered the best of the livers. Prepare like ox liver, but best shallow fried or sauté; not normally braised
Sweetbread	Ris de veau	Two types of glands taken from calves, the long ones near the throat and the round ones near the heart. Soak in cold water to whiten, blanch, refresh, drain, press between two plates or boards for 2–3 hours. After carefully trimming off tubes and sinews, with larding needle stud with truffle, ham or tongue as required. Braise white or brown. Can be cut into escalope and egg washed and crumbed
Calf's lungs	Mou de veau	Beat out all air, cut in uniform piece, blanch. Used for stew, white and brown, or as Lung Hash

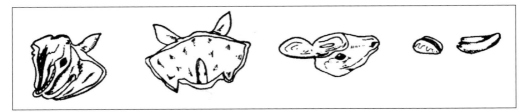

FIG. **6.36** *Preparation of a calf's head (see Table 6.2)*

TABLE **6.3** *LAMB/MUTTON OFFAL* 🍴 *Les abats d'agneau et de mouton*

English	French	Preparation and use
Lamb's brain	Cervelle d'agneau	As for beef and veal brain
Lamb's kidney	Rognon d'agneau	Slit on bulging side and open without separating the two halves, remove the skin, trim tubes, insert skewer to keep kidney open (see Figure 6.37*a*). Use as part of a Mixed Grill, or split in halves or cut in slices for sauté.
Lamb's liver	Foie d'agneau	Prepare as for veal liver
Lamb's sweetbread	Ris d'agneau	Soak in cold water, blanch, trim cook in white stock, with butter and lemon juice for 20 minutes. Cool. Use for stew, pies or garnish in bouchées or vol au vent
Lamb's heart	Coeur d'agneau	As for ox or veal heart
Lamb's tongue	Langue d'agneau	As for ox and veal tongue

TABLE 6.4 *PORK OFFAL*   **Les abats de porc**

English	French	Preparation and use
Pig's brain	Cervelle de porc	As for ox and veal brain
Bath chap	Joue de porc	Treat like ham, usually boiled in stock served cold. A British speciality
Pig's kidney	Rognon de porc	Prepare as for lamb's kidney, can also be used for pies and sauté
Pig's liver	Foie de porc	As for lamb's liver
Pig's tongue	Langue de porc	Prepare as for ox tongue, if brined and cooked showing its red colour useful cut in dice or triangles for inclusion for terrines and brawns and stuffing for boar's head
Pig's trotters	Pieds de porc	Inclusion in making aspic, boiled as salad or boiled and grilled. See more detailed explanation under pork section above

TABLE 6.5 *OFFAL OF POULTRY AND GAME*   **Les abats de volaille et gibier**

English	French	Preparation and Use
Chicken livers	Foie de volaille	Remove gall bladder from all livers, do not break (very bitter). Remove sinews cut into neat pieces according to size
Duck liver	Foie de canard	
Goose liver*	Foie d'oie	Used for pâtes and sauté
Pheasant liver	Foie de faisan	For skewers: season and quickly seal in hot butter, cool, arrange on skewers alternatively with pieces of bacon, mushrooms, onions and/or cherry tomatoes
		Occasionally pieces of liver are added to mixed meat skewers
Venison liver	Foie de gibier	Treat like ox or veal liver. Mostly used for pâtes. In some regions of Europe, slices are sautéed in butter and served as a speciality entrée
Giblets	Abatis	All poultry and game bird have giblets, these are very useful for inclusion in stocks to give game soups and sauces game flavour (see Figure 5.2 in the Poultry chapter)

*Goose liver, besides being made into the famous pâté, is also served as an entrée, like venison liver.

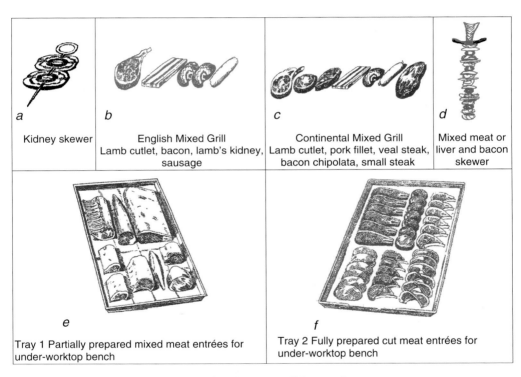

a Kidney skewer	*b* English Mixed Grill Lamb cutlet, bacon, lamb's kidney, sausage	*c* Continental Mixed Grill Lamb cutlet, pork fillet, veal steak, bacon chipolata, small steak	*d* Mixed meat or liver and bacon skewer
e Tray 1 Partially prepared mixed meat entrées for under-worktop bench		*f* Tray 2 Fully prepared cut meat entrées for under-worktop bench	

FIG. 6.37 *Mixed meat and offal preparations*

7

Forcemeats, Garnishes and Seasonings (Les Farces)

In the making of forcemeats it is very important that only the best of fish or meat and other materials are used. All forcemeats should have a good binding but at the same time should be light and not too dry. To get a good binding, bread-crumbs are used for the simpler forcemeats and so-called panadas for the finer ones. To make them smooth, light and white, water, milk, or cream is used according to the forcemeat made.

There are numerous forcemeats, from the simple sausage meat to the finer force-meats used for the making of hot mousses and soufflés. They are usually made from fish and shellfish, the white meats, like veal and pork, as well as from poultry, game, fish and certain vegetables and bread. To call the latter forcemeats would, in English, not be quite correct; those made of vegetables and bread are usually called stuffing, whereas, in French, all of these are known as farces.

A very wide variety of dishes for our menus can be prepared from the various force-meats. Plates 7.1–7.3 offer some examples of the colourful and attractive presentations that can be achieved.

Although they differ in method, there are three basic types:
(1) Forcemeats made of raw fish or meats
(2) Forcemeats made of cooked fish or meats
(3) Cooked forcemeats – stuffings.

RAW FISH FORCEMEATS *Les farces de poisson cru*

In the preparation for the cooking of fish, we often use fish forcemeat in the form of quenelles or as filling/stuffing to both enhance its appearance or flavour. In many cases, we use the various forcemeats to contrast flavours and colours, that is to say, we stuff a portion of white fish such as a paupiette of sole with a pink salmon farce or a salmon portion or salmon trout with a white fish farce to which we may have added some blanched chopped spinach to make it green. Occasionally we add to the farces other ingredients such a diced smoked salmon, asparagus tips, chopped mushrooms and dice or julienne of red or green peppers etc. to further improve appearance and flavour. Some of the better farces allow us to make fish farce dishes in their own right, in the form of fish dumplings or quenelles as they are called in French, as well as mousselines and mousses.

When we make fish farces in small amounts and using fresh fish we can know that the farce recipes given below have been well tried and are reliable. However, when fresh fish or the right fish is not available, or we are making a large amount of the farce, it is best to use a panada (French panade) or binding to make sure the fish farce will hold its shape during cooking.

Bindings or panadas are very important to make a good forcemeat. First in use are breadcrumbs soaked in water, milk or cream, which are used in the making of sausage meats, veal loaf or pojarski. Secondly come the panadas, of which five in everyday use are given below. Some recipes name mashed potatoes, béchamel or veloutés for the binding of certain forcemeats, and although these are widely in use they are in fact only a simplification of the better panadas used in first-class cooking.

THE FISH FARCES

White fish raw forcemeat   Farce de poisson cru blanc

*Ingredients**
500 g white fish, best
   pike or whiting, free
   of bones and skin
3 egg whites
2 egg yolks
1 heaped tsp salt
1 good pinch of white
   ground pepper
500 ml double cream
Juice of half a lemon

Method
1 Mince fish through a fine mincer-blade
2 Place in fridge to be ice cold
3 Place minced fish in food processor, add salt
   and pepper (and add panada if required)
4 Cut fine at high speed for 30 seconds and mix
   well
5 Add lemon juice and egg whites, mix well into
   mixture
6 Gradually add cream a little at a time, with
   pulse button
7 Finally add egg yolk, and if needed correct
   seasoning

*Always poach or fry a small sample to make
sure it holds*

Notes: **The amount of this recipes will produce:*
   4–6 portions of larger quenelles as a main course, 2–3 per portion
   8–12 portions of medium quenelles as a smaller fish course, 2–3 per portion
   10–16 portions of teaspoon-shaped quenelles for fish stews or garnish
   20–24 portions of piping bag shaped fish quenelles for fish soups (see below)

Pink raw salmon forcemeat   Farce de saumon cru

*Ingredients**
500 g salmon fillet free
   of bones and skin
3 egg whites
2 egg yolks

Method
1 Mince fish through a fine mincer-blade
2 Place in fridge to be ice cold
3 Now place fish in food processor add salt and
   pepper (and add panada if required)

Continued

Pink raw salmon forcemeat   Farce de saumon cru—cont'd

*Ingredients**
1 heaped tsp salt
1 good pinch of white
 ground pepper
2 litres double cream
Juice of 2 lemons

Method
4 Cut fine at high speed for a few seconds and mix well
5 Add lemon juice and egg whites, mix well into mixture
6 Gradually add cream a little at a time, with pulse button
7 Add egg yolks, taste, and if needed correct seasoning

Notes: *To both the raw farces certain additions can be made to change colour or/and flavour, e.g.
 150 g of blanched finely chopped dry spinach
 200 g of finely chopped dry very white mushrooms
 100 g of finely chopped dry sun-dried tomatoes or concassé, folded in at the very end.

Fine lobster forcemeat   La farce fine d'homard

Ingredients
300 g raw lobster meat
2 egg yolks
200 g pike or whiting
500 ml cream (approx.)
100 g lobster coral
20–25 g spice salt
2 egg whites

Method
1 Mince lobster meat, pike and coral through a very fine mincer
2 Place and work on ice (see Figure 7.1) or in processor in pulse motion
3 Gradually work in egg whites and spice salt
4 When binding is achieved, gradually work in about half the cream
5 Slightly beat remainder of cream and gently fold into the mixture
6 Correct seasoning and always test before use

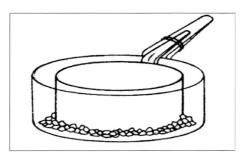

Fig. 7.1 *In the olden day we used to tie two plats a sautés together, with crushed ice on the bottom, for stirring the cream into the minced fish and white of eggs. Today food processors make life much easier, but it is still a useful device*

Panadas or Bindings

The following two panada/binding recipes will be sufficient for the 500–800 g of fish farce recipes given above and can of course be increased in proportion when larger amounts are needed.

All panadas must be very cold before they are used.

Flour panada   Panade à la farine

Ingredients
1 litre of milk
60 g butter
200 g flour
Salt, pepper and
   nutmeg

Method
1 Heat milk and butter in pan
2 Add sieved flour, stir vigorously to smooth paste, simmer for a few minutes
3 Place on a plate, cover with buttered paper and cool (must be very cold before using)

Bread panada   Panade au pain

Ingredients
1 litre milk
200 g white
   breadcrumbs (must
   be made fresh)
60 g butter
Salt, pepper and
   nutmeg

Method
1 Place milk in pan, add breadcrumbs, butter and seasoning
2 Bring to boil, simmer a few minutes
3 Place on a plate, cover with buttered paper, cool (must be very cold before using)

Potato panada   Panade aux pommes de terre

Ingredients
500 g cooked sieved
   potatoes
50 g butter
1 litre milk
Salt, pepper and
   nutmeg

Method
1 Moisten potatoes with milk in a pan
2 Gradually bring to the boil, add butter and seasoning
3 Take to the side, stirring all the time with a spatula until almost dry
4 Place on a buttered tray and cool

Used for large white-meat, quenelles and fricadelles

Rice panada   Panade au riz

Ingredients
4 cups of Caroline rice
50 g butter
10–12 cups good veal
  or chicken stock
1 studded onion
Salt, pepper and grated
  nutmeg

Method
1 Bring the stock to the boil, add the washed
  rice, stir until stock re-boils, gently boil on the
  side of the stove until rice dissolves, pass
  through a fine sieve
2 Return to stove in a clean pan, add butter and
  seasonings, gently simmer on side of stove,
  stirring all the time with a spatula
3 Place on a buttered tray, cover with buttered
  paper and cool

Use for large meat and fish quenelles.

Frangipane panada   Panade à la frangipane

Ingredients
500 ml milk
150 g butter
200 g flour
8 egg yolks
Salt, pepper and grated
  nutmeg

Method
1 Heat milk butter and seasoning
2 Mix yolks and flour in a stainless steel bowl,
  to smooth paste
3 Pour milk over yolk and flour mixture, mix to
  smooth paste
4 Place mixture in a sauteuse, return to stove,
  heat until mixture loosens from bottom of pan
5 Place on a buttered tray, cover with buttered
  greaseproof paper, cool

Ideal for finer farces of fish, chicken, veal and
game

The Shaping and Cooking of Fish Quenelles

Fish quenelles (dumplings) are used in three ways:

(1) Very small quenelles for garnishes of fish soups.

(2) Medium/small quenelles for the garnishing or as part of fish dishes or stews/ragoûts or for salpicons (see next section).

(3) Two or three larger quenelles as main course with a rich sauce/garnish (see poached fish and sauces).

To make the smaller fish quenelles, first put the fish farce into a piping bag with a small plain tube. Holding the piping bag over a plat à sauté with simmering fish stock, cut the fish farce to the required length with a small sharp knife as it is pressed out (see Figure 7.2a). The quenelles will be cooked in a few minutes and as they rise to the top will be ready to be lifted out with a perforated spoon. If larger amounts are required, say for a banquet, the farce can be piped onto a buttered tray with a slight cutting movement on the bottom of the tray. These quenelles are then covered with fish stock and poached in the normal way, after which they are strained and ready for use in soup etc. (see Figure 7.2b).

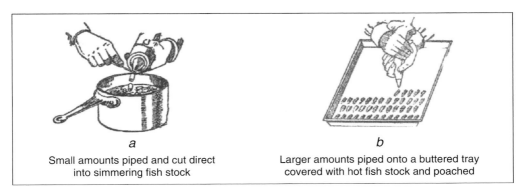

a	*b*
Small amounts piped and cut direct into simmering fish stock	Larger amounts piped onto a buttered tray covered with hot fish stock and poached

FIG. 7.2 *The making of small soup quenelles*

Medium quenelles for fish stews, ragoûts or salpicons are best shaped with a dessert or larger teaspoon in one's hand and than again placed into simmering fish stock to be cooked (see Figure 7.3).

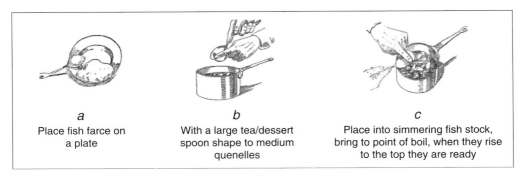

a	*b*	*c*
Place fish farce on a plate	With a large tea/dessert spoon shape to medium quenelles	Place into simmering fish stock, bring to point of boil, when they rise to the top they are ready

FIG. 7.3 *The making of medium quenelles for ragôuts*

Larger quenelles for a main course are best shaped with two soup spoons or one spoon in the palm of your hand and placed for small amounts in a plat à sauté or for larger amounts on buttered stainless steel trays, covered with a good fish stock and a buttered paper. They are gently poached for 10–15 minutes according to size (see Figure 7.4).

Quenelles de Brochette Sauce Homard

The most famous fish quenelles main course dish is the one made from pike, set and served on a lobster sauce – Quenelles de Brochette Sc. Homard. The white of the pike quenelles on a rich red lobster sauce is indeed a striking, attractive and very tasty

a	b
Scrape farce from plate	Shape with two tablespoons or one spoon and palm of hand onto a buttered tray, cover with stock and poach

FIG. 7.4 *The making of large quenelles for a main course*

dish, but quenelles served with a rich white wine, creamy mushroom, asparagus or prawn sauce are equally delicious and attractive dishes of this type.

RAW MEAT FORCEMEATS *Les entrées pour farces de viandes*

However carefully we buy or prepare our various meats, in the average kitchen any butcher will always have some meat trimmings. The larger pieces may be cut into braising steaks or stews. But the smallest, near bone trimmings can be used in no other way than in the form of minced meats, which for a good result should be minced fine and maybe twice with a sharp mincer blade.

These entrées allow us an excellent outlet for the minced meat trimmings, in the form of many tasty and attractive dishes. It is true that these types of minced meat dishes do not have the very best reputation and are considered by many to be dishes best suited to the lower end of catering. It is an interesting fact that most Continental countries accept these types of minced meat dishes much more readily than the British.

Again, however, this is not always true, for when it comes to the British sausage (very much a minced meat dish) it is one of the most popular British dishes, eaten in its various ways, at breakfast, lunch, dinner and suppers.

With the increase in all food costs, particularly meats, we should look again at the uses of forcemeat dishes of all types. With careful initial preparation, not too much fat, good seasoning with fresh herbs and spices and the correct method of cooking, with the right garnishes, sauces and other suitable accompaniments, these simple entrées can be very tasty, attractive and indeed profitable dishes.

We differentiate between two types of forcemeats:

- The **simple forcemeats**, making preparations such as sausage meats of various types, hamburger mixture and its variation (see example list below).
- The **finer forcemeats**, making preparations such as mousses, mousselines, quenelles, terrines, fillings, stuffings etc.

THE SIMPLE FORCEMEATS

Basic simple raw forcemeat **Farce de viande crue**

Ingredients (8–10 portions)
1000 g minced meat (see
  below) free of sinews and
  excess fat
200 g finely diced onions
150 g white breadcrumbs
2 whole eggs
50 g chopped parsley*
500 ml-plus of iced water
1 tsp ground pepper to taste
1 tsp salt to taste
Chopped herbs (optional)
  according to meat or season
150 g margarine/oil/butter or
  mixture thereof**

Method
1 Cook onions in half of fat until golden
  brown, set aside to cool
2 Combine all ingredients in a bowl, add
  cold cooked onions
3 Mix well by hand to a smooth mixture
4 Make a small steak and shallow fry,
  testing the mixture to be holding shape
  and taste for correct seasoning
5 Re-season and shape as required

See different shapes and names below

Notes: *Herbs and seasoning are a matter of choice according to meat used and availability.*
***Fat for cooking is again a matter of choice according to meat used. Margarine/oil is often
a good combination.*

Any of the meats listed below can be made into simple forcemeats using the ingredients and method given for the basic recipe. These can be used for stuffings and simple shaped chopped hamburgers, cutlets, meatballs etc. (see Figure 7.4).

Beef forcemeat	Farce de boeuf	Turkey forcemeat	Farce de dindon
Veal forcemeat	Farce de veau	Lamb forcemeat	Farce d'agneau
Pork forcemeat	Farce de porc	Venison forcemeat	Farce de gibier
Chicken forcemeat	Farce de volaille		

Combination Forcemeats

There are a number of mixed forcemeats used, of which the Austrian veal–pork combination for their Vienna steak and the Scandinavian beef–pork combination fort their famous Köttbultar or meatballs are two examples. Often we also find a combination of the blander chicken or turkey mince, mixed with some minced pork to improve the flavour.

Simply follow the basic forcemeat recipe above replacing the 1000 g of single meat with an equal amount of 500 g of any two meats; the rest of the method can be followed. In the case of the Scandinavian meatballs a little ground all spice will give it its distinct flavour.

In the case of chicken or turkey forcemeats, up to 20–30% of minced pork or bacon is acceptable. As these two forcemeats can be a little bland and dry, add a little minced pork/bacon as well as a little cayenne, which will give a bite to the flavour.

Other Additions

In some countries, fresh tomato dice (concassé), diced peppers, extra onion, diced kidney, dice of fat or speck and cooled rice (to stretch) are sometimes added.

Bread and Water

It may be presumed that the addition of bread and water to our forcemeats is to extend the volume, and naturally this is the case. What is seldom realized and not always understood is that without these additions we would not have a mixture that would bind and hold the various shapes we give it afterwards. Too much of breadcrumbs and water added to these mixtures could do the dish, as well as our reputation, much harm. None of either will make it difficult for the farce to hold and shape.

Various Forcemeat Compositions

The old principle is that for a table d'hôte portion we allow:

125 g of meat without bones
200 g of meat on the bone.

We should then allow about 150 g per portion for any forcemeat dish. In this way the customer will receive 125 g of meat and good value, approximately 25 g or so of the mixture being taken up by the necessary binding in the form of bread and water. In a normal busy kitchen most types of meat trimmings are normally available. Even in supermarkets now minced lamb, minced pork, minced chicken and turkey, and minced beef and veal are easily found.

Table 7.1 offers examples of named minced meat dishes made with the basic simple forcemeat recipe and some its variations given above.

Sausages

The famous British sausage naturally belongs in the group of simple forcemeats. Here are the two basic recipes; the seasonings section of the chapter (see Table 7.5) gives some regional variations.

Pork sausage meat   La farce de porc (Saucisses Anglaises)

Ingredients (30–32 sausages)
1000 g diced pork
500 ml-plus iced water
60 g spice salt or other sausage
  seasonings
400 g white breadcrumbs

Method
1 Moisten crumbs with water
2 Freshly mince meat through a fine
  mincer-blade
3 Mix all ingredients, correct seasoning
  and consistency

TABLE 7.1 *Various Forcemeat Compositions and Shapes*

Type/shape	Preparation	Menu examples	French
Hamburger	Simple beef forcemeat, shaped into hamburgers, shallow fried or grilled served as a snack or small main course	American Hamburger in Bun Grilled Hamburger with Salad and Chips Fried Hamburger with Fried Egg	(No obvious translation)
Bitok	Simple ¾ beef ¼ pork forcemeat, shaped into bitok shape, double the thickness of a hamburger but smaller, often given two per portion, shallow fried and served with garnish and/or sauce	Bitok Russian Style with Sour Cream Sauce Bitok with Tomato Sauce Bitok with Onion Sauce	Bitok à la Russe Bitok sc. tomate Bitok sc. Lyonnaise
Pojarski	¾ veal ¼ pork forcemeats shaped into one larger or two smaller cutlets or steaks, shallow fried or grilled and served with various garnishes or sauces. Can be made with minced chicken or turkey meat	Minced Veal Steak with Asparagus Minced Pork Steak with Tomato Sauce Minced Venison Steak with Red Wine Sauce	Médaillions de veau farci asperge Médaillions de porc farcis sc. tomate Steak de gibier farci vin rouge

Continued

TABLE 7.1 *Various Forcemeat Compositions and Shapes—cont'd*

Type/shape	Preparation	Menu examples	French
Vienna steak	Simple veal–pork mixture, shaped into one or two small steaks which should have an oval shape. Shallow fried, served with a garnish and rich cream-based sauce	Vienna Steak with Sour Cream Sauce Vienna Steak with Asparagus Sauce Vienna Steak with Mushroom Sauce Vienna Steak with Piquant Sauce	Stek farcie viennoise à la crème Stek farcie viennoise à l'asperge Stek viennoise aux champignons
Minced cutlet	Simple lamb or veal forcemeat, rolled in hand into pear shape, than flattened to a cutlet shape (a piece of suitable bone or macaroni can be inserted to represent a bone), pané, shallow fried and served with garnish and sauce	Minced Veal Cutlet with Hunter Sauce Minced Veal Steaks with Celery Sauce Minced Lamb Steak with Tomato Sauce Minced Lamb Steak with Pepper Sauce	Côtelette farcie de veau sc. chasseur Côtelette farcie de veau sc. céleri Côtelette farcie d'agneau sc. tomate Côtelette farcie d'agneau sc. poivre
Meat balls	A simple forcemeat made of a mixture of half pork and half beef, rolled in wet hands into small 2 cm balls and placed on an oiled plate, allowed to set in fridge To cook slide into hot fat in a frying pan and fry until golden brown, or can be poached/boiled in good stock and served with various velouté-based sauces	Fried Meat Balls in Gravy Fried Meat Ball in Tomato Sauce Poached Meat Balls in Caper Sauce Poached Meat Balls in Mushroom Sauce	(No obvious translation)

Beef sausage meat **La farce de boeuf (Saucisses Anglaises)**

Ingredients (3–32 sausages)
1000 g minced beef
500 ml-plus iced water
60 g spice salt or other sausage
   seasonings
400 g white breadcrumbs

Method
1 Moisten crumbs with water
2 Freshly mince meat through a fine
   mincer-blade
3 Mix all ingredients, correct seasoning
   and consistency

Chipolata sausage meat

Ingredients (for 30–32
   sausages)
1000 g diced pork
500 ml-plus iced water
60 g chipolata sausage
Seasonings
400 g white breadcrumbs

Method
1 Moisten crumbs with water
2 Freshly mince meat through a fine
   mincer-blade
3 Mix all ingredients, correct seasoning
   and consistency

Every region has their own sausages which are all basically based on these two recipes, what is different is their seasonings. Sausage meats as given above are often used for stuffing sausage rolls etc. or they are forced into skins with a special machine: normal sausages 8 to a half kilo, for chipolatas smaller, narrower skins are used giving about 10 to a half kilo.

THE FINER FORCEMEATS ***Les farces fines***

In this group belong a number of forcemeats, usually of white meats such as veal, chicken and, of late, turkey. In these cases, as the recipes show, a little minced fat pork or bacon fat should be added to give these somewhat bland meats flavour and bite. Some finer forcemeats are made from venison and lamb for some special preparation or dishes.

The finer farces are sometimes also called farce à la crème.

What is important is that only the best of meats or trimmings are used, free of fat, all skin and gristle, and it helps if the meats are minced twice through the finest mincer-blade available. We can of course not speak of using trimmings in the case of game birds or hare and rabbit; here we purposefully bone these meats for a finer forcemeat dish.

Finer forcemeat for veal and chicken Farce fine de veau et volaille

Ingredients (10–12 portions)
1000 g very finely minced
  veal, chicken or turkey
200 g fat pork or bacon finely
  minced
200 g finely diced shallots
4 egg whites
2 egg yolks
1 litre double cream*
1 tsp freshly ground nutmeg
1 tsp ground pepper to taste
1 tsp salt to taste
Small pinch of cayenne
Fresh chopped herbs
  (optional) according to
  meat or season
150 g margarine/oil/butter**

Method
1 Cook shallots in half of margarine, set
  aside and cool
2 Place minced meat in processor
3 Add seasoning and egg whites, cut and
  mix in short pulses
4 Add panada (see above), cut and mix well
  in short pulses
5 Now gradually add cream, mixing again in
  short pulses. Finally add egg yolks
6 To test-taste, make a small steak sample,
  fry in a little margarine to see that mixture
  holds shape, and taste well
7 Cool and set in fridge, shape and poach
  or fry according to dish.

Serve with various sauces and/or garnishes
(see below)

Notes: *If the finished farce appears too firm add a little more cream, if too loose, don't use all cream.*
       **The fat used for cooking is a matter of choice or custom, margarine/oil is often a good*
       combination, with butter to finish.

Fine game forcemeat Farce fine de gibier

Ingredients (10–12 portions)
1000 g very finely minced
  venison or game bird flesh
200 g fat pork or bacon finely
  minced
1 glass of port wine or
  Madeira
200 g finely diced shallots
4 egg whites
2 egg yolks
1 litre double cream*
1 tsp freshly ground nutmeg
1 tsp ground pepper to taste
1 tsp salt to taste
Small pinch of cayenne
Fresh chopped herbs
  (optional) according to
  meat or season
150 g margarine/oil/butter**

Method
1 Cook shallots in port until almost dry, set
  aside and cool
2 Place minced meat in processor, add
  seasoning and egg whites cut and mix in
  short pulses
3 Add panada, cut and mix well in short
  pulses
4 Gradually add cream, mixing again in
  short pulses, finally, add egg yolk
5 Test-taste by making a small steak sample
  and fry in a little margarine to see that the
  mixture holds. Cool and set in fridge,
  shape, poach or fry according to dish

Serve with various sauces and/or garnishes
(see below)

Notes: *If the finished farce appears too firm add a little more cream, if too loose, don't use all cream.*
       **The fat used for cooking is a matter of choice or custom, margarine/oil is often a good*
       combination, with butter to finish.

MEAT QUENELLES

The making of various types and sizes of fish quenelles has been illustrated above in Figures 7.2, 7.3 and 7.4. From the fine meat farces we can of course again make quenelles of various sizes as garnishes for soups and stews and as dishes in their own right, for example:

Chicken Quenelles with Asparagus Sauce
Veal Quenelles on Creamed Mushrooms
Game Quenelles Chasseur

THE MOUSSES, MOUSSELINES AND SOUFFLÉS

Adding some beaten eggs to the two forcemeats above to make the mixture lighter, we can make three famous fine farce dishes, namely mousselines in individual portions and larger mousses cooked in a bain marie, cooled and served as a starter. Mousselines as a portion and mousses cut into portions within the mousse mould are often served on buffets. The third dish is the soufflé, always served hot, usually in individual moulds or, for a small party, in a large mould.

Mousseline–mousse–soufflé de farce (see Figure 7.5)

Ingredients (10–12 portions)
1 batch of any of the four
    finer farces above (fish,
    veal, chicken or game)
6–8 egg whites

Method
1 Beat egg whites very stiff
2 Work ⅓ of the beaten eggs into freshly made farce to loosen mixture
3 Gently fold in remainder of egg whites as lightly as possible
4 Place mixture into buttered individual or larger moulds
5 Stand in bain marie in boiling water
6 Place in oven at medium to hot heat and cook:
    Individual mould for 20–25 min
    Larger moulds for 30–40 min

Serve cold with suitable cold sauce
Serve hot with rich demi-glace-based sauce, e.g. red wine, port wine, Robert, chasseur, diable; or in case of fish or white meats, with a rich vin blanc or Supreme sauce and its many variations

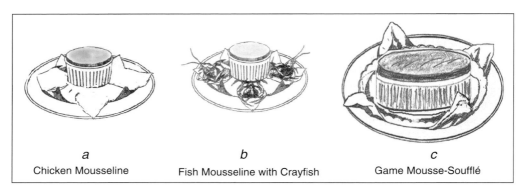

a	b	c
Chicken Mousseline	Fish Mousseline with Crayfish	Game Mousse-Soufflé

FIG. 7.5 *Mousseline and mousse*

The farces and the dishes made thereof are not particularly expensive to produce but need a certain skill in their preparation and cooking. Considering that they are based on minced meat, many would consider their use only at the lower end of catering. But this is not so; on the Continent of Europe these dishes, well prepared and presented, are very popular and are considered excellent dishes even for a festive function or banquet, as can be seen from the following menu from the author's collection. Here we see that a Hot Mousse of Hazel Hen was worthy to be served at a luncheon given by the Swedish Government to the Shah of Persia in 1962 – a simple but truly excellent lunch. More recently, as late as the autumn of 2000 at a dinner party the author attended, we were served a Mousseline of Pheasant with a Port Wine Sauce that could not be faulted and was a most pleasant surprise.

Offert par Le Gouvernment Suède en l´honneur de
Sa Majesté Impérial Le Shah d´Iran

Déjeuner

Menu

Omble chevalier poché aux fines herbes

Meursault 1955

Mousse chaud de Gelinotte

Salades vertes

Château la Tour Haut-Brion 1954

Flan aux fraises Crème Chantilly

Café

A Wealth of Variety

Accepting that it is a fact that minced meat dishes are not very popular, it is also a fact that they can be made into very tasty and attractive dishes, especially in the case of the simpler farces.

> If we use say five meats, e.g. beef, veal, lamb, chicken or turkey = 5 meats
>
> Give them four shapes, e.g. hamburger, Vienna steaks, bitoks, meatballs = 4 shapes
>
> Use four methods of cooking, e.g. poaching, grilling, frying, deep frying = 4 methods
>
> Serving them in four different sauces, Tomato, Mushroom, Capers, Bolognaise = 4 sauces
>
> We have 5 meats × 4 shapes × 4 methods × 4 sauces and garnishes = 320

We thus have some 320 ways of using up our raw or cooked meat trimmings. That gives us almost one for each day of the year; prepared and presented with care, they are a sure way to make a profit.

SIMPLE COOKED FORCEMEATS   ***Les farces (ragoûts) réchauffés***

Forcemeat is a somewhat misleading description for the cooked forcemeats in that they are not forced through the mincer but cut in dice, strips or scallops, the nicer the better, and placed in a binding sauce. After cooling and setting they are shaped and reheated, by shallow frying or deep frying, and served with various sauces and garnishes.

It is often a way of re-using leftover poultry or meats in a profitable way and it is the re-heating aspects of the preparation which gives it its French name, from réchauffer to re-heat. It will of course differ from establishment to establishment, but normally the Larder will only cut-dice-flake the cooked poultry, meats and fish given in to its safe keeping. The preparations described are more normally executed in the Kitchen.

Cooked forcemeats can be formed into many shapes. Figure 7.6 summarizes the four included below.

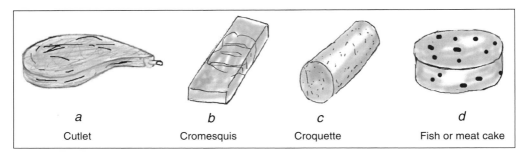

| *a* | *b* | *c* | *d* |
| Cutlet | Cromesquis | Croquette | Fish or meat cake |

FIG. 7.6 *Cooked forcemeat shapes*

COOKED MEAT FORCEMEATS

Cromesquis

Ingredients (10–12 portions)
750 g finely diced any cooked
  meat, usually chicken
4 egg yolks
1 litre chicken velouté or flour
  panada
Pig's cauls or streaky bacon
Salt and pepper to taste

Method
1 Place velouté or panada and seasoning
  into a pan, heat
2 Add chicken, bring to the boil, reduce if
  necessary
3 Bind with egg yolks
4 Spread onto a buttered tray, cool
5 When really cool, cut into neat
  rectangular shapes
6 Wrap each in pig's cauls or bacon, dip in
  butter, deep fry to golden brown

Served as a hot starter, or on a finger
buffet

Chicken Cutlets 　 Les côtelettes de volaille

Ingredients (10–12 portions)
1000 g finely diced cooked
  chicken
4 egg yolks
1 litre velouté
Salt, pepper, nutmeg to taste

Method
1 Place velouté or panada and seasoning
  into a pan, heat
2 Add chicken, bring to the boil, reduce if
  necessary
3 Bind with egg yolks
4 Spread onto a buttered tray, cool. When
  really cold, divide into 8–12 even parts
5 Roll in your hand into pear shape, press
  down to cutlet shape, flour, egg wash
  and breadcrumb
6 Shallow or deep fry to golden brown

Serve as a main course with various
sauces

Chicken and Ham Cutlets 　 Côtelette de volaille et jambon

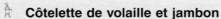

As for chicken cutlets above, replacing 250 g of chicken with 250 g of cooked
diced ham.

Chicken Croquettes Croquettes de volaille

Proceed as for chicken cutlets. When cold cut into 16–20 finger shapes, roll in your hand to a cork shape. Flour, egg wash, breadcrumb and deep fry to golden brown. Serve 2 per portion.

Other cooked meats can be used. Served as a hot starter or on a finger buffet.

COOKED FISH FORCEMEATS

Fish Cakes

Ingredients (10–12 portions)
750 g cooked white fish such as cod, haddock, hake, flaked to be free of *all* skin and bones
1 kg cooked-baked jacket potatoes, peeled and grated
200 g finely diced golden brown cooked onions
50 g chopped parsley or coriander or mixture of both
100 g flour
3 eggs
Salt and milled pepper and nutmeg to taste

Method
1 Place grated potatoes into a large bowl
2 Add onions, parsley, seasoning, eggs and half the flour
3 Work to a smooth mixture, now work in the flaked fish pieces
4 Carefully lift in fish to retain flakes as much as possible
5 Sprinkle remaining flour on a working table
6 Place mixture on flour and shape into 4–5 cm diameter roll
7 Cut into 2 cm thick slices, allow to set
8 Dust with flour* and cook in mixture of oil and butter until golden brown on both sides

*Note: *Fish cakes can be rolled in breadcrumbs, chopped or flaked almonds or nuts or pumpkin seeds to change appearance and flavour. Serve with Tomato, Hollandaise or Béarnaise Sauce. See Figure 7.7*

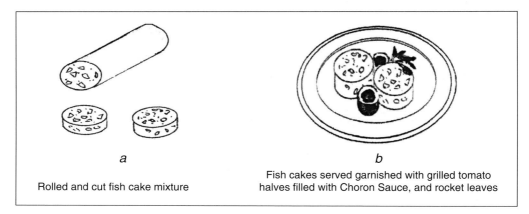

a
Rolled and cut fish cake mixture

b
Fish cakes served garnished with grilled tomato halves filled with Choron Sauce, and rocket leaves

FIG. 7.7 *Fish cake preparation*

Salmon Cakes

Ingredients (10–12 portions)
750 g cooked salmon, can be neck and tail trimmings flaked to be free of *all* skin and bones
1 kg cooked-baked jacket potatoes, peeled and grated
200 g finely diced golden brown cooked onions
50 g chopped parsley or dill or mixture of both
100 g flour
3 eggs
Salt, milled pepper and nutmeg or cayenne to taste

Method
1 Place grated potatoes into a large bowl
2 Add onions, parsley, salt, pepper, eggs and half the flour
3 Work to a smooth mixture, now add the flaked fish, carefully mixing in to retain flakes as much as possible
4 Sprinkle remaining flour on a working table
5 Place mixture on flour and shape into 4–5 cm diameter roll
6 Cut into 2 cm thick slices, allow to set
7 Roll in flour and cook in mixture of oil and butter until golden brown on both sides

Serve with Hollandaise, Béarnaise or Cucumber Sauce

Note: Can be made with most other fish types, e.g. smoked peppered mackerel is rather nice.

Salmon Cutlets   Les côtelettes de saumon

Ingredients (10–12 portions)
750 g cooked salmon, free of skin and bones
1 litre fish velouté or béchamel
4 egg yolks
A little lemon juice
Salt and pepper to taste

Method
1 Bring velouté or béchamel to boil in a pan
2 Add flaked salmon, seasoning and juice, mix well, being careful not to break up salmon flakes too much
3 Add egg yolks, heat and bind
4 Place on a buttered tray, cool
5 When really cold, mould into 8–12 cutlets, flour, egg wash and breadcrumb, deep or shallow fry to golden brown

Serve as a main course with a suitable sauce

Salmon Croquettes Salmon croquettes

Follow basic recipe above, but shape cooled mixture into 16–20 fingers. Floured, egg washed and crumbed, then deep or shallow fry until golden brown.

Note: Other cooked fish can be used, served as a hot starter, or on a finger buffet.

GARNISHES *Les garnies*

During any week, with a daily changing menu, the different chefs de partie need numerous garnishes. The following garnishes, or fillings, as required by the different departments of the kitchen, are just a few examples in each case. They will serve to emphasize their importance and the need for detailed study of this branch of Cold Larder work. Only by being familiar with the whole range of these will the Chef Garde-Manger be able to order all items of food needed, thus promoting a smooth liaison between departments.

With plated service in most restaurants today and a much simpler presentation, the need for classical garnishes in particular is much reduced, but some have been included as a point of interest.

THE SOUP CHEF *Le potager*

Small quenelles of meats
Small quenelles of poultry
Small quenelles of fish
Small quenelles of
  bone-marrow
Slices of bone-marrow

Brunoise of chicken, ham and tongue
Slices, or dice, of chicken, ham and tongue
Julienne of chicken, ham and tongue
Clarification for consommé
Giblets for consommé

THE FISH CHEF *Le poissonnier*

Quenelles fish or main course
Small quenelles
Slice or dice of crawfish and
  lobster
Tails of crayfish and scampis
Stoned olives and grapes
Prawns

Soft roes, plain or pané
Slices or dice of truffles
Oysters and mussels
Fish croquettes, cutlets and cakes
  (fish or main course)
Shrimps

THE SAUCE CHEF *Le saucier*

Salpicons of varying
  compositions
Ragoûts and fillings for
  vol au vent
Sliced, diced or chopped
  truffles
Champignons
Stoned olives

Chicken livers
Dice of pork fat
Lardons
Brunoise of meats, poultry and vegetables
Julienne of meats, poultry and vegetables
Slices of beef-bone marrow

THE ROAST AND GRILL CHEF *Le rôtisseur–grillardin*

Various compound butters
Various cold sauces
Various mayonnaise derivatives

Mirabeau garnish
Holstein garnish
Vienna garnish

THE VEGETABLE EGG CHEF *L'entremetier*

Diced cooked ham – omelettes
Chicken livers – croutons –
   savouries
Oysters – croûtons – savourée

Lamb kidneys – egg dishes Meyerbeer
Crayfish tails – egg dishes Rothschild
Chipolatas – egg dishes Bercy

THE PASTRY CHEF *Le pâtissier*

Filling for sausage rolls
Diced meat for pies and
   puddings, Cornish pasties

Meat, poultry and game farces for en croûte
Chopped suet for pastry
Different salpicons for Dartois ravioli filling

Some Classical Garnishes

Table 7.2 details some of the classical garnishes that still find use today.

TABLE 7.2 *Classical Garnishes*

Menu name	Used to garnish	Typical ingredients
Américaine	Fish	Slices of lobster and truffles
Dieppoise	Fish	Shrimps, bearded mussels, mushrooms
Financière	*	Chicken quenelles, cockscombs, cocks kidneys, truffles, stoned olives
Marinière	Fish	Shrimps or prawns, bearded mussels
Milanaise	*	Julienne of ham, mushrooms, tongue, truffles, tomato
Mirabeau	Grills	Anchovy butter, fillets of anchovy, stuffed olives
Normande	Fish	Bearded oysters and mussels, mushroom heads, crayfish tails, goujons of sole, slices of truffle, croûtons
Régence	Fish	Fish quenelles, crayfish tails, mushrooms, bearded oysters, soft roes, slices of truffles
	Chicken	Chicken sweetbread: chicken quenelles, cockscombs, triangles of foie gras, mushroom heads
	Game	Game quenelles, cockscombs, triangles of foie gras, mushroom heads, croûtons
Réforme	*	Julienne of ham, tongue, beetroot, whites of egg, gherkins
Toulousaine	*	Sweetbread, chicken quenelles, cockscombs, mushrooms, slice or dice of truffles
Viennoise	*	Slices of lemon, anchovy, sieved whites and yolks of egg, parsley
Walewska	Fish	Slices of lobster tails, slices of truffles
Zingara	*	Julienne of ham, mushrooms, tongue, truffles

*For poultry, all meats and pasta.

FRUITS OF THE SEA *Les fruits de mer*

This term means exactly what it says: a mixture of the fruits of the sea, made up from cooked fish and shellfish of all types, including some of the smaller quenelles shown above. It is served:

As a **starter**	e.g. Salade de fruits de mer or Cocktail de fruits de mer
As part of a **sauce**	e.g. in a fish/wine sauce, which we call Sauce fruits de mer
As a **garnish with fish**	e.g. with poached fish
As **fish stew/ragoût**	e.g. as a hot starter or fish course in its own right

Some examples would be:

Salpicon de fruits de mer	Stew
Timbale de fruits de mer, *or*	In a dish
Bouchée Vol au vent	In a puff pastry case
Dartois de fruits de mer	In a puff pastry slice
Crêpes de fruits de mer	In pancakes

CONTENT

What a fruits de mer mixture should consist of is very much a matter of cost. Normally we start with a little firm flesh fish such a plaice, pike, whiting, salmon etc. Often good raw fish trimmings around the tail or head found in every kitchen can be used up. Poached, cooled and flaked they are the base. To this we add some prawns, some mussels, cockles, winkles etc. If there is no limit to our budget, we can of course add the more expensive oysters, clams, scampis, scallops, slices of lobster tail or claw, crayfish, prawns, crawfish and white crabmeat.

Whatever our gastro-geographical region brings forth might be considered for inclusion in fruits of the sea. In England we usually mix some cooked fish flakes with some prawns, some mussels and whole small or sliced scallops.

If our choice or budget is limited it is acceptable to add to our mixture some small or quartered button mushrooms, or asparagus tips or even blanched red or green diced peppers, but these vegetables must not exceed more than a quarter of the mixture.

100 g of the chosen mixture is usually sufficient for a starter in the form of a cocktail or salad

125 g of the chosen mixture is usually sufficient if served as a hot starter or fish course

150 g will make an acceptable portion when serving a fruits de mer mixture for the fish main course.

Three examples of hot fruits de mer presentations are given in Figure 7.8.

| *a* | *b* | *c* |
| Plated served in a rice or piped Duchesse potato border | Fish-shaped puff pastry case filled with fruits of the sea | In timbale as fish course or hot starter |

FIG. 7.8 *Examples of fruits of the sea presentations*

SEASONINGS *Les assaisonnements*

Seasonings play a most important part in the culinary arts and most dishes would be impossible to produce – with a taste to which we are accustomed – without these seasonings. They should always be used with discernment and in well-defined proportions. Thus, the finished food will not be dominated by the seasonings but its own flavour (whatever the food may be) and the associated seasonings will blend to create a perfect harmony of taste.

We group the seasonings as follows:

- Salts (Table 7.3)
- Single spices (Table 7.4)
- Mixed or compound spices and seasonings (Tables 7.5, 7.6)
- Herbs (Table 7.7)
- Condiments, including marinades and pickles

SALTS AND SINGLE SPICES *Les sels et les epices*

TABLE 7.3 *THE SALTS* *Les sels*

English	French	Uses
Salt	Sel fin	Table salt containing sodium phosphate, used in most cooking and baking
Coarse salt	Sel gris	Known also as freezing salt, it is much coarser than table salt, used for culinary purposes and freezing
Celery salt	Sel de céleri	A blend of celery root and table salt, usually purchased ready prepared; may be used wherever celery or celery-seed is used
Garlic salt	Sel d'ail	A blend of garlic and normal table salt, usually purchased ready prepared, used for all dishes where garlic normally is used

Continued

TABLE 7.3 *THE SALTS* *Les sels—cont'd*

English	French	Uses
Monosodium glutamate		Salt-like crystals known as 'MSG'. It is marketed under various brand names and is produced by a special process from wheat, soya and sugar beet. It can be used to enhance the flavours in the cooking of every dish, with the exception of sweets
Saltpetre		A salt-like powder but not really a salt, used in conjunction with salt in the case of pickling or brining meats to retain a good red colour

TABLE 7.4 *THE SPICES* *Les epices*

English	French	Uses
Allspice	Quatre épices	The fruit of the *Pimenta officinalis* is a grain, similar to black pepper in appearance, only twice as large. It combines the properties of pepper, cloves, nutmeg and cinnamon. Used in pickling and sausage making; also found finely ground to a brownish powder
Aniseed	Anis	The dried seed of the plant *Pimpinella anisum*. Has a slight liquorice flavour, cultivated in most European countries. It is grey-green in colour and pear-shaped. It is used in bakery and in the manufacture of liqueurs
Cardamon	Càrdomome	From the plant *Elettaria càrdamomum Maton* from Ceylon and Guatemala; it presents one of the ingredients of curry powder. Used also in the manufacture of sausages and Danish pastries.
Caraway	Carvi	The fruit of the plant *Carum carvi*, cultivated mainly in Holland. It has stimulating and digestive properties, used in the making of cheeses, sprinkled on rolls and bread, cooked in Sauerkraut
Cayenne pepper	Cayenne	The ground pod and seed of hot chilli peppers, finely powdered, with a very hot, zesty flavour; it must be used very sparingly
Chilli	Chilli	Small red very hot peppers, with seed, from Mexico, West Africa, Louisiana and California. Used in Mexican and South American cooking. It is the most pungent of all spices and must be used very carefully. Best known and used in Europe as part of a pickling spice
Cinnamon	Cannelle	The bark of an oriental tree *Cinnamomum zeylanicum*–the best coming from Ceylon, but also grown in China. Commercially sold as stick, ground and cinnamon sugar. Very useful in bakery, syrups, puddings and punches

Continued

TABLE 7.4 *THE SPICES* *Les epices—cont'd*

English	French	Uses
Celery seed	Céleri	Grown in Europe, India and other countries, it is used in pickling and dishes where a celery flavour is desired
Coriander seeds	Coriandre	These seeds are the fruit of the plant *Coriandrum sativum*, cultivated in southern European countries, as well as Asia. A round seed, similar to white peppercorn. Strong aroma but mild flavour and used in the making of jellies, roast pork and certain cakes
Cloves	Clous de girofle	The nail-shaped flower bud of East Indian tree *Eugenia caryophyllus*. The preparation of this spice begins before the buds of the tree are open. Dipped in hot water, they are partly smoked and dried. Used moderately in soups, stocks, sauce studding for onions and braised stews and pies. Found also ground to a fine powder and used in stews and with vegetables
Cumin seeds	Cumin	Resembling caraway seed in appearance. It has quite a different flavour and is grown chiefly in India. It is one of the ingredients and spice of curry, much used in Mexican cookery and most tasteful with all rice dishes. Also available ground
Dill seed	Aneth	A small seed, grey-green in colour and similar to caraway, but round, and used mostly in mixed spices and for pickling. Often new potatoes are cooked with this spice, instead of mint
Ginger	Gingembre	Ginger is the root of the plant *Zingiber officinale*, which grows wild in India. Found cultivated in West Indies, Jamaica and Malabar. In these countries it can be obtained fresh; in Europe, usually only preserved in heavy syrup, as dried root or in powder form obtained from the dried root. It is used as an ingredient for curry powder in confectionery and pickling
Juniper berries	Baies de genièvre	These are the fruit of the shrub *Juniperus communis* cultivated all over Europe. They are of a black-blue colour, twice as large as black pepper-corns. Most famous as flavouring for gin, they are also used for pickling, brining and when cooking Sauerkraut
Mace	Macis	The outer shell of nutmeg *Myristica fragrans* grown in the Far East. It is of similar flavour to that of nutmeg, and orange-red in colour. Its delicate flavour is used for pickling, fish dishes and as a ground fine powder in the seasoning of various types of sausage
Mustard seed	Moutarde	Cultivated in Europe, California and the Orient. It is a seed used mainly in pickling and the making of chutney. When ground it is the base for English, French and German types of mustard commercially manufactured

Continued

TABLE **7.4** *THE SPICES*   *Les epices—cont'd*

English	French	Uses
Nutmeg	Muscade	The seed of the *Myristica fragrans* resembling a brown root grown in the East and West Indies. Also found ground and is used in baking and cooking, especially with potatoes and vegetables
White peppercorns	Poivre en grains blanc	A most universal spice from the East Indies, originated in Malabar. Obtained by soaking the black pepper grains in rye or sea water to remove the black skin. Used with most savoury foods where pepper that doesn't show may be preferred. Ground into a fine white powder for easy use
Black peppercorns	Poivre en grains noir	The dried outer shell of white peppercorns (above) with about the same use, especially in the preparation of charcuterie. Some coloured peppers also
Paprika	Paprika	Sweet Hungarian peppers, dried and powdered. As a member of the pepper family, this one is not strong and has a most sweet, agreeable flavour, and adds a bright red colour to foods
Pimento	Piment/ Poivron	Jamaican and Spanish type peppers. Slightly stronger than paprika but still mild. Used in the flavouring of sausages and manufacture of potted meat and fish preparation
Pistachio	Pistaches	These nuts are the fruit of the shrub *Pistacia vera*, growing in Asia, India and the Near East. The small nuts have a purple skin and bright green inside. The skin is usually removed. The nuts are used in confectionery, soups, potted meat preparations and galantines
Poppy seeds	Pavot	Grown in Europe, especially Holland. Used when fresh for bread rolls and biscuits, as the filling of poppy seed strudle and tasty with buttered noodles of all types
Sesame seed	Sésame grain	Transported from Turkey, India and the Orient, has a mild, nutty flavour. Sprinkled on bread, rolls, biscuits and vegetables
Saffron	Safran	Stems from the plant *Crocus sativus*. Originated in Asia Minor. The flowers are picked when fully open, the stamens removed and dried at a low temperature. They are a light, strong, yellow colour. Used with fish and rice dishes, as well as for confectionery
Turmeric	Curcuma	A root of the ginger family with a bright yellow colour and appetizing odour. Used in the making of curry powder, mustard sauces and pickling

MIXED OR COMPOUND SPICES   *Les epices composées*

There are a great number of spices and seasonings which are mixed and are combinations of different spices, salt and spices, or salt, spices and herbs. Instead of adding offhand a number of different spices to a food, the spices and seasonings are mixed in well-defined proportions beforehand, thus allowing for easy and correct use with different foods. These mixed spices and seasonings may be a simple mixture of salt and ground pepper only, which is extensively used with most savoury foods, or they may be a complicated mixture of spices of up to a dozen or more, and herbs as, for example, curry powder. Tables 7.5 and 7.6 give some examples. Many of these compound spices are bought ready mixed and are often closely guarded secrets of the manufacturers. Others are mixed to one's own taste allowing for personal or regional flavours.

Note that all mixed and compound spices and seasonings should, after careful mixing, be placed in jars of approximate size with a tightly fitting top. This must always be tightly screwed back on after using some of the seasoning.

TABLE 7.5 *MIXED OR COMPOUND SPICES*   *Les epices composées*

Curry powders and pastes	A combination of up to a dozen different spices and herbs, some of which have been named above; their combination is a guarded secret of different manufacturers
Mixed spices	A combination of ginger, cloves, nutmeg, mace, and pepper, etc., bought ready made and used in baking for puddings, cakes and biscuits, usually bought ready-mixed, but can be composed to one's own taste
Pickling spices	A combination of coriander, mace, pepper, etc., bought ready-mixed for pickling. Follow instructions
Spice salt (general)	*Use 15 g for any 500 g meat* 500 g salt 50 g ground black pepper 50 g ground white pepper 25 g ground mace 25 g ground ginger 15 g ground allspice 50 g ground nutmeg
Pork sausage seasoning: basic	*Use 15 g for any 500 g meat* 500 g salt 50 g ground black pepper 50 g ground white pepper 25 g ground ginger 25 g ground mace 50 g powdered sage 50 g ground nutmeg

Continued

TABLE 7.5 *MIXED OR COMPOUND SPICE* 🏃 *Les epices composées—cont'd*

Beef sausage seasoning: basic	*Use 15 g for any 500 g meat* 500 g salt 50 g ground black pepper 50 g ground white pepper 25 g powdered thyme 25 g ground ginger 25 g ground mace 50 g ground nutmeg 15 g ground coriander
Pork sausage seasoning: Cambridge	*Use 15 g for any 500 g meat* 2 kg fine salt 750 g white pepper 10 g ground sage 50 g ground coriander 10 g ground cayenne 40 g ground pimento 40 g ground nutmeg
Pork sausage seasoning: Oxford	*Use 15 g for any 500 g meat* 2 kg fine salt 750 g white pepper 15 g cayenne 25 g ground mace 25 g ground nutmeg 15 g ground coriander 15 g ground ginger 15 g ground sage
Chipolata seasoning	*Use 15 g for any 500 g meat* 4 kg fine salt 750 g white pepper 15 g ground thyme 100 g ground coriander 15 g ground cayenne 75 g ground pimento 75 g ground nutmeg

TABLE 7.6 *Special Dish Seasoning*

Oxford brawn seasoning	*Use 15 g for any 500 g of meat* 2 kg fine salt 1 kg white pepper 25 g ground mace 40 g pimento 40 g cayenne
Lancashire brawn seasoning	*Use 15 g for any 500 g of meat* 2 kg fine salt 1 kg ground white pepper 25 g ground ginger 25 g ground cayenne 25 g ground mace 25 g ground cloves

Continued

Table 7.6 *Special Dish Seasoning—cont'd*

Faggot seasoning	Use 15 g for any 500 g of meat 1 kg fine salt 500 g black pepper 25 g fine thyme, sieved 50 g ground cloves 1 kg fine salt 25 g fine sage, sieved
Hand-raised pie seasoning: Melton Mowbray	Use 15 g for any 500 g of meat 2 kg fine salt 1 kg ground white pepper 25 g cayenne 25 g ground cloves 40 g ground nutmeg
Hand-raised pie seasoning: Nottingham	Use 15 g for any 500 g of meat 1.65 kg fine salt 750 g ground white pepper 25 g ground mace 40 g ground cayenne 25 g ground nutmeg
Hand-raised pie seasoning: Yorkshire	Use 15 g for any 500 g of meat 1.25 kg fine salt 750 g ground white pepper 25 g round nutmeg 40 g ground cayenne
Hand-raised pie seasoning: Lincolnshire	Use 15 g for any 500 g of meat 2 kg fine salt 1 kg ground white pepper 25 g ground fine sage 100 g ground Jamaica ginger
Potted ham seasoning	Use amount given for any 5 kg of meat 100 g fine salt 25 g ground white pepper 15 g ground cayenne 15 g ground mace
Potted turkey seasoning	Use amount given for any 5 kg of meat 100 g fine salt 50 g white pepper 10 g ground marjoram 10 g ground cayenne
Potted salmon and shrimp seasoning	Use 15 g to any 500 g of fish 100 g fine salt 75 g white pepper 10 g ground cayenne 15 g ground mace

HERBS *Les herbes aromatiques*

The culinary herbs and their appropriate uses are described in Table 7.7.

TABLE 7.7 *THE HERBS* *Les herbes aromatiques*

English	French and general description	Foods well suited to these herbs
Basil	**Basilic** *Ocimum basilicum:* a herb of western Europe, very mild and sweet in flavour and used in the flavouring of green beans and pies, as well as green vegetables and pastas. One of the ingredients of turtle herb mixture	Quiche, pasta, lamb, pork, veal, omelettes, lettuce, tomato soup, salads, some white sauces
Bay leaf	**Laurier** *Laura's nobilis:* grown in the eastern Mediterranean countries and used for flavouring in a bouquet garni, pastry and confectionery	Pickles, beetroot, red cabbage, Sauerkraut, braised meats, most stocks and sauces
Caraway	**Carvi** The fruit of the plant *Carum carvi*, cultivated mainly in Holland. It has stimulating and digestive properties, used in the making of cheeses, sprinkled on rolls and bread, cooked in Sauerkraut	Potato soups, beetroot, meats and cheese salads, goulash, braised meats, braised white cabbage, garnish
Chervil	**Cerfeuil** *Scandia ceremonies:* has a most delicate flavour and is used as an ingredient in several mixed herbs and as garnish for certain soups, salads and punch preparations	Potato soups, omelettes, poached fish, many salads, salad dressings, roast chicken, tomato, many stocks and soups
Chives	**Ciboulette** *Allium schoenprasum:* this plant of the onion family has a light, fresh, onion flavour and is used finely chopped on salads, certain sauces and other preparations	Cream soups, salads, bouillions, potatoes, vegetables, kohlrabi, dressings, garnish
Coriander	**Coriandre** Coriander has sweet–sharp leaves, taste salty and should be used sparingly; used in many pickles and brines	Cucumber, pork, omelettes, all dark sauces, beetroot, fish and poultry stock, consommé, garnish

Continued

TABLE 7.7 *THE HERBS* **Les herbes aromatiques—cont'd**

English	French and general description	Foods well suited to these herbs
Dill	**L'aneth** A plant growing to 1.2 m and similar to asparagus fern. It has a delicate mild flavour, its crown or seed of the crown is used in pickling, especially cucumber. It is also used as dried dill seed	Its young, fresh sprigs are most decorative for all fish and shellfish cocktails and can be served with new potatoes instead of mint, crushed stalks form an important part of pickling of Gravad Lax, garnish
Fennel	**Fenouil** *Foeniculum vulgare:* the fresh or dried leaves of this plant are used for flavouring in bakery, pickling and in the manufacture of liqueurs	Pickles, boiled beef, herrings, chicken, dressings, salads, beetroot, cream soups, as vegetable garnish
Garlic	**D'Ail** *Allium sativum:* another of the onion family. It is white and separates into small cloves. The reputation of French and Italian cookery rests, to a large extent, on the use of garlic. It is very pungent and must be used sparingly. It is best crushed and mixed with salt into a garlic paste	Skewers, stocks and sauces, goulash, dressings, chicken, many salads, soups, minestrone, roast lamb, grilled fish
Horseradish	**Raifort** *Cochlearia armoracia:* the roots are used grated as an accompaniment mainly to roast beef and as sauces for various smoked fish. It can also be used for certain other meat dishes and hot and cold sauces. Best fresh, the roots are available from early autumn to early winter, and they can be kept reasonably fresh in a box with damp sand. Also available in jars ready grated under various brand names	Pickles, beetroot, roast and boiled beef, dressings, roast goose, some salads, butters, grilled fish, garnish
Lovage	Coarse parsley-like herb, ideal for all stocks and some soups. Should be infused only for a short time, can be used like chopped parsley	Pastas, rice, spinach, eggs, green salads, dressings, French boiled beef, boiled chicken, roast veal, garnish

Continued

TABLE 7.7 *THE HERBS* **Les herbes aromatiques—cont'd**

English	French and general description	Foods well suited to these herbs
Lemon Balm	Use only fresh, do not boil with foods. Used much in Far Eastern cooking, stir fries, dressings, pickles	Roast veal and lamb, tomato, tomato soup, cucumber salad, blanquette of veal and lamb
Marjoram	**Marjolaine** *Origanum vulgare:* has a very strong flavour and is an ingredient in turtle herbs. It is also used in sausage manufacture, especially liver sausage, and the making of pâtés, where liver is used. Wild marjoram or origanum is used in the preparation of Italian pizza	Green beans, all braised meats, salads, soups, tomato salads, soups and sauces, pasta, pizza, rice
Mint	**Menthe** *Mentha spicata:* this well-known herb is mainly used for mint sauces, peas and new potatoes. Wild mint is also used for the making of peppermint teas and liqueurs	Roast lamb, fried fish, French beans, dressings, salads, sauce, some sweets, garnish
Oregano	**Oregano** Transported from Italy and Mexico and used with vegetables, meat farces and sauces. Important in Italian cookery, wheat dishes and pizza	Lamb, fried fish, many salads, eggs, poached fish, tomato sauces and soups, pizza, pasta, rice
Parsley	**Persil** *Petroselinum sativum*, the best known of all herbs: its stalks are found in bouquet garnis flavouring and nearly all basic cookery. Its sprigs are widely used as garnish or decoration with many foods, fresh or fried	All stocks and sauces, dressings, salads, rice, poached fish, boiled ham
Rosemary	**Romarin** *Rosmarinum officinalis:* the rather tough leaves of this shrub are used mostly with veal, and feature greatly in Italian cooking.	Pickles, veal, lamb, shellfish, rice, pasta, minestrone, tomato salad, soup and sauces, poultry, potatoes, dressings

Continued

TABLE 7.7 *THE HERBS* *Les herbes aromatiques—cont'd*

English	French and general description	Foods well suited to these herbs
Sage	**Sauge** *Salvia officinalis*, has a strong pungent flavour, and is used extensively in English cooking for stuffings and sausage manufacture	Pork, ham, livers, duck, beans, grilled fish, all salads, quiche
Savory	**Sarriette** *Sateureia hortensis:* this herb of the mint family comes from France and Spain and features in these countries' cooking. It is rather strong and rarely used in England.	Farces, lamb, veal, stews, omelettes, dressings, mayonnaise, game, salads, poached fish, red cabbage
Tarragon	**Estragon** *Artemisia dracunculus* has a very pungent flavour and is an ingredient of mixed herbs. When fresh, it is used with salads and sauces, and also as cold larder decoration. It is also available in jars pickled in vinegar in whole leaves, or as flavouring to tarragon vinegar	Dressings, white sauces, Béarnaise, Hollandaise, many soups, poultry, pickles, shellfish
Thyme	**Thym** *Thymus vulgaris:* a well-known herb used extensively in bouquets garnis and is an ingredient of several herb mixtures; it should be used sparingly	All stocks and sauces, many soups, omelettes, grilled and poached fish, potatoes, vegetables, meat salads

CONDIMENTS AND SAUCES *Les condiments et les sauces*

All the preparations mentioned here are manufactured and available in jars, bottles and tins. They are with certain exceptions accompaniments rather than additions to foods and are available to the hotel or restaurant guest on request, to be eaten with ready cooked or cold foods.

Pickles, pickled mixtures and sauces and seasonings do not really represent seasoning and spices as such, although seasoning, spices and herbs are used in their manufacture. The best known are: anchovy essence (essence d'anchois), gherkins (cornichons), Harvey sauce, ketchups, mustards (moutardes), Maggi seasoning, mustard sauces, pickles (achards), pickled capers (câpres), pickled walnuts, Piccalilli, soya sauce, Tabasco sauce, Worcestershire sauce, chutneys. Where the French translation is not given, the produce is known under its English, or same, name.

BRINES, MARINADES AND PICKLES

The Larder uses a number of marinades, pickles and brines, most of which have been known for hundreds of years. Whereas the marinades are always used to give a certain distinctive flavour and/or to tenderize in some cases, the pickles and brines were originally used to preserve food. In modern times of refrigeration and deep freezing, pickling and brining may be thought to be unnecessary, but this is not so; under certain circumstances, this purpose still exists today.

The foods treated by pickling and brining attain a certain colour in the case of brine and, what is more important, flavour in the case of pickles and marinades. People have become accustomed to this and would not care to miss it.

Brines

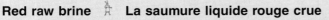

Raw brine   La saumure crue

Ingredients
10 litres water
25 g saltpetre
2 kg salt
100 g brown sugar

Method
1 Dissolve saltpetre in a little water and place with all the other ingredients in a large container which must be made of cement, glazed bricks, slate or earthenware (plastic of special make can also be used)
2 Stir every so often and leave for 24 hours until all salt has dissolved. Add meats to be brined, rubbed in salt
3 Test with salinometer at approx. 60 degrees with an egg, which should float on the surface of the brine. This method is not altogether safe because it only shows that there is enough salt, but not if there is too much

Red raw brine   La saumure liquide rouge crue

Ingredients
10 litres water
50 g saltpetre
2 kg salt
150 g brown sugar

Method
As for raw brine above

Spiced brine   **La saumure aux aromates**

Ingredients
10 litres water
2 kg salt
15 g saltpetre
250 g brown sugar
20 peppercorns
20 juniper berries
4 sprigs thyme
4–6 bay leaves
500 g sliced carrots
500 g sliced onions

Method
As for raw brine above

Cooked brines have salt and diluted saltpetre added to the brine after it has been boiled and strained. All the brines listed here can be brought to the boil and simmered for 10–15 minutes after which the salt and saltpetre is added to dissolve in the still-hot brine. It must be really cold (best cooled overnight) before any meat is added. The spice–brine is usually strained. Raw brines are used when brined meats are used on occasion. The cooked brines will, of course, keep much longer and should be used when brined meats are required continuously. In neither case should they be kept longer than a week.

Cuts of meat weighing up to 3 kg will brine in both raw and cooked brines in 4–6 days. Cuts of meat weighing from 3 to 6 kg will brine in 6–8 days. Cuts of meat weighing more than 6 kg should be left proportionately longer in the brine or should be treated with a pickling syringe; that is to say, cold brine is injected into the middle of the large piece. This technique can also be used if a piece of meat is required quickly.

The Marinades

Uncooked white wine marinade   **La marinade crue au vin blanc**

Ingredients
100 g sliced onions
8–12 peppercorns
50 g sliced carrots
1 clove
1 clove garlic,
   crushed
2 sprigs thyme
25 g sliced celery
   or celeriac
1 bottle white wine
   or wine-vinegar
20 g parsley stalks
500 ml oil
10 g spice salt

Method
1 Rub meat with spice salt
2 Place into a deep dish of china, earthenware, slate, glazed bricks or cement
3 Sprinkle herbs, vegetables and spices over the top
4 Moisten with wine and oil
5 Keep in a cool place for 24–72 hours

Turn the meat frequently so that it absorbs the flavour from all sides

Used for white meats and poultry

Uncooked red wine marinade 🦒 **La marinade crue au vin rouge**

As above, with red wine instead of white. Used for all red meats.

Uncooked red wine marinade for game 🦒 **La marinade crue au vin rouge pour gibier**

As for uncooked red wine marinade, with the addition of 6–8 coriander seeds and 6–8 juniper berries.

Uncooked red wine marinade for lamb–mutton 🦒 **La marinade crue au vin blanc**

As for uncooked white wine marinade with the addition of 8 juniper berries and a generous bunch of rosemary.

Cooked marinades have the advantage of keeping for a long time, provided they are kept in a very cool place and they are brought to the boil, according to the time of the year, every 2nd to 4th day. When re-boiled a little wine or wine-vinegar should be added each time to improve the flavour. Ingredients are the same as for uncooked marinades.

Cooked marinade

Ingredients
As for uncooked
  marinades

Method
1 Place oil in a pan of appropriate size
2 Add vegetables, herbs and spices
3 Sweat and brown slightly, then add wine, or
  wine-vinegar

Must be very cold before marinating meats
(24–72 hours)

Sweet and Sour Raw Pickles

The basic recipe for raw pickles is given below. Some of the many possible foods that can be so pickled are listed in Table 7.8.

Sweet raw pickles (Scandinavian origin)

Ingredients
1 litre white or
  wine-vinegar
1 litre caster sugar
24 peppercorns

Method
1 Combine all ingredients until dissolved (best
  done overnight)
2 Pour over foods to be pickled, which,
  according to firmness, need different times

Some other classical pickles are à la Grecque and à la Portugaise pickles served as hors d'oeuvres, for which recipes and method are given in Chapter 2.

TABLE 7.8 *Sweet and Sour Raw Pickles*

Cucumber	Wash and channel cucumber, slice, place in bowl or dish, cover with freshly chopped parsley or dill, pour over pickle to almost cover, leave for 1–2 hours giving them an occasional stir. Should not be left in pickle for more than 3 hours; must be made more often in batches as use requires Served as a salad, or part of an hors d'oeuvres variés on a buffet selection
Mushrooms	Select small button or closed cup mushrooms, wash, blanch in lemon water for 30 seconds, cool and place in bowl or jars. Cover with the pickle, leave for 24 hours before serving. Will keep firm for 2–3 days in fridge Serve as part of an hors d'oeuvres variés on a buffet selection
Cauliflower	Cut small roses off the cauliflower, blanch for 30 seconds, cool, place into bowl or jars and cover with the pickle, leave for 24 hours before serving. Will keep in fridge for 3–4 days Serve as part of an hors d'oeuvres variés on a buffet selection
Pearl or button onions	Select even onions within type, peel and wash, blanch for 30 seconds, cool and place into bowl or jar, cover with pickle, leave for 24 hours before serving. Will keep in fridge for 3–4 days Serve as part of an hors d'oeuvres variés on a buffet selection
Fennel – Celery – Celeriac	Cut fennel in 4–6 even pieces, celery or celeriac in neat pieces, blanch, place into jar or bowl, cover with pickle, leave for 24 hours before serving. Will keep in fridge for 3–4 days Serve as part of an hors d'oeuvred variés on a buffet selection
Pumpkin	Peel and cut pumpkins into neat strips or dice, not too small, place into bowl or jar, cover, adding 1–2 cinnamon sticks, leave for 24 hours before serving. Will keep in fridge for 2–3 days Serve as part of an hors d'oeuvres variés on a buffet selection
Salted herring fillets	Soak fillets if need be (some are supplied ready for use). Cut fillets in to 3–4 pieces on the slant, place with a pallet knife on to china or stainless steel tray in neat pattern, generously cover with finely sliced red onions, some crushed black peppercorns and allspice corns, pour over pickle mixture to cover. Leave for 36 hours before serving. Will keep in fridge for 2–3 days. A very tasty and popular Scandinavian pickle Serve as single starter or part of an hors d'oeuvres variés on a buffet selection Variations are flavoured with mustard, tomato and mixed herbs (see Chapter 2)

8 The Buffet Chef (Les Buffets Froids)

The function and duties of the Chef du Froid are the preparation, dressing and often the serving of cold buffets. These can range from the elaborate Display Buffet set out in the restaurant or grill room or both, to the Reception Buffet, the Cocktail Party Buffet, the cold luncheons for weddings or other functions, and the preparation of sandwiches for teas, dances, etc.

In other words, the Chef du Froid and his (or her) team are responsible for the **entire Cold Element** on the daily menus, as well as all functions and banquets. To carry out these duties efficiently, he must be familiar with the work concerned with Larder productions. These include the preparation of aspic, chaud–froid sauces, pies, galantines, terrines, pâtés, mousses or soufflés, pressed beef, brawns, boars head etc., as well as the various fillings for sandwiches and cold savouries, canapés, etc. He must also be skilled in the cooking and dressing of fish and shellfish, hams, tongues and other pickled meats, and in the dressing of smoked fish or meats, often showing a special flair and skill for artistic display and presentation.

It is important for the Chef du Froid to maintain close liaison with other departments in the Larder, Kitchen and Pastry so as to obtain the various joints of meat, poultry, game etc., as well as pastry cases, as and when required. He must be skilled in the use of aspic and have an artistic flair, which will enable him to decorate and garnish the various dishes in the pleasant and eye-catching manner that is very important in this branch of Larder work. Some skill in carving fat, or ice, for socles is also desirable.

Finally, the Chef du Froid must be a skilled carver, well able to use carving knives without handling the food with the fingers if it is to be served from a buffet in a dining room. The Chef's general appearance, smartness, cleanliness and manner will also play an important part in this kind of work.

PREPARATIONS

The Chef du Froid will start the day by dressing the various buffet dishes, carefully trimming where necessary, replacing stale items with fresh ones, re-glossing or glazing with aspic any pieces that have become 'tired' through contact with the atmosphere. Having dressed and decorated each dish, the Chef will replace it in the refrigerator until such time as it is required for dressing the buffet in the restaurant. Just prior to sending the food onto the buffet, the Chef will garnish each dish with its appropriate garnishes, e.g. parsley, watercress, hearts of lettuce, tomato, cucumber, horseradish, radishes, etc., to make it look fresh and appetizing.

A record of the number of portions or weight of joints is desirable from the point of control, essential to a well-run buffet. This record is checked on return of the buffet at the end of service, against sales and number of portions or weight returned. This is particularly important.

The rest of the Chef's time is spent in preparing any other cold dishes required for the day, sandwiches, canapés, etc., and in the preparation of the Larder productions for the buffet on the following day. The Chef must of course also ensure that such items as hors d'oeuvres, salads, cold sauces, cold sweets, cheese board, display of fresh fruits for dessert, etc., are available to complement the cold dishes on the buffet.

COLD BUFFETS   *Les buffets froids*

In all European countries a cold buffet is served for such functions as weddings, christenings, birthdays, business or association luncheons, as well as dances and late night suppers. On such occasions as Christmas, New Year, Easter and public holidays a buffet might also be served as a special attraction to the guests, complementing the normal table d'hôte menu. Today, when time seems ever more scarce, more simple self-serving buffets are often served in most hotels, including a breakfast buffet and in many restaurants for lunch to allow a faster service.

When serving a buffet for a function, the average hotel is able to cater for a larger number of guests than is normal for a sit-down meal. Even the number of extra waiting staff can be reduced in proportion, for one of the attractions of a cold buffet is for the guests to help themselves to the delicacies on display.

We differentiate between four types of cold buffets namely:

- **Finger Buffet**
- **Fork Buffet**
- **Modern Buffet**
- **Classical Buffet**

all of which are suited for the above-named functions, according to the host's wishes or requirements, and when planning any of the above buffets we should take into consideration the following:

- price per person agreed
- the number of guests proposed (availability of space for different types of buffets)
- the time, skills and equipment necessary for the made choice
- social grouping, culture and religion of the client considered
- suitability of the choice for the function.

THE FINGER BUFFET

As the name implies, this type of buffet is eaten with one's fingers and **no cutlery** is provided. The caterer must make sure that food items offered on the buffet are of a type and size that can be eaten easily with fingers, in one or at most two bites.

This type of buffet is usually **eaten standing**, seating not normally being provided, except maybe for the senior guests in the party. As no seating is necessary the establishment is usually able to serve a larger number of guests than would be normal and there would be a reduction in the number of service staff needed.

Firms, clubs or association often have their buffet functions on an annual basis, and if they are satisfied will make their bookings in the same local hotel or restaurant. Where this is the case, a record of foods served in the previous year should be kept by the catering establishment, to make sure that the buffet proffered in the following year or occasion has some changes in its content, taking into account the latest popular dishes and fads.

Figures 8.1 and 8.2 offer a list of typical food items and dishes suitable for a Finger Buffet, from the simple and obvious to the more elaborate. According to price charged, any number of dishes may be offered, the range usually being between 6 and 16.

Drinks served with the buffet are very much a matter of price and choice of the host, but are usually selected from the following in order of popularity:

> Champagne, white wine, red wine, sherry, port, punch, cocktails
> Alcohol-free drinks, fruit juices, squashes
> Hot beverages, such as tea or coffee, on special request.

THE FORK BUFFET   *Le buffet à la fourchette*

As the name implies, the guests are now given a **fork** with which to eat the buffet, indeed even the use of a **spoon** is also allowed and included for this type of buffet. We can thus now include foods and dishes somewhat more substantial and varied, but of a type which can comfortably be eaten with only a single item of cutlery. It can be eaten standing, but more often than not **some seating** is provided. It is a matter of space in a given room and numbers accepted.

The food list suited for the Fork Buffet consist of two groups – cold food and hot dishes.

Cold Food

Of course, all the cold foods listed above for the Finger Buffet are suited for the Fork Buffet. But with a fork or spoon now aiding our guests our offerings can be more substantial, and the first thing we should think to include in these days of healthy eating are salads, such as:

> Green and Leaf Salads more finely cut
> Simple Salads more finely cut
> Compound Salads, including their respective dressings (see Chapter 3)

We can also add one or more of:

> Chicken Mayonnaise
> Crab Mayonnaise
> Egg Mayonnaise
> Fish Mayonnaise
> Lobster Mayonnaise
> Prawn Mayonnaise

English sandwiches	Normal English sandwiches with savoury filling, white or brown bread according to fillings, and cut in different shapes, again according to, or to identify fillings	*a* 
Continental sandwiches	Usually made from bread flutes or small French sticks, plain, or with poppy, caraway or sesame seeds, filled with savoury, meat or fish filling, plus salads garnish. Secure with cocktail sticks, and cut into small slices	*b* 
Open sandwiches	Smaller versions of the Smørrebrød open sandwich on different buttered bread bases with suitable savoury filling and delicately decorated	*c* 
Canapés	Normal toast-based canapés with diverse fillings, decorated and glazed	*d* 
Bridge rolls	Small bridge roll, not cut quite open, well buttered with diverse savoury fillings and salad garnish according to type	*e* 
Small bouchées	The smallest of bouchées filled with creamed chicken, meats fish or shellfish. Served cold with lid returned after filling or open with filling shown	*f* 
Barquettes	Boat-shaped barquettes are by custom always filled with fish or shellfish salad or creamed versions of the same	*g*
Tartelettes	These small tartlets are by custom always filled with chicken or meat salads or creamed versions of the same	*h* 
Duchesse	Small blind-baked choux paste balls (profiteroles) about 2 cm in diameter when cooked, cooled and filled with creamed chicken or meats with a very small tube in piping bag through the lower side	*i* 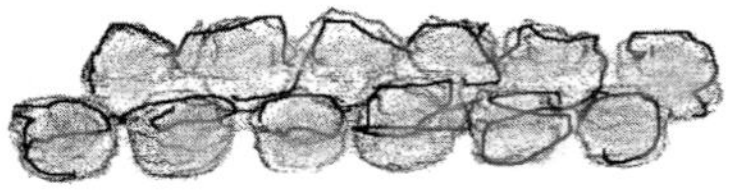
Carolines	Small choux paste éclairs only about 2–3 cm long when cooked, filled with creamed fish or shellfish with a very small tube in piping bag through the lower side	*j* 
Small dartois	Puff pastry filled with a savoury filling, the lid cut into an arrow point to show it is savoury, egg washed, baked golden brown and cut into small portions	*k* 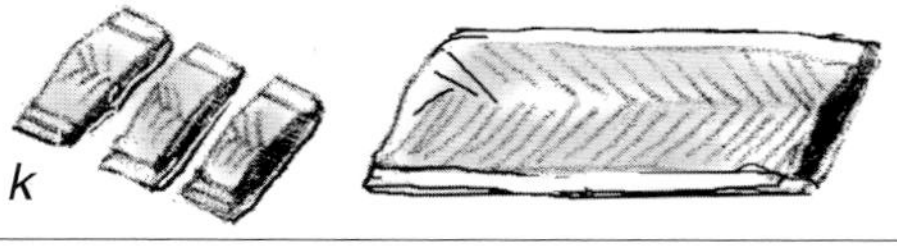

FIG. 8.1 *Examples of cold items for a Finger Buffet*

Cornets of ham (*a*) Cornets of smoked salmon (*b*)	Small triangular slices of ham or smoked salmon, rolled around the finger and filled with various finely cut compound salads, e.g. vegetables, Waldorf, dress on plate or platter	*a* *b*
Roulades of beef (*c*) Roulades of brisket Roulades of tongue(*d*) Roulades of turkey (*e*)	Small neat oblong slices of beef, salt brisket, tongue or turkey filled with various finely cut compound salads, rolled and secured with a cocktail stick, dress on plate or platter	*c* *d* *e*
Stuffed tomatoes	Cut top off small tomatoes, or cut medium tomatoes in even halves, remove inner flesh and pips with a parisienne cutter, fill tomato cavity with compound salads of vegetables, fish, shellfish or meats, dress on plate or platter	*f*
Stuffed eggs	Cut hard boiled eggs in halves, remove yolk, sieve, mix with mayonnaise and seasoning, herbs and spices, pipe back into egg white cavity, decorate (see Cold Starters in Chapter 2 for more variations), dress on plate or platter	*g*
Filled artichokes bottoms	Drain tinned artichoke bottoms, fill cavity with compound salads of vegetables, fish, shell fish or meats, dress on plate or platter	*h*
Potted meat wedges (*i*) Galantines (*j*) Pâté (*k*)	With a small knife dipped into hot water, cut neat small wedges of potted meat, galantine or pâté, place on small slice of toast, or cup of lettuce, decorate with grapes, cranberries, olives etc., dress on plate or platter	*i* *j* *k*
Salamis Beer sausage Garlic sausage Many others	Slice and rolled	See Chapter 2 on Cold Meat Starters

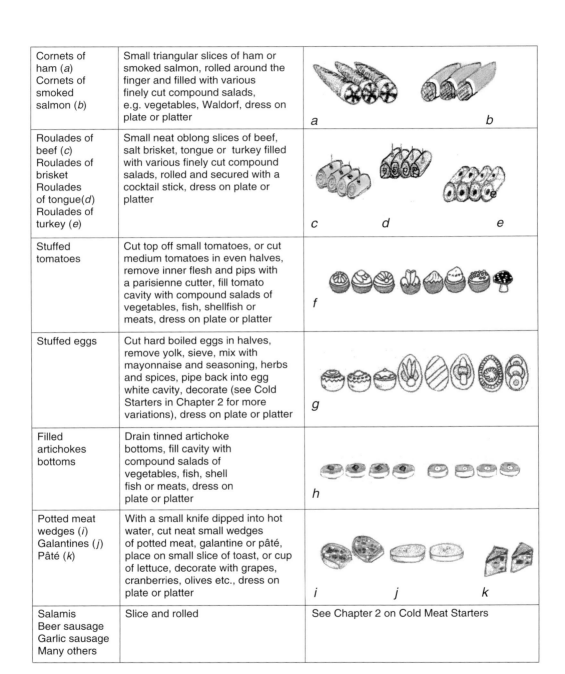

Fig. 8.2 *Examples of finger hors d'oeuvres*

Hot Dishes

As the Fork Buffet is intended as a more substantial meal we can offer additions such as:

Soups	Cream soups, consommés (hot or cold) and Gazpacho (cold), veloutés etc.
Hot starters	Hot quiches, pizzas, artichokes, filled pancakes etc.
Pasta dishes	Risottos, pilaffs, ravioli, gnocchi and noodles with various sauces
Egg dishes	Egg Cocotte, Poached Egg Florentine, Egg Chimay, Croquettes of Eggs etc.
Fish dishes	Poached fish in sauces, fried goujons, scampi or fillets of fish etc.
Entrées	Ragoûts, curry, paprika goulash, sauté or fricassee of chicken etc.

The latter are served and kept hot in chafing dishes. All are easily eaten with a fork and, being more of a meal, are sometimes referred to by the name **Fork-Luncheon Buffet.** This is very popular for business and seminar luncheons, when there is not much time for eating, or any closed function favouring such a self-service arrangement.

Sweets

With a spoon available to the guests we can be a little more inventive in the choice of our sweets, and we may add to the usual fresh fruits of the Finger Buffet cakes and gateaux, such as:

Bavarois
Fruit fools and salads
Ice creams
Coupes, mousses and trifles

Drinks

The choice can be made from the same list as mentioned above for the Finger Buffet. For the Fork Buffet it is more common to have coffee or tea included at the end of the meal.

AIDS TO PREPARATION AND PRESENTATION

We have yet two more buffets to consider – a Modern Buffet and the Classical Buffet. Before we do so, however, it will be helpful to consider some of the preparation and presentation aids which will help to stage and display any buffet in the best and most attractive way,

Aspic ☃ Gelée ordinaire

Ingredients (3 litres, 2–3 items of buffet preparation)

5 litres best beef stock
1 kg best veal bones
  chopped small
2–3 calfs feet blanched
250 g fresh pork rind
  blanched
250 g mire poix
25 peppercorns
Generous bouquet garni
Salt to taste
Glass of Madeira
10–12 sheets gelatine

Method

1 Roast the chopped bones until golden brown
2 Lift into a clean pan, blanch calfs feet, pork rind (for gelatinous properties), cover with cold stock, bring to the point of boil and add mire poix
3 Very slowly simmer on side of stove for 2–3 hours to get a clear stock
4 Gently strain through cloth or chinoise (hair fine sieve) or both. After evaporation should result in about 3 litres. Remove any fat from top
5 Place a ladleful of stock on a plate and place in deep freeze to set. The stock-aspic should be a firm jelly without being rubbery
6 If not firm enough, soak sheets of gelatine in cold water, lift out and dissolve in a litre or so of hot stock/aspic, strain through a fine chinoise. Add to rest of stock-aspic
7 Correct seasoning, add Madeira, store in fridge and use as required

For **chicken aspic,** replace beef stock and veal bones with chicken stock and chicken bone/giblets.
For **game aspic**, replace beef stock and veal bones with game stock and bones/giblets.
For uses, see below under Classical Buffet.

Fish aspic ☃ Gelée de poisson

Ingredients (3 litres, 2–3 items of buffet preparation)

4 litres very good cold fish
  stock
1 kg white fish bone finely
  chopped
8 egg whites
30 g sea salt
1 generous bundle of
  parsley

Method

1 Place fish bones in low wide pan (rondeau), add parsley, salt and peppercorns
2 Beat egg whites very firmly, mix with little cold fish stock
3 Mix with remainder of stock, pour over fish bones, mix all well
4 Place pan on an open flame and bring to point of boil

Continued

Fish aspic   Gelée de poisson—cont'd

Ingredients (3 litres, 2–3 items of buffet preparation)

15 white peppercorns
20 sheets of galantine
½ bottle dry white wine

Method

5 Turn down heat to lowest point or move to side of stove
6 Gently simmer for 20–30 minutes
7 Soak gelatine in cold water, drain, dissolve in 2–3 ladles of the hot fish stock then strain into fish stock/aspic
8 Gently strain through cloth or chinoise (hair fine sieve) or both
9 Correct seasoning and add wine
10 Place a ladleful of stock on a plate, place in fridge to set, the stock/aspic should be a firm jelly without being rubbery. Correct as for basic aspic above if required

For uses, see below under Classical Buffet.

Chicken   Chaud froid sauce

Ingredients (2 litres, 1–2 items of buffet preparation)

1 litre best chicken velouté
500 ml chicken aspic
250 ml single cream

Method

1 Add aspic to hot velouté, combine well
2 Cream, strain through chinoise (hair fine sieve)
3 Correct seasoning, use as required

Other white chaud froids:
Veal: replace chicken velouté and aspic with veal velouté and aspic
Ham: replace chicken velouté and aspic with ham stock-made velouté and aspic

Simple version of chicken chaud froid sauce

Ingredients (2 litres for 1–2 items of buffet preparation)

1 litre best chicken velouté
250 ml cream
6–8 leaves of galantine

Method

1 Soak galantine in bowl of cold water
2 Strain and add to hot velouté
3 Add cream, correct seasoning, strain through fine chinoise

Other simple white chaud froids:
Veal: replace chicken velouté with veal velouté
Ham: replace chicken velouté with ham stock-made velouté

Pink chaud froid sauce Chaud froid Aurore

Cook 25 g sweet paprika powder in little white wine, leave to stand, strain through a chinoise into either of the two chaud froid sauces above. Should be of delicate rose pink colour.

Green chaud froid sauce Chaud froid vert ou vert pré

Cut 100 g of cooked spinach into a very fine puree by passing through a sieve, mix with 30 g of finely chopped blanched herbs and add to either of the two chaud froid sauces above. Should be of a delicate green pastel colour.

Brown chaud froid sauce

Ingredients	*Method*
1 litre best demi-glace or jus lié	1 Soak gelatine in bowl of cold water
	2 Strain and add to hot demi-glace or jus lié
1 glass Madeira	3 Add Madeira, strain through a fine chinoise
8 leaves of gelatine	4 Correct seasoning

Brown glaze

In 1 litre of hot beef aspic (as above) dissolve 3–4 tablespoons of meat glaze/browning until desired rich brown colour is achieved. Used for glazing of the outside of joints of roast meats and boars' heads. For sliced roast meat use normal aspic.

Red glaze

Used for the glazing of red meats, e.g. salt beef, ox tongue and boars' heads. To 1 litre of hot beef aspic (as above) add 1–2 tablespoons of meat glaze and 1–2 tablespoons of fresh beetroot juice or edible colouring. The glaze should be rich dark red in colour.

Mayonnaise collée

To a litre of normal mayonnaise mix in 250 ml of fish aspic and strain. A quick way of achieving a chaud froid sauce, acceptable for the coating of fish. Once set it does not easily soften again.

THE MODERN COLD BUFFET　*Le buffet froid*

The third type of buffet is the modern buffet, sometimes also called the American Buffet. This is a 'buffet proper', with large joints of meat and fish as well as salads and other hors doeuvres. In a colourful presentation with chefs in tall white hats in attendance to carve and serve, it is what most people associate with the word.

For this Modern Buffet the guests need a **knife and fork** to be able to eat and enjoy the meal, which in turn means that **seating must be provided.** As with the previous buffets, the contents of the modern buffet is best presented in groups of dishes which have either method of cooking and/or presentation in common. This grouping will allow us to make the widest possible choice from the greatest number of suitable dishes without too many repetitions of items.

For the Modern Buffet, with its large joints of various meats and poultry as well as often whole decorated salmons and other fish and shellfish displays, it is advisable to have carved portions surrounding the centre pieces (see examples in Figures 8.3–8.5 and 8.8, Plates 8.1 and 8.2). This is to facilitate the early rush on these occasions and to avoid long queues at the start of service. Once this early pressure is over, we can then concentrate on carving the remaining centre pieces for the rest of the service.

Again, price charged and the varying profit margins required will, to a great extent, determine the contents of the buffet. Once these factors are known we can make our choice. A Modern Buffet therefore may consist of only a rib of roast beef and/or a boiled ham and a whole decorated poached salmon plus some salads and bread and butter. Or it can have any or all of the dishes listed below. The choice is yours, or what our customers will be prepared to pay for.

The examples included in Figures 8.3–8.10. below are grouped under the following headings:

> Cold Boiled Meats (Figure 8.3)
> Cold Roast Meats (Figure 8.4–8.6)
> Cold Fish (Figure 8.7)
> Cold Shellfish (Figure 8.8)
> Cold Entrées (Figure 8.9)
> Hors d'oeuvres (Figure 8.10)
> Compound Salads
> Dressings, accompanying Sauces, Condiments
> Breads and Butters

THE CLASSICAL BUFFET

The Classical Buffet consists of very highly artistically decorated food set pieces. These we often see at Hotel Olympia and other food exhibitions, but they are more or less a thing of the past in modern catering. In the average hotel or restaurant they are very seldom produced today except for a very special occasion. We may however present a few Classical pieces as centre pieces for our Modern Buffets. Plate 8.3 illustrates a few examples of Classical presentations.

Boiled ham	The ham on a trivet can be glazed, crumbed or covered with a chaud froid sauce. Surrounding it by cornets of ham will make the presentation attractive and it will help the service in the early rush	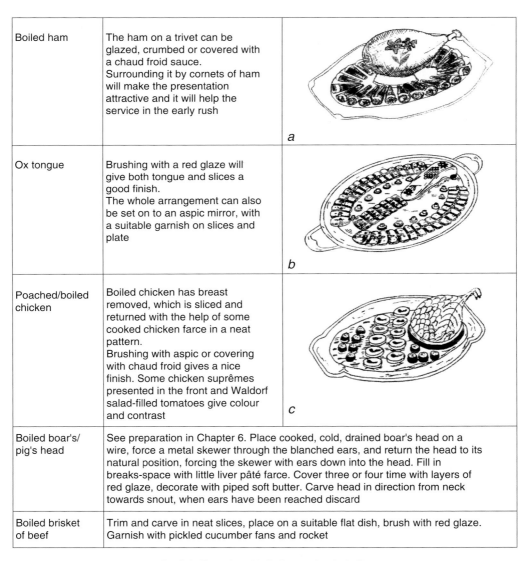 *a*
Ox tongue	Brushing with a red glaze will give both tongue and slices a good finish. The whole arrangement can also be set on to an aspic mirror, with a suitable garnish on slices and plate	*b*
Poached/boiled chicken	Boiled chicken has breast removed, which is sliced and returned with the help of some cooked chicken farce in a neat pattern. Brushing with aspic or covering with chaud froid gives a nice finish. Some chicken suprêmes presented in the front and Waldorf salad-filled tomatoes give colour and contrast	*c*
Boiled boar's/ pig's head	See preparation in Chapter 6. Place cooked, cold, drained boar's head on a wire, force a metal skewer through the blanched ears, and return the head to its natural position, forcing the skewer with ears down into the head. Fill in breaks-space with little liver pâté farce. Cover three or four time with layers of red glaze, decorate with piped soft butter. Carve head in direction from neck towards snout, when ears have been reached discard	
Boiled brisket of beef	Trim and carve in neat slices, place on a suitable flat dish, brush with red glaze. Garnish with pickled cucumber fans and rocket	

FIG. 8.3 *Examples of boiled meats for the buffet*

Rib of beef or sirloin of beef	Rib of beef surrounded by slices of beef. Rib and slices should be brushed according to degree of cooking with red or brown aspic–glaze	*a*
Fillet of Beef Wellington	The Wellington is here simply presented on a board on which it can be carved	*b*
Roast stuffed breast of veal	The stuffed breast of veal has a few slices carved off the front and is brushed with aspic and surrounded with vegetable salad-filled tomatoes. For breast preparation see Chapter 6	*c*
Roast stuffed loin of veal	Here three loins of veal were prepared with veal fillet and kidney in the centre and roasted. Two are presented in the middle, the third carved and placed in slices in the front. Apple salad-filled artichoke bottoms complete the simple presentation. For loin preparation see Chapter 6	*d*
Roast saddle of veal	Saddle and one loin roasted in the normal way. The saddle is taken off the bone and carved and on a paletle knife returned to the bone (a little cooked farce/pâté will help to keep it in place). The loin is carved in neat slices and placed in a circle around the saddle. Each slice has a turned blanched mushroom as garnish on top. Both are brushed with aspic. For carving of saddle see Figure 8.6	*e*

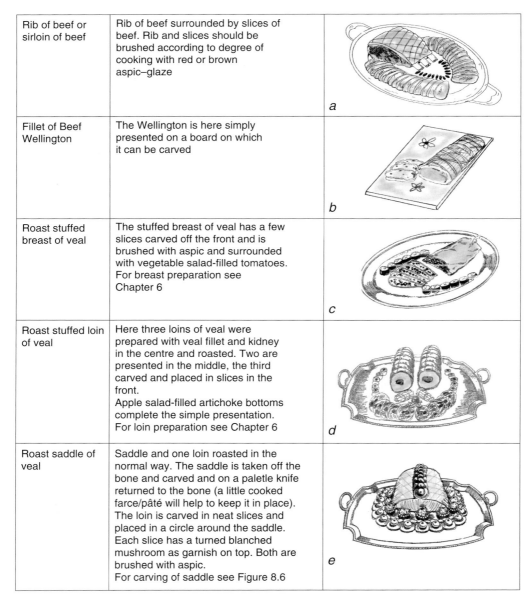

Fig. 8.4 *Examples of roast meats for the buffet: beef and veal*

Crown of lamb	Two crowns of lamb Baskets of mint sauce Tartlets with salad Brush with brown glaze or aspic	 *a*
Guard of Honour	Guard of Honour with a third best end cut ready in cutlets Brush with brown glaze or aspic	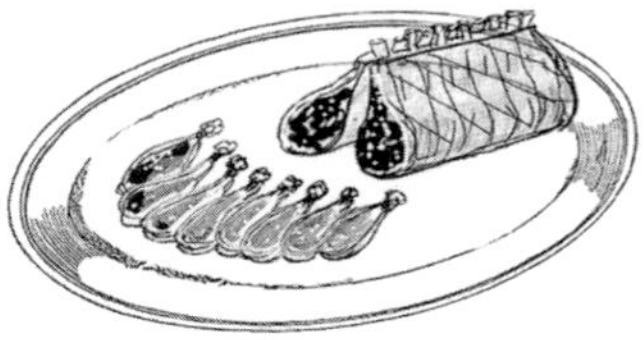 *b*
Short saddle of lamb	Short saddle of lamb with a loin cut in slices around Garnished with artichoke bottoms filled with asparagus tips Brush with brown glaze or aspic	 *c*
Long saddle of lamb	Long saddle of lamb with two loins cut in slices in front Baskets with marinated vegetables, bunch of asparagus Brush with brown glaze or aspic	 *d*
Stuffed loin of pork	Roast stuffed loin of pork with tartlets of mayonnaise-bound apple salad Brush with brown glaze or aspic	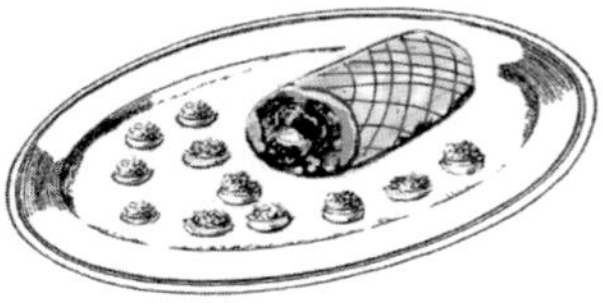 *e*
Roast leg of pork	Roast leg of pork, surrounded by red-coloured baked apples	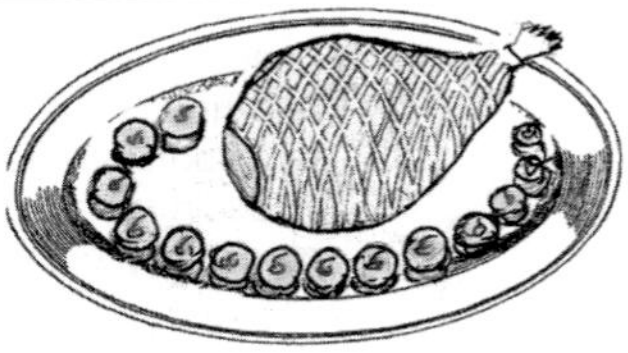 *f*
Suckling pig	Oven or spit roast in normal way, cool, glaze with aspic or brown glaze, serve with apple sauce. Should be carved on buffet in front of guests	

Fig. 8.5 *Examples of roast meats for the buffet: lamb and pork*

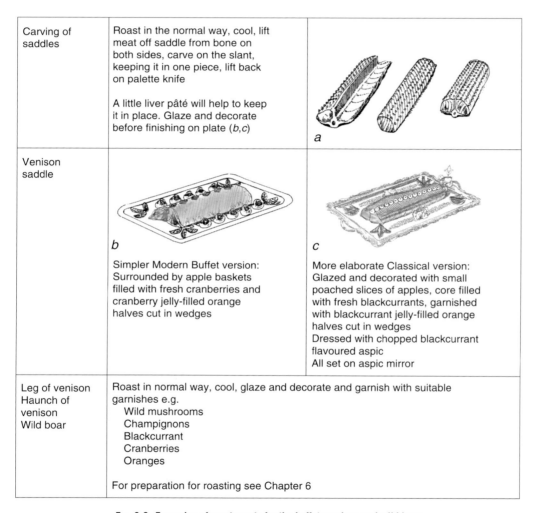

Carving of saddles	Roast in the normal way, cool, lift meat off saddle from bone on both sides, carve on the slant, keeping it in one piece, lift back on palette knife A little liver pâté will help to keep it in place. Glaze and decorate before finishing on plate (*b,c*)	*a*
Venison saddle	*b* Simpler Modern Buffet version: Surrounded by apple baskets filled with fresh cranberries and cranberry jelly-filled orange halves cut in wedges	*c* More elaborate Classical version: Glazed and decorated with small poached slices of apples, core filled with fresh blackcurrants, garnished with blackcurrant jelly-filled orange halves cut in wedges Dressed with chopped blackcurrant flavoured aspic All set on aspic mirror
Leg of venison Haunch of venison Wild boar	Roast in normal way, cool, glaze and decorate and garnish with suitable garnishes e.g. 　　Wild mushrooms 　　Champignons 　　Blackcurrant 　　Cranberries 　　Oranges For preparation for roasting see Chapter 6	

Fɪɢ. 8.6 *Examples of roast meats for the buffet: venison and wild boar*

Whole salmon	Whole poached salmon surrounded by salmon steaks, decorated with blanched tarragon leaves and brushed with fish aspic	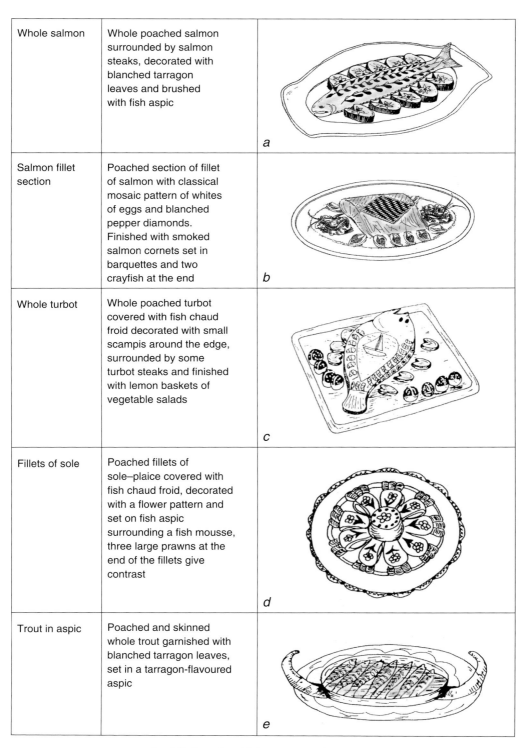 *a*
Salmon fillet section	Poached section of fillet of salmon with classical mosaic pattern of whites of eggs and blanched pepper diamonds. Finished with smoked salmon cornets set in barquettes and two crayfish at the end	*b*
Whole turbot	Whole poached turbot covered with fish chaud froid decorated with small scampis around the edge, surrounded by some turbot steaks and finished with lemon baskets of vegetable salads	*c*
Fillets of sole	Poached fillets of sole–plaice covered with fish chaud froid, decorated with a flower pattern and set on fish aspic surrounding a fish mousse, three large prawns at the end of the fillets give contrast	*d*
Trout in aspic	Poached and skinned whole trout garnished with blanched tarragon leaves, set in a tarragon-flavoured aspic	*e*

FIG. **8.7** *Examples of fish presentation for the buffet*

Lobster Crawfish Crayfish	**Dressed lobster** Normally boiled lobster with whole tails removed, cut in slices, decorated and glazed and presented on empty lobster shell. Claws are left whole. Set on a base of Russian Salad and garnished with stuffed eggs	 *a*
	Lobster display The cooked lobster is separated head–body from tail. The head–body is set upright on a base of Russian Salad. The tails are split in halves, and flesh red side up returned to each half shell. Claws slightly cracked are displayed on either end of a silver flat	 *b*
	Simple split lobster The cooked lobster is split down the middle in a clear cut. The half tails flesh is removed, sliced and returned in the opposite empty shell, red flesh side up	 *c*
Salmon suprêmes	Poached salmon suprêmes, cooled and garnished with slices of cucumber, brushed with fish aspic. Set on lettuce leaves, with a dot of piped mayonnaise. Simple modern presentation	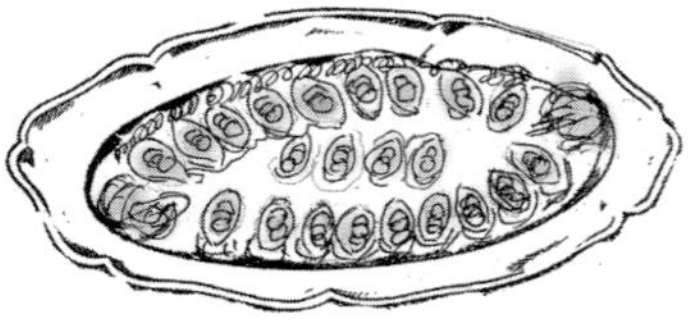 *d*
Crab	The cooked crabs are opened and brown meat from body and white meats from claws removed. Both meats are returned to cleaned shell, dark meat on the bottom, white meat on top. Decorated with hard boiled sieved egg white and yolk and garnished with anchovy fillets, capers and chopped parsley (see Chapter 2)	 *e*

FIG. 8.8 *Examples of shellfish presentation for the buffet*

Mousses/ Mousselines of different meat/fish	Large chicken mousse set in aspic surrounded by individual supreme-shaped mousselines, decorated with truffles or red peppers and with a garnish of bunches of asparagus tips	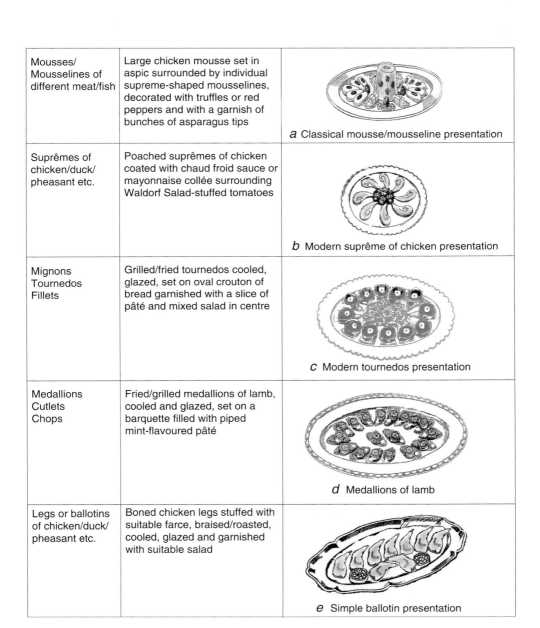 *a* Classical mousse/mousseline presentation
Suprêmes of chicken/duck/ pheasant etc.	Poached suprêmes of chicken coated with chaud froid sauce or mayonnaise collée surrounding Waldorf Salad-stuffed tomatoes	*b* Modern suprême of chicken presentation
Mignons Tournedos Fillets	Grilled/fried tournedos cooled, glazed, set on oval crouton of bread garnished with a slice of pâté and mixed salad in centre	*c* Modern tournedos presentation
Medallions Cutlets Chops	Fried/grilled medallions of lamb, cooled and glazed, set on a barquette filled with piped mint-flavoured pâté	*d* Medallions of lamb
Legs or ballotins of chicken/duck/ pheasant etc.	Boned chicken legs stuffed with suitable farce, braised/roasted, cooled, glazed and garnished with suitable salad	*e* Simple ballotin presentation

FIG. 8.9 *Cold entrées for the buffet*

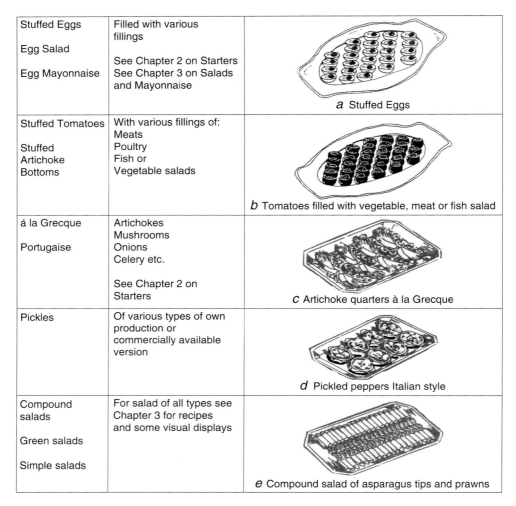

Stuffed Eggs Egg Salad Egg Mayonnaise	Filled with various fillings See Chapter 2 on Starters See Chapter 3 on Salads and Mayonnaise	*a* Stuffed Eggs
Stuffed Tomatoes Stuffed Artichoke Bottoms	With various fillings of: Meats Poultry Fish or Vegetable salads	*b* Tomatoes filled with vegetable, meat or fish salad
á la Grecque Portugaise	Artichokes Mushrooms Onions Celery etc. See Chapter 2 on Starters	*c* Artichoke quarters à la Grecque
Pickles	Of various types of own production or commercially available version	*d* Pickled peppers Italian style
Compound salads Green salads Simple salads	For salad of all types see Chapter 3 for recipes and some visual displays	*e* Compound salad of asparagus tips and prawns

FIG. 8.10 *Hors d'oeuvres for the buffet*

The production of an all-Classical buffet is simply too expensive, both in the materials to be used and more importantly the costly time needed to produce them. However, to show what abilities and skills are involved in this highly accomplished work, the next few pages will give some of the basic understanding needed for the production of Classical Buffet pieces for those who may wish to have a go.

We need several basic preparations. First, the edible decoration aids must be prepared as detailed in Table 8.1. We also need metal cutters of various shapes (Figure 8.11), with which we can produce the flower shapes and other designs characteristic of the Classical Buffet (see Figures 8.12–8.16).

TABLE 8.1 *Edible Decoration Aids for the Classical Buffet*

Decorative colour	Ingredients	Preparation
Black	Truffles Truffle substitutes	In the olden days much buffet decoration was done with slices of truffles. Even if we can get them, the price per kg is now so prohibitive that few of us are able to afford it, in what is already an expensive operation Truffle paste substitutes bought in small tins are acceptable, and can be improved by storing in a glass jar in Madeira
Green	Tarragon leaves Basil leaves Coriander leaves Leeks green tops	Blanch these leaves for a few seconds in boiling water, refresh, drain, store in ice water Trim smaller young leeks and boil whole or split down the middle for 4–6 minutes, refresh, drain, store in ice water
Red	Tomatoes Red peppers	Prepare firm red tomatoes as for concassé by peeling, cutting in half and removing all pips and inner flesh. The now clean flesh can be easily cut in to required shapes Choose smaller, younger peppers, cut in half, remove stalk and all pips, blanch for 1–2 minutes, they should be firm but pliable, drain, refresh
White	Egg whites	Separate white from yolk, place in a buttered dariole mould or small soufflé dish, leave to stand for 2–3 hours to remove any air bubbles, cook very slowly in a bain marie to set firm, cool over night
Brown	Glacé de viande	Slightly warm glacé de viande is placed in a greaseproof paper piping bag and with this a design is piped direct on to the chaud froid background of the item to be decorated. Like using icing sugar on cakes, this needs some experience and artistic skill for it cannot be wiped off

Cooking and Preparation of a Ham for a Classical Buffet Presentation

(1) Cook the ham in the normal way according to size and weight.

(2) Let it slowly cool over night in the cooking stock.

(3) The following day lift the ham out and place on wire to drain for 3–4 hours.

(4) With a sharp knife dipped in hot water remove the skin and excessive fat as well as clear the knuckle bone. In so doing do not disturb the natural shape of the ham or make ridges in the remaining fat.

(5) With a hot knife smooth the fat layer of the ham, *any unevenness will show up,* even after several covers of chaud froid. Place in the fridge to cool well.

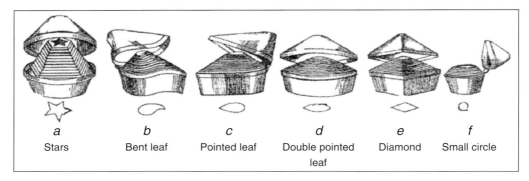

FIG. **8.11** *Various shapes of metal cutters*

a	b	c	d	e	f
Stars	Bent leaf	Pointed leaf	Double pointed leaf	Diamond	Small circle

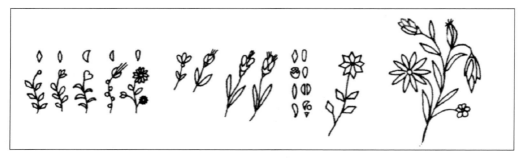

FIG. **8.12** *Simple flower shapes and their assembly. These can be produced using the cutters in Figure 8.11*

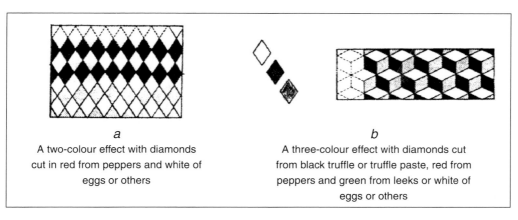

a

A two-colour effect with diamonds cut in red from peppers and white of eggs or others

b

A three-colour effect with diamonds cut from black truffle or truffle paste, red from peppers and green from leeks or white of eggs or others

FIG. **8.13** *Mosaic design effect*

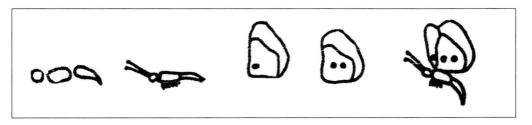

FIG. 8.14 *Butterfly assembly. Here we have for the first time both free hand-cut and cutter-cut decoration material, which shows how decorations can be assembled*

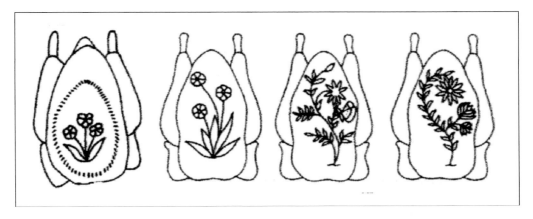

FIG. 8.15 *Various designs of decorations on chaud froid covered chickens. Except for stalks, all are cut with the cutters in Figure 8.11. (For chaud froid sauce covering follow instructions for ham preparation given below)*

FIG. 8.16 *Simple round decoration ideal for tops on mousses or mousselines or ham (follow instructions for ham below)*

(6) Place the ham on wire over a tray. Gently heat the white ham velouté-based chaud froid sauce and with a large ladle pour over the cold ham, any surplus chaud froid will collect and set on the tray and can be scraped off, re-heated and used again. Repeat this process of covering with chaud froid 3–4 times, cooling ham in fridge between each cover applied.

Decorate as shown in Figure 8.17. Follow the method with care.

Garnishes

On any of our flat (platter) presentations, with any of the types of buffets but particularly the Modern and Classical Buffets, we usually employ some garnish to give added colour or finish to the flat. Figure 8.18 gives some garnish ideas. Also, sprigs or bundles of dill, parsley, rocket, tarragon and watercress will complete and give a good finish to our prepared flats.

ROOM LAYOUTS AND BUFFET SHAPES

Not matter how excellent our dishes, for the complete success of our buffet we must also give consideration to two very important aspects of presentation – the shape of buffet table chosen and the layout of the room itself.

Our choice of tables is between round, square and oblong (see Figure 8.19). Having chosen the right type of table, however, it is of utmost importance to place the table or tables in the correct position in a given room. As all busy buffets have to be replenished and cleared, to do this effectively and without the least disruption to the guests, the most basic rule is: *as close to the kitchen area as is possible*. Some examples with different room lay-outs and buffets shapes are shown in Figure 8.20.

The final aspect of a successful buffet presentation is the assembly of the dishes on the tables. Figure 8.21 and 8.22 show some typical examples.

THE SCANDINAVIAN BUFFET OR SMÖRGÅSBORD

The Smörgåsbord serves both cold and hot dishes. The practice can be observed today in many British larger towns hotels, where, at least at lunch time, alongside the cold dishes hot dishes are proffered from chafing dishes.

The layout of the Smörgåsbord is as shown in Figure 8.23 and a particularly fine example is illustrated in Plate 8.4.

Ready chaud froid-coated ham is set on a ham-stand spike	*a*
With a sharp knife cut a thin strip of blanched leek to act as a flower stalk. Dip this in soft aspic and with your hand and the help of a cocktail stick guide into wished position. Repeat on opposite side	*b*
With a leaf cutter, cut the right-size leaves. The leaves may get narrower on top by using a smaller cutter. Dip these again into aspic, and with the help of a cocktail stick, place leaves on either side of stalk	*c*
Repeat on opposite stalk, creating a 'victor's wreath'	*d*
With a larger bend leaf-petal cutter (see Figure 8.11*b*), and possibly two different colours from the green used so far, dip into aspic which acts as an adhesive and place in a flower pattern in the middle of your wreath	*e*
Surround this flower with small circles (cutter 8.11*f*) in the colour of your choice. By free hand cut the shape of a tied bow, possibly in two sections, dip in aspic and place on the base of your wreath. Place the now decorated ham in the fridge for 1–2 hours for decoration to set and adhere	*f*
Now put some warm aspic into a bowl, set this bowl in another bowl on crushed ice and stir with a ladle. The aspic will get slowly firmer. Just at the right moment give your ham (still on a wire and tray) a coat of aspic. *Make sure the aspic is cold but flowing, too warm aspic can drain away your hard work and decoration.* For a good finish place the ham back into the fridge and repeat 2–3 times. Place the ham in the fridge and when you are ready to serve, surround the exposed bone with a ham frill	*g*

Fɪɢ. **8.17** *A simple decoration of a boiled ham*

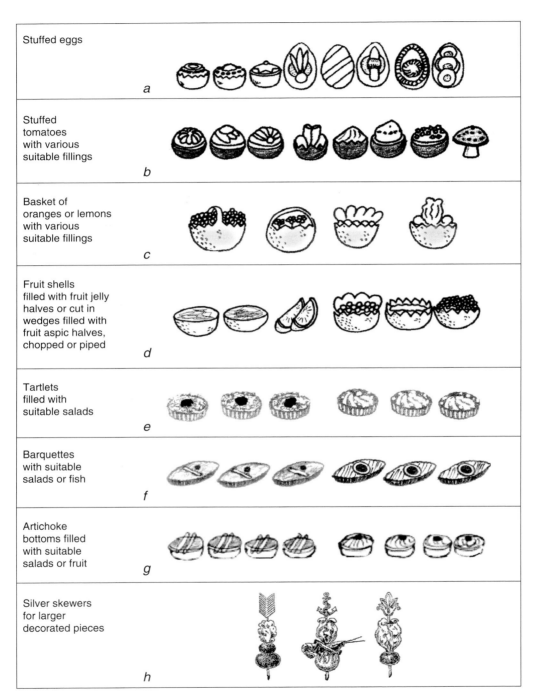

Stuffed eggs	
a	
Stuffed tomatoes with various suitable fillings	
b	
Basket of oranges or lemons with various suitable fillings	
c	
Fruit shells filled with fruit jelly halves or cut in wedges filled with fruit aspic halves, chopped or piped	
d	
Tartlets filled with suitable salads	
e	
Barquettes with suitable salads or fish	
f	
Artichoke bottoms filled with suitable salads or fruit	
g	
Silver skewers for larger decorated pieces	
h	

FIG. 8.18 *Example garnishes for flats*

The round buffet table

Purpose-built for small restaurants or function rooms.

With the advent of self-service Breakfast this table is now common in most small hotels and restaurants.

At luncheons it is often used for the display of hors d'oeuvres and salads or any special cold dishes on offer. There are of course different sizes, but it must never be deeper than the guest can comfortably reach

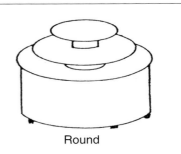

Round

a

The square buffet table

Often purpose-built for restaurants and banqueting halls, with its elevations it is ideal for Lunch and Dinner buffets for small numbers and it can be placed against a wall with a Chef in attendance for carving and serving.

Or with the elevation centred it can be placed in the middle of the room and act as a self-service buffet for small parties with access from all sides. Again, it must never be deeper than guests can reach

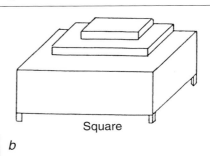

Square

b

The oblong buffet table
The most common shape of buffet table and usually based on trestle tables or purpose-built for most catering operations.

On its own, it may be used as the round or square tables above, or two or more of these tables may be put together or in a protruding 'U' shape.

They are ideal for the larger buffets of all types, especially when placed near a wall with chefs behind the buffet table for carving, serving and portion control.

The elevation can again be flush with the back of the table or centred according to intended use.

On one occasion in the writer's experience 12 such tables were placed side by side to make a buffet 40 metres long on a cruise liner

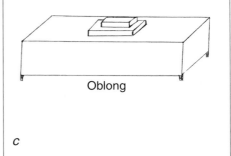

Oblong

c

FIG. 8.19 *The different shapes of buffet tables*

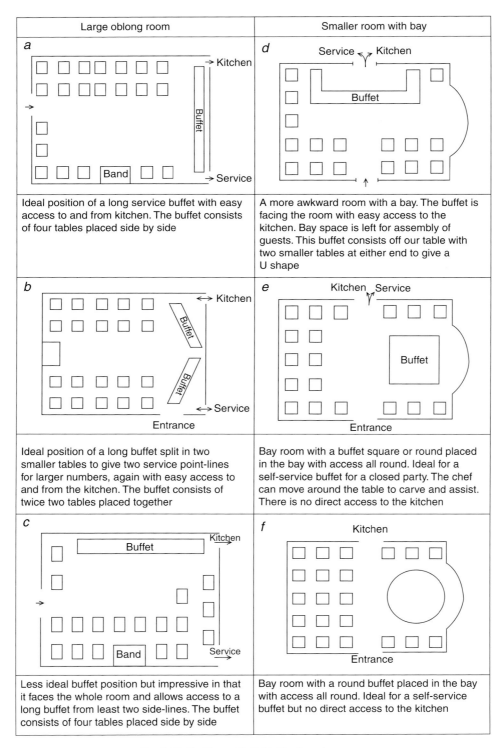

Large oblong room	Smaller room with bay
a — Ideal position of a long service buffet with easy access to and from kitchen. The buffet consists of four tables placed side by side	**d** — A more awkward room with a bay. The buffet is facing the room with easy access to the kitchen. Bay space is left for assembly of guests. This buffet consists off our table with two smaller tables at either end to give a U shape
b — Ideal position of a long buffet split in two smaller tables to give two service point-lines for larger numbers, again with easy access to and from the kitchen. The buffet consists of twice two tables placed together	**e** — Bay room with a buffet square or round placed in the bay with access all round. Ideal for a self-service buffet for a closed party. The chef can move around the table to carve and assist. There is no direct access to the kitchen
c — Less ideal buffet position but impressive in that it faces the whole room and allows access to a long buffet from least two side-lines. The buffet consists of four tables placed side by side	**f** — Bay room with a round buffet placed in the bay with access all round. Ideal for a self-service buffet but no direct access to the kitchen

FIG. 8.20 *Positions of buffet tables in a given room*

a

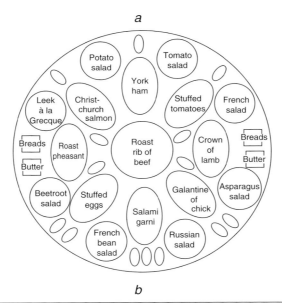

b

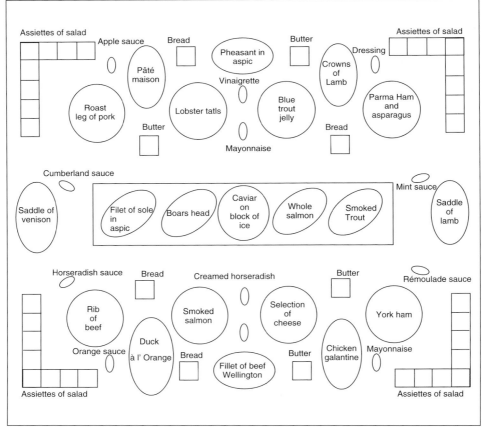

FIG. 8.21 *Assembly and layout of round or square modern buffet tables. A round Modern Buffet may have one or two elevations, it is suited for a centre of the room position with access from all sides and for pre-paid self-service where no control is necessary. A square modern buffet may again have one or two elevations and is also suited to self-service from a centre position. Note that the platters are arranged in mirror effect and salads, sauces and bread and butter are the same on all corners of the table*

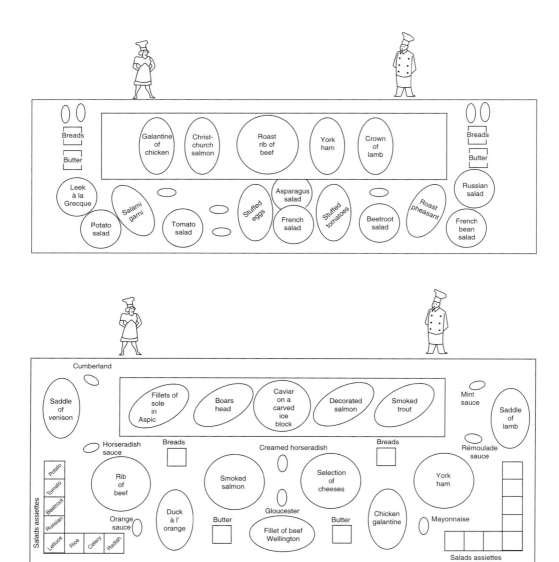

F_{IG}. 8.22 *Assembly and layout of oblong buffet tables against a wall with chefs in attendance to carve and serve the main dishes, guests choosing their own salads and accompaniments. If a larger buffet is needed several tables may be placed side by side. (top) The content here is of a more simple Modern type; (below) the content is more elaborate and Classical*

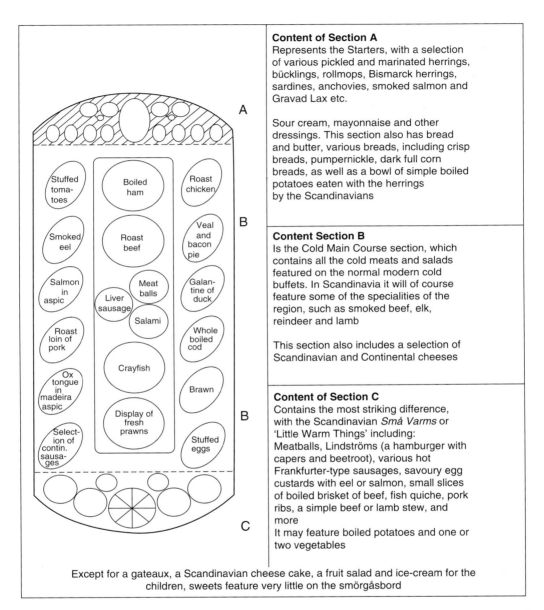

Content of Section A
Represents the Starters, with a selection of various pickled and marinated herrings, bücklings, rollmops, Bismarck herrings, sardines, anchovies, smoked salmon and Gravad Lax etc.

Sour cream, mayonnaise and other dressings. This section also has bread and butter, various breads, including crisp breads, pumpernickle, dark full corn breads, as well as a bowl of simple boiled potatoes eaten with the herrings by the Scandinavians

Content Section B
Is the Cold Main Course section, which contains all the cold meats and salads featured on the normal modern cold buffets. In Scandinavia it will of course feature some of the specialities of the region, such as smoked beef, elk, reindeer and lamb

This section also includes a selection of Scandinavian and Continental cheeses

Content of Section C
Contains the most striking difference, with the Scandinavian *Små Varms* or 'Little Warm Things' including: Meatballs, Lindströms (a hamburger with capers and beetroot), various hot Frankfurter-type sausages, savoury egg custards with eel or salmon, small slices of boiled brisket of beef, fish quiche, pork ribs, a simple beef or lamb stew, and more
It may feature boiled potatoes and one or two vegetables

Except for a gateaux, a Scandinavian cheese cake, a fruit salad and ice-cream for the children, sweets feature very little on the smörgåsbord

FIG. 8.23 *The smörgåsbord. A typical selection is described. To get the best and most original dishes, consult a good Scandinavian cook book*

SANDWICHES

Sandwiches, so the story goes, came first on to the scene in the house of the 4th Earl of Sandwich. He is said to have been a compulsive gambler who so loved his gambling that he left himself no time for eating. One day he asked the butler to serve some bread and cheese, to be eaten while the Earl and his friends went on gambling. His chef, knowing of his master's compulsive affliction, realized he would not stop gambling even while the cheese and bread were eaten, and so to make eating easier, the chef placed the cheese between slices of buttered bread – and thus the first sandwich was born. The actual story may be apocryphal, but certainly sandwiches are named after the 4th Earl of that name.

In catering today there are many types of sandwiches, some of which are variations or improvements on the original above; others are imported from different countries, of which the open sandwich from Scandinavia is the most recent addition.

The conventional, closed, so-called **lunch-box sandwich** consists of two slices of white or brown bread with any filling of meat, poultry, game, fish, shellfish, cheese and eggs. It can be garnished with lettuce, cucumber, tomatoes, watercress, mustard and cress. In the case of meat and fish, certain seasonings like made up English or French Mustard, salt, pepper and mayonnaise may be added where suitable. The sandwich is then cut into two triangles across, without removing the crust. Such sandwiches are served in bars, cafés, snack-bars and restaurants.

Conventional sandwiches

Bread:	Sandwich bread, white or brown
Butter:	Plain, mustard, anchovy, tomato, onion or garlic flavoured
Filling:	Bismarck herring, smoked herring, sardines, smoked eel, smoked trout, smoked salmon, bücklings, prawns, lobster, fresh salmon, shrimps, boiled ham, smoked ham, tongue, brisket, corned beef, roast beef, pork or lamb, salami, mortadella, mettwurst, liver sausage, blood-sausage, roast chicken, duck, game, turkey, chicken liver, liver-pâté, gammon, eggs, as well as all dry and creamed cheeses
Garnish:	Lettuce, tomatoes, watercress, mustard and cress, spring onions, radishes, gherkins, pickled cucumber, fresh cucumber, pickles, chutneys, parsley, as well as mayonnaise, tartare sauce and tomato ketchup
Finish:	Cut into a neat triangle, do not remove crust, serve on a doily or serviette with a little watercress or mustard and cress

The **tea sandwich** has much lighter fillings, and again white or brown bread is used. The fillings may consist of any meat or fish spreads, made in one's own kitchen, or bought commercially: Marmite, tomatoes, cucumber, jams and fruit, as well as mixtures of jam and fruit like bananas with strawberry jam, are very good. The tea sandwich is cut much smaller, into triangles, fingers, and squares, and the crust is always removed. Served in establishments serving Afternoon Tea.

Tea sandwiches

Bread:	Sandwich bread, white or brown, thinly cut
Butter:	Creamy plain butter
Filling:	Tinned and potted meats and fish, fish and meat pastes and spreads, Bovril, Marmite, fresh tomato purée, tomatoes, baked beans purée, cucumber, pickles, dry and creamed cheeses, fruit and jams, eggs, cress

Garnish: As for conventional sandwiches
Finish: Neatly remove crust; cut into even fingers, triangles or squares, or cut into fancy shapes, with a pastry cutter (Figure 8.24). Serve on a silver flat with doily or dish-paper; garnish with sprigs of parsley, watercress or mustard and cress

The **buffet sandwich** is very much the same as the conventional sandwich and similar fillings are used. The sandwich in this instance is cut much smaller, like the tea sandwich, into neat triangles, fingers, or squares. With these sandwiches, a combination of white and brown bread is often used, which will give them the chessboard effect. At times these sandwiches are given fancy shapes by cutting them with different sizes and design of pastry cutters. This method is very wasteful and one should avoid using it, except for children who may find delight in the colourful shapes and designs of these sandwiches.

Buffet or reception sandwiches

Bread: Sandwich bread white or brown, thinly cut
Butter: As for conventional sandwiches
Fillings: As for conventional sandwiches, plus tinned or potted meat and fish
Garnish: As for conventional sandwiches
Finish: Neatly remove crust, cut into even fingers, triangles or squares, or cut with a fancy pastry cutter (Figure 8.24). Serve on a silver flat with doily or dish-paper; garnish with sprigs of parsley, watercress or mustard and cress

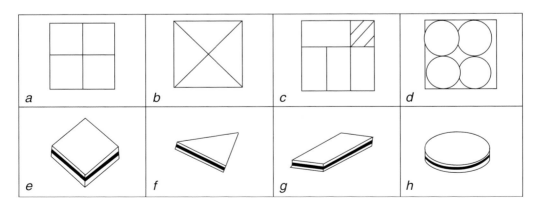

Fɪɢ. 8.24 *Tea and reception buffet sandwich shapes, showing cuts (a–d) producing different sandwich shapes (e–h)*

The **Continental** or **French sandwich** usually consists of a crusty French stick, cut into half and well buttered with either a single savoury filling and garnished with lettuce, tomatoes, cucumber, mayonnaise or a mixture of savoury fillings of meats, fish, poultry, game, cheese and eggs, and again garnished as above. Cut into small strips, secured with a cocktail stick, it can easily be picked up with one's fingers, and eaten in this manner.

Continental or French sandwiches

Bread:	French stick or cottage loaf
Butter:	As for conventional sandwiches
Fillings:	As for conventional sandwiches, one single filling, or a selection of several
Garnish:	As for conventional sandwiches
Finish:	Cut into even, neat strips. Serve on a silver flat with doily or dish-paper, garnish with sprigs of parsley, watercress, or mustard and cress

The **open** or **Scandinavian sandwich** (smørrebrød) is the more recent addition to the sandwich range, at least in England. Very much the same ingredients are used as for the conventional sandwich but here the emphasis is put more on a very attractive and appetizing presentation and, as its name indicates, it is open rather than covered with a second slice of bread. There is a further detailed section on these sandwiches below.

Canapés are not really sandwiches but small pieces of toast, white or brown, or biscuits or sheets of puff pastry, well buttered and covered with fillings of meat, game, poultry, fish, egg and cheese, decorated with flavored or coloured butter; they are finished with a clear glaze of aspic jelly according to their filling.

Canapés

Bread:	Thinly cut toast, *cut horizontally from loaf* to get a larger slice, or sheets of puff-pastry, cut into different shapes (Figure 8.25) or luncheon crackers, Ritz or hotel biscuits
Butter:	As for conventional sandwiches
Fillings:	As for conventional sandwiches
Garnish:	As for conventional sandwiches
Finish:	Piped with flavoured or coloured butter and glazed with aspic jelly. Serve on a silver flat, with doily or dish-paper

Neither do **hot sandwiches** really belong to this category, since they are more a snack or even a meal, but as they are called sandwiches and bread is used they are included here. Their number and variations are enormous, including the English Bookmaker Sandwich, the French Croûte Monsieur and such other internationally famous sandwiches as the Club Sandwich and the American Layer Sandwich, the German Strammer Max, the Swedish Lindström, and the Dutch Hot Beef Sandwich. Some of the Russian hot zakouskis and French brioche, as well as a late addition in the form of the fast food fried hamburger steak in a toasted roll may also be included. The recipes of some of the better known hot sandwiches are given below.

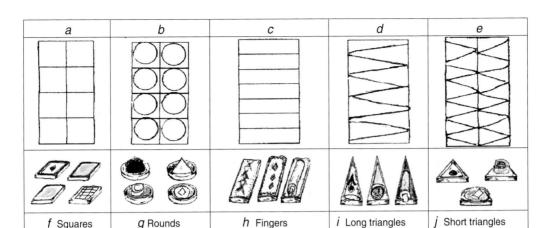

a	b	c	d	e

f Squares	g Rounds	h Fingers	i Long triangles	j Short triangles

Fɪɢ. 8.25 *Canapés cuts (a–e) giving different shapes (f–j). Note that toast is cut horizontally from loaf to get a larger slice*

Club Sandwich

Ingredients (4 portions, hot)
8 slices of toast
4 peeled tomatoes
250 g cooked boneless
   chicken
250 ml mayonnaise
8 grilled bacon rashers
16 cocktail sticks
1 lettuce
100 g butter

Method
1 Toast bread, trim off crust and butter well
2 Place a leaf of lettuce on toast
3 Add chicken, grilled bacon, tomatoes and
   mayonnaise
4 Finish with another leaf of lettuce, and
   second slice of toast
5 Press, secure with 4 cherry sticks, cut into
   4 triangles

Serve upright on a plate or silver flat, with
   doily or dish-paper showing filling

Bookmaker Sandwich

Ingredients (1 portion, hot)
2 slices of toasted bread,
   crust
French stick, or cottage loaf
English mustard
200 g minute steak
1 peeled tomato

Method
1 Season, steak and grill in the normal way
2 Spread liberally with mustard
3 Place between buttered bread
4 Press between two plates or boards
5 Cut in half or into strips

Serve on plate or silver flat with doily or
   dish-paper. Garnish with sprigs of parsley
   and quarters of tomato

Croûte Monsieur

Ingredients (4 portions, hot)
50 g cooked ham four slices
8 slices of slightly toasted
    thin bread
125 g Gruyère cheese, cut
    in 8 slices

Method
1 Place each slice of ham between 2 slices
    of cheese
2 Now place ham and cheese between
    2 slices of bread
3 Press firmly, remove crust and trim, cut into
    2 large or 4 smaller triangles
4 Gently fry until golden brown in clarified
    butter, so that cheese melts (can also be
    dipped in batter and fried, as above)

Serve on a plate or silver flat, with
    dish-paper. Garnish with sprigs of parsley

Strammer Max

Ingredients (1 portion, hot)
50 g lardons of bacon
25 g clarified butter
1 slice of toasted bread
1 egg
1 tomato

Method
1 Fry bread until golden brown, place on a
    warm plate
2 Sauté lardons of bacon, place on bread
3 Fry egg, place on top of bacon
4 Garnish with sprigs of parsley and quarters
    of tomatoes

Serve hot on a warm plate, to be eaten with
    a knife and fork

Sandwich Lindström

Ingredients (1 portion, hot)
25 g clarified butter
1 slice of toasted bread
2 eggs
Little brunoise of beetroot,
    onions, capers
150 g freshly minced
    beef – steak tartare

Method
1 Mix minced beef, onions, beetroot, capers
    and 1 raw egg
2 Season with salt and pepper, shape into
    steak
3 Gently fry in butter
4 Toast and butter bread, place fried steaks
    on the bread, make an indentation
5 Place egg yolk in indentation in steaks

Serve on warm plates, garnished with sprigs
    of parsley and quarters of tomatoes,
    chopped onions, capers

OPEN SANDWICHES (SMØRREBRØD)

This type of sandwich has gained great popularity in Great Britain in the past few years. They are most useful for several types of catering. Most of the open sandwiches originate from old Russia where, when nobility met for important and not so important dinners and dances, these sandwiches were served with drinks, especially vodka. However, it was the Scandinavian countries that adopted the open sandwich to such an extent that it became a real national food in countries like Finland, Norway, Sweden, Northern Germany and especially in Denmark, where it is known as smørrebrød.

In Denmark there are shops selling smørrebrød in more than a hundred varieties and it is not uncommon for a boxful to be bought to provide an easy family supper, in the same way as one might buy cakes or buns to take home for tea. These shops are open from early morning until late at night and smørrebrøds can be eaten on the premises at breakfast with a cup of coffee, at lunch time with a glass of ice cool lager, or one can pop in for snack before going out at night.

Some first class hotels serve these sandwiches in their bars, only smaller, more like canapés, as a sort of hors d'oeuvre with a guest's drink. In Denmark we find restaurants serving nothing but open sandwiches as a speciality. When customers have been seated they are given the Smørrebrød Seddel or Open Sandwich Menu together with a pencil. Customers fill in the menu according to their choices, enumerating the required ingredients, garnishes and breads (see example in Figure 8.26). This menu then goes into the kitchen. Here staff specially trained for this work freshly make the sandwiches. Here 'freshly' is the important word. This needs a very good mis en place in the kitchen. The lettuce and other salad ingredients are ready washed, the butter soft, the breads sliced and possibly buttered, the fish and meats prepared, and the fresh assembly of the chosen sandwich can begin.

When the sandwiches are made, the preparer puts the menu on the edge of the plate or flat, tucked under a doily, arranging the Smørrebrød on top. The waiter takes this to the guest, which allow the guest to check that the order has been correctly prepared. The menu also serves as the bill, to which the waiter only has to add any drinks the guests may have.

Open sandwiches fall into three types:

- **Large:** A normal slice of bread, with crust and fillings as described; this type is usually served in popular cafés, bars and restaurants, as well as smørrebrød shops and restaurants.
- **Medium:** A half slice of bread with the crust removed, cut into oblongs, triangles, half of a small roll, on the slant cut French stick, crisp bread slice, pumpernickel or rye or wholemeal bread slice. Fillings are as requested. This type is usually served in a selection of three or four, representing a meal. The medium size is also extensively used for reception buffets.
- **Small:** A quarter of a normal slice of different bread with the crust removed, cut into oblong squares, triangles, or cut with a pastry cutter, little more than canapés size. Fillings as requested. A selection of six of this small type is given, as a meal, often served as a starter. Now often found in British receptions in place of the normal canapés.

Breads	White	Brown	Rye	Vollkorn	Price
Specials					
Caviar					
Smoked Goose Breast					
Goose Liver Pâté					
Fish					
Smoked Salmon					
Smoked Eel					
Smoked Trout					
Smoked Herring					
Herring Salad with Egg					
Mustard Herring					
Sweet and Sour Herring					
Bismark Herring					
Rollmops					
Smoked Mackerel					
Eggs					
Hard boiled Eggs with Mayonnaise					
Hard boiled Eggs Anchovy					
Hard boiled Eggs Sardine					
Hard boiled Eggs Caviar					
Hard boiled Eggs Prawns					
Egg Scramble with Bacon					
Poultry and Game					
Breast of Chicken					
Turkey and Bacon					
Roast Duck with Apple					
Roast Pheasant Breast					
Roast Goose on Goose Dripping					
Smoked Turkey Breast Cranberries					
Cost					

Breads	White	Brown	Rye	Vollkorn	Price
Meats					
Beef Tartare with raw Egg Yolk					
Beef Tartare with Onions and Capers					
Beef Tartare slightly grilled					
Smoke Ham pickled Cucumber					
Boiled Ham Mixed Pickles					
Salami Tomatoes					
Mettwurst pickled Cucumber					
Boiled Ox Tongue					
Blood Sausages with Apples					
Brisket with Pickles					
Roast Beef Rémoulade					
Roast Beef Horseradish					
Smoked Lamb Cranberries					
Smoked Reindeer					
Liver Sausages					
Roast Pork					
Cheeses					
Danish Blue Grapes					
Camembert					
Stilton					
Flödost					
Hytteost					
Dutch					
Limburger					
Brie					
Stilton					
Cost					
Service Number					Drinks

FIG. 8.26 *Smørrebrød Seddel. The menu has been translated for the English reader. It can be seen that the menu also serves as the bill*

With the larger open sandwiches, a knife and fork must be given to the guest, who sits down. Simplicity as well as combination of ingredients, decoration and expert presentation make all of these sandwiches very attractive and they represent in our hurried modern times a reasonable but excellent nourishing meal.

Figure 8.27 shows 45 drawings of open sandwiches from the Danish Centre for Open Sandwiches. It can be seen that open sandwiches are very often made and sold by particular names, such as Hans Andersen's Favourite, Oliver Twist or Blue Boy. These names denote precise fillings and accompanying garnish, well known to most, and people will order by these names.

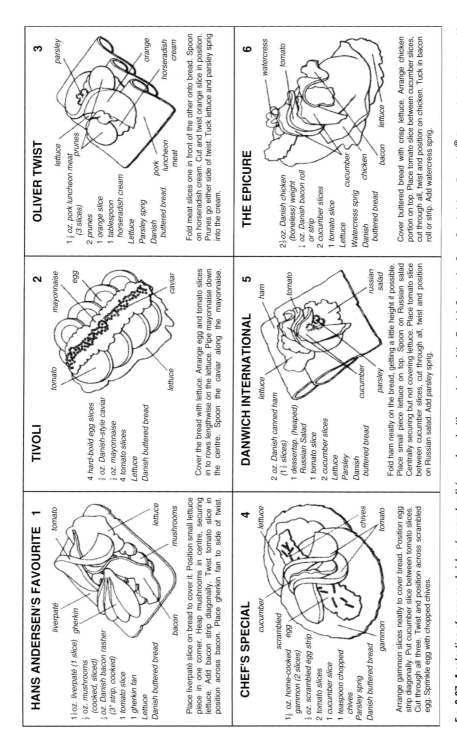

HANS ANDERSEN'S FAVOURITE   1

liverpaté   *tomato*

gherkin

lettuce

mushrooms

bacon

1½ oz. liverpaté (1 slice)
½ oz. mushrooms
(cooked, sliced)
¼ oz. Danish bacon rasher
(3" strip, cooked)
1 tomato slice
1 gherkin fan
Lettuce
Danish buttered bread

Place liverpaté slice on bread to cover it. Position small lettuce piece in one corner. Heap mushrooms in centre, securing lettuce. Add bacon strip diagonally. Twist tomato slice in position across bacon. Place gherkin fan to side of twist.

TIVOLI   2

mayonnaise

tomato

egg

caviar

lettuce

4 hard-boiled egg slices
½ oz. Danish-style caviar
½ oz. mayonnaise
4 tomato slices
Lettuce
Danish buttered bread

Cover the bread with lettuce. Arrange egg and tomato slices in to rows lengthwise on the lettuce. Pipe mayonnaise down the centre. Spoon the caviar along the mayonnaise.

OLIVER TWIST   3

parsley

lettuce

prunes

orange

horseradish cream

pork   luncheon meat

1½ oz. pork luncheon meat
(3 slices)
2 prunes
1 orange slice
1 tablespoon
horseradish cream
Lettuce
Parsley sprig
Danish buttered bread.

Fold meat slices one in front of the other onto bread. Spoon on horseradish cream. Cut and twist orange slice in position. Prunes go either side of twist. Tuck lettuce and parsley sprig into the cream.

CHEF'S SPECIAL   4

cucumber

lettuce

scrambled egg

scrambled egg strip

chives

tomato

gammon

1½ oz. home-cooked
gammon (2 slices)
½ oz. scrambled egg strip
2 tomato slices
1 cucumber slice
1 teaspoon chopped
chives
Parsley sprig
Danish buttered bread

Arrange gammon slices neatly to cover bread. Position egg strip diagonally. Put cucumber slice between tomato slices. Cut through all three. Twist and position across scrambled egg. Sprinkle egg with chopped chives.

DANWICH INTERNATIONAL   5

ham

tomato

lettuce

russian salad

cucumber

parsley

2 oz. Danish canned ham
(1½ slices)
1 dessertsp. (heaped)
Russian Salad
1 tomato slice
2 cucumber slices
Lettuce
Parsley
Danish
buttered bread

Fold ham neatly on the bread, getting a little height if possible. Place small piece lettuce on top. Spoon on Russian salad Centrally securing but not covering lettuce. Place tomato slice between cucumber slices, cut through all, twist and position on Russian salad. Add parsley sprig.

THE EPICURE   6

watercress

tomato

cucumber

chicken

bacon

lettuce

2½ oz. Danish chicken
(boneless) weight
¼ oz. Danish bacon roll
or strip
2 cucumber slices
1 tomato slice
Lettuce
Watercress sprig
Danish
buttered bread

Cover buttered bread with crisp lettuce. Arrange chicken portion on top. Place tomato slice between cucumber slices, cut through all, twist and position on chicken. Tuck in bacon roll or strip. Add watercress sprig.

Fig. 8.27 *A selection of open sandwiches (smørrebrød) (reproduced with permission of the Danish Centre for Open Sandwiches; Danwich® is a registered trademark)*

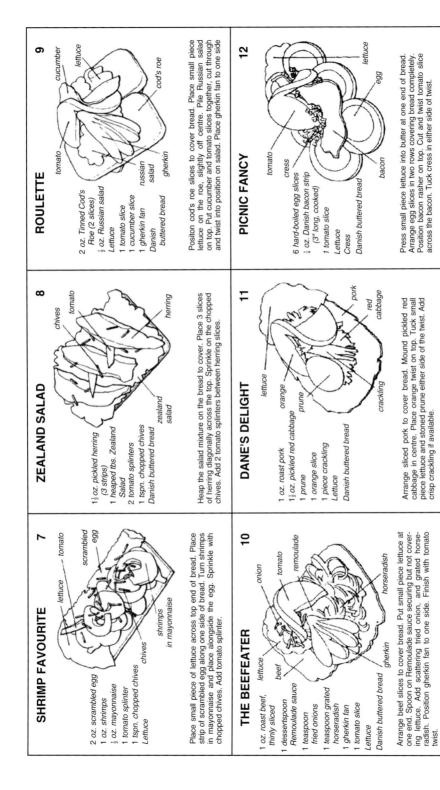

SHRIMP FAVOURITE 7

2 oz. scrambled egg
1 oz. shrimps
½ oz. mayonnaise
1 tomato splinter
1 tspn. chopped chives
Lettuce

Place small piece of lettuce across top end of bread. Place strip of scrambled egg along one side of bread. Turn shrimps in mayonnaise and place alongside the egg. Sprinkle with chopped chives. Add tomato splinter.

(labels: lettuce, tomato, scrambled egg, chives, shrimps in mayonnaise)

ZEALAND SALAD 8

1½ oz. pickled herring (3 strips)
1 heaped tbs. Zealand Salad
2 tomato splinters
1 tspn. chopped chives
Danish buttered bread

Heap the salad mixture on the bread to cover. Place 3 slices of herring diagonally across the top. Sprinkle on the chopped chives. Add 2 tomato splinters between herring slices.

(labels: chives, tomato, herring, zealand salad)

ROULETTE 9

2 oz. Tinned Cod's Roe (2 slices)
½ oz. Russian salad
Lettuce
1 tomato slice
1 cucumber slice
1 gherkin fan
Danish buttered bread

Position cod's roe slices to cover bread. Place small piece lettuce on the roe, slightly off centre. Pile Russian salad on top. Put cucumber and tomato slices together, cut through and twist into position on salad. Place gherkin fan to one side.

(labels: tomato, cucumber, lettuce, cod's roe, russian salad, gherkin)

THE BEEFEATER 10

1 oz. roast beef, thinly sliced
1 dessertspoon Remoulade sauce
1 teaspoon fried onions
1 teaspoon grated horseradish
1 gherkin fan
1 tomato slice
Lettuce
Danish buttered bread

Arrange beef slices to cover bread. Put small piece lettuce at one end. Spoon on Remoulade sauce securing but not covering lettuce. Add scattering fried onion, and grated horseradish. Position gherkin fan to one side. Finish with tomato twist.

(labels: onion, tomato, remoulade, lettuce, beef, gherkin, horseradish)

DANE'S DELIGHT 11

1 oz. roast pork
1½ oz. pickled red cabbage
1 prune
1 orange slice
1 piece crackling
Lettuce
Danish buttered bread

Arrange sliced pork to cover bread. Mound pickled red cabbage in centre. Place orange twist on top. Tuck small piece lettuce and stoned prune either side of the twist. Add crisp crackling if available.

(labels: lettuce, orange, prune, pork, red cabbage, crackling)

PICNIC FANCY 12

6 hard-boiled egg slices
¼ oz. Danish bacon strip (3" long, cooked)
1 tomato slice
Lettuce
Cress
Danish buttered bread

Press small piece lettuce into butter at one end of bread. Arrange egg slices in two rows covering bread completely. Position bacon rasher on top. Cut and twist tomato slice across the bacon. Tuck cress in either side of twist.

(labels: tomato, cress, lettuce, egg, bacon)

FIG. 8.27 cont'd

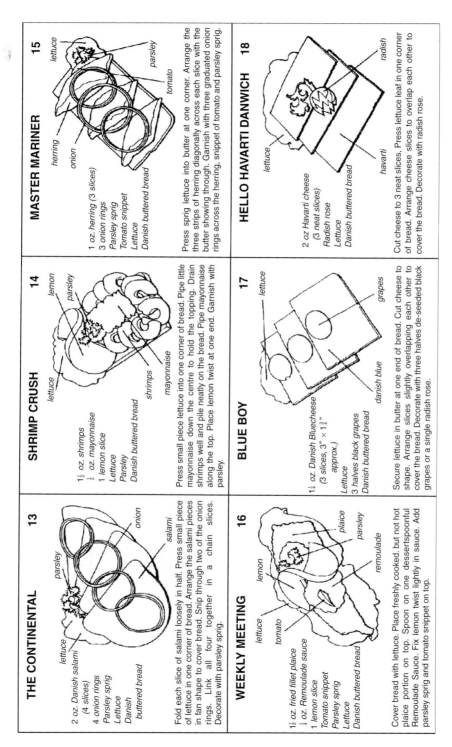

THE CONTINENTAL　　13

lettuce
parsley
salami
onion

2 oz. Danish salami (4 slices)
4 onion rings
Parsley sprig
Lettuce
Danish buttered bread

Fold each slice of salami loosely in half. Press small piece of lettuce in one corner of bread. Arrange the salami pieces in fan shape to cover bread. Snip through two of the onion rings. Link all four together in a chain slices. Decorate with parsley sprig.

SHRIMP CRUSH　　14

lemon
parsley
lettuce
shrimps
mayonnaise

1½ oz. shrimps
½ oz. mayonnaise
1 lemon slice
Lettuce
Parsley
Danish buttered bread

Press small piece lettuce into one corner of bread. Pipe little mayonnaise down the centre to hold the topping. Drain shrimps well and pile neatly on the bread. Pipe mayonnaise along the top. Place lemon twist at one end. Garnish with parsley.

MASTER MARINER　　15

lettuce
herring
onion
parsley
tomato

1 oz. herring (3 slices)
3 onion rings
Parsley sprig
Tomato snippet
Lettuce
Danish buttered bread

Press sprig lettuce into butter at one corner. Arrange the three strips of herring diagonally across each slice with the butter showing through. Garnish with three graduated onion rings across the herring, snippet of tomato and parsley sprig.

WEEKLY MEETING　　16

lettuce
lemon
tomato
plaice
parsley
remoulade

1½ oz. fried fillet plaice
¼ oz. Remoulade sauce
1 lemon slice
Tomato snippet
Parsley sprig
Lettuce
Danish buttered bread

Cover bread with lettuce. Place freshly cooked, but not hot plaice portion on top. Spoon on one dessertspoonful Remoulade Sauce. Fix lemon twist in sauce. Add parsley sprig and tomato snippet on top.

BLUE BOY　　17

lettuce
danish blue
grapes

1¼ oz. Danish Bluecheese (3 slices, 3" × 1¾" approx.)
Lettuce
3 halves black grapes
Danish buttered bread

Secure lettuce in butter at one end of bread. Cut cheese to shape. Arrange slices slightly overlapping each other to cover the bread. Decorate with three halves de-seeded black grapes or a single radish rose.

HELLO HAVARTI DANWICH　　18

lettuce
havarti
radish

2 oz Havarti cheese (3 neat slices)
Radish rose
Lettuce
Danish buttered bread

Cut cheese to 3 neat slices. Press lettuce leaf in one corner of bread. Arrange cheese slices to overlap each other to cover the bread. Decorate with radish rose.

Fig. 8.27 *cont'd*

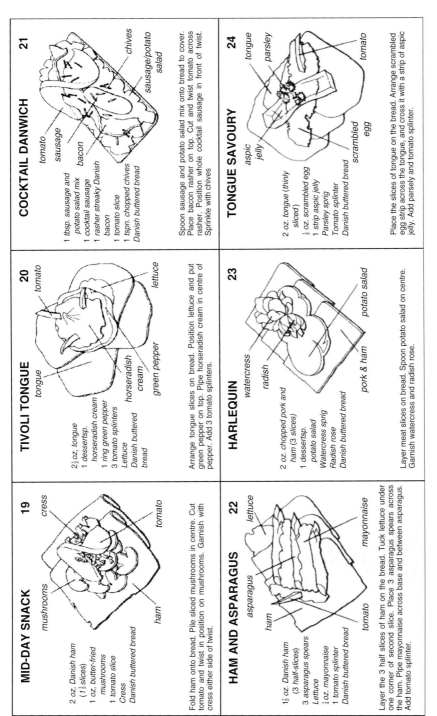

MID-DAY SNACK 19

2 oz. Danish ham
(1½ slices)
1 oz. butter-fried
mushrooms
1 tomato slice
Cress
Danish buttered bread

mushrooms *cress*

ham *tomato*

Fold ham onto bread. Pile sliced mushrooms in centre. Cut tomato and twist in position on mushrooms. Garnish with cress either side of twist.

TIVOLI TONGUE 20

2½ oz. tongue
1 dessertsp.
horseradish cream
1 ring green pepper
3 tomato splinters
Lettuce
Danish buttered
bread

tongue *tomato*

horseradish
cream
green pepper *lettuce*

Arrange tongue slices on bread. Position lettuce and put green pepper on top. Pipe horseradish cream in centre of pepper. Add 3 tomato splinters.

COCKTAIL DANWICH 21

1 tbsp. sausage and
potato salad mix
1 cocktail sausage
1 rasher streaky Danish
bacon
1 tomato slice
1 tspn. chopped chives
Danish buttered bread

tomato
sausage
bacon
chives

sausage/potato
salad

Spoon sausage and potato salad mix onto bread to cover. Place bacon rasher on top. Cut and twist tomato across rasher. Position whole cocktail sausage in front of twist. Sprinkle with chives.

HAM AND ASPARAGUS 22

1½ oz. Danish ham
(3 half-slices)
3 asparagus spears
Lettuce
½ oz. mayonnaise
1 tomato splinter
Danish buttered bread

asparagus *lettuce*

ham

tomato *mayonnaise*

Layer the 3 half slices of ham on the bread. Tuck lettuce under one corner of second slice. Place 3 asparagus spears across the ham. Pipe mayonnaise across base and between asparagus. Add tomato splinter.

HARLEQUIN 23

2 oz. chopped pork and
ham (3 slices)
1 dessertsp.
potato salad
Watercress sprig
Radish rose
Danish buttered bread

watercress

radish

pork & ham *potato salad*

Layer meat slices on bread. Spoon potato salad on centre. Garnish watercress and radish rose.

TONGUE SAVOURY 24

2 oz. tongue (thinly
sliced)
½ oz. scrambled egg
1 strip aspic jelly
Parsley sprig
Tomato splinter
Danish buttered bread

tongue
parsley

aspic
jelly

scrambled
egg *tomato*

Place the slices of tongue on the bread. Arrange scrambled egg strip across the tongue, and cross it with a strip of aspic jelly. Add parsley and tomato splinter.

Fig. 8.27 *cont'd*

SUNSHINE SALAMI 25

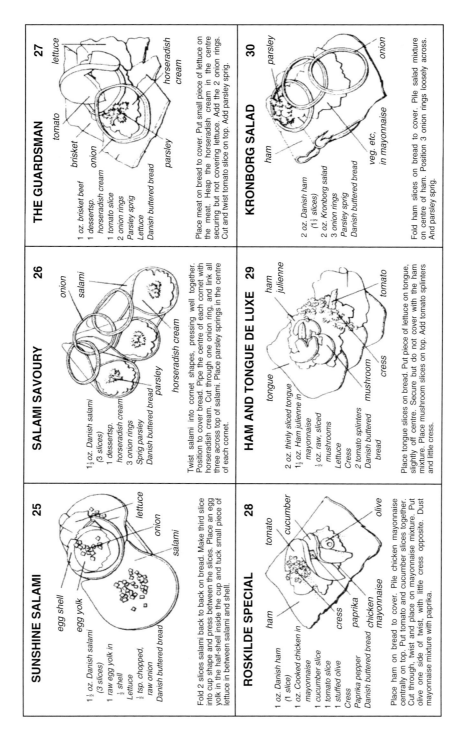

egg shell
egg yolk
lettuce
onion
salami

1½ oz. Danish salami
(3 slices)
1 raw egg yolk in
½ shell
Lettuce
½ tsp. chopped,
raw onion
Danish buttered bread

Fold 2 slices salami back to back on bread. Make third slice into cup shape and press between the slices. Place an egg yolk in the half-shell inside the cup and tuck small piece of lettuce in between salami and shell.

SALAMI SAVOURY 26

onion
salami
parsley
horseradish cream

1½ oz. Danish salami
(3 slices)
1 dessertsp.
horseradish cream
3 onion rings
Sprig parsley
Danish buttered bread

Twist salami into cornet shapes, pressing well together. Position to cover bread. Pipe the centre of each cornet with horseradish cream. Cut through one onion ring, and link all three across top of salami. Place parsley springs in the centre of each cornet.

THE GUARDSMAN 27

lettuce
tomato
brisket
onion
horseradish cream
parsley

1 oz. brisket beef
1 dessertsp.
horseradish cream
1 tomato slice
2 onion rings
Parsley sprig
Lettuce
Danish buttered bread

Place meat on bread to cover. Put small piece of lettuce on the meat. Heap the horseradish cream in the centre securing but not covering lettuce. Add the 2 onion rings. Cut and twist tomato slice on top. Add parsley sprig.

ROSKILDE SPECIAL 28

tomato
cucumber
ham
olive
cress
paprika
chicken
mayonnaise

1 oz. Danish ham
(1 slice)
1 oz. Cooked chicken in
mayonnaise
1 cucumber slice
1 tomato slice
1 stuffed olive
Cress
Paprika pepper
Danish buttered bread

Place ham on bread to cover. Pile chicken mayonnaise centrally on top. Put tomato and cucumber slices together. Cut through, twist and place on mayonnaise mixture. Put olive one side of twist, with little cress opposite. Dust mayonnaise mixture with paprika.

HAM AND TONGUE DE LUXE 29

ham
julienne
tongue
tomato
mushroom
cress

2 oz. thinly sliced tongue
1½ oz. Ham julienne in
mayonnaise
½ oz. raw, sliced
mushrooms
Lettuce
Cress
2 tomato splinters
Danish buttered
bread

Place tongue slices on bread. Put piece of lettuce on tongue, slightly off centre. Secure but do not cover with the ham mixture. Place mushroom slices on top. Add tomato splinters and little cress.

KRONBORG SALAD 30

parsley
onion
ham

2 oz. Danish ham
(1½ slices)
2 oz. Kronborg salad
3 onion rings
Parsley sprig
Danish buttered bread

veg. etc,
in mayonnaise

Fold ham slices on bread to cover. Pile salad mixture on centre of ham. Position 3 onion rings loosely across. And parsley sprig.

Fig. 8.27 *cont'd*

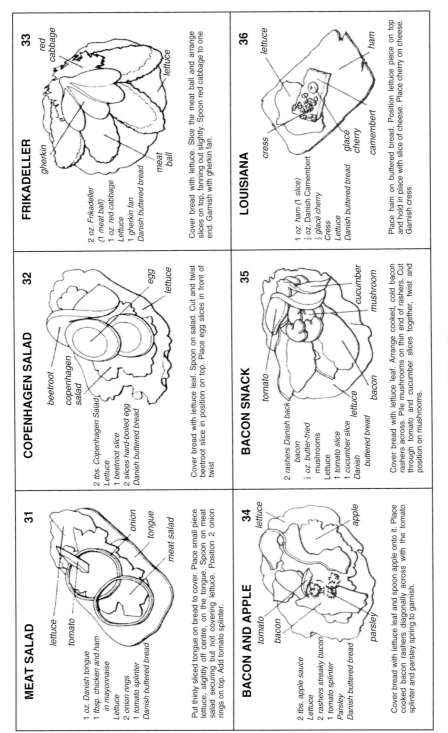

MEAT SALAD 31

lettuce
tomato
onion
tongue
meat salad

1 oz. Danish tongue
1 tbsp. chicken and ham in mayonnaise
Lettuce
2 onion rings
1 tomato splinter
Danish buttered bread

Put thinly sliced tongue on bread to cover. Place small piece lettuce, slightly off centre, on the tongue. Spoon on meat salad securing but not covering lettuce. Position 2 onion rings on top. Add tomato splinter.

COPENHAGEN SALAD 32

beetroot
copenhagen salad
egg
lettuce

2 tbs. Copenhagen Salad
Lettuce
1 beetroot slice
2 slices hard-boiled egg
Danish buttered bread

Cover bread with lettuce leaf. Spoon on salad. Cut and twist beetroot slice in position on top. Place egg slices in front of twist

FRIKADELLER 33

red cabbage
gherkin
lettuce
meat ball
Danish buttered bread

2 oz. Frikadeller (1 meat ball)
1 oz. red cabbage
Lettuce
1 gherkin fan
Danish buttered bread

Cover bread with lettuce. Slice the meat ball and arrange slices on top, fanning out slightly. Spoon red cabbage to one end. Garnish with gherkin fan.

BACON AND APPLE 34

lettuce
tomato
bacon
apple
parsley

2 tbs. apple sauce
Lettuce
2 rashers streaky bacon
1 tomato splinter
Parsley
Danish buttered bread

Cover bread with lettuce leaf and spoon apple onto it. Place cooked bacon rashers diagonally across with the tomato splinter and parsley spring to garnish.

BACON SNACK 35

tomato
cucumber
mushroom
lettuce
bacon

2 rashers Danish back bacon
½ oz. butter-fried mushrooms
Lettuce
1 tomato slice
1 cucumber slice
Danish buttered bread

Cover bread with lettuce leaf. Arrange cooked, cold bacon rashers across. Pile mushrooms on thin end of rashers. Cut through tomato and cucumber slices together, twist and position on mushrooms.

LOUISIANA 36

lettuce
cress
ham
glacé cherry
camembert
Danish buttered bread

1 oz. ham (1 slice)
½ oz. Danish Camembert
½ glacé cherry
Cress
Lettuce
Danish buttered bread

Place ham on buttered bread. Position lettuce piece on top and hold in place with slice of cheese. Place cherry on cheese. Garnish cress.

Fig. 8.27 *cont'd*

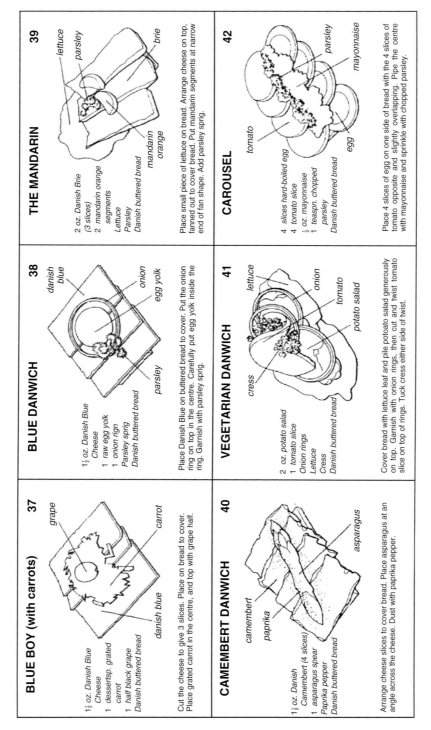

BLUE BOY (with carrots) 37

grape

carrot

danish blue

1½ oz. Danish Blue
  Cheese
1 dessertsp. grated
  carrot
1 half black grape
Danish buttered bread

Cut the cheese to give 3 slices. Place on bread to cover. Place grated carrot in the centre, and top with grape half.

CAMEMBERT DANWICH 40

camembert

paprika

asparagus

1½ oz. Danish
  Camembert (4 slices)
1 asparagus spear
Paprika pepper
Danish buttered bread

Arrange cheese slices to cover bread. Place asparagus at an angle across the cheese. Dust with paprika pepper.

BLUE DANWICH 38

danish blue

onion

egg yolk

parsley

1½ oz. Danish Blue
  Cheese
1 raw egg yolk
1 onion rign
Parsley sprig
Danish buttered bread

Place Danish Blue on buttered bread to cover. Put the onion ring on top in the centre. Carefully put egg yolk inside the ring. Garnish with parsley sprig.

VEGETARIAN DANWICH 41

lettuce

onion

tomato

cress

potato salad

2 oz. potato salad
1 tomato slice
Onion rings
Lettuce
Cress
Danish buttered bread

Cover bread with lettuce leaf and pile potoato salad generously on top. Garnish with onion rings, then cut and twist tomato slice on top of rings. Tuck cress either side of twist.

THE MANDARIN 39

lettuce

parsley

brie

mandarin orange

2 oz. Danish Brie
  (3 slices)
2 mandarin orange
  segments
Lettuce
Parsley
Danish buttered bread

Place small piece of lettuce on bread. Arrange cheese on top, fanned out to cover bread. Put mandarin segments at narrow end of fan shape. Add parsley sprig.

CAROUSEL 42

tomato

parsley

egg

mayonnaise

4 slices hard-boiled egg
4 tomato slice
½ oz. mayonnaise
1 teaspn. chopped
  parsley
Danish buttered bread

Place 4 slices of egg on one side of bread with the 4 slices of tomato opposite and slightly overlapping. Pipe the centre with mayonnaise and sprinkle with chopped parsley.

Fig. 8.27 *cont'd*

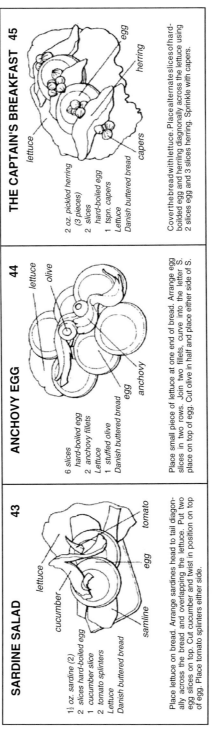

SARDINE SALAD 43

1½ oz. sardine (2)
2 slices hard-boiled egg
1 cucumber slice
2 tomato splinters
Lettuce
Danish buttered bread

Labels: lettuce, cucumber, samline, egg, tomato

Place lettuce on bread. Arrange sardines head to tail diagonally across the bread and overlapping the lettuce. Put two egg slices on top. Cut cucumber and twist in position on top of egg. Place tomato splinters either side.

ANCHOVY EGG 44

6 slices
hard-boiled egg
2 anchovy fillets
Lettuce
1 stuffed olive
Danish buttered bread

Labels: lettuce, olive, anchovy, egg

Place small piece of lettuce at one end of bread. Arrange egg slices in two rows. Join two fillets, curve into the letter S. place on top of egg. Cut olive in half and place either side of S.

THE CAPTAIN'S BREAKFAST 45

2 oz. pickled herring
(3 pieces)
2 slices
hard-boiled egg
1 tspn. capers
Lettuce
Danish buttered bread

Labels: lettuce, egg, herring, capers

Cover the bread with lettuce. Place alternate slices of hard-boiled egg and herring diagonally across the lettuce using 2 slices egg and 3 slices herring. Sprinkle with capers.

Fig. 8.27 cont'd

9 The Cheeses (Les Fromages)

Cheese is possibly the oldest man-made food. There is pictorial evidence of cheese-making from Mesopotamia in 3500–2800 BC. A relief of Al-U-Baid and a stamp seal from Jemdet Nasr also clearly show the Sumerians milking cattle and using the milk for cheese-making. Other archaeological discoveries have been made in Africa, France, Spain and the Libyan Sahara suggesting milk-processing and possibly cheese-making activity as long ago as 20 000 BC. At the height of the Greek and Roman empires cheese was most certainly well established and very much part of the daily diet. Only in the Far East and, in particular, India was milk and therefore cheese considered 'a liquid or sickly excretion unfit for human consumption' and thus for religious reasons cheese was not made.

For the invention and making of cheese man needed two obvious gastro-geographical conditions – a landscape more suited to grazing animals (sheep, goats and later cattle) than agriculture, and a warm climate that facilitated the curdling of milk (by accident rather than design). Milk was stored in large earthenware jars for daily use in what cannot then have been the best of hygienic conditions. These prerequisites for the invention and making of cheese were most strikingly fulfilled in the hilly country around the Mediterranean. It is not surprising, therefore, that the earliest and some of the best-known cheeses have their origins in this part of the world.

Wherever early cheese was made it was very much a hit and miss affair, only gradually improved by trial and error over many thousands of years. The making of cheese was very much a family, or possibly a village, concern, with the technique jealously guarded in the remote valleys or high alpine meadows in which it was produced and enjoyed. Until quite recently it was no more than a cottage industry in all parts of the world. Only in the eighteenth century did the making of cheese become a controllable industry as a result of the work of Justus von Leibig and, later, of Louis Pasteur.

Unlike other foods, cheese has never been considered suitable at one particular mealtime only. It can and is eaten at any time of the day. Some cheeses are better eaten as they come; others are more suitable for cooking and some suitable for both.

The variety is vast. The story goes that French President Charles de Gaulle, in the difficult years of the 1960s, said 'How can you govern a country which has 246 different cheeses?' Although he made a good point, De Gaulle was wrong with the number – France in fact has more than 500 varieties of cheese, most of them very local, many of them we shall most likely never eat, as well as many that are well known and loved in this country. Add to this the many other cheeses made in Europe, and the modern caterer has a very wide choice to offer. Varieties and availability have increased on a considerable scale in the past 20 years and almost every month a new one appears in the shops.

So how to know which cheese is best suitable for table or kitchen, or both? Below is a list of cheeses divided in five distinct groups with some typical examples and their characteristics. Emphasis has been given to the cheeses available in most parts of the British Isles. If cheeses come in great numbers, they also come in many different sizes, from the tiny to the very large, and different shapes. To help with recognition of different cheeses some common shapes and sizes are given in Figures 9.1 and 9.2. If one knows the colour and shape and other characteristics, any local specialities can then easily be placed in any of the groups below.

VARIETIES OF CHEESE   *Les fromages*

FRESH WHITE CHEESES   *Les fromages blancs*

These types of relatively young cheeses are sometimes called raw cheeses. They are made all over Europe from fresh curd with various cream/fat content. They are sold in taps, blocks, or small barrel shapes. Some have cream/butter added, while others have herbs and spices mixed in. Some are covered in vine leaves, most are made from cow's milk some from goat's or sheep's milk. Most can be used in cooking, particularly cheesecake. They are best stored in a fridge. (See Table 9.1 and Plate 9.1.)

SOFT CHEESES   *Les fromages mous*

Into this group fall some of the best-known and liked soft cheeses in the world, including:

> Brie – le roi des fromages, or the king of cheeses
> Camembert – le prince des fromages, or the prince of cheeses

They are probably the most imitated cheeses in the world and now produced in most European countries. But there are considerably more cheeses of this type than these two. They are usually sold in wooden or cardboard cartons, or free of boxes in all manner of shapes, from the large round flat Brie to the small wedges of Camembert. All are in the early stages of being more matured than white cheeses; some can be very strong in flavour and smell, all have an edible crust, a few have a green or blue mould growth. They should be stored in a cool place but never in a fridge. (See Table 9.2 and Plate 9.2.)

BLUE CHEESES   *Les fromages bleus moulés*

The blue cheeses are found all over the world, in all sizes and shapes, and to this group belong some of the most famous cheeses. Induced with *Penicillinum* mould growth, which develops inside from a dark marbled blue as in the case of Stilton to a light green as in the case of Roquefort, the colour may intensify according to the age of the cheese. Even some pink-veined cheeses belong to this group.

Their texture can be crumbly to smooth, their flavour mild to strong. They are highly regarded by cheese lovers and are a must on any respectable cheese board. Stilton and port go together like a horse and carriage or love and marriage. But the custom of pouring port on to the open Stilton half is less to be recommended. (See Table 9.3 and Plate 9.3.)

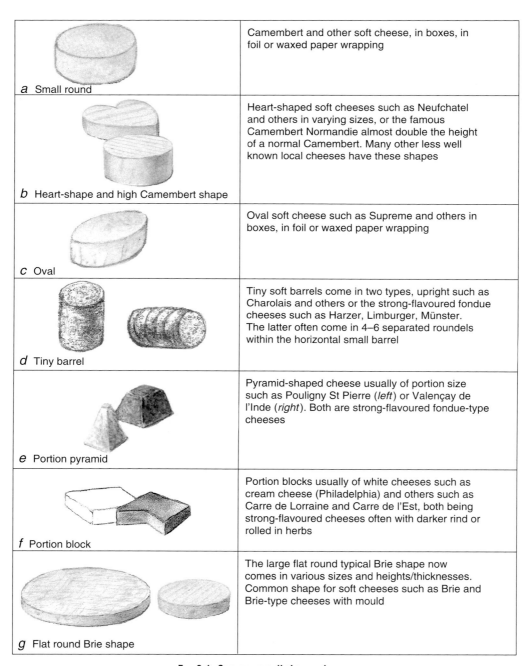

a Small round	Camembert and other soft cheese, in boxes, in foil or waxed paper wrapping
b Heart-shape and high Camembert shape	Heart-shaped soft cheeses such as Neufchatel and others in varying sizes, or the famous Camembert Normandie almost double the height of a normal Camembert. Many other less well known local cheeses have these shapes
c Oval	Oval soft cheese such as Supreme and others in boxes, in foil or waxed paper wrapping
d Tiny barrel	Tiny soft barrels come in two types, upright such as Charolais and others or the strong-flavoured fondue cheeses such as Harzer, Limburger, Münster. The latter often come in 4–6 separated roundels within the horizontal small barrel
e Portion pyramid	Pyramid-shaped cheese usually of portion size such as Pouligny St Pierre (*left*) or Valençay de l'Inde (*right*). Both are strong-flavoured fondue-type cheeses
f Portion block	Portion blocks usually of white cheeses such as cream cheese (Philadelphia) and others such as Carre de Lorraine and Carre de l'Est, both being strong-flavoured cheeses often with darker rind or rolled in herbs
g Flat round Brie shape	The large flat round typical Brie shape now comes in various sizes and heights/thicknesses. Common shape for soft cheeses such as Brie and Brie-type cheeses with mould

FIG. 9.1 *Common small cheese shapes*

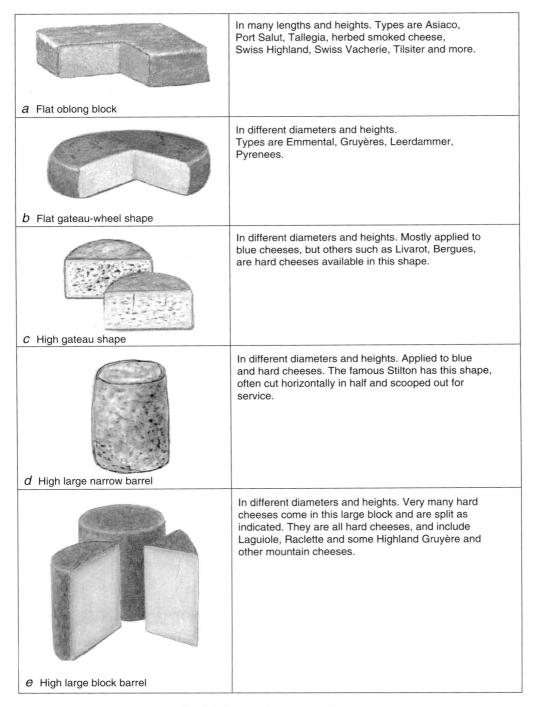

a Flat oblong block	In many lengths and heights. Types are Asiaco, Port Salut, Tallegia, herbed smoked cheese, Swiss Highland, Swiss Vacherie, Tilsiter and more.
b Flat gateau-wheel shape	In different diameters and heights. Types are Emmental, Gruyères, Leerdammer, Pyrenees.
c High gateau shape	In different diameters and heights. Mostly applied to blue cheeses, but others such as Livarot, Bergues, are hard cheeses available in this shape.
d High large narrow barrel	In different diameters and heights. Applied to blue and hard cheeses. The famous Stilton has this shape, often cut horizontally in half and scooped out for service.
e High large block barrel	In different diameters and heights. Very many hard cheeses come in this large block and are split as indicated. They are all hard cheeses, and include Laguiole, Raclette and some Highland Gruyère and other mountain cheeses.

FIG. 9.2 *Common larger cheese shapes*

TABLE 9.1 *EXAMPLES OF WHITE CHEESES* **Les fromages blancs**

Name	Milk	Characteristics	Originated in
Boursin	Cow's	Unripened creamy cheese usually in barrel form, often sold with addition such as with herbs and garlic etc.	France
Cottage cheese	Cow's	Low fat cheese with uneven texture, favoured by slimmers, good for cheesecake	Europe
Chèvre	Goat's	Goat's cheese from France, creamy light, small barrel shapes, but also available in other sizes, some very small and rolled in herbs and spices including cumin and paprika	France
Demi-sel	Cow's	Found in small barrel or square shapes, unripened creamy in texture and taste, a breakfast cheese	France
Feta	Sheep's/Goat's	Firm white cheese sold in a block, rich aromatic sharply tangy in flavour, used much in salads and many cooked dishes	Greece
Fromage fraîche	Cow's	Low fat loose creamy cheese much used for dressings and in cooking in place of cream, useful with liaison	France
Petit Suisse	Cow's	Small barrel shaped unripened cheese, creamy in texture and taste, of late often served with stewed or fresh fruit, in place of cream	France
Philadelphia	Cow's	Sold in square foil box shape, unripened, creamy in texture and taste, a breakfast cheese, commercial brand	England
Quark	Cow's	Not unlike cottage cheese but sieved and finer/smoother, sold in tubs with varying amounts of fat (5–40%), some have herbs added. A breakfast cheese, very good for cheesecakes	Germany
Mozzarella	Buffalo*	Soft creamy, slightly stringy consistency, often used in starter dishes or salads and pastas. A must for pizzas	Italy
Ricotta	Cow's/Goat's	Firmer creamy consistency comes in famous pudding-basin shape, often used in starter dishes or salads and pastas and/or in some regions local pizzas	Italy

Note: *Often now made with cow's milk as well. Not many white cheeses are included in a cheese board.

TABLE **9.2** *EXAMPLES OF SOFT CHEESES* **Les fromages mous**

Name	Milk	Characteristics	Originated in
d'Angloys le Pié	Cow's	Camembert shape and box, very creamy, rich mellow flavour and character	France
Brillât Savarin	Cow's	High barrel shape, akin to Camembert, mature	France
Brie Normand	Cow's	Large round, can be bought in sections, mild and creamy	France
Brie de Melun	Cow's	Smaller round shape, can be bought in sections, creamy but stronger than Brie, full of character	France
Cambozola	Cow's	Creamy with a light blue mouldy growth, sold in gateau-like shape of which sections may be cut	Germany
Camembert	Cow's	Sold in full or half box, creamy and stronger than Brie	France
Carré de Lorraine	Cow's	Small square shape akin to Camembert, strong in flavour	France
Collobrières	Cow's	Sold in rounds like Camembert but larger round somewhere between Camembert and Brie, not boxed, creamy and very tasty	France
De la Creuse	Cow's	Shape like a smaller Camembert, not boxed, strong in flavour	France
Neufchâtel	Cow's	Heart-shaped Camembert-type cheese, but larger and higher than Camembert, creamy and mild in flavour	France
Saint Florentine	Cow's	Slightly larger than a Camembert not boxed, rich and creamy, strong	France
Suprême	Cow's	Oval-shaped Camembert type cheese, not boxed, creamy and very tasty	France

TABLE **9.3** *EXAMPLES OF BLUE MOULD CHEESES* **Fromages bleus moulés**

Name	Milk	Characteristics	Originated in
Bleu de Causses	Cow's	High gateau shape, slight yellow rind, light blue veined creamy and full of flavour with orange outer rind	France
Bleu d'Auvergne	Cow's	High gateau shape, light brown rind, deep blue veined crumbly and with good character of flavour	France

Continued

TABLE 9.3 *EXAMPLES OF BLUE MOULD CHEESES* ⚕ ***Fromages bleus moulés—cont'd***

Name	Milk	Characteristics	Originated in
Bleu de Gex	Cow's	High gateau shape, slight yellow rind, light blue veined, creamy and full of flavour	France
Danish Blue	Cow's	Small barrel shape, rich in mould, strong to sharp in flavour	Denmark
Dolcelatte	Cow's	Distinct blue of Italy, full veined, creamy, often used in the preparation of pasta	Italy
Gorgonzola	Cow's	The most famous Italian blue, has been made for centuries, comes in large cylinder shape	Italy
Roquefort	Sheep's	Famous French blue, light blue sprinkled mould, comes in high gateau shape, good strong flavour and character	France

SEMI-HARD CHEESES ⚕ **Les fromages fondues**

Fondue or fromage fondue is a term referring to semi-hard cheeses and has little to do with the famous Swiss hot cheese dish of the same name. Nearly all of them have a strong, marked flavour and smell, often referred to as 'stinkers', and when placed on a cheese board in a restaurant they, should be covered by a cloche.

They are available in all manner of shapes and sizes. They are usually based on cow's milk or cow's–buttermilk, raw or cooked. They are less well known and liked, or indeed available in the British Isles. (See Table 9.4 and Plate 9.4.)

TABLE 9.4 *EXAMPLES OF SEMI-HARD CHEESES* ⚕ **Les fromages fondues**

Name	Milk	Characteristics	Originated in
Bel Paese	Cow's	Oblong block of cheese in foil, pale yellow colour, strong aromatic	Italy
German red Rind	Cow's	Oblong block or round high Brie-shaped, red veined, mild aromatic	Germany
Harzer Roll	Cow's	Tiny barrel with six sections within, caraway flavoured, highly aromatic	Germany
Limburger	Cow's	Tiny barrel with six sections within, caraway flavoured, highly aromatic	Germany

Continued

TABLE 9.4 *EXAMPLES OF SEMI-HARD CHEESES* *Les fromages fondues—cont'd*

Name	Milk	Characteristics	Originated in
Münster	Cow's	Tiny barrel with six sections within, caraway flavoured, highly aromatic	France, Alsace
Port Salut	Cow's	Oblong block of cheese, creamy but strong aromatic flavour	France
Smoked cheese with herbs	Cow's	Oblong block of cheese, occasionally round in some regions. Found plain smoked or smoked with herbs, strong aromatic flavour	Austria
Swiss Mountain	Cow's	Oblong block of cheese, almost white in colour, very brittle and with strong aromatic flavour	Switzerland
Tallegio	Cow's	Oblong block of cheese, made from salted curd with strong aromatic flavour	Italy

Note: When included on a cheese board must be covered with a cloche.

HARD CHEESES *Les fromages durs*

Among what are considered hard cheeses we find some considerable differences from one cheese to another and from one country to another. Hard ranges from the almost bullet-proof hard Parmesan vecchio to a moist, crumbling Cheddar or Caerphilly. In this group we also find the biggest number of cheeses made, in all sorts of shapes and sizes.

In these types the texture and firmness is a matter of pressure by which they are made and age, and how long they have been stored and matured.

When it comes to cooking, we will, almost certainly, make our choice from this group of hard cheeses, especially if we cannot afford a good and very expensive Parmesan. (See Table 9.5 and Plate 9.5.)

TABLE 9.5 *EXAMPLES OF HARD CHEESES* *Les fromages durs*

Name	Milk	Characteristics	Originated in
Beaufort	Cow's	Large round high gateau shape, firm and aromatic, easily sliced, good for cooking	France
Caerphilly	Cow's	Medium firm cheese, high gateau shape, white and acid, crumbly, dairies in Carmarthenshire produce the best	Wales

Continued

TABLE **9.5** *EXAMPLES OF HARD CHEESES* **Les fromages durs—cont'd**

Name	Milk	Characteristics	Originated in
Cantal	Cow's	Large high barrel-shaped cheese, firm and strong in flavour, good for eating raw and much used in cooking	France
Cheddar	Cow's	The most famous English cheese copied all over the world, produced in England in Somerset, Dorset and Devon. Cheddar is a very good cheese for cooking We differ between two types: **Farmhouse Cheddar**, in cylindrical shape and according to maturity from crumbly mild to mature firm. Farmhouse is considered the best **Oblong block cheddar** can be good when mature	England Now made all over the world
Edam	Cow's	Dutch cheese made from partly skimmed milk with strong dose of rennet, slow fermentation, strong in flavour. Coated with linseed oil and paraffin, always take off rind	Holland
Emmental	Cow's	Full fat Highland cheese, in all respects made in the same way as Gruyère, large high gateau cheese can weigh between 50 and 100 kg Considered creamier than Gruyère and less salty with many holes called eyes. Good for eating and cooking, used in the making of a fondue	Swiss
Gloucester	Cow's	Today produced in Sturminster Newton in Dorset and some Somerset farms. Of two types, Single and Double Gloucester. They are shaped like a grindstone, with a tough crust, they are still used for cheese rolling competitions down Cooper's Hill at the edge of the Cotswolds. Crumbly with a strong but mellow flavour they take 6 months to mature and can weigh between 7 and 12 kg according to the dairy. Excellent for toasting	England

Continued

TABLE 9.5 *EXAMPLES OF HARD CHEESES*   **Les fromages durs—cont'd**

Name	Milk	Characteristics	Originated in
Gouda	Cow's	Dutch full milk cheese, low gateau shape, yellow rind, light yellow inside, good flavour, found fresh or mature	Holland
Gruyère	Cow's	Originated in French Switzerland, but now made in other parts of Switzerland or indeed the world. The large round gateau-shaped cheese can weigh between 40 and 80 kg, the eyes are smaller than those of Emmental. Again a good cheese for eating and cooking. Used in the making of a fondue	Swiss
Red Leicester	Cow's	One of the few red or more correctly pinked veined cheeses. It does not belong to the blues but is more a semi-hard cheese with red marking and mild in flavour. It is sold mostly in oblong blocks, but some small farms still produce 10 kg cylindrical Red Leicesters	England
Parmesan	Cow's	Most likely the most expensive cheese in the world, not surprising when the average Parmesan needs the curd of about 300 litres of milk, after which it matures losing weight all the time. Maturation takes at least 4 years, some are matured up to 5 or 7 years, getting more expensive all the time. Thin slices of 4- or 5-year-old Parmesan can be eaten raw and are much appreciated by the expert. Most Parmesan is used for cooking (what would Italian pasta be without Parmesan!)	Italy

CHEESE ON THE MENU

Cheese is found on all types of menu in Europe, from breakfast to late-night supper. At some point in the past cheese became part of the classical menu and the accepted conclusion or near conclusion to the meal. Research into many old menus does not show cheese used as a course at the conclusion of a meal before the mid-nineteenth century. For this reason the cheese board should be considered a relatively new contribution to the menu.

THE CHEESE BOARD

A cheese board should not be over-laden; it should not be used to impress, but to proffer a small collection of good cheese, including local cheeses of all types, in best state of ripeness and maturity, comprising of:

1–2 hard cheeses in England (beside a Cheddar always include a local hard cheese if possible)

1–2 good ripe blue cheeses (Stilton, Roquefort, etc.)

1 fondue cheese, such as Port Salut, Münster, or a smoked cheese

2–3 soft cheeses such as Brie (always include a local sheep's or goat's cheese if available)

With the cheese board we should offer:

Butter

Breads: French, white and brown rolls

Biscuits for cheese of different types and make

Fruit: apple, apricots, plums, grapes according to season

Vegetables: celery, peppers, chillies, the latter common in South-Eastern Europe

CHEESE DISHES

Cheese is, of course, used for cooking on a considerable scale in and with other dishes. There are also a number of cheese preparation and dishes in their own right, including the famous Welsh Rarebit. Others examples are: cheese straws, cheese fritters, cheese croquettes, deep fried cheeses served as a starter or cheese course, cheese soufflé and the famous cheese fondue. Recipes for all of these can be found in good cookery books. A good fondue recipe is included below.

Swiss Cheese Fondue

Ingredients (4–6 portions)
1 kg grated Emmental,
   Gruyère, Cheddar*
100 g butter
4 cloves garlic, sliced
1 bottle dry white wine
Fresh milled pepper to taste
2–3 tsp corn flour
1–2 sticks French bread

Method
1 Heat butter in fondue pan or low thick bottom sauce pan
2 Add slices of garlic, fry, add ⅚ of the wine, bring to point of boil
3 Add grated cheese, over very low heat to melt, do not stir too much
4 When molten, taste and add milled pepper
5 Finally, dissolve corn flour in remaining wine, stir into fondue. To thicken, take aside, eat with dice of French bread which has been warmed/dried on a tray in the oven

Note: *Half Emmental and Gruyère is the normal recipe, but it works very well with a mature cheddar.*

10 Larder Administration

In this last chapter we shall consider some aspects of Larder administration. Attention to such details is helpful if we wish to do our work as effectively as possible. The chapter comprises five sections:

(1) **A costing sheet:** The costing of our foods and dishes and correct menu pricing is very important. Figure 10.1 will introduce you to a costing sheet and an approach to costing you will find simple and easy to follow.

(2) **Classical menu structure:** A modern classical menu structure is presented in six languages. This will help when writing menus in general, as well as aid understanding of the international language of the menu.

(3) **Vocabulary:** In all kitchens and restaurants there is now an ever-more international personnel, speaking many languages. A wide list of culinary vocabulary has therefore been included here.

(4) **Food in season:** We can nowadays get almost anything at any time of the year, but all foods are best in season, and it should always be our aim to use them at such times, for both the benefit of our customers and our own pockets.

(5) **Consideration of plated service:** A few structured ideas are presented regarding modern plated service of hot and cold food.

THE COSTING SHEET

The first example of a costing sheet (Figure 10.1) is filled out by hard, as you may wish to do as an exercise using the blank version in Figure 10.4. Two further examples of costing sheets for specific menu items are shown in Figures 10.2 and 10.3. These have been completed using a computer. There are many different programs available; the version here gives you a start to learn the basics.

EXPLANATION OF THE COSTING SHEET

(1) Give your recipe a number.

(2) Allocate it to a group of dishes, such as Starters, Soups, Salads, Sauces etc. Put these in a folder or file on your computer.

(3) Always give the last date of your calculations. In times of low inflation re-cost your dishes once a year; in times of high inflation or strong seasonal price changes re-cost more frequently.

(4) Always write out the dish to be produced in full, plus possible accompaniments (see 6 below).

(5) Decide on the number of portions which fits your normal business pattern, or easily multiplied numbers you will usually know from past sales records of a given dish.

(6) Write your needed ingredients clearly and in right amount, weights or measure in the lines provided. In the case of the mayonnaise we have written here (CS-28), which refers to an earlier costing sheet filed under Cold Sauce Recipe No. 28. The cost we therefore know and can just add. This can apply in the writing of many recipes on a new costing sheet, when we need 2 litres of stock or a litre of Béchamel etc.

(7) Add the cost of the ingredients and you will arrive at the most important food cost – **the only known cost**. From this we will derive all other costs, such a labour, overheads and agreed profit in the following way:

(8) Now divide the **food cost** by the determined percentage, which is set by each operation and in this first example is 30% (an average for a British restaurant):

$$\frac{£7.23}{30} = 0.241 = 1\%$$

(9) Now we can work out the other costs and required profit, e.g.
   35% of stated labour cost 35 × 0.241 = 8.435 or rounded to **8.44**
   20% of stated overhead cost 20 × 0.241 = **4.28**
   15% of agreed profit 15 × 0.241 = 3.615 or rounded to **3.62**

(10) If we add these three figures to our **food cost** of 7.23 we arrive at the **cost of production** (here 24.11), or what it has cost us to turn the listed ingredients into a Waldorf Salad.

(11) But these are not all the costs: establishments now add **VAT (Value Added Tax) at 17.5%**, which we have to pay to the government, and of late there has been a tendency to add a Service Charge to our cost so that the price for a given dish is stated on the menu and the guest pays no extra charges added to the bill. This is a trend which should be supported, but it remains the prerogative of any establishment.

(12) Having added VAT and Service Charge, we come to the **final cost** of our Waldorf Salad, which we now divide by the **number of portions produced**, this will often give us an odd figure, as in our example, **2.56**. We can round this down to **2.50** or, in our example, up to a **selling price** of **2.60**.

(13) Finally, it is useful to include the method of preparation. With today's coming and going of staff, it is helpful to print out a copy and give it to a new member of staff with the recipe, method and presentation to be followed.

Over time we could build up on computer or otherwise filed a list of costing sheets for dishes under the following headings: Hors d'oeuvre, Soups, Pasta, Fish, Entrées, Relevés, Vegetables, Potatoes and Sweets, each with its own group and recipe number, and number of portions best suited to our business. It may at first seem a big task, but with two or three worked out in a week, we soon have a valuable reference to the cost of our dishes.

CLASSICAL EUROPEAN MENU STRUCTURE

A modern international menu structure is presented in Table 10.1 with names in six languages. Note that the service of coffee at the end of a meal, associated with most modern meals, did not take place until much later and for this reason it does not appear on the classical menu as a course.

Food Costing Sheet					
Standard Recipe No.	*17*	**Group of Dishes**	*SALADS*	**Last Date of Calculation**	*XYZ*
Name of Dish		*WALDORF SALAD*			
No. of Portion	*12*		*AS STARTER*		
Ingredients		**Unit** kg- l- g	**Price per Unit**	**Cost**	**Method of Preparation**
CELERIAC	*1*	*kg*	*1.68*	*1.68*	*Peel celeriac, cut into neat 5mm*
APPLES RUSSET	*750*	*g*	*1.20*	*0.90*	*dice, blanch. Cool and place*
MAYONNAISE	*0.5*	*l*	*(CG-28)*	*2.10*	*mayonnaise in suitable bowl add*
WALNUTS	*12*	*250g*	*3.60*	*0.90*	*lemon juice now peel and cut*
LEMON	*1*		*0.25*	*0.25*	*apples into neat 5mm dice. Mix into*
FRISÉE LETTUCE	*1*		*1.25*	*1.20*	*mayonnaise as you cut to retain*
SEASONING				*0.20*	*colour. Mix all well. Allow to stand*
					1-2 hours. Dress on leaves of
					Frisée lettuce. Garnish with quarter
					or half walnuts.
Cost of Ingredients or Food Costs			*30% =*	*7.23*	
Divide Food Cost by its percentage to gain 1%. Multiply this with other costs over below to get Cost of Production			$\frac{7.23}{30}$ *=*	*0.241*	
Labour Cost	*35%*		*x 0.241*	*=*	*8.44*	
Overheads Cost	*20%*		*x 0.241*	*=*	*4.82*	
Agreed Profit	*15%*		*x 0.241*	*=*	*3.62*	
Cost of Production				*24.11*	
Plus					
Service Charge	*10%*		*24.11 ÷ 10*	*2.41*	Continue method on back of sheet
VAT	**17. 5%**		*24.11 ÷ 100 x 17.5*	*4.22*	if need be
Sales Cost				*30.74*	-------------------------------------
Divided by Portions		*30.74 ÷ 12*		*2.56*	Latest Calculations
Adjustment to Reasonable Figure				*2.60*	Comments Photo of final dish (optional)
Final Selling Price per Portion				*2.60*	

FIG. **10.1** *Handwritten costing sheet*

Food Costing Sheet						
Standard Recipe No.	10		**Group of Dishes**	Soups	**Last Date of Calculation**	XYZ
Name of Dish			Cream of Celery Soup			
No. of Portion	36		As Soup Course			
Ingredients			**Unit** kg-l- g	**Price Per Unit**	**Cost**	**Method of Preparation**
Celeriac peeled		1½	kg	3.20	4.80	Cut a good $1/8$ of the
Onions peeled		500	g	0.70	0.35	celeriac into neat 5 mm
Leek white peeled		500	g	0.90	0.45	dice, set aside, cut the rest
Margarine		300	g	2.40	0.72	of the celeriac as well as
Flour		250	g	1.20	0.30	onions and leeks into
White Stock		5	l	0.50	2.50	rough 2 cm dice, melt
Milk		2	l	0.82	1.64	margarine in suitable
Cream		½	l	3.80	1.90	sauce pan, add celery
Seasoning					0.50	onions and leeks, sweat, add flour sweat
						Add stock and milk, bring
						to point of boil and
						simmer for 40–50 min.
						Cook celeriac dice in little
						salt water al dente
						Liquidize soup, and or
Cost of Ingredients or Food Costs			40% =		13.16	pass through sieve,
Divide Food Cost by its percentage						correct consistency and
to gain 1%. Multiply this with other			$\dfrac{13.16}{40}$ =		0.329	seasoning, add drained
costs below to get Cost of Production						dice celeriac and finish with cream
Labour Cost	30%	30 × 0.329 =			9.87	
Overheads Cost	15%	15 × 0.329 =			4.94	Replace stock with milk
Agreed Profit	15%	15 × 0.329 =			4.94	or water
						Acceptable for
Cost of Production					£32.91	vegetarians
Plus						
Service Charge		12%	32.91 × 0.12		3.95	
VAT		17.5%	32.91 × 0.175		5.76	*Continue method on back*
Sales Cost					£42.62	*of sheet if need be*
Divided by Portions	36				£1.18	--------------------------------
Adjustments to Reasonable Figure					£1.20	*Latest Calculations*
						Comments
Final Selling Price per Portion						*Photo of final dish*
***or what the market will bear**					£1.50*	*(optional)*

FIG. 10.2 *Example costing sheet for cream of celery soup*

Food Costing Sheet					
Standard Recipe No. 67		*Group of Dishes*	Entrées	*Last Date of Calculation*	XYZ
Name of Dish		Braised Beef Steaks with Mushrooms			
No. of Portion 24		Meat Main Course			

Ingredients	Unit kg-l- g	Price Per Unit	Cost	*Method of Preparation*
Beef Braising Steaks	24 3.5 kg	4.25	14.86	Pass braising steak through
Mire poix	500 g	1.20	0.60	seasoned flour, seal, fry
Tomato puree	200 g	4.10	0.82	golden brown in frying pan,
Fat-Margarine	250 g	1.56	0.40	lift in to suitable braising pan
Flour	200 g	1.20	0.30	
Brown Stock	4 l	(S-S 17)	2.00	Fry mire poix in the same fat
Button Mushrooms	1.2 kg	4.80	5.76	and pan add tomato puree,
Seasoning			1.00	sweat, add to sealed steaks in
				pan, cover with brown stock,
				add bouquet garni, bring to
				point of boil; simmer gently on
				side of stove or in oven, for
				1 hour
				Meanwhile wash button
				mushrooms, sauté in pan,
				drain
				Lift steaks out of sauce into
Cost of Ingredients or Food Costs		35% =	25.74	clean pan, add mushrooms,
Divide Food Cost by its percentage to gain 1%. Multiply this with other costs below to get Cost of Production		$\frac{25.74}{35}$ =	0.735	strain sauce through a fine sieve on to steaks and mushrooms; bring to point of boil; simmer together until steaks are cooked
Labour Cost	30%	30 × 0.735 =	22.05	
Overheads Cost	20%	20 × 0.735 =	14.70	Correct seasoning; an optional
Agreed Profit	15%	15 × 0.735 =	11.00	glass of red wine will put the final touch to the dish
Cost of Production			£73.49	
Plus				*Continue method on back of sheet if need be*
Service Charge	10%	73.49 × 0.1 =	7.35	--------------------------------
VAT	*17.5%*	73.49 × 0.175 =	12.86	*Latest Calculations*
Sales Cost			£93.70	*Comments*
Divided by Portions	24		£3.90	*Photo of final dish*
Adjustment to Reasonable Figure			£4.00	*(optional)*
Final Selling Price per Portion **or what the market will bear*			£4.50*	

FIG. 10.3 *Example costing sheet for braised beef steak with mushrooms*

Food Costing Sheet					
Standard Recipe No.		**Group of Dishes**		**Last Date of Calculation**	
Name of Dish					
No. of Portion					
Ingredients		**Unit** kg- l- g	**Price per Unit**	**Cost**	**Method of Preparation**
Cost of Ingredients or Food Costs			% =		
Divide Food Cost by its percentage to gain 1%. Multiply this with other costs below to get Cost of Production					
Labour Cost	%				
Overheads Cost	%				
Agreed Profit	%				
Cost of Production					
Plus					
Service Charge	%				Continue method on back of sheet if need be
VAT	17. 5%				
Sales Cost					-------------------------------------
Divided by Portions					Latest Calculations
Adjustments to Reasonable Figure					Comments
Final Selling Price per Portion **or what the market will bear*					Photo of final dish (optional)

FIG. 10.4 *Blank costing sheet (may be used for trial calculations)*

TABLE 10.1 *The Classical European Menu Structure*

No.	English	French	German	Italian	Spanish	Swedish
1	Cold Starter	Hors d'oeuvres froids	Kalte Vorspeisen	Antipasti freddi	Entremeses fríos	Kalla Förrätter
2	Soups	Potages	Suppen	Minestra	Sopas	Sopor
3	Hot Starters	Hors d'oeuvres chauds	Warme Vorspeisen	Antipasti caladi	Entremeses calientes	Varma Förrätter
4	Egg and Farinaceous Dishes	Oeufs et farineux	Eier und Teigwaren	Uova e farinacee	Huevos y pasta	Ägg och Mjölrätter Pasta
5	Fish Dishes	Poissons	Fischgerichte	Pesce	Pescado	Fiskrätter
6	Small Hot Meat Dishes	Entrées chauds	Kleine Fleischgerichte	Primi piatti caldi	Primer plato caliente	Små varma Huvudrätter
7	Large Meat Joint	Relevés ou grosse pièce ou Pièce de résistance	Grosse Heiße Hauptgerichte	Piatto forte secondi	Plato princípiale	Stora varma Huvudrätter
8	Small Cold Meat Course	Entrées froids	Kaltes Zwischengericht	Secondi freddi	Secundo plato frió	Små kalla Mellanrätter
9	Sorbet	Sorbet	Sorbet	Sorbetto	Sorbete	Sorbet
10	Roast with Salad	Rôtis et salades	Braten mit Salat	Arrosto con insalata	Asado con ensalada	Stora Stekt med Sallad
11	Vegetable Course	Légumes	Gemüsegerichte	Vendure en legumi	Verduras	Grönsaker
12	Potato Course	Pommes de terre	Kartoffelgerichte	Patate	Patatas	Potatis
13	Warm Sweet Course	Entremets chauds	Warme Süßpeisen	Dolsi caldi	Postre caliente	Varmer Efterrätter
14	Cold Sweet Course	Entremets froids	Kalte Süßpeisen	Dolsi freddi	Postre fríos	Kalla Efterrätter
15	Cheese Course	Fromages	Käse	Formaggi	Quesos	Ostar
16	Fresh Fruit	Desserts	Frische Früchte	Frutta fresca	Frutas fresca del tiempo	Färsk Frukt

CULINARY TERMINOLOGY AND VOCABULARY IN SIX LANGUAGES

English	French	German	Italian	Spanish	Swedish
Alcohol	Alcool	Alkohol	Alcole	Alcohol	Alkohol
Almond	Amande	Mandel	Mandorla	Almendra	Mandel
Almond milk	Orgeat	Mandelmilch	Mandorlato	Horchata de almendras	Mandelmjölk
Anchovy	Anchois	Sardelle	Acciuga	Anchoa	Sardell
Angelica	Angélique	Engelswurz	Angelica	Angélica	Angelika
Aniseed	Anis	Anis	Anice	Anis	Anis
Appetite	Appétit	Appetit	Appetito	Apetito	Aptit
Apple	Pomme	Apfel	Mela	Manzana	Äpple
Apricot	Abricot	Aprikosen	Albicocca	Albaricoque	Aprikos
Artichoke	Artichaut	Artischocken	Carciofo	Alcachofa	Kronärtskocka
Aroma	Arôme	Duft-Aroma	Aroma	Aroma	Arom
aromatic	aromatique	aromatisch	aromatico	aromático	aromatisk
Ashes	Cendres	Asche	Ceneri	Ceniza	Aska
Asparagus	Asperges	Spargel	Asparago	Espárrago	Sparris
Baby chicken	Poussin	Kücken	Pulcino	Pollito	Kyckling
Bacon	Lard	Bauchspeck	Lardo	Lardo	Bacon
Baker	Boulanger	Bäcker	Fornaio	Panadero	Bagare
Banana	Banane	Banane	Banana	Plátano	Banan
Banquet	Banquet	Festessen	Banchetto	Festín	Festmåltid
Barley	Orge	Gerste	Orzo	Cebada	Korn
Basil	Basilic	Basilikum	Basifico	Basilisco	Basilika
Bass	Bar	Barsch	Pesce	Llubina	Havsabborre
Bay leaf	Laurier	Lorbeerblatt	Alloro	Laurel	Lagerbärsblad

Continued

English	French	German	Italian	Spanish	Swedish
Beef	Boeuf	Rinderfleisch	Manzo	Carne de vaca	Oxkött
Beef tea	Fond de viande	Fleischbrühe	Sugo di carne	Jugo de carne	Kött buljong
Beer	Bière	Bier	Birra	Cerveza	Öl
Beetroot	Betterave	Rote Bete Rüben	Barba bietola	Remolacha	Rödbeta
Bell	Cloche	Essen Glocke	Campana	Campana	Mat Klocka
Belly	Ventre	Bauch	Panda	Vientre	Buk
Bill	Addition	Rechnung	Conto	Cuenta	Räkning
Bill of Fare	Carte de mets	Speisekarte	Lista delle vivande	Lista de platos	Matsedel
Biscuit	Biscuit	Biskuit-Keks	Biscotto	Bizcocho	Kex
bitter	amer	bitter	amaro	amargo	bitter
black	noir	schwarz	nero	negro	svart
Black coffee	Café noir	Schwarzer Kaffee	Café nero	Café negro	Svart kaffe
Blackcurrants	Cassis	Johannisbeeren	More	Grosellas	Svart vinbär
Cabbage	Choux	Kohl	Cavolo	Col	Kål
Cake	Gâteaux	Kuchen	Pasticceria	Pastel	Kaka
Calf's feet	Pieds-de-veau	Kalbsfüße	Zampetto di vitello	Monos de ternera	Kalvfötter
Calf's head	Tiède de veau	Kalbskopf	Testina di vitello	Cabeza de ternera	Kalv huvud
Calf's liver	Foie de veau	Kalbs Leber	Fegato di vitello	Hígado de ternera	Kalv lever
Calf's sweetbread	Ris de veau	Kalbsmilch	Animelle di vitello	Molleja de ternera	Kalvbräss
Can	Boite	Dose	Scatola	Lata	Burk
Capers	Carpes	Kapern	Capperi	Alcaparra	Kapris
Capon	Chapon	Kapaun	Cappone	Capones	Kapun

Continued

CULINARY TERMINOLOGY AND VOCABULARY IN SIX LANGUAGES—cont'd

English	French	German	Italian	Spanish	Swedish
Caramel	Caramel	Karamell	Caramello	Caramelo	Karamell
Caraway	Cumin	Kümmel	Cumino	Comino	Kummin
Carcass	Carcasse	Gerippe	Cardo	Carcasa	Kadaver
Carp	Carpe	Karpfen	Carpione	Carpa	Karp
Carrot	Carotte	Mohrrübe,	Carote	Zanahoria	Mo rot
Cauliflower	Chou-Fleur	Blumenkohl	Cavolfiori	Coliflor	Blomkal
Caviar	Caviar	Kaviar	Caviale	Caviar	Kaviar
Cayenne	Poivre de Cayenne	Cayennepfeffer	Pepe di Caienna	Pimienta de Cayena	Kajennpeppar
Celeriac	Céleri-rave	Knollensellerie	Sedano rapa	Nabo	Rotselleri
Celery	Céleri Anglaise	Englischer Seleri	Sedano	Apio	Selleri
Cellar	Cave	Keller	Cantina	Cueva	Källaren
Champagne	Champagne	Schaumwein	Vino Spumante	Champaña	Champagne
Cheese	Fromage	Käse	Formaggio	Queso	Ost
Cherry	Cerise	Kirsche	Ciliegia	Cereza	Körsbär
Chervil	Cerfeuil	Kerbel	Cerfoglio	Perifollo	Körvel
Chestnut	Marron	Kastanie	Castagna	Castaña	Kastanj
Chickpea	Pois chiche	Kirschenerbse	Ceci	Garbanzos	Kikärt
Chicken	Poulet	Huhn	Pollo	Polio	Kyckling
Chicken liver	Foie de volaille	Hühnerleber	Fegato di polio	Hígado de polio	Kycklings Lever
Chicory	Chicorée	Chicoree	Cicoria	Chicoria	Cikoria
Chicory/Endive	Endive	Endivien	Indivia	Escarola	Endiv
China	Porcelaine	Porzellan	Porcellana	Porcelana	Porslin
Chive	Ciboulette	Schnittlauch	Poverino	Cebolleta	Gräslök
Chocolate	Chocolat	Schokolade	Cioccolata	Chocolate	Choklad
Cider	Cidre	Apfelwein	Sidro	Sidra	Äppelmust
Cigar	Cigare	Zigarre	Sigaro	Cigarro	Cigarr

Continued

CULINARY TERMINOLOGY AND VOCABULARY IN SIX LANGUAGES—cont'd

English	French	German	Italian	Spanish	Swedish
Cigarette	Cigarette	Zigarette	Sigaretta	Cigarrillo-pitillo	Cigarett
Cinnamon	Cannelle	Zimt	Cannella	Canela	Kanel
Clams	Clovisses	Venusmuscheln	Conchiglie	Coquillas	Musslor
clean (adj)	propre	rein	puro	limpio-puro	ren
Clear soup	Consommé	Klare Brühe	Chiaro brodo	Claro Caldo	Klar Buljong
Cloves	Girofles	Gewürznelke	Chiodi di Garofani	Cebolleta	Kryddnejlika
coagulated	caillé	geronnen	Coagulato	coujarse	koagulerad
Cocoa	Cacao	Kakao	Cacao	Cacao	Kakao
Coconut	Noisette de coco	Kokosnuss	Cocco	Coco	Kokosnöt
Cod	Cabillaud	Kabeljau	Merluzzo	Bacalao fresco	Torsk
Coffee	Café	Kaffee	Caffè	Café	Kaffe
Coffee pot	Cafetière	Kaffeekanne	Caffettiera	Cafetera	Kaffekanna
Coffee with milk	Café au lait	Milchkaffee	Caffè con latte	Café con leche	Kaffe med mjölk
Cold meat	Viande froide	Aufschnitt kalt	Braciola	Friego fiambres	Kallskuret
cold – cool	frais – fraîche	kalt – kühl	fresco	fresco	kall
cool (verb)	rafraîchir	kaltmachen	raffreddare	refrescare	göra kall
Cook	Cuisinier	Koch	Cuoco	Cocinero	Kock
cook – boil	cuire – bouillir	kochen	cuocere	cocer	koka – laga mat
Cork	Bouchon	Korken	Turacciolo	Corcho	Kork
Corkscrew	Tire-bouchonne	Korkenzieher	Cava-turaccioli	Cava-turaccioli	Korkskruv
Corn flour	Farine	Maismehl - Maizena	Farina	Harina de maíz	Majsmjöl
Cos lettuce	Laitue Romaine	Bundsalat	Lattuga romana	Ensalada romano	Bindsallat
Cover	Couvert	Gedeck	Coperto	Cubierto	Bords skuren
Crab	Crabe	Krabben	Granchio	Camarones	Krabba
Cranberries	Airelles rouges	Preiselbeeren	Mirtillo rosso	Arandino	Tranbär - Lingon
Crayfish	Écrevisse	Krebs	Gambero	Cangrejo	Kräftor

Continued

CULINARY TERMINOLOGY AND VOCABULARY IN SIX LANGUAGES—cont'd

English	French	German	Italian	Spanish	Swedish
Cream	Crème	Rahm-Sahne	Panna	Crema	Grädde
Crust	Croûte	Kruste-Toast	Crosta	Costra	Skorpa Toast
Cucumber	Concombre	Gurke	Cetriolo	Pepino	Gurka
Cup	Tasse	Tasse	Bacinella	Kaps	Kopp
Cottage cheese	Fromage blanc	Quark	Cacio bianco	Cuajada	Kvark
Currants	Raisins de Corinth	Korinthen	Uva di Corinto	Pasa di Corinto	Korinter
Curry	Curie	Currypulver	Curry	Curry	Curry
Cutlet	Côtelette	Kotletten	Costoletta	Chuleta	Kotlett
Dandelion	Pissenlit	Löwenzahn	Dente di leone	Diente de león	Maskros
Date	Datte	Dattel	Dattero	Dátil	Dadel
Daily Menu	Carte du Jour	Tageskarte	Carta del Giorni	Platos del día	Dagens matsedel
Decanter	Carafe	Karaffe	Caraffa	Garrafa	Karaff
Deer	Cerf	Hirsch	Cervo	Ciervo	Rådjur
delicious	delicieux	geschmackvoll	elegante	de muy buen gusto	delikat
different	divers	verschieden	diverso	diferente	olik
Dining room	Salle à manger	Speisesaal	Sala da pranzo	Comedor	Matsal
Dinner	Dîner	Abendessen	Colazione	Comida	Middags (måltid)
Dish	Plat	Gericht	Piatto	Manjar fuente	Plåt
Dough-paste	Boisson	Teig	Pasta	Pasta	Pajdeg
Drink	Boire	Getränk	Bibita	Bebida	Dryck
drink (verb)	boire	trinken	bere	Beber	att dricka
Drop	Goutte	Tropfen	Goccia	gota	Droppe
dry (adj)	sec	trocken	secco	seco	torr
Duck	Canard	Ente	Anatra	Pato	Anka

Continued

English	French	German	Italian	Spanish	Swedish
eat (verb)	manger	Zu essen	mangier	corner	at äta
edible	mangeable	essbar	mangiare	comestible	ätbar
Eel	Anguille	Aal	Anguilla	Anguila	Ål
Egg	Oeuf	Ei	Uova	Huevo Y	Ägg
Egg yolk	Jaune d'oeuf	Eigelb	Tuorlo d'uova	Yema de huevo	Äggula
Egg white	Blanc d'oeuf	Ei weis	Albume	Clara de huevo	Äggvita
empty (adj)	vide	leer	vuoto	vació	tom
Entrails	Intestins	Eingeweide	Intestino	Intestinos	Inälvor
Essence	Extrait – Essence	Auszug – Essenz	Essenza	Extract	Essens
Fat	Graisse	Fett	Grasso	Graso	Fett
Fattened chicken	Poularde	Masthuhn, poularde	Pollastra	Polio	Gödd kyckling
Fennel	Fenouil	Fenchel	Finocchio	Hinojo	Fänkål
Fermented cabbage	Choucroute	Sauerkraut	Crauti	Berzas	Surkål
Festival – Feast	Fête	Fest	Festa	Fiesta	Fest
Fieldfare	Grive	Krammetsvogel	Tordo	Zorzal	Björktrast
Fig	Figue	Feige	Fico	Higo	Fikon
Fillet of beef	Filet de boeuf	Ochsenfile	Filetto di bue	Lomo	Oxfilé
fine	fin	fein	fino – delicato	fino	fin
Fireplace	Fourneau	Kamin-offenes Feuer	Fuoco	Fuego fogón	Eld
first	premier	Erste	primo	primero	öppen spis
Fish	Poisson	Fisch	Pesce	Pescado	Fisk
Fishbone	Arête	Fischknochen-Gräten	Lisca	Espina	Fiskben

Continued

CULINARY TERMINOLOGY AND VOCABULARY IN SIX LANGUAGES—cont'd

English	French	German	Italian	Spanish	Swedish
Fish market	Marché aux poissons	Fischmarkt	Pescheria	Mercado de pescado	Fisktorg
Flounder	Flet-Plie	Flunder	Passera	Acedía	Flundra
Flour	Farine	Mehl	Farina	Harina	Mjöl
Foam – Froth	Mousse	Schaum Mus	Spuma	Espuma	Skum
Forcemeat	Farce	Füssell-Farce	Ripieno	Relleno	Färs (kött)
Fork	Fourchette	Gabel	Forchetta	Tenedor	Gaffel
Fowls	Volaille	Geflügel	Pollame	Aves de corral	Fjäder fågel
French beans	Haricots verts	Grüne Bohnen	Fagiolini	Judía verde	Gröna bönor
Fresh haddock	Aiglefin	Schellfisch	Nasello	Besugo	Kolja
Fried egg	Oeuf sur le plat	Spiegeleier	Uova al tegame	Huevos al plato	Stekt ägg
Fritters	Beignets	Krapfen Beignets	Frittelle	Buñuelo	Bejgnet
Frog	Grenouille	Frosch	Rana	Rana	Groda
frozen	glacé	gefroren	gelato	helarse	frusen
Fruits	Fruits	Obst	Frutta	Fruta	Frukt
Fruit dried	Fruits séchés	Dorrobst	Frutta secca	Fruta seca	Frukt, torkad
Fruit plate	Plat de fruits	Obstschale	Recipiente per Frutta	Compotera	Frukt talrik
Frying pan	Poêle à frire	Bratpfanne	Padella	Sartén paella	Stekpanna
Garlic	Ail	Knoblauch	Aglio	Ajo	Vitlök
Garnish	Garniture	Garnitur–Beilage	Guarnitura	Guanicón	Garnering
Gastronome	Gastronome	Feinschmecker	Buongustaio	Gastrónomo	Gastronom
Gherkins	Cornichons	Essiggurken	Cetriolini	Pepinillos	Ättiksgurka
Giblets	Abats de volaille	Hühnerklein	Frattaglie	Menudillos	Fågel (kräs)
Ginger	Gingembre	Ingwer	Zenzero	Jengibre	Ingefära

Continued

English	French	German	Italian	Spanish	Swedish
Gingerbread	Pain d'épice	Lebkuchen	Pan pepato	Alfajor	Pepparkaka
good	bon – bonne	gut	buono	bueno	god
Goose	Oie	Gans	Oca	Ganso, Oca	Gås
Goose liver	Foie gras	Gänseleber	Fegato d'oca	Higado de oca	Gåslever
Gooseberry	Groseille	Stachelbeeren	Uva spina	Grosella	Krusbär
Grapes	Raisins	Weintrauben	Uva	Uvas	Vindruvor
grated - rasped	râpé	gerieben	grattugiato	rallado	riva
Gravy	Jus	Bratensaft	sugo	Jugo	Stek sås
green	vert	grün	verde	verde	grön
Green cabbage	Chou vert	Wirsingkohl	Verza	Repollo	grön Kål
grey	gris	grau	grigio	gris	grå
Grill	Gril	Rostes-Grill	Gratella	Parilla	Grill
Gristle	Tendron	Knorpel	Cartilagine	Cartílagos	Brosk
Grits	Gruau	Gerstengrütze	Orzo	Engrudo	Krossgryn
Guinea fowl	Pintade	Perlhuhn	Gallina faraona	Pintada	Pärlhöna
Ham	Jambon	Schinken	Prosciutto	Jamón	Skinka
Hare	Lièvre	Hase	Lepre	Liebre	Hare
Hash	Hachis	Gehacktes	Carne tritata	Salpicón	Hackat kött
hashed – minced	hachis	Gemahlen-gehacktes	tritano	piqué	malt kött
Haunch	Cuissot double	Doppelte Wildkeule	Coscia di capriolo	Pernil	Dubbel lår
Haunch of venison	Gigot de chevreuil	Rehkeule	Fianco di gamete	Asada de corzo	Rödjurs dobbel lår
Hazel hen	Gelinotte	Haselhuhn	Gallina regina	Gallina	Brunhöna

Continued

CULINARY TERMINOLOGY AND VOCABULARY IN SIX LANGUAGES—cont'd

English	French	German	Italian	Spanish	Swedish
Hazelnut	Noisette	Haselnuss	Nocciola	Avellana	Hasselnöt
Head	Tête	Kopf	Testa	Cabeza	Huvud
Head Chef	Chef de cuisine	Küchenchef	Capo Cuoco	Jefe de la Cocina	Köksmästare
Head Waiter	Maitred'hôtel	Oberkellner	Primo Cameriere	Jefe de Camareros	Hovmästare
Heat (noun)	Chaleur	Hitze	Calore	Calor	Hetta – värme
Heathcock	Coq de bruyère	Auerhahn	Urogallo	Urogallo	Orrtupp
Herbs	Herbes	Kräuter	Erbe	Hierbe	Örter
Herring	Hareng	Hering	Aringa	Arenque	Sill
Hip – Haw	Églantine	Hagebutte	Rosa canina	Escaramujo	Nyponfrukt
Hock (Rhine wine)	Vin du Rhin	Rheinwein	Vino del Reno	Vino del Rin	Rhenvin
Honey	Miel	Honig	Miele	Miel	Honung
Hops	Houblon	Hopfen	Luppolo	Lóbulo	Humle
Horseradish	Raifort	Meerrettich	Rafano	Rábano	Pepparrot
hot	chaud	heiß	caldo	caliente	het
Hotel	Hôtel	Hotel-Gasthaus	Albergo	Hotel	Hotellet
Hunger	Faim	Hunger	Appetito	Hambre	Hunger
Ice	Glace	Eis	Ghiaccio	Hielo	Is
Ice cream	Glace	Speiseeis	Gelato	Helado	Glass
Icing	Glace	Glasur	Chioccia Reale	Baño de azúcar	Sockerglasyr
Infusion	Infusion	Aufguss	Infusione	Infusión	Avkok
Indian sweetcorn	Mais	Maiskolben	Grano	Turco	Mak
Jam	Confiture	Konfitüre-Marmelade	Marmellata	Salmuera	Sylt-Marmelade

Continued

CULINARY TERMINOLOGY AND VOCABULARY IN SIX LANGUAGES—cont'd

English	French	German	Italian	Spanish	Swedish
Jelly	Gelée	Gelee	Gelatina di frutta	Salmuera	Gelé
Jug – pitcher	Cruche	Krug	Brocca	Jarro	Tillbringare
Kernel	Noyau	Kern	Nocciolo	Hueso	Kärna
Kidney	Rognon	Niere	Rognone	Riñones	Njure
Kitchen	Cuisine	Küche	Cucina	Cocina	Kök
Knife	Couteau	Messer	Coltello	Cuchillo	Kniv
Lamb	Agneau	Lamm	Agnello	Cordero	Lamm
Lamb cutlet	Côtelette d'agneau	Lamm Kohlet	Costolette d'agnello	Costilla di cordero	Lammkotlett
Lambs lettuce	Salade de mâche	Feld Salat	Insalata di raperonzolli	Colleja	Majssallad
Lard	Saindoux	Schweinefett	Lardo	Manteca	Isterflott
Lark	Mauviette	Lerche	Sugna	Alondra	Lärka
lean	maigre	mager	allodola magro	flaco	mager
Leek	Poireau	Lauch, Porree	Porro	Puerro	Purjolök
Leg	Gigot	Keule	Cosciotto	Oierna	Ben (stek)
Leg of lamb	Gigot d'agneau	Lammkeule	Coscia d'agnello	Pata de cordero	Lammstek
Leg of mutton	Gigot de mouton	Hammelkeule	Cosciotto di castrato	Pata de cordero	Fårstek
Leg of veal	Cuisseau de veau	Kalbskeule	Coscia di vitello	Pata de ternera	Kalvstek
Leg of pork	Cuissot de porc	Schweinekeule	Coscia di porco	Pata de cerdo	Fläskstek
Lemon	Citron	Zitrone	Limone	Limón	Citron
Lemon juice	Jus de citron	Zitronensaft	Sugo dl limone	Jugo de limón	Citronsaft
Lemonade	Limonade	Limonade	Limonata	Limonada	Lemonad
Lentil	Lentille	Linse	Lenticchie	Lenteja	Lins

Continued

CULINARY TERMINOLOGY AND VOCABULARY IN SIX LANGUAGES—cont'd

English	French	German	Italian	Spanish	Swedish
Lettuce	Laitue	Kopfsalat	Lattuga	Lechuga	Salladshuvud
light (delicate)	délicate	delikat	delicato	delicado	delikat
light (not heavy)	léger	leicht		lucir	lät
Lights/Lungs	Mou	Lunge	Polmone	Pulmón	Lunga
Lime	Limon	Linde	Lime	Lima	Lime
Liquor	Liqueur	Likör	Liquore	Licor	Likör
Litre	Litre	Liter	Litro	Litro	Liter
Liver	Foie	Leber	Fegato	Hígado	Lever
Lobster	Homard	Hummer	Astice	Langosta	Hummer
living – alive	vivant	lebend	vivo	viviente	levande
Loin of veal	Longe de veau	Kalbslende	Lombata di vitello	Riñonada de ternera	Kainnjurstek
Loin of pork	Longe de porc	Schweinelende	Lombata di porco	Riñonada de cerdo	Kalvskotlettrad-stek
Loin of lamb	Longe d'agneau	Lammlende	Lombata d'agnello	Riñonada de codero	Lamm kotlettrad-stek
luke warm	tiède	lauwarm	tiepido	tibia	ljummen
Lunch	Déjeuner	Mittagessen	Colazione	Almuerzo	Lunch
Macaroni	Macaroni	Makkaroni	Maccheroni	Macarrones	Makaroner
Mackerel	Maquereau	Makrele	Sgombro	Verdel	Makrill
Malt	Malt	Malz	Malto	Malta	Malt
Management	Administration	Leitung – Direktion	Amministrazione	Dirección	Ledning
Manager	Directeur	Leiter Direktor	Direttore	Gerente	Direktör
Marzipan	Massepain	Marzipan	Marzapane	Mazapán	Mars
Margarine	Margarine	Margarine	Margarina	Manteca vegetal	Margarin

Continued

English	French	German	Italian	Spanish	Swedish
Marinade	Marinade	Marinade	Marinare	Marinada	Inläggning
marinate	mariner	marinieren	marinare	marinare	inlägga
Marjoram	Marjolaine	Majoran	Maggiorana	Mejorana	Mejram
Market	Marché	Mark	Fiera	Feria	Torg
Marmalade	Marmelade	Marmelade	Marmellata	Marmellada	Marmelad
Marrow	Moelle	Knochenmark	Midollo	Tuétano	Märg
Mash	Purée	Mus – Püree	Purea	Puré	Mos
Mashed potatoes	Purée de pommes	Kartoffelmaus-Brei	Passato di patate	Puré de patatas	Potatismos
Matches	Allumettes	Streichhölzer	Fiamifferi	Fósforo	Tandstickor
Meal	Repas	Mahlzeit	Pasto	Comida	Måltid
Meat	Viande	Fleisch	Carne	Carne	Kött
Melon	Melon	Melone	Melone	Melón	Melon
Menu	Menu	Menü	Minuta	Menú	Meny
Milk	Lait	Milch	Latte	Leche	Mjölk
Millet	Millet	Hirse	Migro	Mijo	Hirs
Minced meat	Hachis de viande	Hackfleisch	Carne tritata	Picadillo	Köttfärs
Mint	Menthe	Minze	Menta	Menta	Mint
mix (verb)	mélanger	mischen	miscela	mistela	mixa
mixed	mélangé	gemischt	misto	amalgámate	blandad
mixture	Mixture	Mischung	Mistura	Mixtura	Blandning
Mixed fruit	Fruits panachés	Gemischtes Obst	Frutta mastra	Frutas andas	blandad Frukt
mock – false	faux – fausse	Falsch – unecht	falso	falso	falsk
Morello cherries	Girotte	Sauerkirschen	Marasche	Guindilla	Moreller
Morels	Morilles	Morcheln	Spugnole	Colmenillas	Murkla
Mould	Moule	Form	Forma – Stampo	Molde	Form
Mulberries	Mûres	Maulbeeren	More	Moras	Mullbar

Continued

CULINARY TERMINOLOGY AND VOCABULARY IN SIX LANGUAGES—cont'd

English	French	German	Italian	Spanish	Swedish
Mulled wine	Vin brûlé	Glühwein	Vino brûlé	Vino caliente	Glögg
Mushrooms	Champignons	Pilze – Champignon	Funghi	Champignon	Svampar – Champignoner
Mussel	Moule	Muscheln	Muscoli	Almejas	Musslor
Must	Moût	Most	Mosto	mosto	Must
Mustard	Moutarde	Senf	Senape	Mostaza	Senap
Mutton	Mouton	Hammel	Montone	Cordero	Får (kött)
Mutton cutlet	Côtelette de mouton	Hammelkottlet	Braciola di montone	Chuletas de cordero	Fårkotlett
Napkin	Serviette	Serviette	Tovagliolo	Servilita	Serviette
Nettles	Orties	Brennessel	Ortiche	Ortiga	Nässlor
Noodles	Nouilles	Nudeln	Tagharini	Fideos	Nudlar
Nuts	Noix	Nüsse	Noce	Nuez	Nötter
Nutmeg	Muscade	Muskatnuss	Noce Moscato	Moscada	Muskot (Nöt)
Oats	Avoine	Hafer Haferflocken	Avena	Avenal	Havre
Oil	Huile	Speiseöl	Olio	Aceite	Matolja
old	vieux	alt	vecchio	viejo	gammal
Olive	Olive	Olive	Oliva	Aceituna	Oliv
Omelette	Omelette	Omelette	Frittata	Tortilla	Omelett
Onion	Oignon	Zwiebel	Cipolla	Cebolla	Lök
Orange	Orange	Apfelsine	Arancia	Naranja	Apelsin
Ortolan	Ortolan	Fettammer	Ortolano	Verderón	Ortolan (sparv)
Oxtail	Queue de bœuf	Ochsenschwanz	Coda di bue	Rabo de vaca	Oxsvans

Continued

CULINARY TERMINOLOGY AND VOCABULARY IN SIX LANGUAGES—cont'd

English	French	German	Italian	Spanish	Swedish
Ox tongue	Langue de boeuf	Rinderzunge	Lingua di bue	Lengua de vaca	Oxtunga
Oyster	Huître	Auster	Ostriche	Ostra	Östron
Palate	Palais	Gaumen	Palato	Paladar	Gom
Pancake	Pannequet	Pfannkuchen	Frittella	Tortilla	Pannkaka
Parings	Parures	Abfall – Parüren	Ritagli	–	Avfallet
Parsley	Persil	Petersilie	Prezzemolo	Perejil	Persilja
Parsnip	Panais	Pastinaken	Pastinaca	Chirivía	Palsternacka
Partridge	Perdreau	Rebhuhn	Pernice	Perdiz	Rapphöns
Pastry	Pâtisserie	Backwerk – Teig	Pasticceria	Pastinaca	Finare-bakverk
Pastry Cook	Pâtissier	Konditor	Pasticciere	Confitero	Konditor
Peach	Pêche	Pfirsich	Pesca	Albérchigo	Persika
Peacock	Paon	Pfau	Pavone	Pavo real	Påfågel
Pear	Poire	Birne	Pera	Pera	Päron
Pearl barley	Orge perlé	Perlen-Graupen	Orzo brillato	Cebada	Parigryn
Peas	Petits pois	Erbsen	Piselli	Guisantes	Ärtor
Peel – skin	Écorcel – pelure	Schale – Rinde	Scorza – peluria	Corteza – pellejo	Skal
Pepper	Poivre	Pfeffer	Pepe	Pimienta	Peppar
Pepper pot	Poivrier	Pfefferdose	Pepiera	Pimentero	Pepparströare
Peppers, sweet	Poivron doux	Pfefferschote	Peperoni	Pimiento	Paprikaskott
Perch – pike	Sandre	Zander	Picca	Lucio	Gädda
Pheasant	Faisan	Fasan	Fagiano	Faisán	Fasan
Pickle	Pickles	Beize	Conservata	Conservara	Inläggning
pickle (verb)	mariner	beizen	conservare	conservare	konservera
Pie	Pâté	Pastete	Pasticcio	Pastel	Pastej
Pigeon	Pigeon	Taube	Piccione	Paloma	Duva
Pike	Brochet	Hecht	Luccio	Lucio	Gädda

Continued

CULINARY TERMINOLOGY AND VOCABULARY IN SIX LANGUAGES—cont'd

English	French	German	Italian	Spanish	Swedish
Piment (allspice)	Quatre épice	Piment-Gewürzpfeffer	Pimienta-especia	Pimienta	Kryddpeppar
Pineapple	Ananas	Ananas	Ananasso	Piña Tropical	Ananas
Pistachios	Pistaches	Pistazien	Pistacchio	Pistachos	Pistasch-mandeln
Plate	Assiette	Teller	Piatto	Plato	Talrik
Plover	Vanneau	Kiebitz	V'anello	Avefria	Brockfågel
Plover eggs	Oeufs de vanneau	Kiebitzgeier	Uova di v'anello	Huevos di avefría	Brockfågel-ägg
Plum	Prune	Pflaume	Prugna	Ciruela	Plommon
Pomegranate	Grenade	Granatapfel	Mela grana	Granada	Granatäpple
Poppy	Pavot	Mohn	Papavero	Adormidera	Vallmo
Pork	Cochon, Porc	Schweinfleisch	Porco – maiale	Cerdo	Griskött
Pork cutlet	Côtelette de porc	Schweinekotletten	Costolette di maiale	Chuleta de cerdo	Fläskkotlett
Pork trotters	Pieds de porc	Schweinefüße	Zampetti di porco	Manos de cerdo	Grisfötter
Port	Porto	Portwein	Vino di Porto	Oporto	Porlin
Potatoes	Pomme de terre	Kartoffeln	Patata	Patata	Potatis
pound (verb)	piler	zu stoßen	pelare	machacar	banka
Preserve	Conserve	konservieren	conserva	conserva	konsaviera
Pudding	Pouding	Pudding	Budino	Pudín	Pudding
Pumpkin	Potiron	Kiirbis	Zucca	Calabaza	Pumpa
Punch	Punch	Punsch	Ponce	Ponche	Punsch
Quail	Caille	Wachtel	Quaglia	Codorniz	Vaktel
Quince	Coing	Quitte	Cotogna	Membrillo	Kvitten
Rabbit	Lapin	Kaninchen	Coniglio	Conejo	Kanin
Radish	Radis	Radieschen	Campanello	Rabaneta	Rädisa

Continued

English	French	German	Italian	Spanish	Swedish
Raspberry	Framboise	Himbeeren	Lampone	Frambuesa	Hallon
raw	cru	roh	crudo	crudo	rå
Red currant	Groseille rouge	Johannisbeeren	Ribes rosso	Grosella	Röda vinbär
Red mullet	Rouget	Rotbarbe	Triglia	Salmonete	Mullus (fisk)
Restaurant	Restaurant	Restaurant	Ristorante	Restaurante	Restaurang
Rhubarb	Rhubarbe	Rhabarber	Rabarbaro	Ruibarbo	Rabarber
Rice	Riz	Reis	Riso	Arroz	Ris
ripe	mûr	reif	maturo	maduro	mogen
roast (verb)	rôtir	braten	arrostire	asar	ugnsteka
Roast pork	Rôti de porc	Schweinebraten	Arrosto di porco	Asado de cerdo	Fläskstek
Roast loin of veal	Longe de veau rôtie	Kalbsnierenbraten	Arrosto di vitello	Asado de ternera	Kalvstek
Roebuck	Chevreuil	Reh	Capriolo	Corzo	Råbock
Rolls	Petit pain	Brötchen	Panini	Pan	Små Franska
Rum	Rhum	Rum	Rhum	Ron	Rom
Rye bread	Pain seigle	Roggenbrot	Pane nero	Pan moreno	Rågbröd
Saddle	Selle	Rücken	Schiena	Lomo	Sadel
Saddle of venison	Selle de chevreuil	Rehrücken	Lombo di capriolo	Lomo de corzo	Rådjurssadel
Saffron	Safran	Safran	Zafferano	Azafrán	Saffran
Sage	Sauge	Salbei	Salvia	Salvia	Salvia
Salad	Salade	Salat	Insalata	Ensalada	Sallad
Salad dish	Saladier	Salatschüssel	Insalatiera	Ensaladera	Salladsskål
Salmon	Saumon	Lachs	Salmone	Salmer	Lax
Salt	Sel	Salz	Sale	Sal	Saft
Sandwich	Sandwich	Belegtes Brot	Panini imbottiti	Pan cecina	Smörgås
Sardine	Sardine	Sardine	Sardine	Cerdeña	Sardin

Continued

CULINARY TERMINOLOGY AND VOCABULARY IN SIX LANGUAGES—cont'd

English	French	German	Italian	Spanish	Swedish
Sauce	Sauce	Sauce	Salsa	Salsa	Salt
Sausage	Saucisse	Wurst Würstchen	Salsiccia	Salchichón	Korv
Scallop	Escalope	Schnitzel	Stagione	Estación	Årstid
Season	Saison	Jahreszeit – Saison	Carne fredda	Escalopine	Schnitzel
Semolina	Semoule	Gries	Semolino	Sémola	Semllina (gryn)
sharpen	aiguiser	schärfen	affilare	abusar	skarp (kniv)
Sherry	Xérès	Sherry	Sherry	Jerez	Sherry
Shin – knuckle	Jarret	Hesse – Haxe	Garretto	Carvejón	Skenben – lägg
Shoulder	Épaule	Schulter	Spalla	Hombro	Skuldra
Sieve	Passoire	Sieb	Staccio	Tamiz	Såll
Skate	Raie	Rochen	Razza	Raya	(Slatt) rocka
Skin	Peau	Haut – Schale	Pelle	Piel	Hud
Slice	Tranche	Scheibe	Fetta	Loncha	Skiva
small	petit	klein	piccolo	pequeño	liten
Smell	Odeur	Geruch	Odore	Olor	Lukt
smoke (verb)	fumer	rauchen	fumare	humear	röka
Smoked beef	Boeuf fumé	Rauchfleisch	Carne fumare	Carne ahumado	rökt skött
Smoked	Fumée	Geräuchert	Affumicata	Ahumado	Rökt
Starter – appetizer	Hors d'oeuvre	Vorspeise	Antipasti	Entremeses	Förrätt
Table	Table	Tisch	Tavola	Mesa	Bord
Tablecloth	Nappe	Tischtuch	Tovaglia	Mantel	Duk bordsduk
Tail	Queue	Schwanz	Coda	Rabo	Svans
Tangerine	Mandarine	Mandarine	Mandarino	Mandarina	Mandarin
Tarragon	Estragon	Estragon	Serpentario	Estragón	Dragon

Continued

English	French	German	Italian	Spanish	Swedish
Taste	Goût	Geschmack	Gusto	Gusto	Smak
tasteless	goûter fade	geschmacklos fade	gustare insipido	costar insipidez	smaklös
Tavern	Taverne	Kneipe	Taverna	Taberna	Krog
Tea	Thé	Tee	The	Te	Te
Teal	Sarcelle	Knäckente	Alzavola	Cerceta	Krickand
tender	tendre	zart – miirbe	tenero	tierno	mör
Thick soup	Potage lié	dicke Suppe	Minestrone	Sopa	Redd soppa
Thyme	Thym	Thymian	Timo	Tomillo	Timjan
Toast	Pain grillé	Rostbrot	Pane tostato	Pan tostado	Röstat bröd
Tomato	Tomate	Tomate	Pomodoro	Tomate	Tomat
tough	dur	hart – zähe	duro	duro	Seg – hård
Tray	Plateau	Tablett	Vassoio	Bandeja	Bricka
Trout	Truite	Forelle	Trota	Rodaballo	Forell
Truffle	Truffe	Trüffel	Tartufi	Pava	Tryffel
Tumbler	Gobelet	Becher	Calice – coppa	Nabos	Bagare
Tuna fish	Thon	Thunfisch	Tonno	Tortuga	Tunna
Turbot	Turbot	Steinbutt	Rombo	Rombo	Piggvar
Turkey	Dinde	Puter	Tacchino	Trucó	Kalkon
Turnip	Navet	Steckrübe	Nabo	Rapa	Rova
Turtle	Tortue	Schildkröte	Tartaruga	Tortuga	Sköldpadda
under-done – rare	saignant	blutig	sanguinante	sangrante	blodig
Vanilla	Vanille	Vanille	Vaniglia	Vainilla	Vanilj
Veal	Veau	Kalb	Vitello	Ternera	Kalv
Veal cutlet	Côtelette de veau	Kalbsrippe	Costolette di vitello	Costilla de ternera	Kalvkotlett

Continued

English	French	German	Italian	Spanish	Swedish
Vegetables	Légumes	Gemüse	Legumi	Legumbre	Grönsaker
Venison, game	Gibier	Wild	Selvaggina	Caza	Vilt
Vermicelli	Vermicelle	Fadennudeln	Vermicelli	Fideos	Vermicelli
Vermouth	Vermouth	Warmouth	Vermouth	Vermut	Vermouth
Vinegar	Vinaigre	Essig	Aceto	Vinagre	Ättika
Waiter	Garçon	Kellner	Cameriere	Camarero	Kypare
warm up	réchauffer	auf wärmen	riscaldare	calentar	värma upp
Water	Eau	Wasser	Acqua	Agua	Vatten
Water bath	Bain-marie	Wasserbad	Bagno-maria	Baño Maria	Vattenbad
Watercress	Cresson	Brunnenkresse	Crescione	Berros	Vattenkrasse
Watermelon	Pastèque	Wassermelone	Cocomero	Sandia	Vatten Melon
well-done	bien cuit	durchgebraten	ben cotto	bien asado	genomstekt
Whipped cream	Crème fouettée	Schlagsahne	Panna montata	Nata batida	Vispgrädde
White wine	Vin blanc	Weißwein	Vino bianco	Vino blanco	Vitt vin
whole	entier	ganz	completo	entero	hela
Wild boar	Sanglier	Wildschwein	Cinghiale	Jabalí	Vildsvin
Wine	Vin	Wein	Vino	Vino	Vin
Wing	Aile	Flügel	Ala di polo	Ala de pollo	Vinge
Woodcock	Bécasse	Waldschnepfe	Beccaccia	Becada	Morkulla
Woodruff	Aspérule	Waldmeister	Mughetto	Aspérula	Madra
Yeast	Levure	Hefe	Lievito	Levadura	Jäst
yellow	jaune	gelb	giallo	amarillo	gul
young	jeune	jung	giovane	oven	ung
young wild boar	Marcassin	Frischling	Cinghiale novellino	Jabato	ung vildsvin

FOODS IN SEASON

It is true today that we can have most foods at any time during the year, if not fresh, frozen. Or flown in from all over the world when out of season at home.

What they taste like is of course another matter. Strawberries for example in December taste of nothing, and this applies to other foods out of season as well. Concern has also been expressed as to the cost to the environment, and the recent recommendation that airlines should pay fuel tax could make flying food around the world a very expensive business.

Foods in season not only taste better, they give us often a much better yield. A plaice or sole out of season is heavy with roe, and will give 25% less in flesh after filleting, quite apart from the fact that the fish eggs will now not be fertilized, and no new fish will come into being. A lettuce grown in the greenhouse for Christmas uses 125% more energy in growing than it gives us in food value, and all for a few green leaves we think we can't do without at that time of the year. We ignore the many wonderful winter vegetables we can turn into tasty and wholesome salads. Nature has arranged things that the seasons provide us with fresh foods for most of the year, so let us enjoy them at their best in terms of both yield and flavour.

Fruits	Jan.	Feb.	March	April	May	June	July	Aug.	Sept.	Oct.	Nov.	Dec.
Apples	■					■	■	■		■	■	■
Apricots						▨	▨	▨				
Blackberries								■	■	■		
Blackcurrants						▨	▨	▨				
Gooseberries						■	■	■				
Plums						▨	▨	▨	▨			
Raspberries						■	■	■	■			
Red Currants						▨	▨	▨				
Strawberries						■	■	■	■			

Legend: ■ = black (peak season) ▒ = grey (available) blank = not available

Salads	Jan.	Feb.	March	April	May	June	July	Aug.	Sept.	Oct.	Nov.	Dec.
Batavian lettuce					▒	▒	▒	▒	▒			
Beetroot	■	■	■	■					■	■	■	■
Celery	▒	▒	▒						▒	▒	▒	▒
Celeriac	■	■							■	■	■	■
Chicory	▒	▒							▒	▒	▒	▒
Cucumber						▒	▒	■	■	▒		
Iceberg lettuce				▒	▒	▒	▒	▒	▒	▒		
Lambs lettuce	■	■									■	■
Lettuce	▒	▒	▒	▒	▒	▒	▒	▒	▒	▒	▒	▒
Lolla Rossa Lettuce						▒	■	▒				
Oak Leaf lettuce						▒	▒	▒				
Radish		■	■	■	■	■	■					
Tomatoes						▒	▒	▒	▒	▒		

Meats	Jan.	Feb.	March	April	May	June	July	Aug.	Sept.	Oct.	Nov.	Dec.
Beef	■	■	■	■	■	■	■	■	■	■	■	■
Lamb	▒	▒	▒	▒	▒	▒	▒	▒	▒	▒	▒	▒
Mutton	■	■	■	■	■	■	■	■	■	■	■	■
Pork	▒	▒	▒	▒					▒	▒	▒	▒
Veal	■	■	■	■			■	■	■	■		
Venison	▒	▒	▒	▒	▒	▒	▒	▒	▒	▒	▒	▒

Vegetables	Jan.	Feb.	March	April	May	June	July	Aug.	Sept.	Oct.	Nov.	Dec.
Asparagus				■	■	■	■					
Broccoli				▨	▨	▨	▨	▨	▨	▨	▨	
Broad beans					■	■	■					
Cabbage, white	▨	▨	▨	▨	▨	▨				▨	▨	▨
Cabbage, red	■	■	■				■	■	■	■	■	■
Cabbage, Savoy	▨	▨						▨	▨	▨	▨	▨
Carrots	■	■	■				■	■	■	■	■	■
French beans						▨	▨	▨	▨	▨		
Kale	■	■	■							▨	■	■
Kohlrabi	▨	▨	▨	▨	▨	▨	▨	▨	▨	▨		
Leeks	■	■	■	▨	▨		■	■	■	■	■	■
Mange tout						▨	▨	▨	▨			
Mushrooms cultv.	■	■	■	■	■	■	■	■	■	■	■	■
Onions	▨	▨	▨	▨	▨	▨	▨	▨	▨	▨	▨	▨
Peas						■	■	■	■			
Runner beans					▨	▨	▨	▨	▨	▨		
Spinach	■	■	■	■					■	■	■	■
Sprouts	▨	▨	▨	▨					▨	▨	▨	▨
Sweet Corn							■	■	■	■		

Poultry and Game	Jan.	Feb.	March	April	May	June	July	Aug.	Sept.	Oct.	Nov.	Dec.
Capon	▓	▓	▓	▓	▓	▓	▓	▓	▓	▓	▓	▓
Chicken	■	■	■	■	■	■	■	■	■	■	■	■
Duckling	▓	▓	▓	▓	▓	□	▓	▓	▓	▓	▓	▓
Geese	■	■	□	□	□	□	□	■	■	■	■	■
Gosling	□	□	▓	▓	▓	▓	▓	□	□	□	□	□
Grouse (from 12th August)	□	□	□	□	□	□	□	■/▓	▓	▓	▓	▓
Guinea Fowl	□	□	□	□	□	□	□	■	■	■	■	■
Hare	▓	▓	▓	□	□	□	□	□	▓	▓	▓	▓
Partridge	■	■	□	□	□	□	□	□	■	■	■	■
Pheasant	▓	▓	□	□	□	□	□	□	□	▓	▓	▓
Plover	■	■	□	□	□	□	□	□	■	■	■	■
Ptarmigan	▓	▓	▓	□	□	□	□	□	□	▓	▓	▓
Quail	■	□	■	■	■	■	■	□	□	□	□	□
Rabbit	□	□	□	▓	▓	▓	▓	▓	□	□	□	□
Snipe	■	■	□	□	□	□	□	□	□	■	■	■
Turkey	▓	▓	▓	□	□	□	□	□	□	□	▓	▓
Woodcock	□	□	□	□	□	□	□	■	■	■	■	■

Fish and Shellfish	Jan.	Feb.	March	April	May	June	July	Aug.	Sept.	Oct.	Nov.	Dec.
Brill	▨	▨			▨	▨	▨	▨	▨	▨	▨	▨
Dory					■	■	■	■	■	■		
Cod	▨	▨							▨	▨	▨	▨
Crab		■		■	■	■	■			■	■	
Crayfish		▨	▨	▨	▨	▨	▨	▨	▨	▨	▨	▨
Eel	■	■	■		■	■	■	■	■	■	■	
Flounders	▨	▨	▨	▨	▨	▨	▨	▨	▨	▨	▨	▨
Haddock	■	■	■			■	■	■	■	■	■	■
Halibut			▨	▨	▨	▨	▨	▨	▨	▨	▨	▨
Hake						▨	▨	▨	▨			
Herring		■			■	■		■		■	■	■
Lobster	▨	▨	▨	▨	▨	▨	▨	▨	▨	▨	▨	▨
Mackerel					■	■	■	■	■	■	■	
Mullet				▨		▨				▨	▨	
Mussels	■	■	■	■							■	■
Oysters	▨	▨	▨	▨					▨	▨	▨	▨

Continued

Fish and Shellfish	Jan.	Feb.	March	April	May	June	July	Aug.	Sept.	Oct.	Nov.	Dec.
Perch									█	█	█	█
Plaice						▒	▒	▒	▒	▒	▒	▒
Pike								█	█	█	█	█
Prawns	▒	▒	▒	▒	▒	▒	▒	▒				
Salmon		█	█	█	█	█	█	█				
Scallops								▒	▒	▒		
Shrimps	█	█	█	█		█	█	█	█	█	█	█
Skate	▒	▒	▒						▒	▒	▒	▒
Soles	█	█	█	█	█	█	█	█			█	
Sprats	▒	▒	▒	▒						▒	▒	▒
Turbot	█	█	█	█	█		█	█	█	█	█	
Trout					▒	▒	▒	▒	▒	▒		
Whitebait	█	█	█	█	█	█	█	█				
Whiting	▒	▒	▒	▒	▒	▒	▒	▒	▒	▒	▒	▒

PLATED SERVICE

Finally in this chapter we look at the principles of plating. The guidelines here apply to either hot or cold dishes but are of meticulous importance for the Larder, with the many Starters, both single and mixed, served from here at functions.

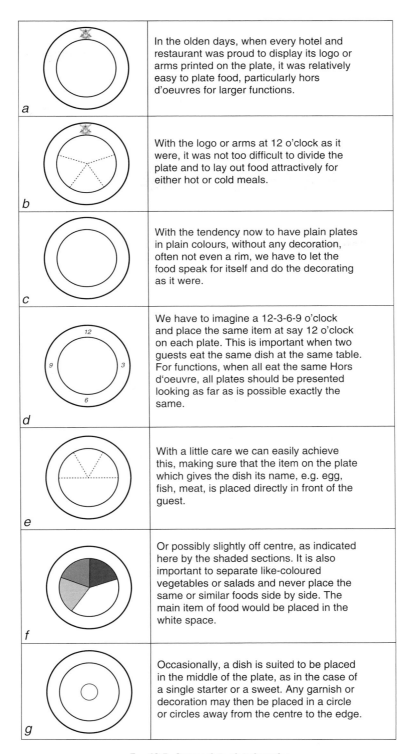

a In the olden days, when every hotel and restaurant was proud to display its logo or arms printed on the plate, it was relatively easy to plate food, particularly hors d'oeuvres for larger functions.

b With the logo or arms at 12 o'clock as it were, it was not too difficult to divide the plate and to lay out food attractively for either hot or cold meals.

c With the tendency now to have plain plates in plain colours, without any decoration, often not even a rim, we have to let the food speak for itself and do the decorating as it were.

d We have to imagine a 12-3-6-9 o'clock and place the same item at say 12 o'clock on each plate. This is important when two guests eat the same dish at the same table. For functions, when all eat the same Hors d'oeuvre, all plates should be presented looking as far as is possible exactly the same.

e With a little care we can easily achieve this, making sure that the item on the plate which gives the dish its name, e.g. egg, fish, meat, is placed directly in front of the guest.

f Or possibly slightly off centre, as indicated here by the shaded sections. It is also important to separate like-coloured vegetables or salads and never place the same or similar foods side by side. The main item of food would be placed in the white space.

g Occasionally, a dish is suited to be placed in the middle of the plate, as in the case of a single starter or a sweet. Any garnish or decoration may then be placed in a circle or circles away from the centre to the edge.

FIG. 10.5 *Approach to plated service*

Index